Reflections on a Troubled
World Economy

Also published for the Trade Policy Research Centre by
Macmillan

Invisible Barriers to Invisible Trade
by **Brian Griffiths**

Public Assistance to Industry
edited by **W. M. Corden and Gerhard Fels**

Agriculture and the State
edited by **Brian Davey, T. E. Josling and Alister McFarquhar**

Tariff Preferences in Mediterranean Diplomacy
by **Alfred Tovias**

Meeting the Third World Challenge
by **Alasdair MacBean and V. N. Balasubramanyam**

Nuclear Power and the Energy Crisis
by **Duncan Burn**

North Sea Oil in the Future
by **Colin Robinson and Jon Morgan**

The Role of Tariff Quotas in Commercial Policy
by **Michael Rom**

East-West Trade and the GATT System
by **M. M. Kostecki**

Trade and Payments Adjustment under Flexible Exchange Rates
edited by **John P. Martin and Alasdair Smith**

Current Issues in Commercial Policy and Diplomacy
edited by **John Black and Brian Hindley**

Anti-dumping Law in a Liberal Trade Order
by **Richard Dale**

Industrial Policies in the European Community
by **Victoria Curzon Price**

Measurement of Agricultural Protection
by **John Strak**

Reflections on a Troubled World Economy

Essays in Honour of Herbert Giersch

Edited by

Fritz Machlup, Gerhard Fels and
Hubertus Müller-Groeling

for the
TRADE POLICY RESEARCH CENTRE
London

First published 1983 by
THE MACMILLAN PRESS LTD
London and Basingstoke
Companies and representatives
throughout the world

ISBN 0 333 35775 2

Typeset and printed in the United Kingdom by
Ditchling Press Ltd
Ditchling, Hassocks, Sussex

195,095

Trade Policy Research Centre

The Trade Policy Research Centre was established in 1968 to promote independent research and public discussion of international economic policy issues. As a non-profit organisation, which is privately sponsored, the institute has been developed to work on

an international basis and serves as an entrepreneurial centre for a variety of activities, including the sponsorship of research, the organisation of conferences, lectures and seminars and a publications programme which includes a quarterly journal, *The World Economy*. In general, the Centre provides a focal point for those in business, the universities and public affairs who are interested in the problems of international economic relations—whether commercial, legal, financial, monetary or diplomatic.

The Centre is managed by a Council, set out above, which represents a wide range of international experience and expertise.

Publications are presented as professionally competent studies worthy of public consideration. The interpretations and conclusions in them are those of their respective authors and should not be attributed to the Council, staff or associates of the Centre which, having general terms of reference, does not represent a consensus of opinion on any particular issue.

Enquiries about membership (individual, corporate or library) of the Centre, about subscriptions to *The World Economy* or about the Centre's publications should be addressed to the Director, Trade Policy Research Centre, 1 Gough Square, London EC4A 3DE, United Kingdom.

Contents

List of Tables

Biographical Notes

ROBERT Z. ALIBER, Professor of International Economics and Finance at the Graduate School of Business, University of Chicago, where he has taught since 1965, was Senior Economic Adviser at the Agency for International Development in the United States Administration (1964-65) and before that was on the staff of the Committee for Economic Development in New York (1961-64). His recent publications include *The International Money Game* (1973, fourth edition 1983), *National Monetary Policies and the International Financial System* (1974), *Exchange Risk and Corporate International Finance* (1978) and (as co-author) *Money, Banking and the Economy* (1981).

BELA BALASSA, a Consultant at the World Bank in Washington, has been Professor of Political Economy at the Johns Hopkins University, Baltimore, since 1967. Between 1953 and 1967, he was Assistant, and subsequently Associate, Professor at Yale University. Professor Balassa has also taught at Columbia University, New York, and the University of California, Berkeley. He is the author *inter alia* of *The Theory of Economic Integration* (1961), *The Structure of Protection in Developing Countries* (1971), *European Economic Integration* (1975) and *The Newly Industrializing Countries in the World Economy* (1981).

KARL BRUNNER divides his time between the United States and Switzerland, being Professor of Economics, and Director of the Center for Research in Government Policy and Business, at the University of Rochester and Professor of Economics, and Director of the Volkswirtschaftliches Institut Abteilung Oekonometrie, at the University of Bern. In addition, he is the Editor of the *Journal of Monetary Economics*; and he is the convener of the annual Interlaken conferences on ideology, the social sciences and policy issues.

W. M. CORDEN, a member of the Council of the Trade Policy Research Centre, London, is Professor of Economics at the Research School of Pacific Studies at the Australian National University, Canberra, to which he returned after a period as Nuffield Reader in International Economics at the University of Oxford (1967-76). Professor Corden has also taught, as a visiting professor, at the universities of California, Minnesota, Princeton and Stockholm. He is the author of *The Theory of Protection* (1971), *Trade Policy and Economic Welfare* (1974) and *Inflation, Exchange Rates and the World Economy* (1977).

JUERGEN B. DONGES, Professor of Economics, and, since 1972, Head of the Development Economics Department, Institut für Weltwirtschaft, at the University of Kiel, is a member of the Advisory Council of the Ministry of Economic Cooperation in the Government of the Federal Republic of Germany. Among his principal publications, he is author of *La Industrialización en España— Politicas, Logros, Perspectivas* (1976) and *Aussenwirtschafts- und Entwicklungspolitik* (1981); and co-author of *Protektion und Branchenstruktur der Westdeutschen Wirtschaft* (1973) and *Aussenwirtschaftsstrategien und Industrialisierung in Entwicklungsländern* (1978).

WILLIAM J. FELLNER, who was a member of the Council of Economic Advisers in the Executive Office of the President of the United States in 1973-75, is Resident Scholar at the American Enterprise Institute for Public Policy Research in Washington. He was Sterling Professor of Economics at Yale University from 1951 to 1973, during which period he was frequently a consultant at the United States Treasury. Among his most notable works have been *Competition Among the Few* (1949), *Trends and Cycles in Economic Activity* (1955), *Probability and Profit* (1965) and *Towards a Reconstruction of Macroeconomics* (1976).

GERHARD FELS is Professor of Economics and Head of the Department of Structural Change and Economic Growth at the Institut für Weltwirtschaft in Kiel. Before joining the institute, he was a research economist at the Council of Economic Experts in the Federal Republic of Germany, later becoming a member of the council itself, relinquishing the post in 1982. Professor Fels has been a member of the Committee for Development Planning at the United Nations since 1978. He is the author of *Der Internationale Preis-*

zusammenhang (1969) and the co-author of *Protektion und Branchen-struktur der Westdeutschen Wirtschaft* (1973) and *Die Deutsche Wirtschaft im Strukturwandel* (1980).

HERBERT GRUBEL is Professor of Economics at Simon Fraser University in Burnaby, Vancouver, Canada. Before joining Simon Fraser University, he was Associate Professor of Economics at the University of Pennsylvania (1966-70), having also taught at Stanford, California and Chicago universities. Professor Grubel was a Senior Policy Adviser in the United States Treasury in Washington in 1970-71. Among his various publications are *Forward Exchange* (1967), *The International Monetary System* (1969) and *International Economics* (1977) and he is co-author of *Brain Drain* (1971) and *Intra-Industry Trade* (1975).

GOTTFRIED HABERLER, who was chairman of the group of experts which produced in 1958 for the signatory countries of the General Agreement on Tariffs and Trade the report *Trends in International Trade* (the Haberler Report), has been a Resident Scholar at the American Enterprise Institute for Public Policy Research in Washington since 1971, having been Galen Stone Professor of International Trade since 1957, and earlier Professor of Economics, at Harvard University. Professor Haberler was an Expert at the Board of Governors of the Federal Reserve System in Washington in 1943-44. Among the major studies he has produced are *The Theory of International Trade, with its Application to Commercial Policy* (1936), *Prosperity and Depression* (1937, reprinted 1958) and *Economic Growth and Stability* (1974).

LUTZ HOFFMANN, Professor of Economics at the University of Regensburg, has been a consultant to the World Bank in Washington on the energy problems of developing countries. Between 1964 and 1970, he was part-time adviser to the West German Council of Economic Experts. In 1971-73, Professor Hoffmann became the Economic Adviser in the Prime Minister's Department, Government of Malaysia, Kuala Lumpur. He is the author of *Importsubstitution und Wirtschaftliches Wachstum in Entwicklungsländern* (1970) and the co-author of *Industrial Growth, Employment and Foreign Investment in Peninsular Malaysia* (1980) and *Wind-energy—an Assessment of the Technical and Economic Potential, a Case-study for the Federal Republic of Germany* (1981).

CHARLES P. KINDLEBERGER, author of *The World in Depression 1929-39* (1973) and *Manias, Panics and Crashes* (1978), was Professor of Economics at the Massachusetts Institute of Technology, Cambridge, Massachusetts, from 1948 until 1976. After serving in the Office of Strategic Services in Washington in 1942-45, he was Chief, Division for German and Austrian Economic Affairs in the United States Department of State in 1945-48. Besides the above titles, he is the author *inter alia* of *International Economics* (1953, 1965 and 1977), *Europe and the Dollar* (1966), *Postwar European Growth* (1967), *American Business Abroad* (1969) and *Money and Power* (1970).

FRITZ MACHLUP (1902-83) had been Professor of Economics at the University of New York since 1971, having been Walker Professor of Economics and International Finance at Princeton University since 1960. Between 1965 and 1977, Machlup was a consultant to the United States Treasury. He was the author of many studies, among his most recent being *International Monetary Systems* (1975), *A History of Thought on Economic Integration* (1977), *Methodology of Economics and Other Social Sciences* (1979), *Information through the Printed Word* in four volumes (1978-80) and *Knowledge and Knowledge Production* (1980).

HUBERTUS MÜLLER-GROELING, who previously taught at the University of the Saarland in Saarbrücken, is Head of the Editorial Department of the Institut für Weltwirtschaft, University of Kiel, in which capacity as Managing Editor of the *Weltwirtschaftliches Archiv*, the quarterly journal published by the institute, he is responsible for the publication of the institute's bi-annual review, *Die Weltwirtschaft*, and the *Kieler Studien* series in which the results of the institute's research projects are published.

ALAN PEACOCK, Chief Economic Adviser to the Departments of Trade and Industry in the British Government from 1973 until 1976, on leave from the University of York where he was Professor of Economics (1962-78), is now Principal and Professor of Economics at University College at Buckingham. He has been a member of the Advisory Council of the Institute of Economic Affairs since 1959. Professor Peacock is the author of *Economics of National Insurance* (1952) and *Economic Analysis of Government* (1979); and the co-author of *Growth of Public Expenditure in the United Kingdom*

1890-1955 (1961), *Economic Theory of Fiscal Policy* (1971) and *Welfare Economics: a Liberal Reinterpretation* (1975).

OLAF SIEVERT has been, since 1976, Chairman of the Council of Economic Experts in the Federal Republic of Germany, having become a member in 1970. He is Director of the Department of Structural and Regional Research at the Institut für empirische Wirtschaftsforschung, and Professor of National Economics, at the University of the Saarland, Saarbrücken. Among his publications have been *Problems of Tax Equalisation Measures for International Trade* (1964), *Giving Economic Policy Advice in the Federal Republic of Germany* (1968), *The Controllability of the Business Cycle by Government* (1979) and *Debt Management without Conflict of Goals* (1981).

ERICH STREISSLER, Director of the Institut für Wirtschafts-wissenschaften, and Professor of Economics, Econometrics and Statistics, at the University of Vienna since 1968, was Professor of Econometrics and Statistics at the University of Freiburg in Breisgau between 1962 and 1968. He has also acted as a consultant to the Osterreichisches Institut für Wirtschaftsforschung in Vienna. Besides his numerous contributions to journals, he is co-editor of *Konsum und Nachfrage* (1966) and the author of *Pitfalls in Econometric Forecasting* (1970).

JAN TUMLIR has been Director of Economic Research and Analysis at the Secretariat of the General Agreement on Tariffs and Trade, Geneva, since 1967. He is also a Professor of Economics at the Institut Universitaire de Hautes Études Internationales, Geneva, a member of the Council of the Trade Policy Research Centre, London, and a member of the European Board of Economists for *Time* magazine. Besides many articles and contributions to volumes of essays, Dr Tumlir is co-author of *Trade Liberalisation, Protectionism and Interdependence* (1977), *Adjustment, Trade and Growth in Developed and Developing Countries* (1978) and *Trade Relations under Flexible Exchange Rates* (1980).

ROLAND VAUBEL is a Research Fellow at the Institut für Welt-wirtschaft at the University of Kiel where he obtained his doctorate in the course of being Assistant to Professor Giersch. Since then and returning to Kiel, he taught at the University of Chicago and, as Professor of Economics, at the Erasmus University in Rotterdam.

He is the author of *Strategies for Currency Unification: the Economics of Currency Competition and the Case for a European Parallel Currency* (1978) and has contributed to professional journals on monetary issues.

Preface

When this volume of Essays in Honour of Herbert Giersch was first being contemplated, it was soon accepted that it was already too late for it to be published as a *festschrift* in time for the sixtieth birthday of the revered President of the Institut für Weltwirtschaft in Kiel. Some asked if Professor Giersch was still not a little too young in any case to be honoured in such a way. Could we not be setting a precedent? Fritz Machlup quickly, and authoritatively, disposed of the question. The question, though, was beside the point. The point was that the approach of Professor Giersch's sixtieth birthday had stimulated the idea of a collection of essays in his honour. But that has been the only connection between 11 May 1981 and this volume.

How is it that the Trade Policy Research Centre produced the volume? To answer the question it is necessary to say something about the Centre's origins. When Harry Johnson and I began thinking about establishing the Centre in 1967, we visualised an entrepreneurial endeavour that would (i) follow developments in the world economy, (ii) anticipate significant policy issues and (iii) plan studies which might help to clarify them, (iv) secure funds for those studies and (v) commission the work in universities, (vi) ensure that the resulting papers were not only analytically sound but also accessible to lay readers and then (vii) have the edited papers published, promoted and disseminated. This has been the Centre's mode of operation, aimed at influencing those who educate public opinion and educating those who influence public policy, and it explains why Johnson once described the Centre as 'ten per cent brains and ninety per cent energy'.

In this respect I am often asked about the size of the Centre's staff. What the enquirer is trying to determine is whether the Centre should be taken seriously. Occasionally I parry the question by recalling Bismarck's reply when asked what he would do if the

British Army landed in Germany. 'I would call out the police and arrest it', he said. The story is possibly apocryphal, but clearly, even in the heyday of the *Pax Britannica*, the British Army was rather small! The moral is, then, that one does not need large numbers of enlisted men to exert influence. The Centre's effectiveness has depended on its ability to draw on specialists in different countries who are well placed, through their professional work and experience, to produce papers on how particular policy issues within and between societies might be resolved or ameliorated.

Professor Giersch understood the Trade Policy Research Centre's purpose and mode of operation from the outset. Shortly before Britain joined the European Community, he called on the Centre and talked of the importance of getting British and German economists to collaborate more, especially on problems of European economic integration. When the Centre began to 'Europeanise' its activities, Professor Giersch joined its Council and, as those activities have been internationalised on a still broader basis, he has either participated himself in its projects or encouraged his colleagues in Kiel to do so. In the nature of things, policy research and analysis involves challenging established positions, which is not as a rule welcomed and can, in practice, be a lonely and dispiriting occupation. Those who have been associated with the Centre over the years have consequently appreciated Professor Giersch's encouragement and support. This volume is a token of their appreciation.

Although Professor Giersch has made a number of contributions to pure economic theory, his work, whether in an official capacity or as an independent commentator, has been oriented towards the important economic issues of the time. Professor Giersch's interest in economic policy issues, however, has been developed in and disciplined by a robust theoretical framework. His major recommendations can thus be said to have been contributions to the theory of economic policy.

When inviting contributions to this volume in honour of Herbert Giersch, we therefore noted the disarray in international economic policy since the collapse of 'the Bretton Woods system' in 1971-73, before the first 'oil shock', and the continuing crumbling of its theoretical foundations since the shortcomings of Keynesian demand management became apparent. This disarray has manifested itself most noticeably in the near continuous negotiations between the leading industrial powers, which have tried to achieve some kind of international compatibility in their domestic policies, bearing on such matters as trade, public subsidies and industrial structure, energy imports and consumption, rates of exchange between currencies and, more recently, interest rates. These negotiations have been conducted with no theory whatsoever to guide them. Their ultimate futility has been depressingly predictable.

The volume does not attempt to address systematically the troubled state of the world economy. That would have been too ambitious an undertaking with contributors scattered so far and wide. In their *Reflections on a Troubled World Economy*, the contributors have addressed different aspects of the present international economic situation, the essays being arranged in six parts. In the first part, on the international economic order, Roland Vaubel dissects the arguments for the coordination of national macroeconomic policies, then Jan Tumlir analyses the problems the European Community has experienced as a result of pursuing policies in conflict, rather than in harmony, with the integration of the world economy as a whole.

The second part of the volume groups three essays on the international monetary system. W. M. Corden sorts out the apparent paradox of logic in what appears to be a non-system. Charles Kindleberger looks at the development and role of key currencies and financial centres. William Fellner discusses why the earlier experience with the gold standard is not an unequivocal justification for dismissing its resuscitation in a modified form. The third part is concerned with international payments and exchange-rate policies with essays by Machlup, Robert Aliber and Olaf Sievert.

General economic policies are dealt with in the fourth part. Gottfried Haberler takes the model of a benevolent and enlightened dictator, applies realistic constraints and points out the policy lessons. Gerhard Fels contrasts the supply-oriented policies pursued in West Germany with those pursued in the United States. Alan Peacock, drawing on British experience, dwells on the failure to assess the full cost of selective public assistance to industry. The fifth part, on policies for industrial development, contains essays by Bela Balassa, Juergen Donges and Lutz Hoffman on the attempts of governments to conduct economic development, which have led to structural adjustment problems in developed and developing countries alike.

The volume ends on a philosophical note with essays by Karl Brunner and Erich Streissler on the great debate between socialists and proponents of the market economy, with the latter discussing the thought of Schumpeter and F. A. Hayek, both of whom have influenced Professor Giersch's thinking.

The final product is considerably larger than planned. Constraints laid down in the beginning resulted in 'regrets' from many who would like to have contributed to the volume. But many of those who did embark on essays found themselves unable to meet the constraints and the editors, in their turn, found themselves unable, for the most part, to resist the arguments for leaving the essays in question unabridged, being the better for being longer than requested.

Fritz Machlup, Gerhard Fels and Hubertus Müller-Groeling grappled with the organising, analytical and diplomatic tasks of editing the volume with the skill, patience and tact which might be expected from three of such formidable experience. Formal thanks are hardly enough. To our deep regret Fritz Machlup, who was the father figure in the enterprise, contributing an essay himself and writing a lively laudatio, did not live to see the volume published. His literary output after he 'retired' from Princeton, back in 1971, was so prodigious that its abrupt end came as a bolt from the blue.

In preparing the typescripts for publication, the editors have been thankful for the diligent assistance of Theresa Hunt, Alexander Noble and Janet Strachan at the Centre in London and Leila Fuchs on Dr Müller-Groeling's staff in Kiel.

As usual, it must be emphasised that the views expressed in this volume do not necessarily reflect the views of the Council or of others associated with the Trade Policy Research Centre which, having general terms of reference, does not represent a consensus of opinion.

HUGH CORBET
Director
Trade Policy Research Centre

London
March 1983

Herbert Giersch: Scholar, Policy Adviser and Public Figure

Fritz Machlup

To honour a scholar with what in Germany would be called a *festschrift* when he is still in his early sixties is rather unusual. I have not tested this statement in a statistical enquiry, but casual empiricism suggests to me that an age distribution curve for recipients of *festschrifts* would have its mode either at the age of seventy or seventy five. In producing a volume of Essays in Honour of Herbert Giersch, we have not quite followed the pattern of a *festschrift*, but an explanation is called for why we have been eager to beat the mode. What I have to say about Herbert Giersch will, I trust, show that he fully merits this early volume of essays in his honour.

A well organised encomium might be divided somehow like this: Giersch, the teacher; Giersch, the writer; Giersch, the exponent of applied economic theory; Giersch, the policy analyst and adviser; Giersch, the testy critic; Giersch, the intrepid leader; and Giersch, the often-denounced public figure. In a scheme of this sort we would find no place for such vital statistics as the date of his birth, an account of his studies and degrees, and of his military service. I shall, at the risk of being less systematic, attempt to do something along both approaches and intersperse my narrative with pertinent or impertinent observations.

Herbert Giersch was born on 11 May 1921 in Reichenbach, a small city at the foot of the *Eulengebirge* (Owl Mountains). These facts elicit a few of the less pertinent observations. First, a lesson in geography: Reichenbach is situated in the district of Breslau, which in 1921 was a part of Prussian Silesia, but after World War II became a part of Poland. Second, a lesson in political history: there was a battle of Reichenbach in 1762, in which the Prussian army won a victory over the Austrian army. As a former Austrian, I might resent this, but I do not blame my friend Giersch for this defeat at the hands of the Prussians. Third, a lesson in monetary history: May 1921 marked a watershed in the German inflation.

Up to this time the stock of banknotes had increased by only 3,250 per cent, or about thirty-three-and-a-half times faster than the price of the American dollar. After May 1921 the inflation of the money supply gathered momentum and the rate of increase of the exchange rate of the dollar began to overtake that of the domestic price level. In the first two years of little Herbert's presence in this world, the stock of banknotes increased by another 19,300 per cent, or about 194 times. This was not yet the end of the German mass production of paper currency. From 13,092,000,000,000 marks in June 1923 the stock increased to 28,229,000,000,000 marks in September, and to 496,500,000,000,000,000,000 marks in December 1923. Young Herbert was two-and-a-half years old when this spectacular inflation was finally stopped. He cannot be blamed for the acceleration of the money creation at the time of his birth, nor can he be credited for eventually having stopped it, but one may wonder whether his elders told him so much about this fantastic experience as to make him the most valiant anti-inflationist in present-day Germany. Incidentally, my information about the phase-change of the inflationary process in May 1921 comes from the article on 'Inflation' that Giersch wrote for the *Handwörterbuch der Sozialwissenschaften*.[1]

Giersch finished secondary school and *Arbeitsdienst* (compulsory labour under the Nazi regime) in 1939 and began his studies in economics at the University of Breslau. He continued at the University of Kiel where he received his diploma (corresponding to a master's degree) in 1942. He served in the German navy, was taken prisoner by the British, and shipped to a camp for prisoners of war in Great Britain. After his return to Germany in 1946 he resumed his study of economics at the University of Münster. He completed a dissertation on 'Der Ausgleich der Kriegslasten'[2]—on the incidence and redistribution of the war burden—and received his degree of *Doctor rerum politicarum* in 1948. The award of a fellowship of the British Council enabled Giersch to spend the academic year 1948-49 at the London School of Economics. In 1950 he worked at Münster as assistant to Walther Hoffmann on 'Economic Growth and Employment', and habilitated as *Privat-dozent* (lecturer). In the years 1950-51 and again in 1953-54 he worked at the Organisation for European Economic Cooperation (OEEC) in Paris. Giersch left the University of Münster in 1955 when he accepted a call to the University of the Saarland in Saarbrücken.

Now I have reached the section in which I may talk about Giersch, the teacher. I shall no longer feel bound by the rules of chronology and hence can talk about Giersch's work as a teacher at different places during various periods: at Saarbrücken, from 1955-69; at Yale University in the United States in 1962-63 and again in 1977-78; at Wiesbaden in the secret meetings and working sessions of the *Sachverständigenrat* (Council of Experts for the Assessment of Economic Developments) from 1964-70; and at the University of Kiel since 1969. The success of a teacher is evaluated chiefly on the basis of the later work and careers of his students. The students whom I have met and whose works I have read are living testimonies to Giersch's effectiveness as a teacher. Another gauge of a professor's success is the quality of the team of fellow-teachers that he manages to assemble and to inspire. The group of scholars around Giersch in Saarbrücken became, in the eyes of academic economists, the 'Saarbrücken School of Economics', recognised abroad as the best place to study in postwar Germany. When Giersch, after almost fifteen years in Saarbrücken, left for Kiel, the local newspaper, praising Giersch's leadership and lamenting his departure, wondered whether this loss might be the end of the '*Saarbrücker Schule*' (*Saarbrücker Zeitung*, July 1969).

Saarbrücken's loss was Kiel's gain. Kiel needed a replacement for the irreplaceable Erich Schneider. Giersch's success as the successor of Schneider is unquestioned. Less well known is the fact that Giersch taught at Yale, where he stimulated and inspired students, who greatly benefited from the exposure to his unconventional ideas. When I included Wiesbaden among the places where Giersch 'taught', I was thinking chiefly of the young people who were working on the staff of the Council of Experts and whose training and learning under Giersch's guidance has created human capital with high returns for the economy of Germany.

The productivity of Giersch, the writer, can be sized up by a glance at his bibliography. I cannot possibly do justice to the richness of this literary output, but I may take the space to comment on his most ambitious books and his most innovative papers. There are two textbooks or, more correctly, two volumes of a text on *Allgemeine Wirtschaftspolitik*: Volume One, *Grundlagen* (Foundations), Volume Two, *Konjunktur- und Wachstumspolitik in der offenen Wirtschaft* (Counter-cyclical and Growth Policies in an Open Economy).[3] Both were widely acclaimed; the author's lucidity, consistency and didactic ability were highly praised. A chapter in the first volume,

'From Diagnosis to Therapy', was singled out by several reviewers for special commendation. They liked the fact that the author did not confine himself to the logic of alternative policies and to purely economic arguments, but considered also the sociological, psychological and political aspects. And they appreciated that he attempted to assess the benefits and costs of compromise solutions, accepting a second-best or third-best alternative when the best was clearly unsaleable. There was an interval of sixteen years between the completion of the two volumes—1960 to 1977—explainable by Giersch's heavy workload as a member of the Council of Experts, as the new Director of the Kiel Institute and by other commitments. Giersch called the intervening years *Lern- und Lehrjahre* and he wrote in the preface of Volume Two: 'Without my learning from the debates about economic policy, the book would have become more formal and poorer in empirical content; and without my ongoing teaching experience, it would have become more concise and less intelligible, and hence more modern'.[4]

Giersch's work is almost without exception policy-oriented and quite ostensibly so. The list of his publications shows that in the years 1960 to 1977 eight titles included the word 'policy' and another the word 'experience'. This commitment to pragmatic relevance does not imply that Giersch is not a first-rate theorist. His essays on 'The Acceleration Principle and the Propensity to Import' (*Weltwirtschaftliches Archiv*, 1953)[5] and on 'Some Controversial Questions on Multiplier Theory' (*Schriften des Vereins für Sozialpolitik*, 1954)[6] are evidence of his ability to generate 'pure' economic theory, although even in these instances he insists or seeking some empirical reference. The same dedication to applied, or at least applicable, theory could be seen when Giersch showed the close connections between the older German theories of economic space and location with modern theories of international trade, on the one hand, and theories of regional income distribution, on the other. I am referring to Giersch's earlier papers on 'Economic Union between Nations and the Location of Industries' (*Review of Economic Studies*, 1949-50)[7] and 'Problems of Regional Distribution of Income' (*Schriften des Vereins für Sozialpolitik*, 1959).[8] Giersch has remained faithful to this theme in later publications: 'Infrastructure and Regional Policy' (*Gespräche der List Gesellschaft*, 1964)[9] and 'Aspects of Growth, Structural Change and Employment' (*Weltwirtschaftliches Archiv*, 1979).[10] In this article he developed a perspective that linked the ideas of Johann H. von Thünen and

Joseph A. Schumpeter in a theory of income differentials in a model based on the notion of 'centre versus periphery'.

Giersch wants to have both feet on the ground and he succeeds admirably in this ambition. This is clearly visible in his collected essays *Wirtschaftspolitik: Kritische Beiträge von 1967-1977*,[11] which presents a retrospective of Giersch's 'critical contributions' to the policy debates over ten critical years. The reader, with the benefit of hindsight, cannot but admire how courageously Giersch warned against wrong-headed policies and how vigorously he argued for alternative policies most unpopular at the time but eventually, often belatedly, adopted by the authorities.

An examination of the titles Giersch has chosen for his books, essays and articles reveals his preference for policies designed to maintain a stable price level. For publications from 1965 to 1971, I counted no less than seventeen titles with the words 'stable', 'stability' or 'stabilisation', and another four with the words 'inflation', or 'decline in the purchasing power of money'. If Giersch had been in charge of actual policy—not just of policy analysis— West Germany could have enjoyed the 1 per cent rate of annual increase of the price level that he would be prepared to tolerate.

With the preceding sentence I have entered the section I had programmed for observations on Giersch as policy analyst and adviser. Several of his functions and positions gave him ample opportunities to engage in policy analysis and advice. In 1960 Giersch became a member of the Scientific Advisory Council at the Federal Ministry of the Economy; from 1963 to 1971 he served on the Scientific Advisory Council of the Federal Ministry of Economic Cooperation; from 1964-70 he was a member of the Council of Economic Experts (*Sachverständigenrat zur Begutachtung der gesamt-wirtschaftlichen Entwicklung*); from 1970-73 he was a member of the German Forum for Development Policy; and in 1970 he became Chairman of the Association (*Arbeitsgemeinschaft*) of the German Institutes for Economic Research. The most widely publicised economic-policy statements were those made by the Council of Experts and by a Joint Working Group of the Association. Perhaps these two bodies should be briefly described, because they are so different from any equivalent agencies, if there are any, in other countries.

The Council of Economic Experts was established by a German federal law in August 1963. This body, whose members are appointed by the President of the German Federal Republic upon

nominations by the Federal Government, is not to advise the
Government but to aid it, as well as the legislature and the general
public, in forming judgments on current economic problems and
policies. The law stresses the complete independence of the Council.
Its mandate is to present, annually, expert opinions on the current
economic situation and on prospective developments, and also on
appropriate ways to attain, 'within the framework of a market
economy, stability of the price level, a high level of employment,
and external balance, with steady and adequate economic growth'.
Alternative ways and means to secure these objectives are to be
weighed and appraised, though no specific recommendations for
policy measures should be made. The annual reports of the Council
are submitted to the West German Government in November of
each year and some special reports are made at other times.

The reports are written by the five members of the Council (or
four if there is a temporary vacancy), with the aid of a small staff
headed by a general secretary, and are therefore collective products.
It happened that, for some time at least, three members of the
Council were from Saarbrücken, as was also the secretary; and
some staff members were students and assistants of Professor Giersch.
Although he was not the chairman of the Council, Giersch was, as
one journalist put it, playing 'first fiddle in the orchestra of experts'.
The press, the daily papers as well as the weekly or monthly
magazines, commonly referred to the Council as 'the five wise men'
('*die fünf Weisen*'); a somewhat irritated journalist once called Giersch
the '*Oberweise*', which I may render as the 'top-sage' or the 'master-
wizard'. In telling this at the present juncture I have anticipated
what I should say only in the section on Giersch, the intrepid
leader, or Giersch, the often-denounced public figure.

The Association of the German Institutes for Economic Research
consists of twenty-five institutes; its Joint Working Group consists
of members of the five large institutes in Berlin, Essen, Hamburg,
Kiel and Munich. They meet every spring and autumn to agree
on a joint *communiqué* on the economic situation, cyclical developments and trends, and offer their judgments regarding desirable
or undesirable economic policies. When, in 1969, Giersch became
Director of the Kiel Institute, the official opinions of the five
research institutes on matters of fixed versus flexible exchange
rates were divided 3:2 against flexible exchange rates. Not long
after Giersch came on the scene, the group agreed that, under
the conditions of the time, flexibility of the exchange rate of the

German mark was the only way to secure the internal purchasing power of the currency against imported inflation.

Giersch's basic principles of policy analysis were firm and consistent throughout his incumbency on the Council of Experts and, subsequently, at the Kiel Institute. In 1967, invited as an independent expert, he presented a concise statement of twenty-five theses at the economic convention of the Christian Democratic Unions (CDU-CSU). I mention only some of the essential points: promoting price competition; restraining wage increases; achieving consensus ('concerted action') among labour unions, employers' associations, government and economic experts on wage guidelines set in conformity with the growth of productivity over a medium-long run (this was called a 'cost-neutral wage policy'); avoiding the waste of attempting income-redistribution through wage-push policies; and securing price-level stability through flexibility of foreign-exchange rates. Supported by steadily refined arguments, this platform was and has remained the implicit philosophy of the Council of Experts.

Almost all the points in this programme were, at the time, controversial. Since Giersch as its vigorous advocate was sharply attacked by official and private opponents, he had to defend his views and found sharp counter-attacks to be the best strategy. Thus I come to talk about Giersch, the testy critic. He and the Council of Experts had to take on the most formidable opponent: the West German Government, represented by the Minister of the Economy, the Minister of Finance or the Chancellor. Some journalists took pleasure in reporting each clash between Council and Government and in counting how often Ludwig Erhard, Karl Schiller, Kurt Georg Kiesinger or Helmut Schmidt were the targets of criticism levelled by Giersch and the Council. The confrontations were sharpest on matters of exchange-rate policy. Chancellor Kiesinger had accepted the advice of German bankers and export industrialists to resist up-valuing the German mark or, 'even worse', allowing it to float in the free market. It had been clear—first to Giersch and the Council of Experts, but subsequently to the overwhelming majority of economists—that an under-valued currency was incompatible with a stable price level and would inevitably accelerate price inflation in West Germany up to the pace of inflation prevailing in other countries. Yet the Chancellor, over-riding the strong appeals by Karl Schiller, his Minister of the Economy, stubbornly stuck to the position of leaving the German mark under-valued, forcing the professors, prompted by Giersch and his Saarbrücken colleague, (the late) Egon Sohmen, to turn to the people by publishing a strongly worded manifesto. The value of the German mark became a decisive campaign issue in the election of 1969. The Chancellor lost the election, and the German mark was revalued, although not freed from its dollar link. This was to come only a few years later.

The leadership of Herbert Giersch in all these matters was, if not clearly visible, easily inferred from the course of events. His influence was paramount in every group of which he was a member. His leadership in making new ideas, new policies or new formulations acceptable was not a matter of charisma, nor of steam-roller tactics, nor of undue pressures brought to bear on colleagues, collaborators, students or subordinates. He got his views accepted on the strength of his arguments and on the steadfastness of his advocacy. The only power he used was the power of his logic.

Leaders of this sort are disliked by many and Giersch had his full share of antagonism. He was attacked, rebuked, abused, threatened, ridiculed and cursed. This part of my research—on Giersch, the often-denounced public figure—was most entertaining. The out-bursts of VIPs (very important persons) stung by Giersch's criti-cisms, or angered by his policy advice, or fuming about his cold-blooded use of logic against their firmly vested interests, made good copy in the newspapers. It makes good reading, especially now, long after the events, when the shooting is over and the historical record is rather clear.

The denouncing of Giersch started with the first Council report in 1964. He and his colleagues on the Council were charged with holding 'unrealistic' views (about the unfixing of exchange rates), sitting in their ivory tower far removed from the real world, reck-lessly endangering the jobs of workers in export industries, making irresponsible declarations liable to induce undesirable flows of speculative capital and lacking the necessary understanding of the sound governmental practice of coordinating the positions of different public bodies. Since the Council, in its subsequent reports, showed that it was unmoved by these strictures, and since it repeated arguments clearly in opposition to the position of the Government, Giersch and his colleagues were accused of having formed an official but not responsible opposition to the constitutional government (*'die Neben-Opposition der fünf Weisen'*). Some of the critics of the Council found this opposition intolerable and proposed that this body become a part of the Government under the Minister of the Economy. An interesting exchange took place in the pages of *Die Zeit*, Hamburg, in November and December 1968, with head-lines reading 'The Unloved Advisers' (*'Die ungeliebten Ratgeber'*), 'Popular or Independent?' (*'Beliebt oder unabhängig?'*) and 'Don't Worry, Mr Giersch!' (*'Machen Sie sich keine Sorgen, Herr Giersch!'*). The first article was by two critics of the Council, the second was a reply by Giersch, the third a rejoinder by Otto Schlecht, a high official in the Ministry of the Economy. The gratifying result of the exchange was that Dr Schlecht defended the independence of the Council in no uncertain terms. He admitted that the Council's statements had been unpopular with private groups, associations, political bodies and the Government, but he made a strong pro-nouncement in favour of the continued independence of the Council and its right and duty to state its views without pulling its punches.

The next clash came in May 1969, when Chancellor Kiesinger announced that he would not accept the Council's views on the exchange rate of the German mark, and when Finance Minister Franz-Joseph Strauss charged the professors with 'manipulating public opinion', using 'terrorist' pressure and arrogating to them-selves the authority of 'super-popes'. His ire had been aroused by the manifesto, which I mentioned before, of 99 (eventually 144) academic economists protesting against the intransigent position of the Government. The *Volkswirt*, Frankfurt a.M., May 1969, reported on the 'May Rebellion of the Professors' (*'Die Mai-Revolte der Professoren'*) and spoke of Giersch and Egon Sohmen as the 'mafiosi of Saarbrücken'.

The recriminations continued. An official of the Chancellor's and Finance Minister's political party denounced Giersch's critique of their position as irresponsible, injurious and a violation of his obligation to loyalty *vis-à-vis* the Government. Giersch replied that 'as an independent expert' he 'did not recognise any obligation of loyalty to the Government, but only an obligation to inform and enlighten the German people' (*Der Spiegel*, 2 June 1969).

The confrontations did not stop with Giersch's transfer from Saarbrücken to Kiel in July 1969, nor with his departure from the Council of Experts in 1970. As Director of the Kiel Institute he had every opportunity to make public pronouncements; and his con-tinued advocacy of a revalued or a freely floating German mark continued to enrage the official and private advocates of an extern-ally under-valued currency. The press reported the outcry of an official trade representative about '*das Rindvieh*' ('that stupid ox, blockhead') who, by advocating a revalued German mark, was making it more difficult to sell export goods payable in German currency. As a matter of fact, in May 1971, the Joint Working Group of the German Institutes for Economic Research came out with a unanimously agreed recommendation for another up-valuation of the German mark or, better still, for letting it float.

There was a short pause in the heated confrontations, probably because of the devaluations of the American dollar in December 1971 and in March 1973. But it was clear to all informed economists that the liberation of the German mark from any fixed relation to the dollar had to be accomplished. Although the Government was considering this move, Helmut Schmidt, then Minister of Finance in the Brandt Government, was furious when Giersch's Institute came out with another plea for a correctly valued currency. Mr Schmidt evidently feared a new flood of dollars if an upward move-ment of the German mark was publicly aired before the Govern-ment took action. He showed his indignation by suggesting that public funds ought to be denied to professors and institutes meddling with the Government's business. The Government should not pay for the ego trips of the professors. Since this clash of views concerned the citizen's right to free speech and the expert's duty to speak out freely, the press was unanimous in siding with Giersch, the de-nounced expert.

I have perhaps given too much space to this aspect of Giersch's activities. By no means should I end the laudation on this note. It is easy to find material for a more appropriate ending: the honours that have come to Herbert Giersch. Here is my list. In 1971 the London School of Economics made him an Honorary Fellow. In 1972 the Council of the International Economic Association elected him to its Executive Committee and in 1974 made him Treasurer. Also in 1974 he was elected for a four-year term as President of the Association d'Institutes Européens de Conjoncture. In 1976 he was elected an honorary member of the American Economic Association. In 1977 he was awarded the Great Cross of Merit of the German Federal Republic. Also in 1977 he received an honorary doctor's degree from the University Erlangen-Nürnberg. And finally, in celebration of his pre-eminence, he has been given this volume of Essays in Honour of Herbert Giersch.

NOTES AND REFERENCES
  1. Herbert Giersch, 'Inflation', in Erwin von Beckerath *et al.* (eds),

Handwörterbuch der Sozialwissenschaften (Stuttgart: Gustav Fischer, Tübingen: J. C. B. Mohr [Paul Siebeck], and Göttingen: Vandenhoeck & Ruprecht, 1956), Vol. 5, p. 290.

2. Giersch, *Der Ausgleich der Kriegslasten vom Standpunkt sozialer Gerechtigkeit*, Soziale Forschung und Praxis, Vol. 8 (Recklinghausen: Bitter, 1948).

3. *Idem, Allgemeine Wirtschaftspolitik, Vol. 1: Grundlagen, Vol. 2: Konjunktur- und Wachstumspolitik in der offenen Wirtschaft*, Die Wirtschaftswissenschaften, Reihe B: Volkswirtschaftslehre, Beiträge Nr 9 und 10 (Wiesbaden: Gabler, 1960 and 1977, respectively).

4. Translation by the present author.

5. Title translated by the present author. The original title reads 'Akzelerationsprinzip und Importneigung' and appeared in *Weltwirtschaftliches Archiv*, Hamburg, No. 2, 1953.

6. Title translated by the present author. The original title reads 'Einige kontroverse Fragen der Multiplikatortheorie' and appeared in Erich Schneider (ed.), *Beiträge zur Multiplikatortheorie*, Schriften des Vereins für Sozialpolitik, Neue Folge Vol. 9 (Berlin: Duncker & Humblot, 1954).

7. Giersch, 'Economic Union between Nations and the Location of Industries', *The Review of Economic Studies*, Cambridge, No. 2, 1949-50.

8. Title translated by the present author. The original title reads 'Probleme der regionalen Einkommensverteilung', in Walther G. Hoffmann (ed.), *Probleme des räumlichen Gleichgewichts in der Wirtschaftswissenschaft*, Schriften des Vereins für Sozialpolitik, Neue Folge Vol. 14 (Berlin: Duncker & Humblot, 1959).

9. Title translated by the present author. The original title reads 'Infrastruktur und Regionalpolitik', in Alfred Plitzko (ed.), *Planung ohne Planwirtschaft*, Frankfurter Gespräche der List Gesellschaft 7-9 June 1963 (Basle: Kyklos, Tübingen: J. C. B. Mohr [Paul Siebeck], 1964).

10. Giersch, 'Aspects of Growth, Structural Change and Employment—a Schumpeterian Perspective', *Weltwirtschaftliches Archiv*, Kiel, No. 4, 1979.

11. *Idem, Im Brennpunkt: Wirtschaftspolitik—Kritische Beiträge 1967 bis 1977*, edited by Karl Heinz Frank (Stuttgart: Deutsche Verlags-Anstalt, 1978).

List of Abbreviations

BIS	Bank for International Settlements
CAP	Common Agricultural Policy of the European Community
CMEA	Council for Mutual Economic Aid (Comecon), embracing centrally-planned economies
CPE	centrally-planned economy
CPI	consumer price index
DFI	direct foreign investment
ECSC	European Coal and Steel Community
EMS	European Monetary System, associated with the European Community
GAB	General Agreement to Borrow
GATT	General Agreement on Tariffs and Trade
GDP	gross domestic product
GNP	gross national product
IMF	International Monetary Fund
LDC	less developed country
MFA	Multi-fibre Arrangement, formally the Arrangement Regarding International Trade in Textiles
NATO	North Atlantic Treaty Organisation
NBER	National Bureau of Economic Research, in the United States
NIC	newly industrialising country
NOW	negotiable orders of withdrawal
OECD	Organisation for Economic Cooperation and Development
OEEC	Organisation for European Economic Cooperation, succeeded by the OECD
OPEC	Organisation of Petroleum Exporting Countries
SDR	Special Drawing Right on the IMF
SITC	Standard International Trade Classification

Part I

International Economic Order

1 Coordination or Competition among National Macro-economic Policies?

Roland Vaubel

'Decisions touching upon monetary policy belong exclusively to the sovereignty of each country.'

—Stresa Conference, 1932, quoted in Jacob Viner, *International Economics* (1951)

'People of the same trade seldom meet together, even for merriment and diversion, but the conversation ends in a conspiracy against the public, or in some contrivance to raise prices.'

—Adam Smith, *The Wealth of Nations* (1776)

One of the most remarkable and perhaps surprising developments of the last few years is the increasing tendency towards international coordination of national stabilisation policies. It is a surprising phenomenon because it occurs at a time of considerable exchange-rate flexibility.

Under the pegged exchange-rate system of Bretton Woods, the need for international coordination of stabilisation policies had been obvious: in order to maintain the exchange rate *vis-à-vis* the American dollar, the n-th currency of the system, each country had to bring the monetary expansion of its currency in line with that of the dollar or to modify the demand for its money through the interest-rate effects of fiscal policy. Coordination took the form of American stabilisation leadership and of adaptive stabilisation policy elsewhere.

Under exchange-rate flexibility, national monetary and fiscal policies are autonomous, except to the extent that countries interfere with each other's money-supply policies through foreign-exchange interventions. But even under 'pure floating', open economies are interdependent in real terms and, thus, with respect to the demand for their monies. International trade makes the demand for money sensitive to changes in the terms of trade and their effects on real income. International capital mobility implies that the demand for money is affected by changes in foreign real interest rates. If different currencies are substitutes for each other and if money does

3

not bear interest or is subject to non-interest-bearing reserve requirements, the demand for a money is even affected by changes in
foreign *nominal* interest rates. Contrary to a widespread belief,[1] these
international interdependencies under floating have neither been
denied nor overlooked by the leading advocates of exchange-rate
flexibility.[2] Indeed, many of them predicted an increase of real
international interdependence, because floating would help to
remove restrictions on international money and capital movements;
and their prediction was borne out by the facts. But, since exchange-
rate flexibility would allow the monetary authorities of each
country fully to compensate foreign-induced changes in the demand
for their money through adjustments of their money supply, they
would be free to attain approximate stability of their national price
level irrespective of foreign monetary policies, international capital
arbitrage and changes in the terms of trade.

How then could the quest for more international coordination
occur under exchange-rate flexibility? I venture to suggest that it
was precisely the result of exchange-rate flexibility. One reason is
the fact just mentioned that real interdependence seems to have
further increased under floating. The second is that national
autonomy over the money supply and the price level was used in
very different ways and thus with very different results in the
various countries and that this natural corollary of freedom alarmed
all those who are used to regarding inequalities of results as inherently
inequitable and intolerable. The view that the marked increase in
the price of oil and other raw materials had affected the various
industrialised countries very differently, and that the 'burden of
adjustment' to this shock had to be 'shared' more equitably, should
also be seen in this context. But the evidence shows, for example,
that the real exchange-rate changes within the European Community increased so little in the 1970s that they may just as well
be attributed to the effect of exchange-rate flexibility and divergent
monetary policies.[3]

The frequent demands for (more) international coordination of
stabilisation policies were voiced by both academic[4] and political[5]
economists and they were magnified by the international organisations (the Organisation for Economic Cooperation and Development
[OECD], the International Monetary Fund [IMF], the Bank for
International Settlements [BIS] and the European Community)[6]
which thereby increased the demand for their product. The dominant interpretation given to coordination was 'to plan jointly broad

economic targets and the general policies to achieve them'[7] and 'to bear in mind the effects on each other of their policies not because of indirect repercussions . . . but because [the governments] have struck a bargain that each take into account the other's interests'.[8] This interpretation should strictly be distinguished from the more modest and *non-controversial* goal of 'adjusting one's own policies to the policies which other countries are about to put into effect and to do so on the basis of dependable current information by others'.[9]

The most spectacular result of the quest for international co-ordination (in the first and wider sense) was a series of 'summit meetings' among the 'Big Five', 'Six' or 'Seven' where national stabilisation policies became the object of international negotiations and commitments. Another remarkable development was that the IMF received explicit responsibility for the surveillance of exchange rates and monetary policies.[10] Finally, the OECD succeeded in drawing attention to its views by popularising the so-called 'loco-motive theory', and later the 'convoy theory', of internationally coordinated demand management.[11] All these efforts differed from what had been typical of coordination under the Bretton Woods system in that:

(a) coordination was no longer achieved through automatic adjustment to American hegemony, but through explicit nego-tiations among governments or IMF surveillance; and

(b) the aim of coordination was not always a more uniform use of the national policy instruments, but sometimes a planned international differentiation (in order, however, to attain a more uniform target performance).

In the following sections we shall ask whether there is an economic case for such *international coordination of stabilisation targets under flexible exchange rates* and whether there are welfare-theoretic argu-ments which might provide a basis for it. We shall distinguish arguments based on (i) assignment theory, (ii) externality theory and (iii) game theory. We shall *not* be concerned with the question whether and how coordination of targets can in fact be achieved[12] and whether there is also a need for international coordination of the use and scope of policy instruments.

INEFFICIENT ASSIGNMENTS

The demand for international policy coordination, that is, for more centralised decision making, must seem puzzling to any neo-classical economist, for, after all, decentralised decision making and automatic coordination through the market are the essence of standard economic theory. With regard to economic policy, the work of James E. Meade, Jan Tinbergen and Robert Mundell has led to the conclusion that decentralised decision making will only be efficient and produce stable solutions if instruments are assigned to those targets for which they have a comparative advantage. In a two-instrument, two-target world, for example, decentralised policy assignment is consistent with efficiency and stability only if the impact coefficients $a_{11} a_{22} - a_{12} a_{21} > 0$ (where the first subscript indicates the instrument and the second subscript the target in the instrument-target matrix). In words, 'if one target is changed by adjustment of the instrument assigned to it, and then some or all other instruments are subsequently adjusted to eliminate the effects on their respective targets of the disturbances initiating from the change in the first instrument, the initial impact of the first instrument on its target is not completely offset'.[13]

Moreover, Jürg Niehans has shown that where the impact coefficients decrease with increasing use (law of diminishing returns), optimisation tends to require equalisation of marginal impact coefficients (per unit of cost of instrument use with respect to the same target) and that targets should not be viewed as fixed, but as partly substitutable—that is, as indifference curves.[14] Thus, decentralised decision making in economic policy matters is subject to precisely the same optimality criteria as decentralised decision making by private economic agents in the market; and it is natural to assume that national decentralised policy making is as unlikely to be sub-optimal as individual decision making in the market.[15]

Nevertheless, some authors have argued that, whatever may be true for the market, 'we can be much less confident that competition among policies will be optimal [and that] joint determination of economic objectives and policies . . . is . . . the most desirable solution'[16] because:

(a) to be attainable, economic objectives must be consistent, for if they are not consistent, no number of policy instruments will suffice to reach the objective;[17]

(b) even if in the end the whole process settles to a point where the various national authorities are satisfied, it will have taken longer than if there had been close coordination between the authorities in the several countries involved;[18] and

(c) it is at least theoretically possible that stability for the

system as a whole would require assignment of one country's
instrument to another country's target, the more so as there
is the 'possibility of reversal in the relative effectiveness of
instruments'.[19]

The first of these arguments is obsolete because it dates from the
pre-Niehans fixed-target assignment theory. Of course, say, in a
two-country world, one country's trade surplus is the other's deficit
and the exchange rate between their currencies must be common to
both. But even if governments have exchange-rate or trade-balance
targets, those targets will not be unconditional; there will be a
preference trade-off with other target variables. Thus, 'the Meade-
Tinbergen-Mundell models lead to the incompatibility problem not
so much because this problem is important in the real world as
because, having fixed targets, they do not provide an automatic
target-adjusting mechanism'.[20]

The second argument is an argument for a speedy and comprehensive exchange of information about current and prospective
government policies and possibly even about the actions which the
individual governments would take under various hypothetical
circumstances. It does not establish a case for *international negotiations
and decision making* about national policy objectives.

Nor does the third argument lead to the conclusion that consensus
has to be established about the *values* which national stabilisation
targets should take; it merely asserts that a consensus may have to
be reached about the *type* of target(s) that should be assigned to the
individual governments. Moreover, there seems to be widespread
agreement that this argument is purely academic and inapplicable
to the real world. Within a Keynesian model, where monetary and
fiscal policy are used to stabilise employment and output, it has been
shown that each country's stabilisation policy has a comparative
advantage over domestic economic activity as long as the Robinson
condition

$$(1/\frac{\delta Y_1}{\delta Y_2} > \frac{\delta Y_2}{\delta Y_1})$$

is met.[21] Given the implausibility of assuming that a given income
change in one country could produce a larger income change in
another country, it is difficult to imagine that the Robinson condition
could fail to be met.

Neo-classical theory would prescribe a domestic assignment that
is different from the Keynesian one:

(a) steady and pre-announced money-supply policy (or a private competitive supply of money) is assigned to the target of price-level stability;

(b) public expenditure policy is assigned to the optimal provision of public goods[22] and possibly to the subsidisation of state-regulated natural monopolies;[23]

(c) citizens are to be taxed in proportion to their marginal benefits;

(d) the choice between tax financing and debt financing serves to optimise the inter-temporal incidence of taxation (along the same lines);

(e) since the demand for public goods must be assumed to be price-elastic and therefore also interest- and wage-elastic, the distribution of public expenditure over time should—if possible —be counter-cyclical (especially with respect to public investment and publicly-produced consumer durables), which is to say the public sector should act as an (output and employment) stabilising speculator if it is capable of doing so; and

(f) any remaining unemployment must be eliminated through an adjustment (in a growing economy: a reduced growth) of the real wages negotiated between labour and employers.

Given that monetary policy has a stronger effect on the domestic price level than (through temporary real exchange-rate changes and international shifts in the demand for money) on foreign price levels, monetary policy is best assigned to the domestic target; as long as public expenditure is to a larger extent directed at domestic output and factors of production than at foreign output and resources, fiscal stabilisation policy must be assigned to domestic targets (an optimal provision of public goods) as well. Since monetary and fiscal policy do not have a comparative advantage in equilibrating the balance of payments, this target must be left to the exchange rate; or, turned around the other way, the exchange rate —which is not an independent policy instrument[24]—is at a comparative disadvantage in providing price-level stability, public goods, *et cetera*.

Finally, it should be emphasised that even if Professor Mundell's principle of effective market classification, or Professor Niehans' optimisation rule led to the conclusion that cross-country assignments would be desirable in terms of technical efficiency and stability, this conclusion would not be conclusive. The conventional assignment literature is partial and defective in that it assumes information to be costless and democratic politicians and voters to be universalist utilitarians who value the (cardinal) utility of others as highly as their own.

First of all, as far as information cost is concerned, it seems plausible to assume with Bentham that, usually, 'everybody is the best judge of his own interest' or at least that if he were given the freedom to make the mistakes from which he can learn, everybody has the highest potential to become, and in the long run is likely to be, the best judge of his own interest. If a foreign government is assigned responsibility for our well being (stability), it is likely to prove more ignorant of our preferences with regard to price-level stability and public goods than our own politicians.[25] Secondly, what is probably even more important, foreign politicians have much less of an incentive—if at all—to pursue our interest than our own politicians have, however loosely the latter may be controlled by their electorate.[26] Any assignment theory which ignores these information costs and incentive aspects is at best technocratic.

INTERNATIONAL STABILITY AS AN INTERNATIONAL PUBLIC GOOD

A welfare-theoretic case for international coordination of stabilisation policies could be established if it could be shown that decentralised competitive policies might produce non-appropriable Pareto-relevant external effects in other countries. If these external effects were the same for all countries and equal to the internal effects in the country of origin, stability would even be an international public good. This view has indeed been taken by Keynesian economists. It found its 'classic' formulation in a 1962 article by John G. Head, of Monash University, Melbourne:

'An economic unit increasing its consumption- or investment-spending, or accepting a substantial money-wage cut in a situation of unemployment equilibrium, can by no means appropriate itself, through private pricing, the full social benefits in the form of multiplier and real balance effects on the incomes and profits of other economic units . . . With the signs changed, a similar argument applies to the inflation case . . . Again, in the case of sub-optimal economic growth, the full benefits in terms of rising real wages from growth-promoting behaviour, such as thrift, risk-bearing, dividend- and wage-restraint, are seldom anything like fully appropriable from the point of view of the economic unit which must bear the full cost of such behaviour . . . In all these cases it would be possible for the community, by means of voluntary cooperative action, to compensate potential losers from socially desirable changes, and still enjoy a net benefit with some members better off and none worse off. Such cooperative effort will seldom be forth-coming in the absence of coercion and the inefficiency due to non-appropriability will therefore persist.

'In a broad but very real and important sense then, domestic and international economic stability, domestic and international allocation of resources in accordance with consumers' wishes and an optimal rate of growth can all quite properly be regarded as public goods, for adequate provision of which public policy must be relied upon.'[27] (Italics in the original.)

This conclusion has been repeated in a somewhat less articulate way by a number of writers on the subject of international co-ordination.[28] Moreover, in line with this conclusion, stability of (full) employment and the price level, being conceived of as public goods, have been treated as standard problem cases of fiscal federalism where a balance has to be struck between the minimisation of external spillovers through the *extension* of the policy domain and the maximisation of taxpayer mobility (Tiebout principle) and of public-good differentiation through a *reduction* of the policy domain.[29]

The problem about this approach is that it fails to make a distinction between technological and pecuniary externalities. This distinction goes back (at least) to the late Jacob Viner;[30] and it has been discussed in some detail, for example by Tibor Scitovsky, of Stanford University, Roland N. McKean, of the University of Virginia, Gordon Tullock, of the Virginia Polytechnic Institute, Blacksburg, and Professor Meade.[31] The distinction is important because, while technological externalities are incompatible with Pareto optimality in competitive equilibrium, 'merely pecuniary' externalities are not. Technological externalities exist where production functions and/or utility functions of individual producers and consumers, respectively, are interdependent. Pecuniary externalities exist where profit or other income functions are interdependent through the price mechanism.

To return to Professor Head's examples, if many consumers increase their demand for, say, blue jeans and reduce their demand for synthetic trousers, this has pecuniary external effects on the profits of both types of producers, on the profits of the producers of their inputs, on the incomes of the factors engaged in those lines of production and on the relative prices charged to consumers. The result is a redistribution of rents, but given the initial shift in tastes, this redistribution through market interdependence is required to achieve Pareto optimality.

Another, more pertinent, example is the following: a producer reduces his price and increases his output because he has made a cost-saving invention. Through market interdependence, other producers will be hurt (that is, they will lose rents), while consumers will gain (consumer surplus). As can easily be shown,[32] however, the gain to consumers and the innovating producer is always larger than the loss to the competing producers. The 'invisible hand' makes sure that 'the sum of consumers' and producers' surpluses will be maximised, although they do not enter explicitly, as part of the maximand, the economic decisions of any producer.[33] The pecuniary spillovers for the profitability of the remainder of production *must not* even be taken into acccount by the innovative producers; for if they were, he would act like a monopolist and output would be sub-optimal.[34]

Given that pecuniary (or distributional) externalities are merely the result of market interdependence, it would indeed be paradoxical to consider them an indication of market failure, when welfare economics tells us that market interdependence serves to bring about a Pareto optimum. Pecuniary externalities have no place in equilibrium theory nor, of course, in cost-benefit analysis.[35] Pecuniary externalities have often been mistaken for technological externalities[36] and this is also true with respect to the tools of stabilisation policy—that is, the production of money and public goods. For example, a growing number of monetary analysts argue that money-holding exerts Pareto-relevant external effects or even that money is a public good because:

(a) 'the individual who adds to cash balances confers a benefit on his fellows for which he cannot collect compensation [because] he would make the price level slightly lower than it would otherwise be'[37] and induce a 'restructuring of the whole system of payments and transactions';[38]

(b) 'the holding of cash balances by an individual . . . yields liquidity services to other individuals as well';[39] or because

(c) 'money is a device for economising on the cost of information required for transactions'.[40]

These arguments have been refuted in considerable detail,[41] but even without going into details, it is obvious that money meets neither the non-excludability criterion nor the non-rivalness criterion.[42] The external effects of a change in the demand for, or supply of, money on the holders and users of money are purely pecuniary; and they are likely to be smaller, the more competitive the supply of money.[43]

As for fiscal policy, non-market interdependence exists with respect to taxation and the supply of public goods; that is, in those fields where, rightly or wrongly, governments interfere with the market process. Such direct external effects may, however, provide a basis for *international* cooperation only to the extent that a country taxes foreigners or supplies public goods to them.

Moreover, since the need for international cooperation in this case arises not *qua* stabilisation policy but *qua* non-market interdependence, it does not establish a case for international coordination of stabilisation policies as such, but merely for *cooperation in fields where Pareto-relevant international externalities are important* (such as protection of the environment, the law of the sea and space, international security, international property rights, rules of conduct in international trade policy, exchange of all other information about past experience and future policy[44] and international aid to the extent that utility functions are interdependent internationally). In fact, as Herbert Stein, of the University of Virginia, has pointed out, there is a danger that a misplaced emphasis on international coordination of stabilisation policies may distract governments' attention from these vital fields of international cooperation: 'the supply of willingness to cooperate internationally is not unlimited and it should be conserved for use in the most productive areas'.[45]

Two concrete examples may show the pecuniary nature of the international external effects of national stabilisation policy. In the first case, let us assume an expansionary monetary policy abroad; that is, an unexpected increase in the production of foreign money by a foreign money-producing monopolist. From the monetary approach to exchange rates we know that the exchange rate will adjust faster than the foreign price level so that the *real* exchange rate will temporarily change (*ceteris paribus*). If the foreign interest rate falls before it starts rising and if the short-run response of foreign output to the monetary shock is weak, there may even occur an overshooting of the *nominal* exchange rate.[46] If the real exchange rate (which in this context may be identified with the terms of trade) deteriorates for the foreign country temporarily, foreign demand for our exports will fall temporarily, and our demand for imports will increase temporarily. Thus if prices and/or wages in our export- and import-competing industries remain unchanged and if profits are reduced for longer than their buffer function can sustain, the home country may experience a temporary reduction of employment.[47]

Our problem, however, is purely one of inadequate adjustment to market interdependence; for if the prices of domestic tradeables were temporarily reduced and if wages were adjusted to the temporarily reduced marginal value productivity of labour, no temporary unemployment would arise.[48] This explains why, for example, W. M. Corden, of the Australian National University, Canberra, rests his case for coordination squarely on the vague possibility that 'there may be rigidities in real factor prices'.[49]

But does it make sense for the government to step in whenever some economic agents refuse or at least fail to adjust to changes in the market situation—the more so as the government can only avoid the temporary real exchange-rate change if it creates more inflation at home, either by imitating the foreign monetary expansion[50] or by adopting a bond-financed expansion of public expenditure (on excess public goods or possibly even for wage subsidies), thus raising the domestic interest rate and reducing the demand for the domestic money? In both cases, it would, of course, create expectations of more interventions in the future, thus rigidifying the economy even further. Or finally, should the domestic government put pressure on the foreign government to refrain from its monetary expansion although the latter, after thorough consultation (exchange of information), believes that such action would be in its best interest? After all, the cause of the temporary exchange-rate change is not only that the foreign authorities have modified their monetary policy, but also that the domestic authorities want to follow a different monetary policy. The case against such disregard of the right of national self-determination is, of course, at least as strong if the foreign authorities decide to reduce monetary expansion.

Up to now we have ignored that, other things unchanged, the foreign expansion also has implications for our price level. Since our import prices fall temporarily, our price level will temporarily be lower than it would otherwise be—to the extent that, in addition, the demand for money shifts from the foreign currency to our currency once and for all, our price level will (*ceteris paribus*) be lower permanently. These price-level effects, however, would be avoided almost completely if the domestic monetary authority satisfied the increased demand for its (base) money[51] and if, in addition, it temporarily increased its monetary expansion by a fraction of the foreign increase in monetary expansion, the fraction being equal to the effective weight which import prices have in the national price index.[52]

As a second example, assume a reduction of bond-financed public-goods supply abroad. To the extent that the reduction of the foreign real rate of interest increases the foreign demand for money and consequently causes the foreign money to appreciate and, with a lag, the foreign inflation rate to fall, the foreign disturbance is transmitted to our home country through the same channel, namely a temporary change (deterioration) in the latter's real exchange rate. The reduction in the foreign interest rate will, however, also cause a capital movement from the foreign to the home country, thus requiring a largely temporary decrease in the current account and hence an improvement of the real exchange rate of the home country. Whether and in which direction its real exchange rate (its terms of trade) will temporarily change cannot therefore be determined through theoretical analysis.

Although market participants have it in their power to prevent such market interdependence through the real exchange rate from affecting employment and although the domestic authorities can (very nearly) prevent the foreign policy change from affecting the domestic price level (or from affecting employment in the short run), this is not to deny that real exchange-rate fluctuations that are induced by (international differences in) monetary disturbances pose a real cost to the world economy.[53] But is it not also true that consumers suffer when producers are inefficient and do we for that reason demand 'summit meetings' between consumers and producers or consumer 'surveillance' over producers? The reason why we do not is that, especially in a competitive economy, producers have a sufficiently strong incentive to avoid inefficiencies because such inefficiencies reduce their profits. Similarly, precisely because no country can gain from temporarily destabilising income and/or employment in its export- and import-competing sector or even from distorting its structure of production through temporary real exchange-rate signals that are due to monetary disturbances and, above all, because such monetary disturbances also destabilise the domestic sector of the economy, each country must be interested in avoiding them. In other words, as is typical of pecuniary externalities, the 'invisible hand' assures that each country has a sufficient incentive to maximise world welfare because by doing so it would also maximise its own welfare.

International differences in stabilisation policies lead to temporary real exchange-rate changes only if stabilisation policies are volatile and unexpected. Thus all countries have an incentive to avoid unexpected stabilisation policies: monetary expansion, public expenditure and public debt 'management' should all be pre-announced.[54] By pre-announcing their policies, or the rules by which they are formed, governments would ensure an optimal supply of the only (international and national) public good that is at stake with regard to stabilisation policy as such: the public good of knowledge about government behaviour. But there is no welfare-theoretic argument to the effect that such knowledge should be supplied on the basis of joint international decision making.[55]

So far this section has purported to show that from the point of view of externality and public-good theory, internationally nego-tiated decision making is not superior to independent and com-petitive decision making. It will now be argued that competition among national stabilisation policies is in fact preferable to co-ordination because competition provides a public good which coordination fails to provide. The Nobel laureate, Friedrich von Hayek, has emphasised time and again that competition is a mechanism of discovery.[56] The diversity of competitive efforts and of their results sets a process of 'natural selection' in motion. Since the more successful competitors can be (and are!) imitated by the less successful ones, competition produces more of the public good of knowledge than the uniformity which tends to result from co-ordination.[57] For example, if Switzerland and West Germany had been prevented from pursuing their disinflationary stabilisation policies over the last few years, citizens in Italy, the United Kingdom and elsewhere might not have realised as clearly that inflation in their own countries was and is due to the inappropriate monetary policies conducted by their own governments and, consequently, the public pressure on these governments to reduce inflation would have been much weaker.[58]

Diversification of stabilisation policies may also provide know-ledge or more predictability in another way. If, say, the theory of the political business cycle is applicable and if, for this reason, there will always remain a nest of discretionary, non-announced and destabilising 'stabilisation' policies in democracies, policy competition is a way to de-synchronise business cycles or even to randomise the underlying policy shocks internationally and thus to reduce business-cycle uncertainty and risk through diversification.[59]

A GAME-THEORETIC CASE FOR COORDINATION OF NATIONAL STABILISATION POLICIES

The previous section has assumed that national stabilisation policies could come close to being genuinely competitive. It may be objected that some countries are too large and that the number of countries and policy domains is too small to warrant this assumption.[60] There may, therefore, be a game-theoretic argument in favour of coordination and this should strictly be distinguished from the arguments examined in the previous sections.[61] The difference between the argument based on public-goods theory and the one based on game theory stands out most clearly if consideration is given to the fact that the dilemma case in game theory arises because the number of participants is *small*, while the free-rider problem in public-goods theory is more severe the *larger* the number of people who participate in the public good's benefits.

Game-theoretic analyses of decentralised stabilisation policies have been presented by, for example, Richard Cooper, of Harvard University, Professor Niehans, and Koichi Hamada, of the University of Tokyo.[62] They invariably use two-player (duopoly) models, and they find that whenever both parties have targets which must be identical or mirrored between both of them (the change in foreign-exchange reserves or the real rate of interest)[63] the intersection of their reaction curves (the Nash point) in the myopic, non-cooperative Cournot case may not lie on the Pareto-efficient contract line connecting the points of tangency of their indifference curves. Moreover, they demonstrate the familiar point that the Stackelberg leadership solution may improve on the Nash point, but that the contract line will not be reached in this way. Thus, they conclude, a cooperative solution has to be sought and this solution may require direct bargaining between the two players and an agreement to avoid 'beggar-thy-neighbour' stabilisation policies. Since notably discretionary monetary policy, regardless of whether it operates through foreign-exchange interventions or in other ways (say, through domestic open-market operations), temporarily affects the real exchange rate, the composition of the balance of payments and even the real world interest rate, it is classified as a policy to be coordinated internationally.

There are a number of problems with this line of reasoning. In the first place, one might emphasise that the game-theoretic case for coordination of monetary policy breaks down under the neo-classical assignment:

(a) If monetary expansion is always pre-announced and expected (as would be in the interest of each country), there are no temporary (and later offset) real exchange-rate changes, current-account changes, *et cetera*, that are due to monetary policy.[64] The real exchange-rate changes which then still take place are due to market forces and international market interdependence and there is no good reason for trying to suppress them.

(b) Even if foreign monetary expansion were not pre-announced and if temporary real exchange-rate changes did result, the home government would be ill advised to pursue a real exchange-rate target, for it would have to give up its price-level target and it would not know which real exchange rate is the long-run equilibrium rate. On the other hand, the domestic authorities would still be free to achieve approximate price-level stability through compensatory monetary-policy adjustments. The discretionary monetary policy abroad, it is true, would prevent the domestic monetary authorities from fixing a certain rate of monetary expansion in advance; but it would not in principle prevent them from attaining approximate price-level stability. Needless to repeat, adjustment of prices and wages in the market would have to take care of full employment.

Secondly, one may wonder whether a two-person game situation is a better approximation to the real world than a competitive model. After all, competition need not be atomistic and perfect to bring about a Pareto-optimum; for example, an approximately equal degree of imperfection might do as well. Indeed, any game-theoretic approach which treats (two or more) governments as the only parties affected by the game is entirely misleading. Governments are producers who sell public goods and natural-monopoly goods (like money)[65] to their electorates. If governments collude, they will collude at the expense of the consumer.[66] They will raise the joint 'profits' of the politicians participating in the cartel, but they will reduce output and raise prices regardless of whether the standard of comparison is perfect competition, oligopoly[67] or a duopolist Cournot solution.[68]

It is well known from public-choice theory that, to some extent, rational politicians and bureaucrats have an incentive and the power in a democracy to act against the interest of the majority of their voters, let alone the welfare of society at large. What is only gradually coming to be known is that international collusion strengthens this power. As Professor Hayek and others have argued,[69] international monetary-policy cartels (in the extreme case fixed exchange rates) enable the producers of money (the national central banks) to increase their profits (seigniorage) by raising the price of holding money (the inflation rate and hence the nominal interest rate) at the expense of their customers (money holders); and real output (real cash balances) will fall as a result. It is more currency competition (less monetary-policy coordination) which, by increasing product (currency) substitutability, raises the price elasticity of demand faced by each producer (central bank). The hypothesis has been tested for Western Europe in 1968-78; the evidence shows very clearly that the average rate of monetary expansion in Western Europe was lower, the more the national rates of monetary expansion differed across countries.[70] In other words, coordination raised the inflation rate.

The theory of currency competition does not pre-suppose that monetary-policy makers aim at the maximisation of seigniorage. Even if they try to use unexpected monetary expansion and inflation to raise employment, an increase in the degree of currency competition has the welcome effect of deterring them from inflation:

(a) As was mentioned already, public opinion in the more inflationary countries is impressed by the example of the less inflationary countries (competition as a process of discovery and imitation).

(b) Where 'voice' does not help enough, 'exit' does. As the demand for money shifts from the more inflationary to the less inflationary currencies, the monetary policy domain of the more inflationary central banks, and hence their power to affect the level of employment in the short run, is reduced.

(c) Exchange-rate flexibility speeds up the price-level adjustment to an expansionary monetary policy and thereby reduces its output effects.

NOTES AND REFERENCES
1. See, for example, Marc A. Miles, 'Currency Substitution, Flexible Exchange Rates, and Monetary Independence', *The American Economic*

Review, Menasha, Wisconsin, June 1978, p. 428, and Arturo Brillembourg and Susan M. Schadler, 'A Model of Currency Substitution in Exchange Rate Determination', *International Monetary Fund, Staff Papers*, Washington, No. 3, 1979.

2. The following is a good example: 'Flexible exchange rates are a means of combining interdependence among countries through trade with a maximum of internal monetary independence: they are a means of permitting each country to seek for monetary stability according to its own lights, without either imposing its mistakes on its neighbours or having their mistakes imposed on it': Milton Friedman, 'The Case for Flexible Exchange Rates', in *idem, The Optimum Quantity of Money and Other Essays* (Chicago: Aldine, 1969), p. 200. Flexible exchange rates will not provide complete insulation unless money and capital movements are assumed to be zero and unless terms-of-trade changes do not affect desired expenditure, the demand for money and the cost of production. See Michael Mussa, 'Macroeconomic Interdependence and the Exchange Rate Regime', in Rudiger Dornbusch and Jacob A. Frenkel (eds), *International Economic Policy, Theory and Evidence* (Baltimore and London: Johns Hopkins Press, 1979).

3. For references and the evidence, see Roland Vaubel, 'Real Exchange-Rate Changes in the European Community: a New Approach to the Determination of Optimum Currency Areas', *Journal of International Economics*, Amsterdam, May 1978, and *idem, Strategies for Currency Unification: the Economics of Currency Competition and the Case for a European Parallel Currency*, Kieler Studien, 156 (Tübingen: J. C. B. Mohr, for the Institut für Weltwirtschaft an der Universität Kiel, 1978).

4. See notably Richard N. Cooper, 'Worldwide versus Regional Integration: Is There an Optimum Size of the Integrated Area?', in Fritz ¡Machlup (ed.), *Economic Integration: Worldwide, Regional, Sectoral*, Proceedngs of the 4th Congress of the International Economic Association held in Budapest, Hungary (London: Macmillan, 1976), pp. 47-49; Paul McCracken *et al., Towards Full Employment and Price Stability*, a Report to the OECD by a Group of Independent Experts (Paris: OECD Secretariat, 1977), p. 237; Charles P. Kindleberger, 'International Policies for the Coordination of Economic Growth', *Journal of International Affairs*, New York, No. 2, 1969, pp. 302 and 310-11, and *idem*, 'Dominance and Leadership in the International Economy: Exploitation, Public Goods and Free Rides', in *Hommage à François Perroux*, sponsored by the Centre National de la Recherche Scientifique (Grenoble: Presses Universitaires, 1978), p. 285. Peter B. Kenen, in 'Flexible Exchange Rates and National Autonomy', *Rivista Internazionale di Scienze Economiche e Commerciali*, Padua, No. 2, 1976, p. 120, even concludes from his formal analysis that, in a world of high international capital mobility, 'there may . . . be more need to harmonize monetary policies under the current exchange-rate regime than there was when rates were pegged'.

5. 'Each country has to make allowance for the external effects of [its] policy and to work with other countries toward achieving some consistency and compatibility in the interests of broad stability', Paul A. Volcker, 'Contribution to Session 1: "The Role of Monetary Policy Coordination to Attain Exchange-Rate Stability"', in Robert A. Mundell and Jacques J. Polak

(eds), *The New International Monetary System* (New York: Columbia University Press, 1977), p. 35. 'What can be expected is that countries recognize the external impact of their national monetary policies, and that in pursuing their domestic policies they take this impact on other countries into consideration': Otmar Emminger, 'Contribution to Session 1', *ibid.*, p. 18. '[Countries] have an international responsibility to conduct monetary policies with external factors in mind': Rinaldo Ossola, 'Comment on Session 1', *ibid.*, p. 39.

6.   See notably *Economic Outlook*, Paris, OECD Secretariat, December 1976, pp. 11-12; *ibid.*, July 1977, p. 11; H. Johannes Witteveen, 'Scenario for Coordinated Growth and Payments Adjustment', address to the IMF Interim Committee, Mexico, 29-30 April 1978, published as 'Witteveen Analyzes Economic Prospects, Offers Basis for Coordination of Policies', in *IMF Survey*, Washington, 8 May 1978; *Annual Report of the Bank for International Settlements*, Basle, 1976, p. 7; Resolution of the Council of Ministers of the European Community, November 1976; and the Commission of the European Community, *Die Wirtschaftslage der Gemeinschaft*, Brussels, No. 4, 1977, p. 4.

7.   Marina von N. Whitman, 'Coordination and Management of the International Economy: a Search for Organizing Principles', *Contemporary Economic Problems* (Washington: American Enterprise Institute, 1977), p. 321.

8.   W. M. Corden, 'The Coordination of Stabilization Policies among Countries', in Albert Ando, Richard Herring and Richard Marston (eds), *International Aspects of Stabilization Policies*, Conference Series No. 12 (Boston: Federal Reserve Bank of Boston, 1974), p. 139.

9.   William Fellner, 'International Coordination of National Economic Policies, a Commentary', in Samuel I. Katz (ed.), *US-European Monetary Relations* (Washington: American Enterprise Institute, 1979), p. 232.

10.   Guidelines for surveillance were adopted in June 1974. In April 1978 they were revised and incorporated in the new Articles of Agreement, IV, Section I.

11.   Support for the locomotive approach came also from the International Monetary Fund, the Bank for International Settlements, McCracken *et al.*, *op. cit.*, and Cooper, *op. cit.*

12.   Whitman, 'The Locomotive Approach to Sustaining World Recovery: Has it Run Out of Steam?', *Contemporary Economic Problems*, (Washington: American Enterprise Institute, 1978), p. 283, and Herbert Stein, 'International Coordination of Domestic Economic Policies', *The AEI Economist*, Washington, June 1978, pp. 4-5, argue that international coordination cannot be implemented satisfactorily because too little is known about international interdependencies and because the policy-making process would be 'overburdened'. Their scepticism is shared by Gottfried Haberler, 'Flexible-Exchange-Rate Theories and Controversies Once Again', in John S. Chipman and Charles P. Kindleberger (eds), *Flexible Exchange Rates and the Balance of Payments: Essays in Memory of Egon Sohmen*, Studies in International Economics, Vol. 7 (Amsterdam, New York and Oxford: North-Holland, 1980), p. 32.

13. John D. Patrick, 'Establishing Convergent Decentralized Policy Assignment', *Journal of International Economics*, No. 1, 1973, p. 42.

14. Jürg Niehans, 'Monetary and Fiscal Policies in Open Economies under Fixed Exchange Rates: an Optimizing Approach', *Journal of Political Economy*, Chicago, 1968, No. 4, pt 2, pp. 899 and 908-9.

15. This is what Corden, in 'The Coordination of Stabilization Policies among Countries', *op. cit.*, pp. 139-40, calls the simple argument: 'It can be argued that if countries make adequate use of the policy instruments available to them, there is no need for coordination of stabilization policies among countries ... One can thus imagine countries reacting continually and atomistically to the events from outside them, including the consequences of other countries' stabilization policies. And if their policies are intelligent and speedy, they will achieve whatever stabilization they wish to achieve.'

16. Cooper, *The Economics of Interdependence: Economic Policy in the Atlantic Community* (New York, Toronto and London: McGraw-Hill, for the Council of Foreign Relations, 1968), pp. 171, 262 and 264.

17. *Ibid.*, p. 155. See also *idem*, 'The Assignment Problem: Comment', in Robert A. Mundell and Alexandre K. Swoboda (eds), *Monetary Problems of the International Economy* (Chicago and London: University of Chicago Press, 1969), p. 237; Corden, 'The Coordination of Stabilization Policies among Countries', *op. cit.*, p. 143; Robert Solomon, 'The Allocation of "Oil Deficits" ', *Brookings Papers on Economic Acitivity*, Washington, No. 1, 1975, p. 70; Michael Mussa, 'The Exchange Rate, the Balance of Payments and Monetary and Fiscal Policy under a Regime of Controlled Floating', *The Scandinavian Journal of Economics*, Stockholm, No. 2, 1976, pp. 238-40; *idem*, 'Macroeconomic Interdependence and the Exchange Rate Regime', *op. cit.*, pp. 180-81; Volcker, 'The Role of Monetary Policy Coordination to Attain Exchange-Rate Stability', *op. cit.*, p. 28; Whitman, 'Coordination and Management of the International Economy', *op. cit.*, p. 323; Assar Lindbeck, 'International Coordination of National Economic Policies: a Commentary', in Katz (ed.), *op. cit.*, pp. 225-26; Jacques L. Pelkmans, 'Economic Cooperation among Western Countries', in Robert J. Gordon and Pelkmans, *Challenges to Interdependent Economies: the Industrial West in the Coming Decade* (New York: McGraw-Hill, for the Council of Foreign Relations, 1979), pp. 91-92; and Niels Thygesen, 'International Coordination of Monetary Policies, with Special Reference to the European Community', in John E. Wadsworth and Francois L. de Juvigny (eds), *New Approaches in Monetary Policy* (Alphen: Sijthoff & Noordhoff, for the Société Universitaire Européenne de Recherches Financières, 1979), pp. 211 *et seq.*

18. Cooper, *The Economics of Interdependence*, *op. cit.*, p. 158. See also Niehans, 'Monetary and Fiscal Policies in Open Economies under Fixed Exchange Rates', *op. cit.*, p. 908; Cooper, 'The Assignment Problem: Comment', *op. cit.*, p. 237; *idem*, 'Macroeconomic Policy Adjustment in Interdependent Economies', *The Quarterly Journal of Economics*, Cambridge, Mass., No. 1, 1969, pp. 14-23; and Corden, 'The Coordination of Stabilization Policies among Countries', *op. cit.*, p. 140.

19. Cooper, 'The Assignment Problem: Comment', *op. cit.*, p. 237.

20.   Niehans, 'Monetary and Fiscal Policies in Open Economies under Fixed Exchange Rates', *op. cit.*, p. 909.

21.   Jay H. Levin, 'The International Assignment of Stabilization Policies under Fixed and Flexible Exchange Rates', *Journal of International Economics*, No. 1, 1979.

22.   Note that redistribution and merit goods may be public goods if utility functions are interdependent. As the economic theory of government failure shows, however, public-good status is not a sufficient, but merely a necessary condition for a good to be optimally provided by the government rather than by the private sector. In the international context, inter-dependence of utility functions may, of course, induce the government of one country to care about the rate of unemployment and the political stability in other (allied) countries. The rational response, however, would be voluntary unilateral cash grants instead of 'negotiations' about a stabilisation policy that would be sub-optimal for the donor country.

23.   Whether the 'natural monopoly' should be a private or a state monopoly or be fragmented under anti-trust policy depends largely on the relative X-inefficiencies which arise under private and public monopoly.

24.   The exchange rate is certainly not an instrument additional to monetary and fiscal policy; for if the exchange rate and fiscal policy are given, money supply is endogenous.

25.   This argument should be distinguished from the more *ad hoc* objection (used especially against the locomotive theory) that 'placing pressure on a *well-performing* country to serve the interests of others by engaging in more rapid expansion than it considers desirable is an ill-conceived policy', Fellner, *op. cit.*, p. 236. For similar statements, see Emminger, *op. cit.*, p. 4. Herbert Giersch, 'Comments on the Report', in McCracken *et al.*, *op. cit.*, p. 248, and Stein, *op. cit.*, p. 6. The difference is that the Benthamite rule of thumb does not presume that there is agreement and absolute knowledge about whose performance is best in a given situation. For a similar view, see Norbert Walter, 'Koordinierung der Konjunkturpolitik der westlichen Industrieländer: Notwendigkeit oder Gefahr?', *Europa-Archiv*, No. 8, 1977, p. 233. Also see Ryutaro Komiya, 'Is International Coordination of National Economic Policies Necessary?' in Peter Oppenheimer (ed.), *Issues in International Economics*, Essays in Memory of Harry G. Johnson (Stocksfield and Boston: Oriel Press, 1980), pp. 19-21.

26.   This argument goes back to James Mill, 'Essay on Government' (1820), in Jack Lively and John Rees (eds), *Utilitarian Logic and Politics* (Oxford: Clarendon Press, 1978), p. 90: 'They who have a fixed, invariable interest in acting ill, will act ill invariably. They who act ill from mistake, will often act well, sometimes even by accident, and in every case in which they are enabled to understand their interest, by design . . . The evils which are the produce of interest . . . are altogether incurable . . . The evils which arise from mistake are not incurable.' The incentive aspect is recognised by Dietmar Gebert and Joachim Scheide in *Die Lokomotiven-Strategie als wirtschaftspolitisches Konzept: Argumente und Gegenargumente*, unpublished preliminary project report, Institut für Weltwirtschaft, Kiel, 1978, p. 13, and Koichi Hamada, 'Macroeconomic Strategy and Coordination under

Alternative Exchange Rates', in Dornbusch and Frenkel (eds), *op. cit.*, p. 299. Moreover, it constitutes one of the main reasons why the neo-classical economists assign the full-employment objective to labour. For workers and even trade unions have a stronger incentive to reduce unemployment than to avoid inflation or excessive public expenditure.

27. John G. Head, 'Public Goods and Public Policy', *Public Finance*, The Hague, No. 3, 1962, pp. 217-18.

28. 'A main argument for concerted action is that part of the benefits of policy actions tend to wind up in other countries . . . A main purpose of coordinated action is to prevent governments from trying to take "free rides" on anti-inflationary policies in other countries': Lindbeck, *op. cit.*, p. 223. 'With Keynes, the list of public goods was enlarged to include stability of national income sought through fiscal as well as monetary policy . . . The analysis of public and private goods is also applicable to the international economy. For private goods, read national benefits, and for public, cosmopolitan goods, or the maintenance of the world economy': Kindleberger, 'Dominance and Leadership in the International Economy', *op. cit.*, p. 285. He also refers to 'the public good of increasing efficiency', *ibid.*, p. 287, and 'leadership to provide the public good of stability', *ibid.*, p. 289.

29. *Cf.* Cooper, 'Worldwide versus Regional Integration', *op. cit.*, p. 49, and Whitman, 'Coordination and Management of the International Economy', *op. cit.*, p. 307. Among the 'fiscal federalists', notably Stanley Engerman, 'Regional Aspects of Stabilization Policy', in Richard A. Musgrave (ed.), *Essays in Fiscal Federalism*, Studies of Government Finance (Washington: Brookings Institution, 1965), pp. 53 and 56, and Wallace E. Oates, *Fiscal Federalism* (New York, Chicago and San Francisco: Harcourt Brace Jovanovich, 1972), p. 30, have argued that, owing to the existence of spillovers, stabilisation policy cannot be left to 'lower level governments'.

30. Jacob Viner, 'Cost Curves and Supply Curves' (1931), in George J. Stigler and Kenneth E. Boulding (eds), *Readings in Price Theory* (London: Allen & Unwin, 1953).

31. Tibor Scitovsky, 'Two Concepts of Externality', *Journal of Political Economy*, No. 2, 1954; Roland N. McKean, *Efficiency in Government through Systems Analysis* (New York: Wiley, 1958), Ch. 8; Gordon Tullock, *Private Wants, Public Means: an Economic Analysis of the Desirable Scope of Government* (New York and London: Basic Books, 1970), Ch. 7; and James E. Meade, *The Theory of Economic Externalities: the Control of Environmental Pollution and Similar Social Costs* (Leiden and Geneva: Sijthoff, 1973). Meade (pp. 20 *et seq.*) makes the same distinction by re-labelling technological externalities 'real-income externalities' and pecuniary externalities 'distributional externalities'.

32. See, for example, Tullock, *op. cit.*, pp. 163-64.

33. Scitovsky, *op. cit.*, p. 147.

34. See McKean, *op. cit.*, p. 139, and Tullock, *op. cit.*, pp. 166-67.

35. In a later section (*cf.* note 33), Scitovsky, *op. cit.*, p. 149, argues that, owing to the absence or thinness of futures markets, dynamic pecuniary externalities lead to sub-optimal outcomes: 'When an investment gives rise to pecuniary external economies, its private profitability understates its

social desirability'. But, as McKean, *op. cit.*, p. 141, has shown, the case of dynamic externalities differs from that of static ones only in that producers should try to anticipate the adjustment of others and the repercussions for themselves; nevertheless they should be guided by their own expected profits.

36.   See McKean, *op. cit.*, pp. 141 *et seq.*, and Tullock, *op. cit.*, pp. 162-63.

37.   Friedman, 'The Optimum Quantity of Money', in *idem*, *The Optimum Quantity of Money and Other Essays*, p. 15.

38.   Harry G. Johnson, as quoted in Emil M. Claassen and Pascal Salin (eds), *Stabilization Policies in Interdependent Economies* (Amsterdam and London: North-Holland, 1972), p. 97.

39.   David E. W. Laidler, 'The Welfare Costs of Inflation in Neoclassical Theory: Some Unsettled Problems', in Erik Lundberg (ed.), *Inflation Theory and Anti-Inflation Policy*, proceedings of a conference held by the International Economic Association at Saltsjöbaden, Sweden (Boulder, Col.: Westview Press, 1977), pp. 321-22. For a similar view, see Serge-Christophe Kolm and Mundell, as quoted in Claassen and Salin, *op. cit.*, pp. 96-97, and John G. Gurley and Edward S. Shaw, *Money in a Theory of Finance* (Washington: Brookings Institution, 1960), p. 195.

40.   Hamada, 'On the Political Economy of Monetary Integration, A Public Economics Approach', in Robert Z. Aliber (ed.), *The Political Economy of Monetary Reform* (London: Macmillan, 1977), p. 16.

41.   Vaubel, *Strategies for Currency Unification*, *op. cit.*, pp. 75-79.

42.   *A fortiori*, it is not true that 'the provision of a convertible currency is an international "public good" ', Ronald I. McKinnon, *Money in International Exchange: the Convertible Currency System* (New York and Oxford: Oxford University Press, 1979), p. 3.

Some authors do not (only) call *money* a public good but (also) 'international money' and 'international monetary stability' (Kindleberger, 'The Benefits of International Money', *Journal of International Economics*, No. 4, 1972, p. 435; *idem*, 'Lessons of Floating Exchange Rates', in Karl Brunner and Allen H. Meltzer [eds], *Institutional Arrangements and the Inflation Problem*, Carnegie-Rochester Conference Series on Public Policy, Vol. 3 [Amsterdam, New York and Oxford: North-Holland, 1976], pp. 62 and 72, and *idem*, 'Dominance and Leadership in the International Economy', *op. cit.*, p. 287) and the 'consensus on a money' (Tullock, 'Competing Monies: a Reply', *Journal of Money, Credit and Banking*, Columbus, Ohio, No. 4, 1976, p. 524) or the benefits thereof (Hamada, 'On the Political Economy of Monetary Integration', *op. cit.*, pp. 16 and 25). But, since these are aspects of the quality of money and since each unit of money is privately owned and confers benefits only to its owner, they cannot be public goods either. Consensus on a money, it is true, is the result of a social interaction process involving considerable social economies of scale, but as Kindleberger, in 'Lessons of Floating Exchange Rates', *op. cit.*, emphasises himself, this social process can be left to the market ('monetary Darwinism').

43.   See Friedrich A. von Hayek, *Denationalisation of Money: an Analysis of the Theory and Practice of Concurrent Currencies*, Hobart Special Paper No. 70 (London: Institute of Economic Affairs, 1976), p. 44; Lance Girton and Don Roper, 'Theory and Implications of Currency Substitution', May

1978, p. 23, unpublished revised version of International Finance Discussion Paper No. 56 (Washington: Federal Reserve System, 1976), and Vaubel, *Strategies for Currency Unification, op. cit.*, p. 77.

44. The welfare-theoretic case for an international exchange of information is recognised by most authors. See, for example, Michele Fratianni and John C. Pattison, 'The Economics of the OECD', in Brunner and Meltzer (eds), *Institutions, Policies and Economic Performance*, Carnegie-Rochester Conference Series on Public Policy, Vol. 4 (Amsterdam, New York, Oxford: North-Holland, 1976), p. 121; Giersch, 'Comments on the Report', *op. cit.*, p. 248; Stein, *op. cit.*, p. 5, and Fellner, *op. cit.*, p. 232. The case for international rules, laws, rights and sanctions, even where they are enforced by a leader acting as a 'world policeman' ('gunboat diplomacy'), derives also, at least partly, from the public-good nature of knowledge and its approximation, predictability. Since, however, knowledge is a public good, there is no reason to exchange it secretly on the occasion of international summit meetings. Secrecy is superior to public pre-announcement only if the aim of stabilisation policy is to surprise (deceive) the public.

45. Stein, *op. cit.*, p. 6.

46. See Dornbusch, 'Expectations and Exchange Rate Dynamics', *Journal of Political Economy*, No. 6, 1976. Another transmission mechanism relying on systematic expectational errors in the foreign-exchange market is discussed by Dornbusch, 'The Theory of Flexible Exchange Rate Regimes and Macroeconomic Policy', *The Scandinavian Journal of Economics*, No. 2, 1976.

47. Note that the reduction of net exports and employment in the home country will not only be temporary, but will also be followed by a temporary increase of net exports and employment above their initial level. This is because when the foreign price level catches up with foreign monetary expansion, foreigners hold excessive claims on the home country as a result of their increased net exports. In re-establishing their real portfolio proportions, foreigners will depreciate the home currency (either by trying to sell the home currency itself or by trying to sell financial claims on the home country, thus raising the home interest rate and thereby reducing the demand for the home currency). The home currency remains depreciated until the capital movements induced by the initial monetary expansion are reversed and the initial claims in net exports and employment are offset. See, notably, Niehans, 'Exchange Rate Dynamics with Stock/Flow Interaction', *Journal of Political Economy*, No. 6, 1977, pp. 1249-51, and *idem*, 'Purchasing Power Parity under Flexible Rates', in Oppenheimer (ed.), *op. cit.*

48. See Egon Sohmen, 'The Assignment Problem', in Mundell and Swoboda (eds), *Monetary Problems of the International Economy* (Chicago and London: Chicago University Press, 1969), p. 185; Giersch, 'Comments on the Report', *op. cit.*, p. 248; and Pieter Korteweg, 'Assessment and Critical Appraisal of the OECD Views on Economic Policy', *Aussenwirtschaft*, Zurich and Saint Gall, No. 4, 1977, p. 366.

49. Corden, 'The Coordination of Stabilization Policies among Countries', *op. cit.*, p. 142.

50. This objection to monetary policies designed to stabilise real exchange rates is elaborated in some more detail by Niehans, 'Dynamic

C

Purchasing Power as a Monetary Rule', in Chipman and Kindleberger (eds), *op. cit.*, pp. 220-23 and 225-27, and Vaubel, 'A Europe-wide Parallel Currency', in Katz (ed.), *op. cit.*, p. 182. Niehans, in 'Dynamic Purchasing Power as a Monetary Rule', *op. cit.*, pp. 15-18, even shows in a plausible numerical example that an adaptive monetary policy which stabilises the real exchange rate tends to destabilise domestic output more than an entirely non-adaptive monetary policy or, put differently, that stabilisation of employment would require only partial (but permanent) adjustment of domestic monetary expansion and inflation to foreign monetary expansion and inflation so that the temporary real exchange-rate change should not be avoided completely.

51. For a detailed analysis of how monetary policy should respond to international shifts in the demand for money, see Vaubel, 'International Shifts in the Demand for Money: Their Effects on Exchange Rates and Price Levels and Their Implications for the Preannouncement of Monetary Expansion', *Weltwirtschaftliches Archiv*, Kiel, No. 1, 1980. His article also presents econometric evidence on the extent of (demand for) currency substitution and its effect on exchange rates and price levels.

52. I owe this point to discussions with Reinhard Fürstenberg, of the Institut für Weltwirtschaft, Kiel.

53. 'The presence of "unstable floaters" is detrimental not only to their own welfare which is depressed by undervaluation of their exchange rates as well as excessive inflation, but also to the welfare of their trading partners, whose trade and investment relationships are disrupted', Stanley W. Black, *Floating Exchange Rates and National Economic Policy* (New Haven and London: Yale University Press, 1977), p. 187. See also Thomas D. Willett, 'Alternative Approaches to International Surveillance of Exchange-Rate Policies', in *Managed Exchange Rate Flexibility: the Recent Experience*, proceedings of a conference held at Melvin Village, N.H., October 1978, sponsored by the Federal Reserve Bank of Boston and the International Seminar in Public Economics, Conference Series No. 20 (Boston: Federal Reserve Bank of Boston, 1978), p. 168. For a different view, see Sohmen, *op. cit.*, p. 188.

54. The case against sudden changes of stabilisation policies and their terms-of-trade effects is also stated by Corden, 'The Coordination of Stabilization Policies among Countries', *op. cit.*, p. 140, and *idem*, 'Expansion of the World Economy and the Duties of Surplus Countries', *The World Economy*, London, January 1978, pp. 128 and 132.

55. For the opposite view, see Volcker, *op. cit.*, p. 33: 'Floating rates provide some new degree of freedom for domestic policy in the short run provided that expectations about the future are reasonably firm. But those expectations will not be firm unless monetary-policy harmonization or coordination is taken seriously.'

56. See notably Hayek, *Der Wettbewerb als Entdeckungsverfahren*, Kieler Vorträge 56 (Kiel: Institut für Weltwirtschaft, 1968).

57. *Cf.*, for example, *idem*, *The Constitution of Liberty* (London: Routledge & Kegan Paul, 1960), pp. 43-49: 'In the long run, the existence of groups ahead of the rest is clearly an advantage to those who are behind' (*ibid.*, p. 46). 'So long as some countries lead, all the others can follow, although the conditions for spontaneous progress may be absent in them' (*ibid.*, p. 48).

'Knowledge, once achieved, becomes gratuitously available for the benefit of all' (*ibid.*, p. 43). With respect to economic policy, this point is emphasised by Jan Tumlir, *Weltwirtschaftsordnung: Regeln, Kooperation und Souveränität*, Kieler Vorträge 87 (Tübingen: J. C. B. Mohr, for the Institut für Weltwirtschaft an der Universität Kiel, 1979), pp. 16 and 14.

58. Somehow, this argument has also found its way into the *Annual Report of the Bank for International Settlements*, Basle, 1977, p. 95.

59. On the other hand, Lindbeck, *op. cit.*, pp. 223 *et seq.*, argues that coordination of stabilisation policies is needed to bring about more desynchronisation of macro-economic fluctuations than policy competition can provide. This implies that, in spite of his own work on the political business cycle, he believes that discretionary stabilisation policy—if coordinated—tends to be stabilising rather than destabilising.

60. 'The standard prescription . . . let competition prevail and if it will not prevail enforce it—is not only irrelevant but downright misleading in the international monetary context, since it assumes that atomistic competition is possible whereas the international economy more nearly resembles a situation of oligopolistic competition. It is misleading because it encourages the notion that institutional devices can be found to reduce large national oligopolies to the status and performance of atomistic firms under perfect competition': Harry G. Johnson, 'Political Economy Aspects of International Monetary Reform', *Journal of International Economics*, No. 4, 1972, p. 406. For similar criticisms of competitive assumptions in the field of stabilisation policy, see Cooper, 'Economic Interdependence and Foreign Policy in the Seventies', *World Politics*, Princeton, New Jersey, No. 2, 1972, p. 180; Frenkel, 'Reflections on European Monetary Integration', *Weltwirtschaftliches Archiv*, No. 2, 1975, p. 219; Whitman, 'Coordination and Management of the International Economy', *op. cit.*, p. 313; Lindbeck, *op. cit.*, p. 224; and Hamada, 'Macroeconomic Strategy and Coordination under Alternative Exchange Rates', *op. cit.*, p. 292.

61. An author who keeps jumping from game-theoretic analyses to conclusions about 'the public-good nature of monetary assets' is Hamada, 'Alternative Exchange Rate Systems and the Interdependence of Monetary Policies', in Aliber (ed.), *National Monetary Policies and the International Financial System* (Chicago and London: University of Chicago Press, 1974), p. 24; similarly, *idem*, 'A Strategic Analysis of Monetary Interdependence', *Journal of Political Economy*, No. 4, 1976, pt 1, p. 685.

62. Cooper, *The Economics of Interdependence*, *op. cit.*, pp. 172-73; Niehans, 'Monetary and Fiscal Policies in Open Economies under Fixed Exchange Rates', *op. cit.*; Hamada, 'Alternative Exchange Rate Systems and the Interdependence of Monetary Policies', *op. cit.*; *idem*, 'A Strategic Analysis of Monetary Interdependence', *op. cit.*; *idem*, 'On the Political Economy of Monetary Integration', *op. cit.*; and *idem*, 'Macroeconomic Strategy and Coordination under Alternative Exchange Rates', *op. cit.*

63. Other targets which belong in this category are current-account targets and nominal or real exchange-rate targets. Only with regard to such variables can 'zero-sum game' situations arise.

64. This supports Hamada's conclusion that 'one possible course of conflict lies in a wrong conception of national interests' (*idem*, 'A Strategic

Analysis of Monetary Interdependence', *op. cit.*, p. 699). It can in fact be argued that it is the only source in the case of stabilisation policy.

65.   For the arguments from which this hypothesis is derived, see Vaubel, 'Free Currency Competition', *Weltwirtschaftliches Archiv*, No. 3, 1977, pp. 456-458; *idem, Strategies for Currency Unification, op. cit.*, pp. 71-74; Claassen, 'Monetary Integration and Monetary Stability: the Economic Criteria of the Monetary Constitution', and Salin, 'The Political Economy of Alternative Approaches to Monetary Integration', both papers presented at the Colloquium on 'New Economic Approaches to the Study of International Integration: Applications of Economic Analysis to Political Decision Making', European University Institute, Florence, 31 May-2 June 1979.

66.   Ironically, collusion at the expense of third parties is also the essence of the classical example of game theory, the 'prisoners' dilemma'.

67.   As has already been shown by Edward H. Chamberlin, in *The Theory of Monopolistic Competition: a Re-orientation of the Theory of Value* (Cambridge, Mass.: Harvard University Press, 1865), pp. 32-46, 'if each [oligopolist] assumes his competitors' supplies to be unchanged, the equilibrium price is continually lower than the monopoly one as the sellers are more numerous . . . If each assumes his competitors' prices unchanged, and if competitive bidding, or "recontract", continues until no further price change can be made without disadvantage to someone, the equilibrium price is the purely competitive one for only two sellers, and, of course, for any greater number' (*ibid.*, p. 54).

68.   See, for example, James M. Henderson and Richard E. Quandt, *Microeconomic Theory: a Mathematical Approach* (New York, Toronto and London: McGraw-Hill, 1958), p. 179.

69.   See Hayek, *Choice in Currency: a Way to Stop Inflation*, Occasional Papers No. 48 (London: Institute of Economic Affairs, 1976); *idem, Denationalisation of Money: an Analysis of the Theory and Practice of Concurrent Currencies, op. cit.*; Vaubel, 'Free Currency Competition', *op. cit.*; *idem, Strategies for Currency Unification, op. cit.*; Girton and Roper, *Theory and Implications of Currency Substitution, op. cit.*, and *idem*, 'Substitutable Monies and the Monetary Standard', forthcoming.

70.   See Vaubel, 'The Money Supply in Europe: Why EMS May Make Inflation Worse', *Euromoney*, London, December 1978.

2 Strong and Weak Elements in the Concept of European Integration

Jan Tumlir

'It is the price of democracy that the possibilities of conscious control are restricted to the fields where true agreement exists.'
—Friedrich von Hayek, *The Road to Serfdom* (1944)[1]

An early encounter with the analysis of the concept and conditions of economic order, as then developed in German-language literature, was decisive in my choice of career. The original interest was never lost and, in time, became the basis of many memorable discussions with Herbert Giersch, whose own work now constitutes an important contribution to that distinctive analytical tradition.

It is thus appropriate to turn on this occasion to the theory of economic order.[2] Interest in it is reviving again and the volume of new work is growing rapidly. As recently as the mid-1960s, I had difficulties in trying to convey to my English-speaking colleagues the main concerns—the flavour, so to speak—of this approach to economics.[3] But since then American economics has been converging on the same concerns from many different directions: economics and the law in general and the economics of property rights in particular; public choice and the concern with monetary and fiscal constitutions; economic theories of public goods, democracy, bureaucracy, the state, federalism *et cetera*. This new interest, which is beginning to amount to a radical shift in the focus on economic inquiry, is not difficult to understand. The emergence of the systematic law-and-economics approach from the collaboration of Franz Böhm and Walter Eucken at Freiburg in the 1930s was prompted by the experience of constitutional failure. The bulk of the American work just mentioned is also guided by an explicitly constitutional interest. In recent works by D.C. North,[4] of the University of Washington, and Dan Usher,[5] of Queen's University, Kingston, Canada, we even have the beginning of a theory of constitutional failure, or erosion.

In the present essay I want to demonstrate the relevance of this theorising by using it (i) to explain the nature of the long crisis of European integration and (ii) to indicate the direction of the steps by which the crisis might be overcome. It is a political crisis which has developed from economic arrangements and malfunctions. It is thus difficult to deal with in the framework of neo-classical or mainstream analysis which is designed to trace the economic consequences of political decisions, not the political consequences of economic changes, whether spontaneous or policy induced. The theory of economic order, concerned with the political conditions and implications of different economic systems, traces the consequences of economic policy not only for the allocation of resources, levels of activity and prices and distribution of income but also, through these refractions, back into the political system itself.

The central question of the theory as well as of the two particular strands of it on which I shall touch—the theories of federalism and of constitutional failure—is basic to all constitutional reasoning. What are the kinds of issues on which large groups of free individuals, who owe such welfare as they have attained to more or less extensive division of labour, cannot only agree but maintain agreement over time? Here it must suffice to mention the two essential attributes of issues 'agreeable' in this sense. First, they must lend themselves to articulation in the form of *general* propositions which are largely formal or procedural in nature and related mainly to securing civil equality or—better—maximum equal freedom for all individuals. Discussion of particular substantive arrangements tends to engage the self-interest of individuals; agreement is thus difficult to achieve and even more so to maintain. Second, the agreement can be maintained over time only if the system composed of the agreed general proposition 'works' to the satisfaction of a large majority of participants. It must, in other words, make possible, and indeed promote, Pareto-type improvements (external economies, economies of scale, gains from specialisation and trade).

The satisfactory working of the system depends on the consistency of the rules composing it. Essentially, both legal and economic systems can be described as sets of incentives and disincentives intended to guide the self-interested conduct of individuals in such a way that it is compatible with, and conducive to, social welfare. The problem of legislation is to avoid setting up incentives for behaviour inconsistent with that which the rest of the system seeks to promote. Legal analysis alone does not suffice to ensure such an effective, as against merely formal, consistency. Hence the need for close collaboration between the two disciplines, to which economics brings its closely elaborated positive theory of the process by which independent maximising decisions in a given legal framework are brought into mutual consistency and overall coherence.

THE THEORY OF ECONOMIC ORDER

In a world of continuous and uncontrollable change, economic order can be maintained only by continuous adjustment to novelty. The institutional order of an economy consists of arrangements or rules under which such necessary changes in the deployment of available resources can be expected to proceed with minimum waste. The different kinds of economic orders in actual operation can be judged as to their efficiency in this respect. Private property rights can be viewed as a system of organisation[6] ensuring a high degree of adjustment efficiency and hence of overall stability in the flux of change. The markets which arise from transactions in such rights signal occurring or impending changes, the foreseen future consequences of which are promptly capitalised into present prices and asset values. Thus private property rights provide both signals and incentives for adjustment. The protected private domains which they—together with other laws—create, also contain all the freedom necessary to carry out the adjustment with optimal speed.

While the working of the economic order depends on the internal consistency of its general rules, the democratic political process is largely concerned with securing exceptions for particular groups. The rules are always threatened by erosion, which explains the continuous search in every society for institutional means of entrenching the order against political pressures. The German-language literature traditionally maintains a strict distinction between the society and the state or between the private economic process and its public institutional framework. In the felicitous expression of Ernst-Joachim Mestmäcker, of the Max-Planck-Institut für ausländisches und internationales Privatrecht, in Hamburg, the problem is 'how to order the economy so that it can become neither the servant nor the master of the state'.[7]

The standard constitutional techniques of protecting the private and the public realm against each other need only be mentioned here: specification of those individual rights which are to be placed beyond politics; enumeration and strict division of powers among the branches of government, accompanied by insistence on proper delegation of legislative power; and judicial review to ensure internal consistency of the legal system. It is not adequately understood, however, that the international economic order, though necessarily articulated in less detail and with less effective enforcement than the national orders, likewise serves primarily to bolster the latter against internal disintegrative pressures.

The commitments which states accept, as participants in the international order, are generally thought of as constraints on economic sovereignty—more or less painful concessions of national interest made for the sake of international comity. The first thing to emphasise here, however, is that the rules which constitute the international order have been designed and voluntarily accepted by these sovereignties themselves. They felt a need for them. These rules and commitments are intended to protect governments in the exercise of their sovereign powers against the pressure of interest groups which want these powers exercised to their own benefit. Such use of sovereign power, involving transfers of benefits between social groups, is inherently conflictive. The adversely affected groups are often located abroad and appeal to their own government to protect their interest. The purpose of the international rules can thus be seen to parallel closely that of a municipal legal system. The international order is intended to guide the self-interested conduct of sovereign collectivities so that they can avoid conflicts among themselves and so that the pursuit of national interest can be compatible with, and conducive to, a more general interest which they share.[8]

The comparison of national and international order provides a more general insight into this issue. There exist any number of intermediate orders both within a nation and between individual nations and the international order. Municipal and regional economies exhibit regularities and rules of their own, even though they depend on, and merge into, the national order—and there are regional groups of sovereign nations expressing their common interest through agreed rules. In fact, as the preceding discussion has suggested, order in general can exist only as a stratified structure. This insight was articulated by the Nobel laureate, Friedrich von Hayek, as follows:

> 'Societies differ from simpler complex structures by the fact that their elements are themselves complex structures whose chance to persist depends on (or at least is improved by) their being part of the more comprehensive structure. We have to deal here with integration on *at least* two different levels, with,

on the one hand, the more comprehensive order assisting the preservation of ordered structures on the lower level, and, on the other, the kind of order which on the lower level determines the regularities of individual conduct assisting the prospect of the survival of the individual only through its effect on the overall order of the society'[9] (emphasis added).

By virtue of its unique institutional structure, the European Community is a nearly perfect example of an intermediate order in the Hayekian sense. It depends for its own stability on the normative force of the comprehensive international order with which its own rules are, with a few exceptions, fully compatible. More than that, most of the Community rules are more rigorous, and more effectively enforceable than the international rules, because they reflect a more complete understanding of the conditions of economic order than could be achieved at the level at which all sovereignties were represented with their diverse cultures and political traditions. Since the Community encompasses a large part of the world economy, its more strongly entrenched rules make it capable of greatly strengthening the higher-level order. A corresponding interdependence exists between the Community and the lower-level national orders. The effectiveness of Community institutions depends on the orderly functioning of political and administrative processes in the member countries. When national governments are over-extended and weak, they tend to chisel at the rules; and the powers of the Community authorities are impaired. Only routine common decisions are then possible, or decisions which go against the logic of the basic contract—'package deals', or decisions appealing to the atavistic zero-sum mentality, in that they appear to secure some benefit for the members at the cost of third parties. But there is also a great potential in the Community order for strengthening orderliness at the lower level. The Community rules protect member governments by proscribing those activities which are most likely to lead to an erosion of their authority domestically and thus to conflict with other governments.

THE THEORY OF FEDERALISM

The notion of a 'layered' or stratified order leads into the theory of federalism. Only a rudimentary version of such a theory can be sketched out here, consisting of four main elements.

The first concerns the range of political arrangements which can be subsumed under the heading. The comprehensive international

economic order, or a defensive military alliance like the North
Atlantic Treaty Organisation (NATO), are contractual in nature.
Sovereignties commit themselves to observe agreed rules in their
conduct of economic or military policy. They remain sovereign,
however, in that they reserve for themselves the right to interpret
the terms of the contract. Federal arrangements begin at the point
at which formerly sovereign polities accept a superior authority to
interpret the terms of their contract. Clearly, the enumeration of
the particular aspects or powers of sovereignty depends on each
analyst and his purpose; no finite number can be agreed upon.
There being 'n' aspects of sovereignty, the range of federal arrangements extends from one to $(n-1)$ of them being ceded, to be exercised by a common authority. If all aspects of sovereignty were
to be centrally exercised on behalf of (and over) the formerly
independent polities, no federal element would be present. In this
case we would be concerned with a unitary state.[10]

Next we have to deal with the question: what aspects of sovereignty will independent polities of free citizens be willing to cede
first? Historically it is difficult to determine whether military security
or economic considerations played the more important role in the
forming of federations. Note, however, that in both considerations
economies of scale and gains from trade play an important part.
There are savings on unnecessary defence against each other, as
well as gains from comparative advantage in common defence
arrangements. When economic considerations predominate, the
leading motive is the Smithian one of increasing the scope for
specialisation by extending the market. In either case, the polities
would be renouncing and pooling those aspects of their sovereignty
most likely to cause unnecessary conflict, uncertainty and waste.

The third element deals with the question of how far in the range
of possible federal arrangements the formerly fully sovereign polities
will be willing to go. There is a divide in this range which is of major
importance to my theme. Some sovereign powers can be jointly
administered on behalf of several polities without a common political
process; some cannot. In the decision to form a common market,
for example, the formerly independent governments need to cede
only those aspects of economic sovereignty which are inherently
conflictive in the sense that their exercise, while it may be politically
convenient to the government of the moment, cannot benefit, and
indeed is costly to, the society at large. A market always exists
among fully sovereign countries; it is, however, burdened by the

risk of disruption by any one government exercising its sovereign right to restrict a particular flow of imports, or destabilise the exchanges by inflating to spend its way out of unemployment. The international market can be made more efficient by reducing or eliminating risks of this kind. In a common market, the sovereign powers generating these risks are pooled (in effect, mutually cancelled) and replaced by rules which can, at least in principle, be judicially enforced. In arrangements of this kind, governments of the participating polities simply renounce specified powers. The administration of the general rules replacing these discretionary powers is professional rather than political.

On the other hand, where common substantive policies are the object of federation, a common political process is called for. Defence policy is a good example here. Discretion is of its essence; it cannot be conducted according to pre-announced rules. In a military alliance, free-riding is thus a constant temptation. A federation formed on defence considerations would be able to enforce the allocation of the joint cost, but only because its central authority would be backed—which also means controlled—by a common public opinion. Furthermore, a common defence implies a common foreign policy which, again, cannot be effective unless it reflects (a large majority of) common public opinion. Thus there must be regular procedures for ascertaining what the common public opinion demands or is unwilling to support.

We shall therefore speak of a proto-federal arrangement where certain aspects of sovereignty can be pooled and jointly administered through a system of rules. Federal arrangements proper involve joint formulation and conduct of substantive policies, for which a common political process is required.

There is thus a point in the range of possible federal arrangements at which an important qualitative change occurs and a common political (electoral) process must be instituted. The fourth and last element of the theory of federalism has to specify the conditions which make common politics possible. When would the free polities posited at the outset be willing to elect a common legislature? The answer is simple: once none of them had to fear being systematically out-voted on an issue of over-riding importance to it. In other words, there has to be a sufficiently strong perception by the individuals composing the federated polities of shared interests and values. This is a demanding condition, usually requiring a community of language or religion and/or a long experience of living together in

proto-federal arrangements.[11] If the issue on which one or several
polities fear being out-voted can be specified with sufficient
precision, it can be constitutionally removed from the reach of
politics. This, however, is a perilous undertaking in view of the
demonstrated latitude of constitutional interpretation.[12] Non-
constitutional compacts and arrangements, however solemnly
undertaken, cannot be maintained against a majority opinion, as
the issue of slavery in the constitutional and political history of the
United States demonstrated.

INTEGRATION IN WESTERN EUROPE

I have finally reached the central subject of this essay. This
section will present what I consider the dominant elements in the
original 1950s version of an integrated—or, rather, re-integrated—
Western Europe, a vision which attained its fullest expression in the
Treaty of Rome, signed in 1957. These elements seem to me to have
been derived from a clear conception of a proto-federal order;
together, they compose a nearly self-sustaining arrangement of that
kind. This is what I shall call the 'strong conception' of European
integration—strong because it was sufficient to the concerns of the
founders and because it was realistic. The idea of a common political
process in Western Europe was clearly premature. The strong
elements, however, were combined with aspirations less clearly
thought out, conditioned on a common political process which the
founders themselves realised to be unattainable. These 'soft spots'
of the conception will be analysed in the following sections.

One generation has already grown up in the European Community. Its members may be more or less familiar with the complexities and difficulties of 'constructing Europe', but most of them
would probably be surprised by the simplicity of the purpose the
original founders had in mind. The six countries—Belgium, France,
the Federal Republic of Germany, Italy, Luxembourg and the
Netherlands—were to be joined, by an irreversible constitutional
act, into a common market, so that it would become forever impossible for any member state to abuse the economy of its people for
adventures in foreign policy. The protection of the private economy
from the government was the eminent idea in forming the European
enterprise. What must be emphasised again is that it was an idea of
governments. The six governments themselves recognised that they
needed an effective restraint on those powers of their sovereignty
the use of which had caused so much enmity and suffering in the

past. In reaching the agreement, they defined the supreme interest of their nations. In working out the institutional details of the agreement, they set up a framework within which the politics and policy of each nation could pursue the national interest more safely, with less risk of collision than had been possible in all the European systems and 'concerts' preceding World War II.

The strong conception in which the need for greater security of national interest was implemented consists of the three principles of the common market, the detailed legal expression they were given and, most importantly, the enforcement mechanism behind them. The principles are (i) freedom of movement of goods, services, labour and capital, (ii) undistorted competition and (iii) non-discrimination, implied in the preceding two but re-emphasised separately as a general category for unforeseen instances of obstruction.

What makes the European Community a distinct, indeed unique, order is the fusion of the legal or legislative sovereignty of member states, which makes possible an effective enforcement of the three principles. The Treaty of Rome's provisions relating to the common market principles have constitutional status. Their interpretation by the three central authorities, the Commission, the Council of Ministers and the European Court, develops a Community law which over-rides national law relating to these common concerns. The primacy of Community law is necessary to ensure uniformity in the interpretation of the Treaty of Rome by national courts. This, in turn, is required by the other revolutionary aspect of the agreement. While international treaties are strictly a matter of public law, binding only governments, the Treaty of Rome's provisions relating to the three principles create private rights which the national courts must protect. It is here that the special power of enforcement of the Community rules resides. Formulating international commitments as directly applicable treaty provisions is the ultimate guarantee one government can give to another that it will honour the obligation. Society itself enforces the commitment on its government.

HARMONISATION OF POLICIES

Two major weaknesses mar the concept of integration embodied in the Treaty of Rome. The lack of a monetary constitution has just been mentioned. The second weakness consists in the range of provisions for the coordination, progressive approximation and harmonisation of economic policies, culminating in the three mandated common policies (for agriculture, foreign commerce and transport). It is now an accepted interpretation of Article 2 of the Treaty of Rome that it not only states the ends of the common undertaking but also specifies two distinct means or ways to them: the establishment of a common market and the progressive approximation of economic policies. Accordingly, these have been considered to be two distinct fields of activity for, or two distinct tasks entrusted to, the Community authorities. We shall see that a different reading is possible. At any rate, the subsequent text of the Treaty reveals a striking contrast between the precision of the provisions relating to the former means and the vagueness of those relating to the latter. On closer consideration, the two classes of provisions—for the establishment of a common market and for the approximation of economic policies—actually appear incongruent. The latter is not only unamenable to precise specification (co-ordination, for example, seems a strange word to use in a contract) but also unnecessary and ultimately unhelpful for the attainment of the stated ends. It is perfectly logical that the private rights which the Treaty creates arise only from the provisions implementing the three common market principles.

One could go further and say that the two classes of provisions reflect two different conceptions of the European undertaking, one emphasising the word 'common', with its political implications, the other the word 'market'. The latter is, of course, what I call the strong conception. The former unified the 'federalists' in their confused debate with the 'nationalists holding onto sovereignty'. In the temper of the time, the provisions for policy unification were interpreted, perhaps intended, as a mandate for political activity at the centre, the more extensive the better. The federalism of the Europeans could not be anything other than centralising. It is regrettable, nonetheless, that the European federalists chose the United States as their ideal and rallying slogan, a polity which was already then approaching the dividing line between a federal and a unitary state. Switzerland would have furnished a much more useful model. But Orson Welles' *The Third Man* was playing to rapt European audiences at the time and Switzerland, however instructive she might have been, was politically unglamorous to say the least.

There are reasons to believe, however, that the desire to approximate and harmonise economic policies also reflected some less idealistic convictions. In part at least, I suggest, it derived from the ancient continental European tradition confounding sovereignty with power, and thus vastly over-estimating the power of sovereignty. An aspect of this tradition has been the (often virulent) continental resistance to classical economics—the belief that sovereignty not only can but would humiliate itself if it did not over-ride the law of comparative advantage. The first flush of Jean Monnet's European inspiration can be traced to this source.[13] French industry had always believed itself inferior to Germany's because the Germans could produce and deliver steel more cheaply. Why not, then, Monnet reasoned, establish for both economies an 'equal starting base' in this respect? Indeed, equalisation of the cost of steel production, and of delivered prices by what was essentially a basing-point system, became the most difficult issue in the negotiation of the European Coal and Steel Community (ECSC) in the early 1950s. The legal regime for coal and steel established by the Treaty of Paris, signed in 1951, actually bears a close resemblance to the American legal model of regulated industry. A direct United States input into the ECSC negotiation would be explained by the fact that the West German negotiators were representing an occupied country whose coal and steel industries were still operating under a special Allied Control Commission. The Treaty of Rome, by contrast, relies on competition to control industry. By 1956 the West German economic experiment had restored a considerable degree of trust in the effectiveness of markets as an integrative as well as a control mechanism, and the Federal Republic of Germany was negotiating as a sovereign country. Nonetheless, the over-riding concerns of the earlier negotiations continued to influence the professional Europeans administering the Treaty. Several statements, as for example the following, suggest that the Commission of the European Community considered *similarity* of national policies and institutions to be desirable in itself:

'Un des principaux problèmes . . . est celui des moyens permettant d'atteindre *un degré suffisant de similitude* des systèmes de politique economique dans les Etats membres, notamment sur le terrain de la politique conjoncturelle et de la planification à moyen terme'[14] (emphasis added).

It may be noted here that the possibility of a conflict between policy harmonisation or unification and a socially beneficial exploitation of comparative advantage was pointed out in a 1965 Saarbrücken dissertation written under the supervision of Herbert Giersch.[15]

The economic purpose of having similar policies is not at all obvious. The relevant distinction is between similarity and compatibility. All micro-economic policies, for example, would be compatible as long as they conformed to the three principles of the common market. To secure such compatibility, the European Community authorities have legal powers and do not have to rely on negotiations. Indeed, there is a close parallel between economic policies and law itself. With respect to Treaty provisions—or federal constitutions more generally—there must be uniformity of interpretation by state courts, but beyond that, compatibility is all. Efficient money and capital markets existed in the United States prior to the unification of the law of negotiable instruments. How much more perfect they have become since then, and how much of the improvement is due to legal changes, is impossible to determine. As long as the field is free of outright conflicts, inter-state transactors may be thought to derive an additional degree of freedom from such diversity as exists in national commercial law, choosing to contract under that which best suits the nature of their transaction.

Another aspect of the strong conception is that it excludes any possibility of a systematic income redistribution. The Treaty of Rome has created a Social Fund for the purpose of helping individual governments to comply with their Common Market obligations. The European Investment Bank was intended to utilise the enhanced creditworthiness of six governments acting jointly. Its functions, however, were not sufficiently specified in advance. It was never clear in what respects it could improve the operation of the private capital markets and its operations remained, by and large, insignificant. The European Community's Regional Fund, created later, implied a degree of redistribution, but has been in fact used mainly to help even out the differences between national financial contributions and national receipts from statutory entitlements. The recent political developments in the Community vindicate the original conception; they suggest that a proto-federal order cannot survive if some members consistently have to put more into the common coffer than they receive from it.

The strong conception of the Treaty of Rome was incomplete in one important respect. A common market implies a common money—or the equivalent of it; that is, firmly fixed exchange rates. The founders took the existing international monetary system for granted and made no additional provisions for monetary discipline in member countries. A common monetary system comparable in the rigour of its rules to the disciplines derived from the three common market principles would, for example, have complemented the general obligation to maintain fixed parities by a requirement that exchange-market interventions by central banks of member countries be fully reflected in their domestic monetary base. With such a monetary constitution, the European Community could have avoided the great inflation of the 1970s simply by allowing its (effectively unified) currencies to float against the dollar.

Coming back to economic policies, another relevant, although not absolutely precise, distinction is between day-to-day 'process' policies, such as monetary policy, and those which set the framework of the economic process for a period of time and are changed only by discrete reforms. The tariff or the competition law are examples of the 'framework' policies. Since there is no single, simultaneous business cycle running through the whole common market (which presumably would be unwanted, even though it would provide a striking symbol of unity), there would be little point in 'approximating' monetary policies. The view that they need to be 'coordinated' beyond the degree customary among the central banks of independent countries rested on the fallacy, widespread at the time, that monetary policy could stabilise employment directly. It is now generally recognised that it can advance that goal only indirectly, by stabilising the price level. Thus again, if each national monetary policy concentrated fully on what it can actually control, namely the price level, they would be perfectly coordinated by their objective. Had the Treaty of Rome contained provisions for an effective common monetary order, national monetary policies would have been coordinated by its rules. Alternatively, we may say that there would be little scope for discretion requiring explicit coordination.

As to the framework policies, the full effects of each of them depend on all the other policies and institutions in existence. Given this lack of precise knowledge about the effects of particular policies in a national context, a negotiated harmonisation of them across the Common Market could hardly amount to more than mindless averaging, more likely than not to entail significant welfare losses for the societies concerned. Klaus Stegeman, of Queen's University, Kingston, Canada, concluded from his investigation that 'harmonization of national cartel policies towards an average degree of stringency would allow more national cartels to remain effective than would be possible if the existing policies, differing from country to country, remained in force'.[16]

So far the analysis has relied on economic theory alone. A consideration of the political process—of the incentives and constraints facing the negotiators—strengthens the probability of the results of a negotiated policy harmonisation being deeply suboptimal. These results are likely to be inferior not only to those of a spontaneous approximation of policies that otherwise might be expected to occur in a vigorously competitive common market, but even to those of what we have termed 'mindless averaging'. The negotiation takes place among the executives of national governments only imperfectly controlled by their legislatures in what is, in effect, foreign policy. The results produced do not have to face a common electoral sanction. Harmonised or common policies agreed upon under these circumstances run the risk of aggregating the worst features of the previously independent national ones. This danger can best be demonstrated by the Treaty-mandated common policies.

It is true that, prior to the establishment of the European Community's common agricultural policy (CAP), agricultural prices and trade were strictly controlled in all member states. In each state, however, only the prices most important to the domestic farmers were relatively high while the others were closer to world market levels, as a politically necessary concession to consumers. At Community level, consumer interests are more difficult to defend and those of producers more strongly represented. Log-rolling among producer interests inevitably results in a price structure which is more uniformly high.

The case is similar with the European Community's common commercial policy. It would pose no problem if it consisted only of the administration and periodic renegotiation of the common external tariff. Non-tariff barriers, especially quantitative import restrictions, were initially (and, to a considerable extent, still are) administered by the member states. In so far as liberal trade is desirable, it is easy to show that it is better if non-tariff protection against third countries remains decentralised. As long as trade within the common market is free, no national industry can be more than temporarily helped by its government through the restriction of national imports from third countries. The corresponding industries in the more liberal member states, whose governments refused to grant similar protection, would have to meet third-country competition by increased efficiency, which would soon raise their exports into the member country which maintained restrictions on external imports. With the possibility of the whole common market being protected by quantitative restrictions on particular imports, the political data change fundamentally. Industries, which otherwise would compete, organise for lobbying. Each national lobby is strengthened *vis-à-vis* its government whose executive, in turn, has less incentive to resist the pressure. If a government were to grant protection nationally, it would have to deal with the opposition of consumers or industrial users of the product in question. Presenting a decision agreed upon in Brussels, it has an argument which it could not deploy in a purely national debate, namely that its agreement to the import restriction was a concession to European unity. For this reason, it is impossible to maintain that the Community authorities are the main champions of liberal trade, minimising the damage to it that the more protection-minded member governments would otherwise cause by independent actions; nor, indeed, that the agreements made at the centre reflect the average strength of the protectionist forces in the member states.

In combination, these economic and political considerations suggest that a significantly different reading of the Treaty of Rome is possible. Coordination, gradual approximation and harmonisation of national policies need not be seen as specifically mandated objects of a common effort. Virtually all that is really needed in this respect—with the major exceptions of a more effective monetary order and a reform of the CAP—would be achieved spontaneously, with a minimum of formal negotiation among all member states. As long as they conform to the Community law, the diversity of national policies is an advantage. Political change is constantly taking place, each country constantly adjusting its policy in the light of its own circumstances and traditions, learning from its own experience as well as that which other countries have made with their different policies and institutions. Nobody knows which policies are best; and competition is a process of discovery. In a large and vigorously competitive market, national policies could be expected to adjust spontaneously to each other, at a rising level of efficiency. I believe, with Herbert Giersch, in the need for competition among policies.

CHANGES IN ATTITUDE TOWARDS
POLICY MAKING

In the course of the 1960s the tide of Western political opinion turned. One set of axioms which formed the basis for the conduct of public affairs yielded its place to another. Except perhaps for its speed, there was nothing historically unusual about the change. Western intellectual tradition from the Greeks onwards has consisted in an alternation of two basic attitudes. The terms classicism and romanticism are one way of describing them. Correspondingly, there are two conceptions of law, one as a rational perception of necessity, the other as an expression of sovereign will; and two conceptions of order, one as a condition existing prior to government, which governments have to respect if they are to be effective, the other as the creation by the state out of pre-existing chaos. To these basic positions there also correspond two conceptions of economics. One views the decentralised economy, structured by a system of private property rights, as a sturdily self-stabilising system; this view has traditionally gone hand in hand with the belief in the capacity of individuals to shape their own life. The other views the market as inherently unstable, needing constant attention from and intervention by the government if it is to maintain anything like full employment.

What happened in the 1960s was that the romantic propositions replaced the classical ones as basic assumptions of policy making. Two consequences followed. First, the time horizon of national policy making began to shrink rapidly. National economic policies became more encompassing, seeking to control more variables. They also became more changeable and for both reasons more frequently inconsistent with each other. Second, because inconsistencies of domestic policy manifest themselves most promptly in an economy's foreign transactions, national policies began to conflict internationally. Unfailingly, although without warrant, such conflicts were presented as clashes of national interests.

This change posed an important question as to the role the European Community's authorities should play in the integration process. They could assume an essentially constitutional role, concerned only with carrying out the Treaty of Rome which was largely a programme and a time-table of measures by which the common market was to be created. This activity would be guided by the three principles and would be mainly judicial. Where the Treaty calls for common policies, the main effort of the Community authorities would be to ensure that they conformed to the three basic principles as closely as possible.

According to the alternative conception, the central authorities, in addition to being endowed with functions flowing from the strong provisions of the Treaty, were to be the pioneers of unification. In the sense of the vague preambular language, they should generate initiatives for a continuing movement from the 'foundation' in the form of a common market towards an 'even closer union'. It is easily understandable with hindsight why the European Community's authorities opted for this role. National governments were beginning to act on the romantic set of political assumptions which seemed to promise more power and prestige to the political and administrative elites. The Community authorities were only human to want a piece of the action. Indeed, the conception of integration by coordinating and centralising the new powers and responsibilities that national governments were soliciting for themselves appeared to promise not merely a piece but the bulk of the action to Community authorities.

The French protest in 1965-66, seen at the time as an attempt to block integration altogether, now appears to have been motivated by a correct perception of the threat to the operation of the Treaty of Rome's arrangements which was implied in this view of the functions and mission of the Community authorities. The political tactics chosen to emphasise the protest failed to induce the kind of discussion and joint analysis which the alternatives demanded. The public debate that followed was dominated by an issue of secondary importance—majority voting in the Council of Ministers. The issue is secondary because the Treaty of Rome admits of majority voting only on technicalities arising in the implementation of a specifically laid out programme. Any initiative beyond that programme, especially if it involves an assignment of additional functions to the central authorities, requires a unanimous vote according to Article 235.[17] It should be noted that the wording of this Article includes under the unanimity requirement all substantive policies.

Since the Luxembourg compromise, the process of 'European construction' has been characterised by an increasingly hectic improvisation. That there was no clearly conceived purpose guiding it is now obvious; what is puzzling is the sense of urgency that has been animating it. After all, the programme of work agreed upon in the Treaty of Rome was far from complete. Besides, it is not as if a common market could be created once and for all;

maintaining and perfecting it, seeing to it that there was sufficient competition and that it was not distorted by government measures would require a steady, demanding political effort. There were thus no compelling reasons, external or internal, for new initiatives while past commitments were still unfilled. Nonetheless, towards the end of the 1960s a new political rhetoric developed, as ambitious as it was vague. It stressed the need to advance from the negative, merely economic phase of integration to a positive, political one. The contrast between the negative and the positive, the economic and the political phase, appears in numerous variants. It is implied in *First and Second Europe* by Ralf Dahrendorf, of the London School of Economics,[18] and most notably in the mystical resolve of the 1972 Paris Summit conference to convert the European Community into an economic and monetary union before the end of the decade. The only practical or plausible interpretation of these arcane pronouncements would seem to be that they referred to a transition from a proto-federal to a federal arrangement, to an institution of a common political process. Yet this is clearly not what the speakers meant.

The anti-market bias of the rhetoric is obvious.[19] Could it be that, as the basic political assumptions shifted, both national and Community authorities became afraid of the difficulties of trying to implement more fully the strong Treaty of Rome provisions implying a severe constraint on governmental discretion? Since nobody could politically afford to appear to be giving up on existing Treaty commitments, it would be understandable that national politicians as well as Community authorities started looking for more dramatic but less constraining forms of 'unification'. The bolder the announcements of new initiatives, the more difficult it would be for the political public to realise that significant elements of the original, underlying agreement were being abandoned. The direct election of the European Parliament is probably best seen in this light. The body's powers are severely restricted; it is not at all clear why it should be preferred to an assembly composed of national legislators; and should it gradually acquire more powers, as elected assemblies are in the habit of doing, there would be the threat of a paralysing conflict with national legislatures.[20] The agreement on direct elections was a politically spectacular, although constitutionally unpremeditated, gesture.

A considerable amount of literature emerged in those years on how to 'develop Europe' further. All these proposals were conceived in terms of new common policies. Jelle Zijlstra, then Prime Minister of the Netherlands, and later President of the Netherlands Bank, Michel Waelbroeck, of the Institute for European Studies in Brussels, Pierre Werner, Prime Minister of Luxembourg, Professor Dahrendorf and Leo Tindemans, then Prime Minister of Belgium, and a former President of the European People's Party, were mainly preoccupied with the question of which additional issues the ministers of the member states could jointly decide on or coordinate. It occurred to none that common policies cannot be conducted for long without a common political process. Implementation of substantive policies negotiated among executives of national governments will eventually be frustrated by the lack of public understanding and support; it may, indeed, endanger the national democratic consensus itself. When French farmers block roads and destroy imported produce, they find the cohesion needed for such defiance of public authority only by presenting their action as a protest against the 'policy of Brussels'. The Council's decisions on agricultural policy, it may be noted here, are still unanimous; what would happen if the common policy were adopted by a majority over-riding the vote of the French representative need not tax the reader's imagination excessively. Surely it would be much more difficult to organise a comparable protest against a policy decided by a national government. It may not be kind, but it is a perfect illustration of my point, to recall here that, at the end of 1975, Mr Tindemans, in his report on European Union,[21] recommended the establishment of a common European energy authority empowered to decide on the siting of nuclear power plants in the European Community.

PROBLEMS WITH POLICY HARMONISATION

The main result of Community policy in this period has been a paradox. In the beginning there was a well-founded expectation that the participating economies through their opening and exposure to undistorted competition in the Common Market would indeed become more similar, not necessarily in any concrete sense, but in their mode of organisation—in what a German-language economist would call their 'order'. Instead, while the European Community authorities were—ineffectively—devising new common projects through which to coordinate and perhaps control the multiplying economic interventions of member states, the national economic systems grew apart to such an extent that today these economies cannot adjust to mutual change without political friction. With respect to such vital features as the extent of indexation, the proportion and status of nationalised industries, the degree of subsidisation, the effectiveness of the labour market in indicating the skills needed and those becoming redundant, job-security legislation, labour-union rights and responsibilities, the financial state of social security funds, the extent of government's presence in money and capital markets and many others, there can be no doubt that differences between the participating economies are far more pronounced today than they were twenty years ago. How is the paradox to be explained?

The first explanation might be that most of these changes occurred in response to rising but divergent rates of inflation against which the European Community 'order' had provided no effective defences. More generally, however, one would note that the original expectation presupposed general compliance with the principles of the common market. The progressive approximation of economic systems could have been expected as a result of competition, including competition among policies. This suggests that the policies which actually produced opposite results were not exposed to such competition and were indeed shielded from it by means incompatible with the conception embodied in the strong provisions of the Treaty of Rome.

Even though economic growth in the European Community slowed down sharply after 1973, changes in the world economy were proceeding at an undiminished pace. The global change impinged on the Community's national economies, so to speak, 'from the same direction' so that proper adjustment to it could be expected to contribute to a progressive approximation of these economies. If, under these conditions, the member states not only maintained but even widened the systemic differences among themselves, the conclusion is at hand that they had to resort to policies increasingly isolating them from (i) the rest of the world economy and (ii) each other.

These policies were perhaps mainly national, but it is impossible to overlook the role which certain European Community policies played in this period. In particular, trade, industrial and competition policies virtually merged into a single complex of measures directed at facilitating (for facilitating, read slowing down or delaying) adjustment. Trade policy provided external protection for such industries as textiles, clothing and steel, as well as for a number of particular products of other industries.

Industrial policy, both generally and in the particular way it has been practised in the European Community, is difficult to define. Perhaps the most important thing an economist can say about it is that in a democratic country it must always be a surreptitious policy. It is a policy of the executive, essentially unamenable to legislative control. In one way or another it has to do with industrial structure, both in terms of the relative sizes of industries and their spatial distribution. For the effective control of such a policy, the legislature would need to have an agreed notion of the optimal industrial structure and distribution, something an assembly whose members represent a country's different regions and interest groups is intrinsically unable to agree upon. The history of the Community authorities' effort in this area reflects the irremediable lack of a firm theoretical basis and guidance. It started with the promotion of large European enterprises in response to the then fearsome *défi americain*. Several years were spent in an effort to elaborate a European company statute. After 1973 the policy consisted almost entirely of *ad hoc* attempts to coordinate national schemes and devise Community schemes to assist particular industries in difficulty. The Treaty of Rome vested the control over national subsidies in the central authorities. This power is, of course, essential for securing the principle of undistorted competition; but it is still impossible to speak of the Community authorities exercising effective control over subsidies. Instead, the last phase of its industrial policy has brought the Commission into another conflict with the principles of undistorted competition. Schemes of assistance to particular industries are most difficult to design when the anti-cartel provisions of the Treaty itself and of at least one national competition law have to be respected. The negotiation of the synthetic fibre industry scheme in 1978, and the still unclear legal status of its result (the cartel has been 'notified but not approved'), provide a case in point.

The converging development of the Community's trade, industrial and competition policies illustrates the point already made about the dangers of trying to formulate a common substantive policy without a common political process. As Professor Mestmäcker has noted, 'the economic order based on liberty and the rule of law, which the Treaty or Rome is to secure and develop further, would be seriously endangered if an executive operating without parliamentary control were to seek its political backing primarily from those economic groups which are directly affected by its decisions'.[22]

Another way of viewing these developments has already been

suggested in this section. Taken together, the growing systemic differences, and the rapid relative expansion of the public sectors which has accompanied their emergence, represent a substantial reduction in what might be called the adjustment capacity of the economies participating in the common market. If this reduction were uniform, internal cohesion on a generally lower growth path could be secured by gradually rising protection against the more flexible and dynamic economies outside the European Community, admittedly at the cost of some political friction with them. Significant disparities in adjustment capacity, however, have also emerged among the participating economies. This is the main reason for the inability of the central authorities to enforce the Community law integrally. The backlog of the adjustments needed has grown too large; if a truly undistorted competition were to be instituted now, changes in particular industries in different countries might be too painful.

One must also expect that within the European Community, as well as countries of the Organisation for Economic Cooperation and Development (OECD) as a whole, there will be differences between countries with respect to the rate at which the various impairments of the economic adjustment capacity can be corrected. The disparities will persist, in other words, at least in the current decade, and so will the political tensions which they generate within the Community and between it and other parts of the Western world. In these circumstances, to strive for greater unity among the Community countries, and for their greater 'international effectiveness', through new mechanisms for a common foreign policy (or any other common policy for that matter) is like beginning to work on the roof of a house before its foundation has been completed. Proponents may believe that confrontation with external problems will promote accord on internally disputed issues. But external 'problems' are not given objectively: they are in the eye of the beholder, shaped by the beholder's interests. A common reaction to external problems *presupposes* an identity of interests which in turn depends on a satisfactory functioning of the common market.

THE ROLE OF GOVERNMENTS

In the early years, the unification of Western Europe was often debated in instrumental terms: was it more promising to start with economic integration, which could be considered a roundabout way to political union, or to tackle the political objective directly?

From the late 1960s onwards the latter view has been ascendant. Approaching conclusion, we may now draw from the foregoing discussion three reasons why economic integration was, in fact, the most promising road to unity among the peoples of Western Europe.

Those scornful of the 'negativism' of the original conception—of its concern, that is, with removing obstacles and enlarging the freedom of action and choice—had a more positive blueprint, a true construction, in mind. It was to be accomplished by political will and, where necessary, by political cunning. But we have seen that, in the present European circumstances, the political will needed for the purpose cannot be formed, exercised and controlled democratically. It is perhaps more appropriate to speak of consensus than of will. The federal consensus could only emerge from an experience of polities living together in a less ambitious common order whose functioning satisfied all. Only such an experience, through which each polity comes to understand and trust the interests others have in the common arrangement, will make it possible for each to accept decisions made by a majority of the common vote. In Western Europe, the requisite less ambitious common arrangement, however, has not yet been fully implemented. The functioning of the rudimentary existing arrangements was in the 1970s and early 1980s far from satisfactory.

There are more basic difficulties. The ease or difficulty of forming a consensus in support of a common authority clearly depends on the nature of the functions the authority is supposed to discharge. A judicial authority, endowed with powers to ensure compatibility between national legal systems and a multilateral treaty, will find general support more easily than a legislative and administrative authority empowered, for example, to redistribute income between the component polities. The main obstacle in the way of European federation may thus be said to consist in the currently prevalent views of the legitimate functions of government. These views have become so loose that in economic matters, at least, it is now impossible to discern any effective limit to what a government should or is entitled to do. One may well ask whether the thirteen colonies would ever have come together had the American Founding Fathers explicitly postulated for the federal government some of the economic powers which it exercises today. The unique political feat of the Swiss, welding into a nation three population groups with ties of language and culture to three large neighbouring nation states, would never have been possible had the central government possessed half the economic powers which national governments elsewhere exercise as a matter of fact. So it is no wonder that old historical nations such as the French or the English, let alone the younger and smaller ones such as the Belgians and the Dutch, are balking at arrangements under which a common authority would be established and endowed with—or would eventually come into the possession of—the panoply of powers which their national governments wield today and would be directed in the exercise of these powers by a West European electoral majority which could be formed even against their unanimous national opposition.

The difficulty goes deeper still. The loose conception of the legitimate functions of government is proving increasingly unsatisfactory even on the national level. For the high cost of government we seem to be governed rather miserably; and we are beginning to understand why this is no paradox. The truth of the matter is that the authority and effectiveness of democratic government has been greatly reduced by the loosening of the legal constraints on its economic powers. When a government budget begins to approach one-half of the national product, its influence on the private transactions in the other half is such that the whole economy may be said to be controlled by the government. 'Controlled' may not be the right word, though. The government has virtually all the powers needed for central planning or guidance of the economy except that, being a democratic government, it cannot prepare a coherent plan. That would require judging and ranking the needs of all the groups in society and, in fact, determining their relative incomes—something democratic assemblies are inherently unable to agree upon, even by simple majority. 'Whatever we assume, it turns out that the attempt to assign incomes by voting gives rise to consequences so unsatisfactory that the voting mechanism itself would sooner or later be abandoned.'[23] The democratic political process is, however, equally overloaded by the unplanned and unsystematic use by the government of its extensive powers to regulate production and transfer income. Everybody feels affected by such political decisions and, worse, has at least a plausible reason to feel discriminated against; the overall results of the sum of interventions are indeterminate. This process, too, is unsustainable over a long period.

Democracy is a political method of accommodating change without a revolution. It must therefore rely mainly on procedural rules and have only a minimum of substantive content. When the state comes to be so involved in the processes of society that it becomes the necessary support of the existing economic and social structures, it has become identified with the *status quo*. The basic function of democracy—change without upheaval—has become undischargeable.

OVERCOMING THE CRISIS

How, then, can the crisis be overcome? If my impression that the ideological wave which provided its main impulse has already crested, is correct, the remaining difficulties are purely economic and well understood. As the period of Western Europe's easy afflu- ence follows the *Pax Americana* into history, the socially satisfactory performance of national economies will require more saving, greater scope for entrepreneurial initiative and a much improved function- ing of the price mechanism or, in other words, greater care by governments for undistorted competition.

No doubt all this will be difficult in political practice and I have little to suggest in terms of the practical 'how'. This is only to say that the politician's profession is as difficult as any other—when taken seriously. But the analysis presented here does lead to one practical suggestion. The national difficulties can be alleviated by the existing Community 'order'. What has to be done nationally can be achieved more easily if it is presented as an implementation of the existing Treaty commitments. For what has to be done nationally is what the strong elements of the Treaty of Rome have provided for. Indeed, a fuller development of these provisions would be an adequate response to most of the problems into which democratic welfare states have manoeuvred themselves.

Returning to the strong conception entails two immediately obvious steps:

The first consists in asserting, or reasserting, the European Community law in its integrity. Rescuing a law from abeyance is always a delicate problem, as past precedents have created equitable claims. How can a government refuse a new claimant a subsidy or protection it has granted to so many in the past? The precedents themselves must be attacked and deprived of their political force. Systems of trade restrictions can be gradually dismantled through an international agreement. Phasing out subsidies is politically more difficult since in this area neither international nor European Community rules have yet taken hold. Here the Community law derived from the principle of undistorted competition could provide important assistance to national governments. It undeniably creates private rights which the courts must protect. The possibility of private suits against restraints of competition and the abuse of dominant position constitute the heart of competition law. Can it be maintained that the same principle of undistorted competition does not create equivalent private rights in situations where enterprises are damaged by subsidies granted to their competitors, whether in the national economy or in that of another member state?

Second, there is an equally pressing need to unify and complete the legal system outlined in the Treaties. Where different systems of rules for coal and steel, other industries, agriculture and service activities exist, the same or at least more consistent rules should apply. Agriculture will remain a special problem, but not an insoluble one. Several proposals for a more economical organisation of European agricultural production and trade are under discussion. They may provide a suitable basis for the overdue reform of the CAP.

Taking these two steps may well imply a revision of the basic legal instruments. Those who say that it is politically impracticable may be too sceptical of the human capacity to learn. But it must be admitted that we know very little about the learning capacity of democratic societies. At the end of the decade we may know more. The question is whether societies can learn fast enough to avoid a crisis they see coming, or whether a calamitous breakdown in international relations continues to be the instrumental part of the learning process, necessary to drive the lesson home. It is now for the European statesmen to disprove the latter hypothesis. If it cannot be rejected, the whole adventure of European integration, in which such a vast fund of political idealism has been invested, may yet prove to have been only another episode in our *Zeitalter der Misserfolge*, our age of failures.

NOTES AND REFERENCES

1. F. A. von Hayek, *The Road to Serfdom* (Chicago: University of Chicago Press, 1944), p. 69.

2. The views expressed here are strictly personal and in no way implicate the GATT Secretariat.

3. Despite the fact that Frank H. Knight and Henry Simons represent its indigenous version.

4. D. C. North, 'Structure and Performance: the Task of Economic History', *Journal of Economic Literature*, Kingsport, Tennessee, No. 3, 1978.

5. Dan Usher, *The Economic Prerequisite to Democracy* (Oxford: Basil Blackwell, 1981).

6. *Cf.* Kenneth Minogue, 'The Concept of Property and Its Significance' in J. Roland Pennock and John W. Chapman (eds), *Property*: *Nomos XXII* (New York: University Press, 1980).

7. Ernst-Joachim Mestmäcker, *Recht und ökonomisches Gesetz: Uber die Grenzen von Staat, Gesellschaft und Privatautonomie* (Baden-Baden: Nomos Verlagsgesellschaft, 1978), p. 79, my translation.

8. The parallel is not perfect. For a major difference see Jan Tumlir, 'International Economic Order: Rules, Cooperation and Sovereignty', in Peter Oppenheimer (ed.), *Issues in International Economics, Essays in Memory of Harry G. Johnson* (Stocksfield and Boston: Oriel Press, 1980), pp. 5-6.

9. Hayek, *Studies in Philosophy, Politics and Economics* (London: Routledge & Kegan Paul, 1967), p. 76. Walter Eucken's notion of 'interdependence of orders' is, by contrast to the vertical stratification discussed here, horizontal in nature: he stresses the interdependence of the economic, legal, political, constitutional and possibly also cultural or other orders; *cf.* Walter Eucken, *Grundsätze der Wirtschaftspolitik*, edited by Edith Eucken and K. Paul Hensel (Tübingen: Mohr, 1952; and Bern: Francke, 1952), pp. 180-84.

10. *Cf.* David Whymes and Roger A. Bowles, *The Economic Theory of the State* (Oxford: Robertson, 1981), p. 182.

11. It is even more demanding than suggested in the text. If the value consensus were perfect, or even if the minority adhering to different values were evenly spread throughout the common territory, there would be no point in having a federal arrangement. The point in having it is that the constant tension between regional and national, national and still more general interests and values is politically creative. But the two must remain in some balance, and balancing them is always difficult.

12. Which is, in turn, due to the fact that it is at best large majorities, rather than whole polities, which consider particular issues of importance above politics, and that any majority may dwindle in time.

13. Jean Monnet, *Mémoires* (Paris: Fayard, 1976), pp. 345-47.

14. Jelle Zijlstra, *Politique économique et problèmes de la concurrence dans la CEE et dans les pays membres de la CEE*, CEE Etudes, Série Concurrence—Rapprochement des Législations, No. 2 (Brussels: Commission of the European Community, 1966), p. 5.

15. Klaus Stegemann, *Wettbewerb und Harmonisierung im Gemeinsamen Markt* (Köln: Heymanns, 1966).

16. *Ibid.*, p. 76, my translation.

17. 'If any action by the Community appears necessary to achieve, in the functioning of the Common Market, one of the aims of the Community in cases where this Treaty has not provided for the requisite powers of action, the Council, acting by means of a unanimous vote on a proposal of the Commission, and after the Assembly has been consulted, shall enact the appropriate provisions'. Article 235 of the Treaty of Rome.

18. Ralf Dahrendorf, *Plädoyer für die Europäische Union* (Munich and Zurich: Piper, 1973), Ch. 14.

19. One may recall that the conservative, the romantic and the socialist critics of industrial society in the first half of the nineteenth century were

united in condemning the liberals for their 'purely negative' conception of freedom.

20. *Cf.* Andrew Shonfield, *Europe: Journey to an Unknown Destination*, an Expanded Version of the BBC Reith Lectures 1972 (Harmondsworth: Penguin, 1973), pp. 70-72.

21. Leo Tindemans, *The European Union*, Tindemans Report, Bulletin of the European Communities, Supplement 1 (Luxembourg: European Communities, 1976).

22. Mestmäcker, *op. cit.*, p. 97, my translation.

23. Usher, *op. cit.*, p. 16.

Part II

International Monetary System

3 The Logic of the International Monetary Non-system

W. M. Corden

It has been said that the present international monetary system is really a 'non-system'. It emerged unplanned out of the chaos of the Great Inflation, the breakdown of the Bretton Woods system and the Oil Shock. It has no relationship to anything considered or proposed by the Committee of Twenty that was supposed to produce an outline of a new system and that gave up the job at the end of 1973. It is neither a system of agreed fixed rates of exchange—even if fixed only for limited periods—nor a system of free floating. As a system of managed floating rates of exchange it is a system of many managers who appear to operate subject to no explicit rules, whether self-imposed or laid down by some central agreement.[1]

This rather negative characterisation can be developed further if one looks at this chaotic system through the eyes of a Soviet central planner. Who decides the prices—that is, the exchange rates and the interest rates—in the system? Who ensures that when one price is changed by one manager the other prices change in a compatible way? Who decides the quantities? For example, when the members of the Organisation of Petroleum Exporting Countries (OPEC) decide to increase their current-account surpluses, who allocates the inevitable total 'oil deficit' of the rest of the world? How much of this deficit is to be borne by the United States, for example, and how much by the non-oil developing countries? When the corporations of a major country like Japan decide to reduce investment because of their pessimism about the future, who ensures that the resultant excess savings of the Japanese people are absorbed? And so on. Presumably the present non-system—like the chaotic decentralised capitalist system itself—would be the despair of such a central planner who put his mind to understanding it. It is certainly a system which, in the minds of many, cries out for reorganisation, central direction and frequent reconsideration at summits of wise international statesmen. It is noteworthy that of the many plans for international monetary reform that were developed in the 1960s and early 1970s none emerged that can be said to describe the present system. It is indeed a miracle that it works at all. Perhaps there is some 'hidden hand' that continuously guides it away from breakdown.

The purpose of the present essay is to seek out the logic of the system. This should help in understanding its points of friction and in finding ways of improving it. The essay does not attempt to deal with all aspects of the question since the study of the international monetary system is a complex subject and has spawned a vast literature. The purpose is really just to make a simple point, one which is implicit in much current discussion, but usually fails to be made explicit. Herbert Giersch, in whose honour this essay is written, showed consistently in his writings two characteristics, namely *realism* and *a belief in the market* and—as the reader may already have detected—the present essay has the same two characteristics.

A SYSTEM OF INTERNATIONAL LAISSEZ-FAIRE

The key feature of the present system is that it is a form of international *laissez-faire*. First of all, it allows free play to the private market, not just to trade in goods and non-financial services but, above all, to the private capital market. Secondly, it allows free play to governments and their central banks to operate in the market and —if they wish and where they can—to influence and even fix its prices or its quantities. Thus it is a fairly free market where many governments, acting in their own presumed interests and not necessarily taking much account of the interests of other governments, are participants.

Governments are quite free to borrow and lend and to determine their own monetary policies. Above all, they are free to intervene as much or little as they wish in the foreign-exchange market. From the point of view of the present discussion this is the most important way in which governments participate in the system. This latter freedom was clearly established in the Jamaica Agreement of January 1976 reached by the Interim Committee of the Board of Governors of the International Monetary Fund (IMF). The Jamaica Agreement in fact ratified the new system that had evolved since early 1973. It provided 'principles for the guidance of members' exchange rate policies' and for 'surveillance' of such policies by the IMF. But, for all practical purposes, countries could do what they liked. The proposed guidance was rather general and no element of compulsion was intended.

In practice, governments and central banks act subject to many constraints, whether constraints of credit-worthiness in the international capital market, ability to control their domestic monetary policies or self-imposed constraints on their exchange rate policies. They may choose to fix their own rates relative to some other currency, relative to a currency basket, or to the value of the Special Drawing Rights (SDRs). But, like the constraints which the members of the European Monetary System (EMS) have imposed on themselves, these are self-imposed and—above all—do not take into account the international system. The essential feature of the present system is thus *decentralisation* and absence of uniform, worldwide rules of any real significance.

In assessing this apparently chaotic 'non-system' one must deal with three questions. First, what motivates the various decentralised interventions of governments? Secondly, how is a world equilibrium established; in other words, how are targets—whether exchange-rate targets, current-account targets or official-reserve targets—reconciled? Thirdly, is there some element of optimality, some logic from a world welfare point of view, in the system?

SYSTEM OF FREE FLOATING EXCHANGE RATES

Before pursuing these three issues it seems desirable to clarify the nature of the present system by describing an alternative model where governments and central banks are not actors in quite the same sense. This is the model of a free-floating exchange-rate system—*with no management of exchange rates*—which many of us envisaged until the early 1970s as the alternative to the Bretton Woods system. I assume that this is, broadly, the model that Milton Friedman and James Meade had in mind when they put their cases for flexible exchange rates in the 1950s.[2]

In this model each country chooses its fiscal and monetary policies with no concern for the exchange-rate or current-account outcomes. Let us assume for the moment a passive fiscal policy taking the form of exogenously determined government expenditure combined with either constant tax rates and an endogenous bond-financed government deficit or, alternatively, with variable tax rates designed to maintain a constant deficit. Monetary policy could be determined in a number of simple ways: there may be a constant or predetermined rate of growth of the money supply, the actual rate of growth being determined by domestic considerations; alternatively, nominal wages may be assumed given and monetary policy may be aimed along Keynesian lines to achieve a constant level of employment or a given unemployment rate; and, finally, monetary policy may be directed to maintain a constant domestic nominal interest rate. With monetary policy decided on the basis of any of a number of possible domestic considerations—and with fiscal policy passive, with international capital mobility and with the exchange rate freely floating—there will then be unplanned exchange-rate and current-account outcomes. There will be no need for official reserves and if they exist their levels will not change.

The world capital market will equilibrate through interest-rate changes. In any given period the algebraic sum of net capital outflows of all the countries must equal zero for the world as a whole; the obverse is that the algebraic sum of current-account surpluses must equal zero. This would not just be a statistical result: interest-rate flexibility in the world capital market would make it a true equilibrium. It might be noted that the existence of a world capital market does not mean that interest rates throughout the world must be uniform. Expectations of exchange-rate changes will bring about divergences between interest rates. In addition, since not all bonds are traded, a country's monetary policy can still aim to fix or influence the prices of its non-traded bonds even when the prices of traded bonds are determined in a world market.

A change in a country's monetary policy will alter its exchange rate and possibly its capital (and hence current) account. Thus governments influence the foreign-exchange and capital markets even in a system where they do not directly intervene in the foreign-exchange market. As long as there is publicly supplied money, this cannot be otherwise. But the 'free floating' paradigm has an implicit view about motivation: monetary policy does not have exchange-rate or current-account objectives.

An active fiscal policy can easily be introduced. Again, it is necessary to assume that fiscal policy is not consciously directed to influencing the exchange rate or the current account. Given this assumption, it is not really necessary to set out the various possible motivations of fiscal policy changes, whether they are concerned with employment, with domestic interest rates and with the achievement of some budget balance target, or whether fiscal policy is the outcome of pressures from various interest groups.

This brief description of a hypothetical 'free-floating' system where governments do not concern themselves with their countries' exchange rates nor with the magnitudes of the various components of their balances of payments, provides background for the subsequent discussion. We can now turn to the three questions listed earlier that arise in an assessment of the current 'non-system' of managed floating.

MOTIVES FOR INTERVENTION IN THE FOREIGN-EXCHANGE MARKET

What motivates the various decentralised interventions of monetary authorities in the foreign-exchange market? There appear to be two main motivations.

'*Smoothing*' Intervention

The first is to smooth out fluctuations whether in the very short or the medium term. Short-term intervention is usually described as avoiding 'disorderly conditions' in the market. Such smoothing intervention, if it is successfully stabilising, should be profitable to central banks. It has been much discussed in the literature and raises the question of whether public authorities have more resources or better information, or are more rationally motivated, than private operators in the market. In any case, governments widely intervene on these grounds not because they wish their central banks to make profits from foreign-exchange speculation, but because they believe that they can successfully smooth out exchange-rate movements and because they regard this result as desirable for trade and capital flows.

In practice there is not much debate about the legitimacy of this type of intervention. It does not give rise to conflicts between governments because they usually welcome the smoothing activities of other countries' central banks. At the same time some academics doubt that such intervention is usually successful—that is, that it smoothes and is profitable—and even if it is, they question its necessity in the presence of private speculators.

Exchange-rate Protection

A second motivation for intervention in the foreign-exchange market is by far the most important for the present discussion. This is 'exchange-rate protection', a special case of which is 'leaning against the wind'.[3] Governments intervene in the market in order to affect the domestic inter-sectoral or inter-factoral income distribution. Usually the aim is to prevent or moderate a redistribution that would otherwise have taken place as the result of changes in the real exchange rate. If the net effect is neither to bring about an actual redistribution relative to a recent period, nor to prevent completely one that would have taken place in the absence of intervention, but only to brake it or slow it up, then the policy can be described as 'leaning against the wind'.

It may be observed that a country's exchange rate is appreciating in real terms and, at the same time, foreign-exchange reserves are being accumulated (which prevents even greater appreciation). Then we know that a leaning-against-the-wind policy is being followed. The same applies if the exchange rate is depreciating in real terms and reserves are being run down. There is evidence that this has been the main type of medium-term intervention since generalised floating began in 1973. For example, Japanese intervention in 1977 and 1978 slowed up the yen appreciation that was actually taking place; and this intervention appeared to be motivated by a concern for the adverse effects on export and import-competing industries that an even greater yen appreciation in real terms would have had. British intervention in 1974 and 1975 was designed to prevent further depreciation of sterling that would have reduced real wages and so would have accelerated a wage-price spiral. In general, the governments of appreciating countries worry about the adverse effects on profits and employment in their export and import-competing industries and governments of depreciating countries worry about the effects on wage demands and hence inflation. In the era of the Bretton Woods par-value regime these worries gave rise to reluctance to alter exchange rates—as Professor Giersch well knows from his experience as an advocate of appreciation in the Federal Republic—while in the era of managed floating they give rise to leaning-against-the-wind interventions.

Intervention of this kind can create problems and international conflicts, as Japanese intervention did in 1977 and 1978. A part of Japan's export industry was booming, capturing world markets and generating a current-account surplus for Japan. Appreciation of the yen moderated the adverse effects on competing industries in other countries. At the same time it *created* adverse effects for other Japanese export industries and for import-competing industries. Intervention designed to brake the appreciation then had a leaning-against-the-wind effect domestically in Japan, while preventing such an effect for industries in other countries that competed with Japan's boom industries.

In principle, exchange-rate protection could be more than leaning against the wind. It could aim to prevent an exchange-rate change altogether, or it might be directed to allowing some change, but then stabilising the rate at a new level other than the equilibrium rate which a free market would generate. Advocates of an exchange-rate policy in Britain designed to prevent so-called 'de-industrialisation' seem to have something like this in mind. It should also be stressed that intervention motivated by exchange-rate protection assumes that nominal exchange rates and real exchange rates move together. It is assumed that domestic wage and price movements do not fully offset the effects of nominal exchange-rate changes. There seems to be good evidence that, in general, for the short and medium run this is actually so. Of course, there is usually partial offsetting, especially in the case of depreciation, so that the extent of a real depreciation is less than the nominal depreciation which gave rise to it.

Exchange-rate protection—like other forms of protection—has a cost to the country practising it, even though there are presumably also perceived benefits. In the case of a deficit country this is the cost of running down reserves or of official borrowing beyond levels that would otherwise be optimal, taking into account the world interest rate, political conditions attached to special loans, the domestic social rate of return on investment and the domestic rate of time-preference. In the case of a surplus country, it is the cost of excess lending on the world market, taking into account again the world interest rate as well as the potential social return if the funds were used domestically. The greater the borrowing or lending, the greater not only the total cost, but also the greater the marginal costs are likely to become, especially if the country is a large borrower or lender on the world capital market. Even in the case of a small borrower the market's perception of the country's credit-worthiness is likely to deteriorate as more is borrowed and so the interest cost will rise.

Apart from smoothing intervention and leaning against the wind there is a third possible category of motives for exchange-rate interventions, namely to attain certain quantitative targets, whether of levels of official reserves or of current accounts. The implications of such motives will be discussed below. Nevertheless, it is difficult

to explain a significant proportion of interventions in recent years—
as measured by changes in official reserve levels—in these terms.

The objectives just discussed could also be achieved or influenced
by domestic monetary and fiscal policies. For example, exchange-
rate protection can be brought about by a contractionary fiscal
policy which lowers domestic interest rates, induces capital outflow
and thus depreciates the exchange rate. Similarly, a monetary
expansion can bring about this result. The net exchange rate and
current-account results can thus be achieved in a number of ways,
although often intervention in the foreign-exchange market seems
the most direct for the purpose. In any case, the motivation and the
final results, rather than the instrument, are crucial.

HOW IS WORLD EQUILIBRIUM ESTABLISHED?

With different monetary authorities intervening in the foreign-
exchange market as they choose and no centralised agreement about
the exchange-rate pattern (like the Smithsonian Agreement of
December 1971) or about the pattern of current accounts (as was
widely advocated in 1974), how does the system equilibrate?

United States 'Benign Neglect'

The simple and well known answer is that—subject to some
qualifications—the United States has acted as the residual net buyer
or seller of financial claims in the world capital market. It has been
passive in the foreign-exchange market, following a policy of 'benign
neglect'. Every other country can determine its own exchange rate
relative to the dollar if it wishes or, alternatively, can use a manipulation of its exchange rate combined with monetary and fiscal
policies to bring about a desired current-account outcome. But the
United States stands by and lets things happen. Essentially, this
was also the situation under the Bretton Woods regime, except that
other countries were not quite so free as they are now. The world
system is thus closed by the introduction of a major asymmetry.
This does not mean that other countries can have the bilateral
exchange rates they want—even though these may often be their
main concerns. It obviously takes two to settle a bilateral rate. But
the system does allow immense flexibility—coping, for example,
with the OPEC surpluses by means of decentralised adjustments.

Two qualifications to this asymmetrical 'benign neglect' model
have to be noted. First, in November 1978 the United States did
intervene in the market in response to an apparently precipitous

depreciation of the dollar. The intervention itself and—more important—the expectations generated by the intervention stabilised the dollar. This was a major departure of policy since floating began. It was an abandonment of 'benign neglect' and suggests the possibility of frequent or regular interventions in the future. Nevertheless this episode has not put the basic system to the test. The reason is that the objective of intervention was clearly not to establish an exchange-rate pattern different from that desired by other major countries—especially West Germany and Japan—but to put an end to what policy makers regarded as 'disorderly conditions' in the foreign-exchange market. The intervention took place with the enthusiastic support of monetary authorities in the other major countries and was in the same direction as their own interventions. Thus there was no element of international conflict.

The second qualification is that there have been times when the authorities have had views about the medium-term value of the dollar—especially relative to the yen—which were influenced by concern for American industries that compete with Japanese exports. Thus an element of exchange-rate protection thinking has existed in the United States. For example, it influenced the American advocacy of yen and German mark appreciation in 1977. This type of thinking also played a part in the realignment of exchange rates forced by the United States in 1971. But at these times the American authorities have not actually intervened in the market directly; rather they have sought by exhortation and political pressure to influence the intervention policies of other countries.

Equilibrium in a Symmetrical System

The interesting question next arises whether it is possible to conceive of a completely symmetrical system where the United States does not follow a passive policy. In such a system all governments act in a decentralised way—with no role for exhortation, cooperation or centralised decision making. Can such a system yield a world equilibrium? In such a system governments, like private firms, can be buyers and sellers not only of goods but also of financial claims in the world market. They can be concerned with levels of real exchange rates and the interests of their export and import-competing industries to varying extents—varying between countries and at different times for any given country. In such a system, the United States authorities must be allowed to have an exchange rate protection view—or a view about the desirable change in the level of net liabilities to foreigners in any given year.

In considering this hypothetical symmetrical international monetary world, the first point to make is simple. If all countries including the United States had fixed current-account targets a problem of incompatibility of targets would be likely to arise. Some countries would end up not attaining what they wanted. Similarly, if all housewives and shopkeepers went into the market on a particular day with a fixed view of how many apples they intended to buy or sell that day, irrespective of the price of apples, a problem of incompatibility of targets would arise. The essential feature of this supposed incompatibility problem is that it leaves out of account the possibility that targets can be influenced by prices.

Exactly the same problem would be generated if all countries wished to fix either their nominal or their real exchange rates. This point is so well known that it need hardly be laboured. If all countries other than the United States fixed their nominal exchange rates relative to the dollar, the United States would be left with nothing to decide.

What, then, is the resolution to this apparent difficulty? The answer is that a role must be given to the usual market forces acting through prices. The relevant prices in this case are interest rates. The problem is to reconcile the desires of different countries to buy and sell financial claims on the world market, the potential transactors including central banks that are intervening in the foreign-exchange market. The system will equilibrate, if the demands or supplies of at least some transactors' financial claims are responsive to interest rates. Given some elasticity, price changes in this market can reconcile targets that initially seem incompatible, just as changes in the prices of apples can equilibrate the apple market.[4]

Two out of many possible stories can be envisaged. In the first case governments (and central banks) have fixed targets which are not responsive to the interest rate, but equilibrium is attained through the interest-rate responsiveness of private-sector demands or supplies. In the second case governments have exchange-rate targets, but these are responsive to the interest rate.

In the first case we assume that the United States authorities do not wish to change the supply of bonds (financial claims) in the hands of the public, domestic as well as foreign, and use fiscal policy to ensure this. Foreign governments then intervene in the foreign-exchange market to build up their foreign-exchange reserves, which we can suppose to take the form of dollar financial claims of various kinds. They aim at a fixed target increase in reserves in a given period. The reason for this desired increase in reserves need not concern us here. The interest rate will fall (bond prices will rise) and this will induce private holders to part with bonds just sufficiently to satisfy the extra demands of the world's governments. Governments thus have fixed targets, while market forces operate through the interest-rate responsiveness of the private sector in various countries.

The current-account outcomes will be incidental. The American current account will deteriorate as the United States private sector moves marginally out of bonds into goods. On balance the current account of any particular country other than the United States could move in either direction. On the one hand, the accumulation of official reserves and the associated depreciations will improve the current account. On the other hand, private-capital inflow will result from the stimulus to borrowing (sale of bonds) brought about by the reduced world interest rate, and this will tend to appreciate the exchange rate and worsen the current account. For all countries together (with the United States excluded) there must be a net improvement in the current account.

In the second case we assume that government targets are interest-rate responsive. We assume that all governments other than that of the United States have an exchange-rate target relative to the dollar which they have initially attained, the United States having been passive. The result has been a particular pattern of current-account imbalances, perhaps adding up to a net deficit for the United States. The combined public and private sectors of other countries are building up financial claims on the United States. The American authorities then end their passivity. They may wish to reduce the accumulation of foreign claims on the United States. More likely, they may wish to bring about depreciation of the dollar to assist United States export and import-competing industries, the motive thus being exchange-rate protection.

The Federal Reserve can bring about the desired result by engaging in open-market operations designed to lower American interest rates. This will lead to private capital outflow and—for given official net purchases in the foreign-exchange market by foreign monetary authorities—to the desired dollar depreciation. But foreign official intervention cannot be taken as given since we are supposing that the foreign authorities have exchange-rate targets. If the foreign exchange-rate targets were absolutely fixed, foreign intervention would then be increased in order to restore the original exchange rate pattern.

It is at this point that the cost of exchange-rate protection—to which reference was made earlier—must be recalled. In the case of a surplus country this is the cost a country incurs by lending abroad more than is justified by the usual optimal lending considerations. The lower the American interest rate, the greater the cost of excess lending and, hence, the greater the cost of exchange-rate protection. It is reasonable to presume that exchange-rate targets would be modified by this cost consideration. To take an extreme case, if a country like Japan found that she was obtaining negative real rates of interest on her dollar-denominated claims, she would be likely in due course to moderate a policy of exchange-rate protection that was leading to the official accumulation of such claims. If such a mechanism operates, then market forces are at work through their influence on official policies. United States policies which lower American interest rates will alter the exchange-rate targets of foreign governments and so bring about the dollar depreciation desired by the United States. It might be added that, as the interest rate falls, the concern of the United States over the growth of its indebtedness to foreigners might also be moderated, and that the benefits to the United States from cheap borrowing might be set against the adverse effects on American export and import-competing industries which would result from the exchange rate that goes with such borrowing.

The United States authorities could bring about a dollar depreciation not by open-market operations that involve the purchase of American bonds, but by intervening in the foreign-exchange market directly—for example buying yen and hence pushing down yen interest rates. In both cases the American money supply is increased. Given capital mobility, and with some substitutability between yen-denominated bonds and dollar-denominated bonds, the lower interest rates on yen-denominated bonds will also lead to lower interest rates on American bonds; the question then is whether this will affect the Japanese exchange-rate target. If the lower interest rates did not induce the Japanese to reconsider their exchange-rate target there would be a clear case of incompatible exchange-rate policies—with the Japanese buying dollars to keep the dollar up and the Americans buying yen to get the dollar down. On the other hand, a non-cooperative equilibrium would be established when these operations lead to a reconsideration of exchange-rate targets and, in particular, when the lower interest rate induces the Japanese to moderate their accumulation of dollars.

IS THE SYSTEM EFFICIENT?

In assessing the market economy as a method of economic organisation it is usual to assume that households and firms are the best judges of their own interests and then to consider the role of the market system as a coordinator or integrator of the various decentralised decisions of households and firms. The principal argument for the market is that decentralised decision making is more efficient and flexible than the alternative central-planning approach. Theory does not suggest that the free market necessarily leads to an 'optimal' result—that is, that it cannot be improved upon in various ways. In particular, monopolistic and oligopolistic elements may distort the outcome, externalities may generate effects which by-pass the market and, finally, no firm judgment can be made about the income distribution effects which are a by-product of the market system.

It is also accepted that all firms do not necessarily know how to maximise profits or organise themselves efficiently. This gives rise to the study of business management, to consulting services and also to conditions imposed by creditors upon firms that get into financial difficulties. In addition, households and individual persons may need information and guidelines to make wise decisions in their own interests. Furthermore, it is also thought appropriate in many countries to impose a few firm rules to protect citizens from themselves.

All these ideas which have been formalised in modern welfare economics can be, should be, but have not been applied to the assessment of the international monetary system. The parallel will no doubt appear obvious to the readers of this essay. The current *laissez-faire* international monetary system is simply a market system which coordinates the decentralised decisions reached by private *and public* actors and is likely to be as efficient in this as the market system is within the domestic economy. In formal terms one might make the assumption that when governments intervene in the foreign-exchange market and when they practise their monetary and fiscal policies they are trying to maximise a national social welfare function in the same way as households are presumed to be maximising a utility function and firms are presumed to be efficiently maximising profits. With regard to the international trade by private and public transactors in financial claims the crucial prices are interest rates and the question has to be considered to what extent these prices are equated to relevant marginal costs and returns. Current-account imbalances simply indicate the net trade by each country in financial claims in exchange for goods.

In assessing the system one has to consider whether there are externalities—that is, connections between the actors in the system that do not pass through the price system—and whether the outcome is significantly affected by monopolistic or oligopolistic elements, which in the present case must presumably refer to the dominant role of the United States monetary authorities. It should be noted that if a particular policy of one country—such as an intervention that brings about depreciation of its exchange rate—has an adverse effect on another, this does not necessarily mean that there is an externality. After all, if a housewife goes into the market and buys a thousand kilos of apples, hence forcing up the price of apples, this has an adverse effect on other apple-buying housewives and yet it is not an externality because all the adjustments operate through the market. Similarly, if Japan boosts her exports of goods so that her government can import more bonds (that is, build up foreign-exchange reserves), this will have an adverse effect on competing foreign producers of these goods and on foreign buyers of bonds, but there need be no element of externality.

It is not possible here to carry out an analysis along these lines in any detail, but perhaps it can be suggested as an agenda for research. In particular, what are the external diseconomies in the international monetary system, if any? It seems to me that the proper approach is to start with the assumption that this particular form of international market is reasonably efficient. It is likely to be more efficient and flexible than a system of coordinated or centralised decision making of the type that was uniquely and unsuccessfully attempted in 1971 at the Smithsonian Agreement with regard to nominal exchange rates. The focus should be on improving the information and signalling process, on correcting for specific well defined distortions and, in general, on 'making the market work'.

There is presumably a role for an international body like the IMF to give guidance to countries as to how to pursue and assess their own interests more effectively. In addition, the Fund plays, of course, the usual role of a creditor with respect to the countries, that borrow from it on conditional terms.

In my view it cannot be automatically assumed that attempts to 'manipulate' exchange rates because of concerns over domestic sectoral or factor incomes—that is, exchange-rate protection—are never legitimate. Such a concern could be part of a reasonable national social welfare function. But perhaps this matter should be left as an open question, calling for more consideration. In any case, for the purposes of thinking clearly about the international monetary system, it seems convenient to separate those issues that are concerned with the optimal or efficient policies for individual countries from their own points of view (maximising their social welfare functions) and those issues that are concerned with the efficiency of the international system as a whole. Many international monetary problems fall under the first category—for example, the problem of a country that has engaged in excess borrowing owing to an inability or reluctance to bring about needed reductions in real incomes and now faces either bankruptcy or a need for drastic and domestically unpopular measures as a result. The focus of this essay is on the second aspect. The suggestion here is that, with regard to the system as a whole, the concept of the market and the methods of modern welfare economics for assessing markets are highly relevant.

At the beginning of this essay I said that the aim is really to make a single and simple point. This simple point is that the current system of managed floating, with its large and changing current-account 'imbalances' and its exchange-rate 'manipulations', should be seen and assessed in terms of familiar market concepts, bearing in mind that governments can be actors in such a market. In particular, the role of the interest rate in the adjustment mechanism must not be neglected. It is only a beginning for analysis, but suggests an appropriate framework both for discovering 'non-optimal' or inefficient aspects of the current international monetary system and finding ways of improving it.

NOTES AND REFERENCES

1. The term 'international monetary non-system' comes from John Williamson, 'The Benefits and Costs of an International Monetary Non-system', in Edward M. Bernstein *et al.*, *Reflections on Jamaica*, Essays in International Finance No. 15 (Princeton: International Finance Section of Princeton University, April 1976). Unlike the present author, Williamson viewed the absence of 'system' with disapproval.

2. Milton Friedman, 'The Case for Flexible Exchange Rates', in *idem*, *Essays in Positive Economics* (Chicago: University of Chicago Press, 1953). James E. Meade, 'The Case for Variable Exchange Rates', *Three Banks Review*, Edinburgh, September 1955.

3. On 'exchange-rate protection', see W. M. Corden, 'Relationships between Macro-economic and Industrial Policies', *The World Economy*, London, September 1980. On 'leaning against the wind', see Peter J. Quirk, 'Exchange Rate Policy in Japan: Leaning Against the Wind', *International Monetary Fund Staff Papers*, Washington, November 1977 and Paula A. Tosini, *Leaning Against the Wind: A Standard for Managed Floating*, Essays in International Finance No. 126 (Princeton: International Finance Section of Princeton University, December 1977).

4. This is, perhaps, the main point of this essay. The idea seems to have been neglected in the literature on the international monetary system. The only exceptions of which I am aware are Assar Lindbeck, 'International Coordination of National Economic Policies', in Samuel I. Katz (ed.), *US-European Monetary Relations* (Washington: American Enterprise Institute for Public Policy Research, 1979) and Joanne Salop and Erich Spitaller, 'Why Does the Current Account Matter?', *International Monetary Fund Staff Papers*, Washington, March 1980.

4   Key Currencies and Financial Centres

Charles P. Kindleberger

The subject of key currencies would seem to be more closely associated with the work of John H. Williams than with Herbert
Giersch. It is nonetheless an appropriate subject for this volume
since Professor Giersch is a key economist in a key country with
what may well be the next key currency. I propose in this essay to
discuss the question of whether the arrangements for international
money should be organised hierarchically, with a single key currency
standing at the apex of a world system—whether two or more such
currencies can serve effectively if no single currency stands out
following the weakening of the dollar—and to explore a bit of
European financial history in search of insights, analogies or
contrasts with the present.

In 1944, John Williams testified in the Congress of the United
States against the Bretton Woods proposals on the grounds that it
was a superior strategy in restoring a well-functioning world
monetary economy to focus on key currencies, presumably one or at
most a few, and one at a time, instead of seeking to construct a
convertible world at one swoop with a worldwide organisation
such as the International Monetary Fund (IMF).[1] The concept,
which went back to a phrase he had used as a member of the
Preparatory Commission of the League of Nations for the World
Economic Conference of 1933—'key country'—underlay the Anglo-
American Financial Agreement of 1946, the so-called 'British loan',
designed to restore the pound to financial health first, and through
it other currencies, starting perhaps with the sterling area. As it
happened, the British loan failed to provide durable sterling convertibility—exchange restrictions were reimposed in the summer
of 1947, a few weeks after the pound had been made convertible—
and the IMF itself was sidetracked after a wobbly start in 1946,
spending its time, until convertibility was finally achieved in 1958,
largely in tendering advice to less developed countries. The task of

75

monetary and economic reconstruction in Western Europe was assigned to the European Recovery Programme, also known as the Marshall Plan.

It is not widely known that the United States had an opportunity to apply the key-country approach to European recovery. When the Ambassador to Britain, Lewis Douglas, and the Under Secretary of State for Economic Affairs, William L. Clayton, visited Europe in June 1947, less than three weeks after Secretary Marshall's speech, they called on Britain's Foreign Secretary, Ernest Bevin, who suggested that the United States undertake a large programme of aid to Britain and thereafter that Britain and the United States together turn their attention to recovery on the Continent. The 'special relationship' between the United Kingdom and the United States proved not to be sturdy enough to support this proposal and Britain became another recipient of Marshall Plan aid to Europe along with the Continental states.[2]

Whatever the immediate postwar experience, the insight of John Williams and the question of key currencies are still unresolved. Questions remain open whether a key-currency approach to international monetary arrangements is valid; if so, whether there should be a single key currency, or a series; if more than one, whether these should be arranged hierarchically or on an equal level; and finally, if it be efficient to have a single key currency— or one key currency *primus inter pares*—what Susan Strange, of the London School of Economics, might call from her political-science perspective a 'top currency' or a 'master currency'[3]—how a change can be made from a tired and worn-out top currency to a youthful and more capable one.

In the immediate postwar period at the Massachusetts Institute of Technology (MIT), all social sciences were gathered into a single department and economists would sometimes find themselves more or less unintentionally edified by having to listen to practitioners from other and not always closely-allied fields. One experimental social psychologist used to organise small groups in various ways for problem-solving and was persuaded that when task forces were grouped in circles, each connected only with members of the group to his or her right and left, communicating by writing on slips of paper in some constrained way and unable to see the faces of the group, the problem—the nature of which now escapes me—could be solved in many fewer steps than if the group were forced to communicate in hierarchic fashion, through a centralised message centre. I no longer recall whether time constraints played a role. In crisis, it is reasonably clear that strong leadership without extended discussion is desirable. Goodman's novel, *Delilah*, suggests what may happen when enlisted men converse freely with their officers and believe themselves in a position to discuss and question orders in a crisis. Examples more apposite for international economics are the three weeks of discussion insisted upon by the French at the time of the Hoover Moratorium of 19 June 1931, raising the question whether it applied to the unconditional payments provided under the Young Plan of 1929 or only to the conditional ones— a valid legal point, which, however, delayed the rescue of the German money market for so long that its banking system collapsed.[4] Or again, years of discussion and what seemed interminable delays were required by the point, raised by the French on 'disparities' (*encrêtements*) in the Kennedy Round of negotiations under the General Agreement on Tariffs and Trade (GATT), whether it was equitable for a country with a narrower range of customs duties, that is, less disparities, to be required to reduce tariffs by the same percentage as one with the same average level, but a wider range of duties.[5] The point remains a fascinating conundrum for economists, but came within an ace of ruining the Kennedy Round by exhausting the five years of lee-way given by the Congress to the executive branch before the presidential powers under the legislation lapsed. Equality of participation may be best in the production and exchange of ideas under normal, unstressful times, but it is likely that strong leadership and docile followership are optimal in crisis.

FINANCIAL CENTRES AND ECONOMIES
OF SCALE

Some years ago in a paper on financial centres I concluded that there were strong economies of scale associated with centralisation in a single financial centre in a country and presumably, by extension, in a region like the European Community and in the world as a whole.[6] These economies are similar to those in an agglomeration of markets, that is, the reduction of transactions costs, especially those of search. A lesser region with excess savings finds it effective to send them to a financial centre where demanders for savings gather. Conversely, demanders are attracted to a central source of excess supply. Local financial institutions cannot be altogether dispensed with, to be sure. One of the most important

requirements in finance is credit information; and this is available
in detail about small participants in the market only in the village,
town or provincial city. Central stapling markets for goods—
Antwerp, Amsterdam, Hamburg, London—lost their eminence as
trade relays, when knowledge of what goods were produced and
wanted where became widely diffused and when the cost of trans-
porting from producers to the centre and from the centre to consumers could be reduced by direct dealings. The costs of transferring
money to and from a central place, however, are far less, which
argues in favour of retaining financial centres and their economies
of scale. On the other hand, as computers and the cost of electronic
communication become drastically cheaper, and reduce search
costs in the field of money to trivial levels, there may be an argument for direct trade in money and securities as in goods, with
supply and demand unified worldwide by electronic bands without
assembly in geographic centres. (At the moment, it should be noted,
new issues of Euro-bonds are marketed worldwide, whereas the
secondary market, where search costs have to be absorbed by small
transactions, tends to locate in a single place.) For the time being,
the N-1 argument for money as a unit of account, rather than each
good being priced in terms of every other, applies both to currencies
and to financial centres. It is more efficient to pick a single (or
perhaps a limited number of financial centres) and deal with all
transactions above some considerable size in it (or them) than to
search the world for outlets or available supply. The same argument
applies to selecting one currency as international money and, to
shift to another medium of exchange, to conducting international
discourse for the most part in a single language. The currency
should be one already in use, like the dollar, rather than an artificial
one like the Special Drawing Right (SDR), just as the language
used as a medium of exchange cannot be Esperanto or a dead
language such as Latin.

One puzzle in the study of financial centres was why Canada and
Australia were so slow in converging on Toronto and Sydney,
respectively, and why Montreal and Melbourne hung on for so long
as doughty rivals. Considerations of history, geography and
especially the association of a given centre with a certain industry,
as St James Street in Montreal was the financial centre for Canadian
railroads, each doubtless played a part. Professor S. H. Butlin, the
Australian economic historian, suggested in a private letter, however, that there might be a significant difference between federal

and unitary states, a difference inherent less in constitutional arrangements, I should think, than in sociology. That this is so is demonstrated, I believe, by German and United States experience, where the formation of a single financial centre took place in the face of national policies directed at preventing it. The Federal Reserve System was set up in 1913 with twelve regional banks which were intended to serve as foci for twelve regional money markets. It was quickly evident after World War I, however, that the system was unified with a dominant financial market in New York and subsidiary markets in Chicago, San Francisco and Los Angeles. In Germany, the occupation authorities after World War II sought to diffuse monetary and banking direction to the *Länder*, and especially to build up Hamburg and Düsseldorf as rivals to Frankfurt, which was the heir-apparent to Berlin's pre-war eminence. The gesture was futile as the centripetal tendencies of money and capital markets in unified states asserted themselves and the main capital market gravitated towards Frankfurt.

THE RISE AND DECLINE OF FINANCIAL
CENTRES

Key countries and key currencies are by no means new, although historians tend to illustrate their importance by reference to the contemporary scene. Pierre Vilar asserts that the Florentine florin and the Venetian ducat were the dollars of the Middle Ages, and the Dutch currency the dollar of the seventeenth century.[7] (Analogously with English, Italian was the commercial language of the Mediterranean,[8] and Dutch prevailed as the commercial language in the Baltic ports and elsewhere in the seventeenth and eighteenth centuries.)[9] World financial markets were dominated successively by Florence, Venice, Genoa, Bruges, Antwerp and London, but there have always been strong pulls in other directions. From time to time it appears that there have been financial axes, Florence-Lyons, Venice-Augsburg-Bruges, Augsburg-Antwerp, Amsterdam-London and London-Hamburg. Financial distinction appears to have followed temporally after supremacy in trade and to have been causally connected with the decline in trade. Men with fortunes made as merchants chose to reduce their risks by shifting into loans and securities. In one city after another the lament was voiced that merchants were turning their backs on the sea and commodities in favour of money, bills of exchange, securities and country estates, to reduce both trouble and risk.[10] The shift from trade to finance appears to be largely an internal process, associated with accumulation of wealth by merchants.

The decline of financial centres and their supersession by others is more complex: it may come from some inner weakness or decay of the sort that seems to afflict the dollar today; it may reflect an aggressive challenge; or both may apply. Until about 1670 the Dutch considered themselves superior to the British in ability, energy, capital and material resources and the British admitted their inferiority.[11] But by then the position had begun to change. After a false start early in the century, the Navigation Acts were passed in 1651 and strengthened in 1660. The British coveted Dutch trade: as his country prepared aggressively for the second Anglo-Dutch War, the Duke of Albermarle stated that 'What we want is the trade the Dutch now have'.[12] The Dutch trade advantage went down first—various sources debate exactly when—but between the last quarter of the seventeenth century and 1730. The Dutch advantage in finance declined sometime after the fourth Anglo-Dutch War in 1784, perhaps with Napoleon's occupation of the United Provinces in 1795. Without making a distinction between trade and finance, Braudel states that between 1780 and 1815 the economic centre of Europe, which had remained for two hundred years in Amsterdam, moved to London (and in 1929 crossed the Atlantic to New York).[13] The occupation of the United Provinces of Holland by Napoleonic armies underlines the fact that military power can play an important role in shifts of currencies and financial centres. The shift from Bruges to Antwerp was slow in the latter part of the fifteenth and early sixteenth centuries as Portuguese pepper and German copper came to be traded in the latter and Flemish cloth spread from Bruges to many places visited by the Hanseatic League.[14] Antwerp's yielding of place to Amsterdam (and to a lesser extent to Hamburg and Frankfurt) occurred suddenly as the Spanish invaded the Scheldt in 1585 and cut off its access to the sea. Both rise to financial eminence and decline from it can occur either rapidly or slowly.

It is not inevitable that any financial centre that tries to displace another in the world hierarchy can do so. The Deutsche Bank was started in 1872 with the express purpose of challenging British leadership in world finance. It got caught up in the domestic boom associated with the founding of the German Reich and the receipt of the Franco-Prussian indemnity.[15] Paris challenged London's supremacy several times in the nineteenth century, but especially in the 1850s. In some views, it achieved success.[16] For the most part, however, scholars agree with Walter Bagehot, who concluded that the abandonment of convertibility in 1870 at the outbreak of the Franco-Prussian War spelled the end of French hopes to dominate the finances of Europe.[17]

KEY CURRENCIES OR KEY FINANCIAL CENTRES?

Should one say key currency or key financial centre? Is New York the world financial centre or is it London with its enormous business in Euro-dollars? In a sense the market for the dollar has no location, as it travels around the world each weekday, starting out west of the international dateline (to be arbitrary) in Singapore, moving thence to Bahrain and on to Europe, before crossing the Atlantic to New York and ending up in San Francisco.[18] This fact complicates the management of a leading currency which is now a 24-hour-day affair during the week which starts on Sunday afternoon in the United States as Singapore is opening on Monday morning. Most financial authorities work from 9 to 5, but news of the sort to disturb the market, such as that of President John F. Kennedy's assassination, can occur in any place in the world and at any time.[19]

A financial centre has certain functions and, I would add, certain responsibilities, notably that of acting as a lender of last resort in crisis. Financial integration may be said to be a good thing if the trouble starts at home and integration into a world market diffuses it over space—a bad thing if it arises abroad and is communicated to a given centre from the outside. In either event, the world centre presiding over a key currency presumably has the function of trying to halt it. The lender-of-last-resort function is generally associated with the name of Bagehot, who articulated a rationale for it in *Lombard Street*, although he left some residual ambiguity by writing from time to time that the system by which the Bank of England held the reserves for the London money market as a whole was an 'unnatural' one that would not have been constructed *de novo* had it not happened to have evolved that way.[20] I demur from this line of argument, believing that the insurance principle dictates great economies from centralised reserves, although one must recognise that moral hazard is implicit in any system having ultimate responsibility yet divorced from operating units. Revealed historical preference, however, seems to show that the dangers of moral hazard from relieving banks of too much responsibility are less than those in having no lender of last resort. Where there is no clear financial centre, there may be failure to discharge the duty of halting spreading collapse in the international monetary system, such as occurred, in my judgment, in 1929-33, in the midst of the transfer of financial leadership from London to New York.[21]

There is a complex disability to the system if the failure starts with the dominant financial centre itself. Paris came to the rescue of Britain at least four times between 1815 and 1914. In 1825 it swapped gold for silver to help the Bank of England meet a run that was ultimately checked by finding some of the £1 and £2 notes left over from the period of inconvertibility that halted with resumption of specie payments in 1819. It did so again on two occasions between 1836-39, when the Bank of England drew on Paris for £400,000 the first time and £2 million, along with £900,000 from the State Bank of Hamburg, the second. In 1890, when the Bank of England was about to announce the collapse of Baring Brothers, it sought assurance from the Russian Government that it would not withdraw its deposit of £2.4 million at the Bank, and arranged for loans of £3 million from the Bank of France and £1.5 million from the State Bank of Russia. Yet again, the Bank of France helped the Bank of England by selling gold to the London market in the crisis of 1907, although British historians assert that this was not a rescue operation, since the Bank of England did not ask for help, and did not need it.[22]

Sometimes a government or its central bank acts as the lender of last resort. Sometimes it merely opens its market to permit a foreign institution in trouble—government, central bank, outstanding banker acting as a chosen instrument of the government— a Rothschild or a Baring—to borrow in the private capital market. Many lender-of-last-resort loans in the nineteenth and twentieth centuries were of this type. In these cases governments proposed, the market disposed—and not always favourably. Italy sought a stabilisation loan in 1881 as she was prepared to return to gold following the depreciation of the lira from 1866—the so-called *corso forzoso*, or forced circulation. The loan was opened in Paris and failed miserably, to such an extent that it was transferred to London.[23] The French capital market happened to be bemused by the boom that collapsed the next year with the failure of the *Union Générale*. Moreover, French investors were in the process of turning their attention away from involvement with Italy, Spain and Austria, to shift their interest to Russia and South-eastern Europe.[24]

THE DOLLAR AS A KEY CURRENCY

We come shortly to the problem of the financial difficulties of the dollar. First, however, it may be observed that, historically, financial centres have been aided by winning the role of distributing additions to world monetary reserves. German silver moved to Venice during the Renaissance. African gold went originally to the Levant and then to Europe via Venice or Genoa, often exchanged for silver which was more highly valued in the East. When Spanish treasure arrived at Seville, it was already owed to German, Genoan and later Flemish and Dutch bankers, and had to be shipped out. Small amounts stayed in Spain; a trickle went into France by way of Biarritz.[25] The silver of Spanish America went largely to Flanders in the second half of the sixteenth century, along the Atlantic route. From 1568 it became diverted to Genoa and the so-called Besançon fair at Piacenza.[26] With the collapse of Genoa as a financial centre after 1620 'for a multitude of causes that occurred simultaneously',[27] the flow went to Amsterdam, which carried off up to 25 per cent of the treasure brought in by the *flota* and redistributed it to the Far East and Europe.[28] Portuguese discoveries of gold in the 1680s— which Spooner is bold enough to ascribe to the causes of the Industrial Revolution a century later— led the British to conclude the Treaty of Methuen and helped divert gold to London. In the mid-1850s, the yield of California and Australia arrived in London to be redistributed to the Continent, much of it to be exchanged by France against silver for shipment to the Far East.[29]

The contrast, of course, is with the dollar standard after World War II, when gold production was first cut by retaining a fixed price when mining costs had risen sharply owing to the war and then went into hoarding rather than being distributed by the leading financial centre. A number of economists, notably Milton Gilbert, wanted to raise the price of gold to correct what he saw as an anomaly.[30] The world was not short of liquidity, as economists such as Robert Triffin thought would occur; on the contrary, world liquidity was produced on demand by borrowing dollars in New York up to the imposition of the Interest Equalisation Tax in 1963 and then in the Euro-dollar market. The difficulty was that the United States reserve ratio was continuously in decline. It was not in 'deficit', lending long and borrowing short as banks normally do, but with a fixed and later a declining amount of gold in the face of mounting dollar liabilities, its reserve ratio dwindled. United States assent in 1965 for the adoption and distribution of SDRs was dictated, in my judgment, by the necessity seen to add to United States quick assets. In the process, other countries including those with excess dollars gained reserves as well, in the absence of recognition of the principle that the leading financial centre is different.

THE PROBLEM OF LENDER OF LAST RESORT

But to return to the lender of last resort. The function is normally discharged by the key-currency centre. What if it is that centre which finds itself in trouble and it cannot be helped with gold as Paris helped London? What especially if the leading centre committed a blunder of monetary policy, as the Federal Reserve System did in 1971, in trying to lower interest rates (to help President Richard Nixon's chances for re-election) when the next largest monetary power, West Germany, was trying to hold interest rates up, or raise them, to restrain inflation, both at a time when the two money markets were joined through the Euro-dollar market? Money created to lower interest rates in the United States would flow to the Euro-dollar market centred in London. German firms finding local interest rates high and rising would replace loans from German sources by borrowing in dollars in London and selling the dollars to the Bundesbank. The 'liquidity deficit' of $2,000 to $4,000 million a year experienced from the mid-1950s to the end of the 1960s, and tolerable despite the downward path of the reserve-to-foreign-deposits ratio, rose to $20,000 and $30,000 million yearly.

When the dollar was strong and countries in trouble needed dollars, they could be provided in leisurely fashion by the IMF or, if the crisis was more exigent, by the General Agreement to Borrow (GAB) and ultimately by the swap lines. Swaps were devised at the time of the March 1961 British crisis in the Basle agreement and used later for Canada, Italy, a second time for Britain, and for France. The United States spearheaded the operation. But when the crisis was that of the dollar, rescue called not for a single or leading lender of last resort, or many lenders operating in a single currency, but for a whole variety of other currencies sought by the entities quitting the dollar—German marks, Swiss francs, sterling—

especially those sought by some countries belonging to the Organisation of Petroleum Exporting Countries (OPEC) which at one time had given allegiance to the sterling area—not to mention yen, French francs, *et cetera*. When the leading centre is in trouble, and there is a variety of assets into which its currency might be converted, the lender-of-last-resort function becomes more complex.

A further important complication arises if the secondary centres do not share the sense of responsibility of the primary one. This is partly a question of conditionality, in which it is difficult to distinguish technical economic and financial conditions—what the country in trouble needs to do to correct its position—from ideological and political ones. In addition there may be conditions of a purely foreign-policy nature, such as those demanded by the French as a *quid pro quo* for acceding to the second tranche of the Bank for International Settlements (BIS) led loan to the Creditanstalt in May 1931—that Austria withdraw from the Zollunion with Germany—or the demand that the Germans abandon construction of the Panzerkreuzer (armoured cruiser), then under way, before the French could consider a stabilisation loan in June 1931.

Political considerations may of course dictate the granting of a rescue loan which could not be justified on economic and financial grounds. In April 1906, the French market was opened to a loan of Fr. 1,500 million for Russia, immediately after the defeat of Russia by Japan in war, a failed revolution and the prospective bankruptcy of the Czar.[31] And even when the supporting centres come to the rescue without hesitation, the possibility of last-minute holding back gives rise to nervousness. Britain felt humiliated by the need to appeal to France in 1839, and the French found vainglory in having helped, albeit resolving never to do so again. In 1873, flushed with pride of victory in the Franco-Prussian War, the Germans offered to help the Bank of England through a gold loan and were thought insulting. In 1890, when Britain needed the help of France and Russia, the appeal gave rise to great uneasiness: 'Suppose for some political-financial reason, they had been unwilling to oblige'.[32]

It is sometimes suggested that the IMF should act as the lender of last resort, and remove that necessity from private financial centres and their national monetary authorities. For the less developed countries this has the obvious advantage that there is at least the superficial appearance of no imperialistic tutelage. Less developed countries do chafe at the conditions laid down for their borrowing by the IMF, and tend from time to time to penetrate the international form to detect the imperialist guidance of the major powers. They accept these conditions—and those of the Euro-currency bankers—more readily, however, than they would those of national governments.

For the major financial powers, however, the IMF is typically too slow and too limited in size. The slowness arises from the voting procedure and the need to consult domestic monetary authorities, often of a long list of countries. The process takes three weeks at a minimum, and financial crises may blow up in hours. The size limitation had its origin in the initial view that IMF borrowings would meet deficits on current account because capital movements would be subjected to controls. In the event, financial crises are associated with large capital movements, permitted under con-vertibility, and in any case uncontrollable because of leads and lags. The IMF cannot perform the other functions of a financial centre and in crises operates best in mopping-up operations in the rear rather than at the vortex.

On the national front, an important step was taken at the BIS in Basle in 1975, following the Herstatt and Franklin National bank crises, in the agreement that each major financial country in case of trouble would take care of its own banks, no matter where they operated abroad, and would prevent any failure from spreading to banks or firms of other nations. The agreement spreads responsi-bility widely: it does not eliminate completely the need for some direction to the system by a leading financial centre. There remains a small and declining problem of consortium banks, owned by other banks in a number of countries for which, in time of trouble, rescue methods would have to be devised *ad hoc*. And there remains, too, the need for international help in cases of sudden switches of hot money from one to another financial centre which it is thought unwise to handle through exchange-rate changes because of irreversible effects on prices, costs and hence on inflation—a prob-lem which the newer generation refers to as 'currency substitution' by contrast with the pre-war expression 'hot money'.

But it is time to conclude. History shows, at least in my judgment, that financial centres and national currencies—no longer completely congruent as national currencies are traded worldwide—tend to organise themselves in hierarchical order, with one key currency serving as numeraire for much of the world's business. In earlier times when, say, sterling meant London, the financial centre asso-ciated with the leading currency had certain functions to perform:

the distribution of additions to world reserves, the accumulation and allocation of short- and long-term capital and, in time of crisis, serving as a lender of last resort.

Today, key currencies and financial centres cannot be matched so readily, and the capital-accumulation process can take place, for the most part, worldwide in a leading currency. The financial centre responsible for that currency—New York in the case of the dollar—cannot, however, escape its lender-of-last-resort function.

Change in key currencies and leading financial centres seems to follow a law of growth. It may take place slowly, in a long drawn-out process, or suddenly because of the aggressive rise of a new centre, or the collapse of the old in war. One is unable to say much based on either theory or history about what happens with no financial centre in charge, or with two. I have argued that the slow transfer and especially the slow acceptance of responsibility from London to New York in the inter-war period were responsible for the width, depth and length of the world depression of the 1930s, but the case is not proven. London was supported on occasion in the nineteenth century by Paris, but it can hardly be said that the two centres operated a duumvirate: Paris reigned supreme in a narrow area that changed, but London was clearly the dominant centre, and sterling the dominant currency.

This leaves us unable to say whether the dollar and the German mark and New York and Frankfurt can operate as dual key currencies and dual financial centres, sharing responsibility for world financial crises—although I have doubts; or whether the dollar and the world Euro-dollar market, centred perhaps in London, are *en route* to being replaced by the German mark and Frankfurt. Gresham's law, which states that a system with two monies is unstable, is easily extended to the proposition that a world with two key currencies of equal worth, or two key financial centres on a par, is equally unstable. The ageing of the American economy is clear, but the German economy in 1980 has lost some of the energy and drive it had two years earlier.[33] One responsible centre or the other would be satisfactory, possibly but probably not both would be, or perhaps a third country that emerges (maybe soon) as a dark horse and takes over. What strikes this observer as dangerous is a long period with no one in charge.

NOTES AND REFERENCES
1. See John H. Williams, *Postwar Monetary Plans and Other Essays*, 3rd rev. and expanded ed. (New York: Knopf, 1947) *passim*. The index for this

edition has almost four inches of citations under the headings 'key countries' and 'key currencies'.

2. *Foreign Relations of the United States, 1947*, Vol. III (Washington: US Government Printing Office, 1972), pp. 268-70.

3. Susan Strange, *Sterling and British Policy: a Political Study of an International Currency in Decline* (London: Oxford University Press, 1971).

4. See Charles P. Kindleberger, *The World in Depression, 1929-1939* (Berkeley: University of California Press, 1973), pp. 154-55.

5. See Gerard and Victoria Curzon, 'Options after the Kennedy Round', in Harry G. Johnson (ed.), *New Trade Strategy for the World Economy* (London: Allen & Unwin, for the Trade Policy Research Centre, 1969), pp. 34-36.

6. See Kindleberger, *The Formation of Financial Centers: a Study in Comparative Economic History*, Princeton Studies in International Finance, No. 36 (1974), repr. in *Economic Response, Comparative Studies in Trade, Finance and Growth* (Cambridge, Mass.: Harvard University Press, 1978), pp. 66-134.

7. Pierre Vilar, *A History of Gold and Money, 1450-1920*, transl. by Judith White (London: NLB, 1976), pp. 2-5.

8. Fernand Braudel, *The Mediterranean and the Mediterranean World in the Age of Philip II*, Vol. I (New York: Harper, 1973), p. 131.

9. Elizabeth E. de Jong-Keesing, *De economische Crisis van 1763 te Amsterdam* (Amsterdam: Intern. Uitgevers en H. Mij, 1939), p. 220.

10. On Antwerp, see Richard Ehrenberg, *Capital and Finance in the Age of the Renaissance: a Study of the Fuggers and their Connections*, transl. from the 1929 German text by R. M. Lucas (New York: Brace, 1928), p. 243; for two others, see Peter Burke, *Venice and Amsterdam: a Study in Seventeenth Century Elites* (London: Temple Smith, 1974), p. 104; Charles Wilson, *Anglo-Dutch Commerce and Finance in the Eighteenth Century* (Cambridge: Cambridge University Press, 1941), Pt II, Ch. III. Wilson deals here with the transition of Amsterdam from trade to finance.

11. Charles R. Boxer, 'The Dutch Economic Decline', in Carlo M. Cipolla (ed.), *The Economic Decline of Empires* (London: Methuen, 1970), p. 245.

12. E. Neville Williams, *The Ancien Regime in Europe, Government and Society in the Major States, 1648-1789* (New York: Harper & Row, 1970), pp. 44 and 484.

13. Braudel, *Afterthoughts on Material Civilization and Capitalism*, transl. by Patricia M. Ranum (Baltimore: Johns Hopkins University Press, 1977), p. 86.

14. See Jean-François Bergier, 'From the Fifteenth Century in Italy to the Sixteenth in Germany: A New Banking Concept', in Center for Medieval and Renaissance Studies, UCLA (ed.), *The Dawn of Modern Banking* (New Haven: Yale University Press, 1979), pp. 107-8; and Philippe Dollinger, *The German Hansa*, transl. and ed. by D. S. Ault and S. H. Steinberg (Stanford: Stanford University Press, 1970), p. 203.

15. Karl Helfferich, *Georg von Siemens, Ein Lebensbild aus Deutschlands grosser Zeit*, rev. and shortened ed. (Krefeld: Scherpe, 1956), pp. 32-34, 41 and 56.

16. Jean Bouvier, *Un siècle de banque française* (Paris: Hachette Lit-

térature, 1973), p. 238, calls Paris the international clearing house in 1820-1840, citing Maurice Lévy-Leboyer, *Les banques européennes et l'industrialisation internationale dans la première moitié du XIXᵉ siècle* (Paris: Presses universitaires de France, 1964), pp. 437-44. Most writers date the challenge as occurring in the 1850s, see for example Hans Rosenberg, *Die Weltwirtschaftskrisis von 1857-1859* (Stuttgart and Berlin: W. Kohlhammer, 1934), p. 38. Oskar Morgenstern, *International Financial Transactions and Business Cycles* (Princeton: Princeton University Press, for the National Bureau of Economic Research, 1959), p. 128, states that Paris emerges as the *strongest* (his italics) financial centre in the world before 1914 if the fact that its short-term interest rate is the lowest is an indication of strength. Franco Bonelli simply asserts that Paris was the real centre for regulating world liquidity at the beginning of the second half of 1907, but this may reflect a particular Italian view since Italian finances were tied to Paris; see *La crisi del 1907: una tappa dello sviluppo industriale in Italia* (Turin: Fondazione Luigi Einaudi, 1971), p. 42.

17. See Walter Bagehot, 'Lombard Street', in *The Collected Works of Walter Bagehot*, Vol. IX, ed. by Norman St John-Stevas (London: The Economist, 1978), p. 63.

18. See Marcia Stigum, *The Money Market: Myth, Reality and Practice* (Homewood, Ill.: Dow-Jones-Irwin, 1978), Ch. VI, esp. pp. 108-10 and 427.

19. See Charles A. Coombs, *The Arena of International Finance* (New York: John Wiley, 1976), pp. 96-98.

20. *The Collected Works of Walter Bagehot, op. cit.*, Vol. IX: pp. 197, 377, 428, 444, 451 and 453; Vol. XI: pp. 109, 135 and 139. The principle of the lender of last resort was asserted at the beginning of the nineteenth century by Henry Thornton in *An Enquiry into the Nature and Effect of Paper Credit of Great Britain* (1802), ed. with an introduction by Friedrich A. von Hayek (London: Frank Cass, 1962), pp. 187-88.

21. Kindleberger, *The World in Depression, op. cit.*

22. For details of these operations and sources, see Kindleberger, *Manias, Panics and Crashes* (New York: Basic Books, 1978), Ch. X, 'The International Lender of Last Resort'.

23. See Lévy-Leboyer, 'La balance des paiements et l'exportation des capitaux français', in Lévy-Leboyer (ed.), *La position internationale de la France, Aspects économiques et financiers, XIXᵉ-XXᵉ siècles* (Paris: Ed. de l'Ecole des Hautes Etudes en Sciences Sociales, 1977), p. 129.

24. *Ibid.*, p. 251.

25. Frank C. Spooner, *The International Economy and Monetary Movements in France, 1493-1725* (Cambridge, Mass.: Harvard University Press, 1972), pp. 5, 125.

26. See Braudel, *Afterthoughts on Material Civilization and Capitalism, op. cit.*, p. 87; and José-Gentil da Silva, *Banque et credit en Italie au XVIIᵉ siècle* (Paris: Ed. Klincksieck, 1969), pp. 38-40.

27. Braudel, *ibid.*, p. 25.

28. Violet Barbour, *Capitalism in Amsterdam in the Seventeenth Century* (Ann Arbor: University of Michigan Press, 1966), p. 50.

29. Jonathan R. T. Hughes, *Fluctuations in Trade, Industry and Finance: a Study of British Economic Development, 1850-1860* (Oxford: Clarendon

Press, 1960), pp. 243 *et seq.* and esp. p. 247. Michel Chevalier, *On the Probable Fall in the Value of Gold*, transl. by Richard Cobden, 3rd ed. (Manchester: Alexander Ireland, 1859) calls the exchange of gold for silver in France a 'parachute' that retarded the fall in the price of gold.

30.   See Milton Gilbert's posthumous study, *Quest for World Monetary Order, The Gold-Dollar System and its Aftermath*, a Twentieth Century Fund Study (New York: John Wiley & Sons, 1980).

31.   René Girault, 'Investissements et placements français en Russie, 1890-1914', in Lévy-Leboyer (ed.), *op. cit.*, p. 251.

32.   Sir John Clapham, *The Bank of England: a History* (Cambridge: Cambridge University Press, 1958), Vol. II, pp. 170, 291-94, 329-30 and 344; and Jacob Viner, *Studies in the Theory of International Trade* (New York: Harpers, 1937), p. 273.

33.   See 'Bonn's World Role: Recession is Limiting Leverage', *New York Times*, 7 November 1980, p. 2.

5 Gold and the Uneasy Case for Responsibly Managed Fiat Money

William Fellner

In a world in which policy makers who are short-run oriented persist in creating inflationary pressures at rates that cannot be predicted without large margins of error, floating provides the only acceptable exchange-rate arrangement. Lack of predictability is an essential property of such an inflationary setting, because even the limited, short-run stimulus derived from inflation would be unattainable if the inflation rate were correctly foreseen. Thus, to maintain the stimulus, inflation must be accommodated for a while at an accelerating rate, but full accommodation must occasionally be interrupted to prevent the process from getting out of hand at a very early stage. The resulting environment is one of heightened uncertainty and of lowered efficiency.

Floating rates are much better suited to the requirements of such an undesirable environment than any other exchange-rate system. One of their several advantages is that they permit some countries to resist the inflationary policy pressures to a greater extent than that to which others are capable of resisting it. Furthermore, in such an inflationary world, attempts to adjust 'fixed' rates properly by occasional administrative decisions would miscarry. The attempt to avoid floating by that method would be apt to result in the rationing of currencies and even in the occasional closing of exchange markets. This is because of the insufficient flexibility of administratively adjusted rates when excess demand develops.

Whereas this essay takes the advantages of floating in an environment of this sort for granted, it is not concerned with the requirements of such an undesirable international setting. Instead it is concerned with a specific problem relevant to the overdue effort to put an end to these difficulties by restoring non-inflationary conditions. With that objective in mind, the essay argues for the validity of the following three propositions.

(1) In a future near enough to serve as a basis for present policy

planning, re-establishing the gold standard (to be defined for our purpose specifically later in this essay) can play no useful role in restoring a policy package that performed a significant function in an earlier era. This package included in the past, in addition to the gold standard, policies that can safely be called non-inflationary as compared with recent Western practices.

(2) The unavailability at present of the gold standard as an element of such a package will make the return to an essentially non-inflationary course considerably more difficult, although it is crucially important that we should make a determined effort to achieve the objective in spite of the greater difficulty.

(3) The reasons why the techniques for defining the gold standard can at present not be used constructively by any group of countries are not necessarily 'here to stay'. I therefore consider it important to keep open the debate not only over the past performance of the gold standard but also over the possible future role of gold in the monetary system.

I will refer to the foregoing three paragraphs as my three 'numbered propositions'. Jointly, these propositions are highly controversial. Those agreeing with the first proposition make up a large majority of my professional colleagues, but they are likely to disagree sharply with the third and, in many cases, even with the second proposition.[1] Those agreeing with the second and the third propositions are likely to disagree with the first. I will argue for the joint validity of all three propositions.

Attributing significance to the second and the third propositions, in spite of the validity of the first, derives its justification from the substantial element of truth involved in the assertion that fiat money has been misused throughout history, which has always led to the corruption of the currency. Further, it is no distortion of the truth to add that when conditions under inconvertible currencies deteriorated far enough, countries usually coupled a return to healthier monetary conditions with a return to the convertibility of paper money. The reason why the concept of convertibility into gold enters here in connection with the avoidance of monetary irresponsibility is that in modern economic history the essential method of debasing the currency has ceased to be the reduction of the metallic content of coins; instead, it has become the excessive creation of means of payment in the form of bank notes and particularly of bank deposits. These are created in terms of currency units for which under some systems it *is* and under others it is *not* possible to acquire an officially determined quantity of gold. If we had earlier phases of modern economic history in mind, we should presumably say 'gold or silver', but for well over a century now this has amounted to gold.

The fact that, as an element of a package involving essentially non-inflationary demand management, gold convertibility did play an important role in the past and that during that time it added considerably to the credibility of such a policy package, has to do primarily with the *simplicity and easy ascertainability of the behavioural rule prescribing constancy of the nominal price of gold*. That rule cannot be disregarded (or even bent) more or less unnoticed, when short-run considerations would make it convenient to do so. Abandoning the rule is a major and 'dramatic' political decision. This is an essential property of such a system. Yet it is equally important to remember that observing that rule is not a reasonable objective for its own sake. It is a reasonable objective or is not depending on whether its observance does or does not serve other directly desirable objectives. This is the case in some circumstances, but not in others, as will be argued in these pages.

As these introductory remarks may suggest to the reader, I propose to take an unemotional look at some of the main issues involved in a problem that has given rise to highly emotional controversies. Sometimes I have the feeling that the debate about gold has moved increasingly into a name-calling stage: 'gold bugs' are facing 'debauchers of currencies'. From that stage the debate should progress into one of rational economic-theoretical analysis with reliance on the available data.[2]

I will end this introductory section with a word about the concepts of rationality and irrationality. One may be inclined towards the position that, even if it were possible to return to the gold standard in the predictable future, or even if it were possible to do so in the more distant future, such possibilities do not deserve detailed analysis, because tying monetary management to gold is an irrational arrangement in any event, even if such a system turns out to work satisfactorily most of the time. I have no quarrel with the 'irrationality' thesis *per se* which is involved in that position, but I find it difficult not to be greatly impressed by the very large damage done to the economies of the industrialised world, and indirectly to other countries as well, by the 'irrationality' of the monetary management that has *followed* the era of convertibility. In this newer era, it has so far proved impossible to overcome the consequences of highly inflationary techniques focussed on a short run that tends

to become increasingly short and that creates the need for uncomfortable adjustments which become increasingly uncomfortable
as the political process postpones them further and further. This is
the irrationality of the new era and it has placed the Western
economies in acute danger.

Yet, as concerns the options we are facing at present, I feel
convinced of the validity of the first of my numbered propositions
as well as that of the other two and will provide here a somewhat
detailed justification for all three. Largely because of space limitations, I will not discuss projects that purport to get around the
difficulties to be considered here by establishing a more generally
based commodity-reserve currency. Moreover, I would find it
difficult to add anything of interest to Herbert Giersch's detailed
and predominantly negative appraisal of these projects,[3] although
some recent contributors take the position that systems belonging
in this category should also be kept in mind as carrying potential
promise for the future.[4]

DEFINING THE GOLD STANDARD FOR THE
PRESENT PURPOSE

The gold standard is a somewhat ambiguous concept, the precise
definition of which is often made dependent on the specific list of
gold-related obligations which the monetary authorities accept
under a system. I consider this an unnecessary difficulty and will
circumvent it by regarding a system adopted by a country (or by a
group of countries) as a system belonging in the gold-standard
category if the following condition is satisfied: the purchase and sale
of gold at a fixed price by the monetary authority of any participating country keeps the price of gold continuously constant at that
level not only in the transactions to which the authorities themselves
are committed but also in market transactions in general in which
the public at large is free to participate.

Achieving this objective without interruption requires a stockpile
('reserve') of gold held by the monetary authorities not only for
sales to and purchases from the monetary authorities of other
countries, but also for sales to and purchases from private market
participants. The institutionally prescribed or otherwise generally
accepted rules of behaviour, however, must be such that very little
room should be left for influencing the free-market price of gold by
sustained reserve gains or losses of the authorities, except for the

influence exerted by gradual reserve accruals along the time paths of growing economies. As for the little room that can be left for *sustained* reserve movements beyond this, increases in reserves can be sterilised, within limits, over periods of considerable duration and this can perform the function of diminishing the supply available to private holders. From this it follows that in some circumstances it is possible to engage in the inverse operation involving reserve losses over periods of considerable duration as a means of increasing the supply to the private sector. But continuing such operations in one direction indefinitely is even physically impossible and, if the system is to function efficiently, reliance on them over periods of appreciable duration must be held within narrow limits. Such operations endanger the system particularly because the second of the two operations—reliance on major reserve losses for holding on to a price that would otherwise be changed by the market—removes the anti-inflationary discipline which the system is intended to create.

In other words, the general rule which the system enforces must be such that the gold-price support commitment, and the changes in reserves which the official support operations bring about, should induce the authorities to allow the overall demand for goods and services to rise and to fall along with the gold stock. The general rule requires making the official price acceptable to the market by an adjustment of the nominal demand for goods and services in such a way as to keep the real price (relative price) of gold corresponding to its official nominal price at the demand-supply equilibrating level in the market.

In the interpretation of the mechanism on which the proper functioning of such a system is based, the emphasis thus belongs on the influence of the overall demand for goods and services in determining whether a given nominal price of gold corresponds to the correct *real* price by market criteria. Reduction of the general price level through demand policies will raise a real price of gold that was initially too low by the criteria of the market, and even if a tightening of demand-management policies does not reduce the general price level, it reduces or eliminates any excess demand for gold at a real price that was initially too low (hence, will tend to make that real price reflect the changed market forces more accurately). For analogous reasons, general demand expansion will, by raising the price level, reduce the real price of gold corresponding to a given nominal price that was initially too high or will, even aside from this, diminish or eliminate the excess supply that develops at such a real price.

It is with the conditions faced by gold-standard countries in the aggregate (or globally) in mind that I stated the requirement that, given any official price of gold, central-bank policies must be such as to ensure that demand and supply in the gold market should tend to balance at the corresponding real price of gold. But the essential content of these propositions is not altered if the analysis is focussed on the country-to-country aspect of the problem, as this reflects itself in the balance of payments of individual countries.

The position of deficit countries can always be expressed by the statement that given the exchange rates, and given the international capital movements and the unilateral transfers, they have developed an excess demand for the goods of the surplus countries, that is, the latter have developed relative demand insufficiency for the goods of the deficit countries (excess supply to these countries). This dis-equilibrium tends to lead to a change in exchange rates which, however, the gold standard suppresses. The method by which the exchange-rate movements are suppressed involves substituting gold for part of the other exports of the deficit countries since the demand insufficiency of the surplus countries for the goods of the deficit countries cannot apply to gold, as long as the monetary authorities of all countries concerned are willing to buy and sell gold in un-limited quantities at constant prices. Hence, while at the given exchange rates the deficit countries' goods *other than gold* are over-priced from the point of view of the surplus countries, the gold of the deficit countries does not exhibit the behaviour of an overpriced commodity but shows the behaviour of a commodity *in relation to which* the other goods of these countries are overpriced. At the official nominal price the real price of gold is too low in the deficit countries and too high in the surplus countries. If the system is to function properly, however, the resulting gold movements will lead to the adjustment of the demand for goods and services in general in such a way as to eliminate the deficit countries' excess demand for the goods (other than gold) of the surplus countries, and thus to eliminate the surplus countries' demand insufficiency for the goods (other than gold) of the deficit countries. The overpricing and underpricing relative to gold will then also disappear. The real price of gold will be set right again by the criteria of the market and, given the nominal price of gold, its real price and the general price level are two sides of the same coin.

The gold-exchange standard, by contrast with what sometimes is considered the gold standard proper, is described by the practice of some participating countries of substituting for monetary gold reserves, in part at least, claims on the monetary authorities of other countries that are maintaining gold reserves for keeping the price of gold constant in terms of their own currency. Yet this raises no question of principle beyond that already pointed out, namely, whether there is a sufficient stockpile of gold behind the system as a whole to maintain the price of gold continuously fixed at the officially announced level, without permitting a discrepancy to develop between this price and the gold price tending to develop in the free market.[5]

As concerns the official dollar price and the private-market price of gold, the Bretton Woods system kept the United States close to the requirements of the gold standard in the sense explained above, even if two qualifications will subsequently have to be added to this interpretation. In the entire post-World War II period up to the collapse of the Bretton Woods system in 1971, the official price of gold remained at $35 an ounce and deviations of the free market price from this level did remain small in all years except 1968. Whereas the United States was obligated to buying and selling gold at this price only in its relations with foreign official agencies, and while the official agencies of the other countries were settling with each other mostly in dollars, the participating countries achieved near equality of the free market price with the official dollar price of gold by transactions in the world market whenever that was needed.

Yet if for this reason we interpret the United States as having been 'essentially on gold' not only up to World War II but through the Bretton Woods era, two qualifications need to be added. One of these is that in the late part of that era quite a bit of pressure was placed on foreign dollar-holding agencies not to convert their dollar reserves into gold and thus not to speed the depletion of the American gold stock. This was an antecedent of the collapse of the system with a gold price that had been kept constant since 1934 and with a price level that had, from that year, already more than doubled by the early part of the 1960s. The other qualification is that from 1933 to the mid-1970s the ownership of unfabricated gold by American citizens was made illegal. Yet it is in the nature of such regulations that it is not very difficult to get around them even without violating the provisions of the law. Hence, by the criteria

I am applying here, the United States was 'essentially on gold' throughout the Bretton Woods gold-exchange-standard era, with some qualifications, the essential one of which relates to symptoms of an impending collapse at a time when gold was becoming increasingly under-valued relative to other goods and services. The under-valuation became particularly pronounced in the years following 1965 when the American inflation rate started steepening.

For most other countries the question arises with what frequency the fixed price of gold can be adjusted to a different level without the country being 'off gold'. In the United States the price of gold was adjusted only once in about nine decades beginning in 1879— and this happened in the 1930s. From 1879, when after the Civil War the country returned to gold, until March 1933, the official price was $20.67 an ounce; then, after about eleven months of inconvertibility of the dollar, the country was again on gold at $35 an ounce. I will deal with this by regarding the American system as one belonging in the gold-standard category up to *1933*, and then again as one belonging in that category from *1934* on, with a discontinuity developing at the time of the 1933-34 revaluation. I favour the analogous terminological practice, postulating a discontinuity, also for countries which (unlike the United States in 1933-34) moved from one specific gold parity to a different parity without an intervening period of inconvertibility, and I also favour the same terminological practice for countries which changed the official price of gold in terms of their currencies more frequently than the United States—changed it during, as well as before, the Bretton Woods era.

Leaving semantics aside, it needs to be stressed that adjustments of the official gold price express that 'something has gone wrong' with the system. While adjustments, on very rare occasions, may simply suggest that no system can be expected to work perfectly, frequent adjustments by administrative decisions are a sign of malfunctioning.

THE REAL PRICE OF GOLD

I suggest that the usefulness of coupling a return to monetary stability with a return to gold depends on whether the *real price* (relative price) of gold would tend to remain reasonably stable in the market—at least in the sense of changing only very gradually in a more or less predictable fashion. In this case the general price level would tend to remain reasonably stable, or, at least, its slow and gradual movements would bring few surprises, so that the simple device of fixing the nominal price of gold would at the same time achieve what is usually meant by reasonable price stability. Alternatively expressed, in terms of central-bank operations: with the *real* market price of gold tending to remain reasonably stable, or tending to show only a mild and roughly foreseeable trend, the degree of tightness or ease of monetary policy which is required for observing a simple and well-defined rule—that of keeping the nominal price of gold constant with reliance on a stockpile of 'reserves'—*would be the same degree of monetary tightness or ease that would ensure reasonable general price stability*. On the other hand, with an underlying tendency of the real market price of gold to change at a significant rate, the gold standard would malfunction by becoming associated with significant changes in the price level, and these changes would be very likely to be sufficiently unpredictable to generate substantial uncertainty and inefficiency.

In the preceding pages it was explained that by the appropriate central-bank policies the authorities are able to avoid discrepancies between the official gold price and the price reflecting the market forces. Sustained discrepancies of this kind would make the official price untenable. At this point it needs to be added that the expansionary or contractionary moves required for attaining these objectives are apt to become large, and the important requirement of a reasonably stable price level is apt to be violated in a major way, if the gold output shows little responsiveness to the demand for gold. It may be taken for granted that by market criteria the 'correct' real market price of a *fixed supply* of gold would change significantly along the time path of growing economies and that predictions of the rate of change would be surrounded by substantial uncertainty. Hence, with the output irresponsive to demand and with the nominal price of gold held constant, large pressures would be generated on the price level in an environment of high risk.

This proposition places the emphasis on market forces and on the supply as well as the demand which they generate rather than on decisions of the monetary authorities to absorb more or less of the gold output and of the gold stock. One's inclination, to place the emphasis in the analysis of trends on the public's basic preference functions rather than the rate of change of monetary reserves along the time path of growing economies, is supported by economic history. We shall soon see that in the United States the real price of gold had a moderate downward trend over a period of roughly

ninety years, and that was a period during which the monetary
authorities were absorbing a high proportion of the gold output—
a proportion which was, at times, rising. More recently, the real
price of gold has been rising steeply, although the authorities have
been decreasing their gold holdings. In the interpretation of these
trends the emphasis belongs on private market behaviour.

In a matter of such complexity, however, few generalisations hold
without a qualifying comment. As for the emphasis on the demand-
supply relations in the private sector, rather than on the demand
originating from the monetary authorities, it must be taken into
account that the reduction of the real market price of gold in the
era of substantially *rising* official holdings would have been smaller,
or would have been turned into a rising real price, if various
innovations in the management of gold-standard type systems as
well as in the private financial markets had not gradually increased
the amount of money compatible with any given official gold stock.
The importance of these innovations must not be overlooked; but
recognising their importance does not contradict the statement
that in the era of significantly rising official stocks the market forces
generated a mild downward trend in the real price of gold and that
in a subsequent period of declining official stocks the market forces
generated a steeply rising real price. This directs attention primarily
to the market forces, and to the large role which the private demand
for gold and the responsiveness of the output to the total demand
have played in shaping these forces.

As concerns the general price trend, the American record of the
post-1879 gold-standard period up to 1965 was certainly far more
satisfactory than the subsequent record has been. For the period
1879-1965 as a whole, during which there occurred one instance of
gold revaluation, there was a 1.4 per cent average yearly compound
rate of increase in the Consumer Price Index (CPI)—see Table 5.1.
This 86-year period does, to be sure, include sub-periods for which
the behaviour of the American price level cannot be properly
described as expressing reasonable stability and for which the
behaviour of the real price of gold can also not be so described. But
most of this instability of behaviour during various sub-periods can
be explained by wars and the events following them. The inflation
of World War I was followed by a downward-moving price level
with deflation becoming sharp and highly damaging during the
Great Depression. Nevertheless, only partially did the cumulated
deflation of the post-World War I sub-period offset the general price

increases of the war years (that is, the earlier decrease of the real price of gold), and yet gold was not revalued until 1934. The

TABLE 5.1
The Real Price of Gold
(Average yearly rates of change, 1879–1965)

	Official dollar price of gold per troy ounce	Average yearly rate of increase of CPI (%)	Average yearly rate of change of real price of gold (%)
1879–1965[a]	Revalued in 1934 by 69.3%, from 20.67 to 35.00	1.4	−0.8
1879–1933	20.67	0.6	−0.6
1879–1929	20.67	1.2	−1.2
1879–1896*[b]	20.67	−0.7	0.7
1896–1913*	20.67	1.0	−1.0
1913–1929	20.67	3.4 } jointly	−3.4 } jointly
1929–1933*	20.67	−7.0 } +1.3	7.0 } —1.3
1929–1965	Revalued in 1934 by 69.3%, from 20.67 to 35.00	1.7	−0.2
1934–1965[c]	35.00	2.8	−2.8
1934–1951	35.00	3.9	−3.9
1951–1965*	35.00	1.4	−1.4

Source: United States Department of Commerce and Bureau of the Census, *Historical Statistics of the United States* (Washington: US Government Printing Office, 1975). CPI data based on series E 135, pp. 210–11. Explanation of methods used for the computation of these and of wholesale price data to be referred to is found in *ibid.*, pp. 183 *et seq.* All yearly rates of change are continuously compounded.
[a]For the entire period 1879–1965 the cumulated decline in the real price of gold amounted to about 50 per cent of its initial value.
[b]The four periods marked with an asterisk (*) are the only ones uninfluenced by major wars.
[c]Roughly the second half of the period 1934–1965 falls in the Bretton Woods era in which the United States was committed to converting on demand into gold at the official price any dollar balances presented by the other central banks. The currencies of many other countries were devalued and some were revalued upward relative to the dollar during that period. While the central banks of the other countries were accumulating large dollar balances, several were converting part of their reserves into gold. From 1949 to 1965 the United States official gold stock declined from about 700 million to about 400 million ounces. In the remaining five years of the Bretton Woods era, when inflation started accelerating in the United States, there was a further rapid decline. The aggregate official gold stock in the system rose mildly up to 1965, and declined somewhat subsequently. Prior to 1971, the free-market price of gold differed significantly from the official price only in 1968 (though by the late part of 1970 there was again a non-negligible 6 per cent difference).

inflation of World War II and that of the Korean War were never offset by any subsequent decreases of general price level—indeed, they were followed by a renewed flare-up of the American inflation after 1965—and yet gold was not revalued during the quarter-century following the war. Thereafter the system collapsed.

Furthermore, the difficulties caused by wars for American monetary management are given insufficient weight by any such account which limits itself to the United States. After World War I, it took most major European countries several years to return to gold, and they did so after going through a period of severe inflationary disorder. When stabilisation did occur abroad, the gold parity of most currencies corresponded to a lower real price of gold than had been the case prior to World War I—but to a different extent in different countries and, thus, typically to a different extent than in the United States. In the 1930s many countries abroad went off gold again and, with the likelihood of imminent war greatly increasing, capital movements into the United States assumed a very large size.

I have not carried the table beyond 1965 because the span from that year to 1971 was the immediate antecedent of the collapse of Bretton Woods, with the average yearly rate of price increase in the United States already starting to accelerate noticeably and the real price of gold thus declining in those final years of the system at an average yearly rate of more than 4 per cent. The collapse of Bretton Woods was followed by a brief period in which unsuccessful attempts were made to stabilise exchange rates at various administratively adjusted levels and early in 1973 this period was followed by generalised managed floating.

The entire period, as here decomposed, includes only four spans (marked in the table with an asterisk) that are not affected by major wars. Two of these particular spans (1896-1913 and 1951-65) show a decline of the real price of gold at a moderate yearly rate while the other two (1879-96 and 1929-33) show a rise of the real price. The first of the latter two (1879-96) shows a rise of the real price at a very moderate rate; the second of these two (the four-year span 1929-33) brought a steep yearly rise of the real price. But this brief span, ending in 1933, coincides with the Great Depression, and the rise in the real price (reduction of the price level) during these four years of substantial hardship was insufficient to prevent gold's real-price trend from being negative for longer periods, ending in

1933. For instance, the real price of gold was lower (the price level higher) in 1933 than either in 1879 or in 1913. After 1933 the price of gold was revalued upwards belatedly, by a substantial margin. Even with allowance for this revaluation we obtain a moderate yearly downward trend of gold's real price for the entire period covered in the table. But, as was suggested above, this real-price trend was greatly influenced by wartime inflations, followed in one case (after World War I) by partially offsetting and thereafter by belated gold revaluation, and followed on the next occasion (after World War II) by a further increase of the price level. During the period 1951-65, but not thereafter, this price increase remained mild.

The entire close-to-90-year period covered by the table shows a 0.8 per cent average yearly rate of decline of the real price of gold (see the first span listed). If, instead of using the CPI series referred to in the identification of sources under the table, I had used whole-sale price data based on Series E23 and E52 in *Historical Statistics* (pp. 199 and 201), almost the same rate of decline of the real price of gold would have been obtained for the entire period 1879-1965. The average yearly rate of decline would have come out at 0.9 per cent instead of the 0.8 per cent yearly decline shown in the table.

The *cumulated* decline of the real price of gold over the long period covered in the table is, of course, large—about 50 per cent. By the end of the Bretton Woods era (1971) the real price of gold had lost about 60 per cent of its 1879 level and this suggests one of the reasons for the insufficiency of the gold output to prevent a very steep price increase subsequently. But aside from interludes signifi-cantly affected by major wars, the long-run trend of the real price of gold was proceeding at a very moderate yearly rate.

There is no need to conclude that during the period covered by the table this record of the real price would have disappointed the expectations of the holders of gold. The record implies merely (i) that from the implicit rate of return which jewellery, art objects and the like provided to the owners through their use value, a *deduction* needs to be made to reflect the gradual downtrend in the real price, and (ii) that the price which hoarders of gold in the usual sense were paying for better protection of part of their assets from various risks in specific emergencies tended to include a real capital loss (as compared with full maintenance of their real wealth but, of course, not as compared with all available specific alternatives). This relates to the period ending in the late 1960s.

The record of the real price of gold becomes very different for the recent decade. From 1969, when the free-market price was still in the close neighbourhood of $35 an ounce, to December 1980, the real price of gold rose *six- to seven-fold*, which corresponds to an average yearly rate of increase of 15 per cent or more. The rise was exceedingly steep in several years of the 1970s, with occasional interruptions by phases of sharp but temporary decline. In the brief interval from the end of 1978, when the nominal price was about $220 per ounce, until December 1980 when it was in the $550 to $600 range (after having hit the $800 to $900 range in January 1980), the real price rose about 2.5-fold, that is, at an annual rate of 45 per cent.

To put it differently, if at present the real price of gold were the same as it was in 1879, then its nominal price would be about $200 an ounce; if its present real price were the same as in 1929, then its nominal price would be not more than $100; and if its present real price were the same as in 1934, then its nominal price would be about $225. The nominal price would be in the neighbourhood of $70 an ounce if, from 1879 through to the end of 1980, the real price had declined at an average yearly rate of 1 per cent which, according to the table, used to be more or less the rate characteristic of longer spans not affected by major wars.

For long intervals ending in 1980 we obtain in reality an *increase* in the real price at the average yearly rate of about 1 per cent since 1879, about 3 per cent since 1929 and 2 per cent since 1934. The average yearly rise since 1879, or since the gold revaluation of 1934, corresponds to merely a mild upward trend in the long run, but the recent price increases have been sharp and the fluctuations of the price have been large. The belief, that the recent sharp price increases and the fluctuations are explained almost entirely by inflationary psychology, implies that it would be unreasonable to attribute a large part of these price increases and their effect on the long-run trend to changed market appraisals of basic demand-supply relations in the gold market. I will suggest that, in view of what so far appears to be irresponsiveness of the gold output to a steeply rising real price, much of the emphasis does belong on changed appraisals of these basic demand-supply relations which, even quite aside from inflationary psychology, are apt to produce instability of the real price of gold around a rising long-run trend. This change of appraisals is likely to have developed from the nature of the incentives to hold gold in the private sector of growing economies, on the one hand, and from the recent trend in the output of gold, on the other.

INCENTIVES TO HOLD GOLD

I will distinguish two incentives which motivate private owners to hold gold in one form or another, adding subsequently a comment on why a third incentive is not explicitly listed, and a further comment on the relation of the two listed incentives to each other. In this discussion gold money in circulation can by now be disregarded.

First Incentive (use-value incentive): attractiveness of the implicit rate of return developing to the owners through a flow of *use value* from highly durable objects containing gold. This is illustrated by jewellery and art objects.

Second Incentive (asset-composition or 'portfolio-mix' incentive): attractiveness of including gold in the owner's portfolio of assets in view of a prospective change of the real value of gold or of gold-containing objects. This may provide a positive incentive over a considerable range of possible expected rates of real capital gain, often including even negative gains (losses). Even an asset with an expected moderate real capital loss may have a legitimate place in a portfolio if other assets expected to yield a positive real return carry a larger risk of major loss—either a larger market risk *or* a larger political risk.[6] But, other things being equal, the Second Incentive will be more powerful the higher the expected rate of real capital gain is on gold.

Comment on why the industrial inventory-holding incentive is not added explicitly: somewhere between 10 and 15 per cent of the world's current gold output is conventionally classified as going to industry rather than as becoming incorporated into jewellery and art objects or as being hoarded. Much of this industrial absorption requires no discussion beyond recognition of the fact that the gold held in response to the First and Second Incentives must, of course, be mined and processed and that at the industrial level this obviously creates an inventory-holding incentive that is the corollary of our First and Second Incentives. Even the gold acquired by industries such as that manufacturing dental products (rather than jewellery and art objects) falls into this category, since it is ultimately incorporated into objects which yield the owner (patient) use value in the form of an implicit return from highly durable goods, and which the owner therefore holds in response to the First Incentive. But, if the matter is interpreted in this fashion, then the 10 to 15 per cent of the world's gold output going to industries should be said to contain a component that does not fit a categorisation limiting itself to the First and the Second Incentives. This component consists of the gold acquisition of industries incorporating gold into equipment used in the production of final goods containing no gold. The electronics industries illustrate this. The incentive leading to these particular gold purchases by industry is not simply a corollary of the First Incentive, because here no implicit returns from gold-containing durable consumer goods are involved in the process—computers are not typically owned by consumers. But from the viewpoint of the analysis that follows in this essay the small proportion of the gold output and of the gold stock that does not 'fit' in this sense has the same effect as do the gold holdings acquired in response to the incentives which were listed in the preceding paragraphs. I will limit myself to those incentives.

Relation of the First to the Second Incentive: the First Incentive is almost always either strengthened by the Second Incentive or is weakened by it (the latter if the Second Incentive is negative, suggesting disinvestment). In other words, the buyers of jewellery and art objects containing gold are aware of the durability and marketability of these objects which they do consider part of their 'wealth'. On the other hand, the Second Incentive may be effective without this having any bearing whatever on the First Incentive. For instance, gold bars in a safe create no flow of use value for the owner. Yet, not all 'hoards' are held exclusively in response to the Second Incentive, as is gold held in a safe. Gold coins of various sorts are usually included in the estimates of hoarded gold, and these are not held exclusively in response to the Second Incentive In part they are held in view of their aesthetic quality, and thus they also yield use value (implicit return to the owner) in a sense similar to that in which jewellery and art objects do.

REASONS FOR STRESSING OUTPUT
LIMITATIONS . . .

. . . In the Analysis of the Process Generated by the Two Incentives

In the decade of the 1970s the average yearly gold production of the world—*declining* gradually from about 47 million to 40 million ounces, including a crude allowance for the rising Russian component—seems to have been about 1.4 times as high as four decades earlier (in the 1930s). This corresponds to an annual rate of increase of only 0.8 per cent over the four decades. Going back another forty years, and comparing the decennial output of the 1930s with that of the 1890s, we observe a 3.1-fold increase (instead of the more recent roughly 1.4-fold rise) which corresponded to an average yearly rate of 2.8 per cent (instead of the recent 0.8 per cent).

While we thus see that for the past four decades the world output has not risen at any substantial rate, the data to be surveyed indicate that the private gold holdings, now estimated at 1,650 million ounces, have been rising significantly. Of the 1,650 million ounces, about 1,100 million ounces are supposed to be in jewellery, art objects and industrial inventories, with the remainder in 'hoards'. The privately-owned gold stock could rise significantly in a period in which output rose little and, indeed, has recently *declined* because while in earlier times the monetary system of the world often absorbed more than one-half of the current gold output, the gold held by the monetary authorities has recently been declining. The monetary component of the stock has declined from about two-thirds of the world's total gold stock in 1959 to little more than 40 per cent by the end of the 1970s—and since 1965 the monetary component has declined even absolutely.[7]

Over the past fifty years private gold holdings have risen at an average rate of 2.5 per cent. The present yearly world output of 40 million ounces is barely sufficient for accommodating a continued 2.5 per cent increase in the privately-owned stock. The present Western output (that of the non-Communist countries), which amounts to about 30 million ounces, is sufficient for accommodating only a 1.8 per cent yearly increase and Russian sales to the West, which, along with sales of official agencies have been making up the difference between private accumulation and the recent Western output, have varied greatly from year to year. Given the rate of increase of the world population and, we hope, its standard of living, the growth rate of the private stock which the Western output— or even the world output—can accommodate is modest, particularly in an era in which substantial international uncertainties would presumably not disappear even if inflation were eliminated. But this leaves open the question to what extent the price at which the past accumulation took place has been raised by inflationary psychology and to what extent by a reappraisal of future demand-supply relations in view of the irresponsiveness of output to demand.

If the price has been raised mainly by inflationary psychology— essentially by the expectation that the price of gold will keep up with inflation in an environment in which real returns on many other available assets tend to become negative—then the restoration of a henceforth non-inflationary trend would lower the price of gold significantly. Even in that case, though, the growing demand for gold which is developing in growing economies would thereafter raise the real price of gold at hard-to-predict and probably variable rates *provided* the output remained irresponsive (or insufficiently responsive) to the growing demand. An output sufficient for, say, a 2 per cent annual growth rate of the stock would have to rise at an annual rate of 2 per cent to remain sufficient for that growth rate of the stock. Another way of expressing this is to say that if in such circumstances an attempt were made to return to the gold standard along with restoring a non-inflationary general price trend, then feeling out the proper nominal price of gold would lead to setting the price at the outset much lower than any recent market price, but keeping the nominal price constant would from there on produce a downward-tilted general price trend at hard-to-predict and probably variable rates.

In the next section it will be seen that even to the extent that the recent rise in the gold price has resulted from the reappraisal of normal demand-supply relations in the gold market in view of the irresponsiveness of output—that is, disregarding any additional role of inflationary psychology—the resulting price movement would in all probability still not be monotonically upward. The general outline of the price developments would in all probability be similar and the essential conclusion would still be that after a phase of price fluctuations the relative fixity of the output in growing economies would dominate the trend. This would in any event be an upward trend in the real price of gold which, under the gold standard, would show in a downward trend of the price level.

Hence, if we take it for granted that transitional difficulties associated with price readjustments after initial impacts are inevitable, output limitations make up the core of the story. Quite aside from what could reasonably be called inflationary psychology, the basic facts suggest that the market participants have reason to anticipate the advent of a long-run upward trend in the real price of gold *provided* the prospect of significantly delayed major output-raising effects of the increased real price of gold is considered too uncertain to be weighted heavily. In this case they have reason to anticipate also that this trend will not reassert itself monotonically and, depending on their attitude to risk (variance about expected values), they will react to this differently.

It is possible to take the position that the consequences of tightness could be postponed over an extended period because, at any gold price approximating those recently prevailing and at any price that might initially seem 'just right' by market criteria, the monetary authorities could afford to lose gold to private owners over an extended period and thereby they could make up for any output deficiency. The authorities could indeed afford to do this, and if they wanted to depress the market price of gold they could obviously do so by selling part or all of the 1,100 to 1,200 million ounces of gold they now possess. Thereby they could depress the market price significantly for a long time. But, as has already been suggested, doing this outside the framework of the gold standard is very different from trying to operate a system, belonging in the gold-standard category, by sustained losses of monetary gold reserves. Trying to rely on sustained reductions of the monetary gold stock for making a restored gold standard immune to the tightness developing from an inflexible gold output would be basically inconsistent with the proper functioning of any variety of that system. This is so not only because the functioning of the system would be based on a temporary makeshift, but also because, during the entire intervening period of gold-reserve losses, the extent to which the authorities engage in inflationary operations would depend on *ad hoc* political decisions, *as is the case with fiat money.*

As long as the system would be made to work by the makeshift of gold-reserve losses, the avoidance of inflation would have nothing to do with constraints imposed on the authorities by gold convertibility. The authorities could go on losing gold reserves during an intervening period so conceived by policies leading to a rise in the general price level; and by thus reducing the real price of gold, rather than by merely keeping the real price unchanged in the face of a demand that would be rising even at the unchanging real price. They could generate inflation without any dramatic and promptly observable departure from the behavioural rule making them responsible for the nominal price of gold. Reliance on the makeshift of gold-reserve losses over an extended period would destroy the discipline of the gold-standard mechanism up to the time when, following that period, the system would start relying on the responsiveness of the gold *output* to demand—or, in the absence of such responsiveness, would become faced with upward pressures on the real price of gold.

BARE BONES OF THE PROCESS . . .
. . . Gold-stock Adjustment, Flow Effects and Price Movements aside from Inflationary Psychology and from Gold Sales by the Authorities

Let us now briefly follow through the consequences of a newly developing expectation that the gold-output trend will be insufficient, by a substantial margin, to match the rising trend in the demand for gold at a real price that initially reflects the market forces. This problem will first be considered without regard to the question of inflationary psychology and the monetary authorities' modes of behaviour—questions to which I shall return subsequently. The final section of the essay will stress the possibility of delayed output responsiveness, such as could influence the outlook for the role of gold significantly.

With the output flow showing little or no flexibility, the price-raising effect of the rising demand for gold, as determined by population growth and the rise in living standards, would become automatically supplemented by another price-raising effect which is apt to cause major upward and downward movements around a rising trend. This additional effect would be generated by gold purchases motivated by expected capital gains. In this context I refer back to the foregoing discussion of incentives for the private acquisition of gold. Once we assume that, given the supply of gold, the First Incentive (use-value incentive) suggests a substantial change in the trend of the real price, the Second Incentive (portfolio-mix incentive) will reinforce the real-price effect. The price of gold would have to rise to the level at which the acquisition of the use-value of objects containing gold becomes expensive enough to reduce purchases motivated by the First Incentive; and this to the extent needed for making room for purchases motivated by the strengthened Second Incentive (portfolio-mix incentive).

If the markets were heedless of the mechanics of the successive price developments so described, there would first take place a steep increase in the price to suppress a substantial amount of purchase motivated by the use-value incentive, thereby enabling the asset rearrangement towards gold to take place in response to the portfolio-mix incentive. After the completion of the stock adjustment the price would decline steeply to make room again for satisfying the use-value incentive; yet, subsequently, the price would rise as population growth and rising living standards raise the amount of gold demanded in response to the use-value incentive.[8] The more predictable the details of this time sequence become, however, the more will the sequence become modified by anticipatory market behaviour which, in the limiting case of full predictability, would lead to a monotonic rise in the real price from the outset. Market participants would obviously not shift to gold in view of a long-run rise in its real price, if they knew the near future would bring a passing phase of a declining real price. With full predictability of the course of events, the monotonicity of the rise in the real price would result from slower portfolio rearrangement in the early phases and from subsequent substitution of a rising use-value-motivated demand for the portfolio-mix-motivated demand as the portfolio rearrangement is gradually completed.

Full predictability represents, of course, an unrealistic limiting case. On realistic assumptions concerning foresight, the initially described time sequence of price movements—a very sharp *up and down* followed by a *gradual rise*—may be smoothed out to a considerable extent as compared with the account given above, but the instability will not be removed. And quite aside from the initial up and down and the extent to which it may become smoothed by foresight, it would be Utopian to attribute to experts, or markets in general, the ability to predict with much accuracy the rate of the subsequent gradual rise in the price—the rise resulting from an inflexible or insufficiently flexible gold output as against a gradually rising demand motivated by the use value of gold-containing objects and, to some extent, by the amount of hoarding that would take place even aside from inflationary psychology.

This alone suggests the emergence of an environment in which the present outlook is unpromising for associating a return to non-inflationary demand management with a return to a fixed nominal price for gold. The data surveyed here suggest that fixity of the nominal price of gold would run a serious risk of having as its corollary not a reasonable degree of price stability, but first major swings while the 'present' appropriate price is felt out and *thereafter* general price deflation at variable and unpredictable rates. It is inevitable that such general deflationary price trends should become associated with a fixed nominal price for gold, whenever the real price of gold has a basic tendency to rise at rates which it would be very difficult to predict for successive intervals.

So far no attention has been paid to several further complicating factors. The effect of inflationary psychology is clearly one of these but, as will be argued in the next section, it is not the only complicating factor. On the other hand, in the final section it will be stressed that it would be a mistake to overlook an essential qualification to which the negative attitude concerning the future of gold is subject.

ADDITIONAL COMPLICATING FACTORS

While I do not believe that it is *logically* necessary to bring inflationary psychology into the picture to explain the recent instability in the gold market, it is safe to conclude that inflationary psychology has in fact played an additional role. Financial assets that in a non-inflationary world carry predictably positive (or at least non-negative) real rates of interest, have in our recent environment often yielded negative real rates and this must have tilted the desirable portfolio mix towards a number of physical assets including gold. This supplementary gold-price raising factor, the weight of which cannot be appraised at present, must have accentuated not only the recent steep rise in the price of gold but also the instability of the price. Still, this factor is not at the root of the difficulties standing in the way of returning to any variety of the gold standard in circumstances such as the present. If the basic demand-supply forces in the gold market were compatible with a policy package aiming jointly for the restoration of general price stability and for that of the gold standard, then the knowledge that such a policy package is about to be adopted would suppress the inflationary gold-price raising and destabilising factor which in the present circumstances does play an additional role. As I see it, the real difficulty develops because the basic demand-supply forces are not shaping up the way in which they were in the era of the efficient functioning of the policy of fixed nominal gold price, at which time these forces were compatible with an acceptable approximation to long-run general price stability under the gold standard. The basic forces are apt to produce an upward-tilted long-run trend in the real price of gold, but one that would not manifest itself in a monotonic rise in the real price—even if changing inflationary expectations and possible major gold sales of the authorities could be disregarded.

Beyond this, there are further complicating factors in the present circumstances. One of these is the instability of the portfolio-mix preferences, including gold-holding preferences, of foreign owners of very large funds some of whom are in a politically sensitive position and whose risk appraisals are apt to be highly variable. To the extent that these foreign owners are monetary authorities (in form or in essence), this essential complicating factor can alternatively be expressed by saying that even adequate responsiveness of output to demand would not satisfy the requirements of the proper functioning of the gold standard, as long as sudden large gold accumulations and sales by major gold-holding authorities are not excluded.

The other adverse factor not taken into account in the foregoing discussion is the additional demand for gold that would develop in the future if, along the growth paths of economies, the monetary authorities were gradually to acquire again part of the current gold output. Of this last-mentioned factor the discussion has not as yet taken account, since so far attention has been paid primarily to the possibility that the future era of gradually rising monetary gold stocks would be preceded by a period of gold-reserve losses on the part of initially 'overstocked' authorities. This possibility introduces another complicating factor discussed earlier in this essay, because during such an intervening period essentially the same kind of lee-way would be created for inflationary policies as is created by inconvertible paper money—but what needs to be added here is that, from some future point of time on, the monetary authorities of growing economies would have to absorb part of the gold output. Ultimately, the system would have to be kept going by significant responsiveness of the output to demand; that is, to the real price of gold.

INCONCLUSIVENESS OF THE NEGATIVE
ARGUMENT FOR THE LONG RUN . . .
. . . and the Need to Keep the Debate Open

The reader might wonder why he was asked to go through a piece of reasoning of some complexity for the purpose of doing justice to the case for a return to gold, if the analysis ends with a negative note about the outlook for such a policy shift in any future for which it would be possible to develop plans at the present time. The answer is that the unfavourable basic demand-supply conditions which were explained in my analysis and which were assumed to last into the predictable future *could* change, as supply conditions have on various past occasions changed and have made a significantly enlarged quantity of gold available without much advance notice. Discoveries of new ore deposits, and major technological improvements enabling producers to win gold profitably from poorer quality ores have, after all, played a very major role in modern monetary history, and these events have in large part been concentrated into periods during which the real price of gold had been rising in response to supply limitations. For the nine decades covered by the table the great discoveries of the late 1880s and 1890s illustrate this point. Even as of now about 70 per cent of the Western output comes from South Africa, the gold mines of which were discovered in the final ten to fifteen years of the last century, along with improved methods of obtaining gold from the ore found there. The South African discoveries of the late nineteenth century and the subsequent Alaskan, Canadian and other finds, came after a period of a significant tightening of the gold supply relative to the demand for gold as compared with the 1850s, when the Californian and Australian discoveries had temporarily put an end to the earlier tightness.

It is easy to find illustrations of positive output effects touched off by scarcities, even if with a lag. It is even possible to take a stronger position on those supply effects by stating that a large price-raising excess demand for gold has, so far, always led to technological improvements and new discoveries that brought the real price of gold down again. But the lags with which this has happened in different phases of history have been of very different duration. With any reasonable time horizon in mind it is therefore preferable to suggest here the existence of a major potential output-raising effect of gold scarcity rather than to predict such an effect on the grounds of past experience.

These are the considerations leading to the conclusions briefly expressed in the three 'numbered propositions' in my introductory remarks. To repeat briefly: at present the demand-supply conditions required for making gold a reasonably good 'proxy' for goods in general, and thus for a successful return to gold convertibility, are not satisfied; the possibility exists that for a group of countries these conditions will become satisfied in the future; the general argument against the gold standard, that it is irrational to tie the currencies of a group of countries to gold (a single commodity), is inconclusive because the political process by which fiat money is managed also has major irrationalities which have proved highly damaging. I will add that jointly these considerations make me feel opposed to the resumption of gold sales by the American authorities.

NOTES AND REFERENCES

1. I believe that Robert J. Barro belongs among the exceptions, in that I would interpret one of his recent writings as expressing a spirit similar to that motivating this essay. See Robert J. Barro, 'United States Inflation and the Choice of Monetary Standard', Working Paper Series No. PPS 80-30, Graduate School of Management, University of Rochester. This working paper contains the text of a talk presented by the author on 9 April 1980. A matter-of-fact recent analysis of the obstacles standing at present in the way of returning to gold, without (it seems to me) any attempt to judge the prospects for the more distant future, is also found in Edward M. Bernstein, 'Back to the Gold Standard?', *The Brookings Bulletin*, No. 2, Washington, 1980. For Bernstein's contribution to the debate see also note 2.

2. Aside from the sources listed under the table, I made use largely of data found in W. John Busschau, *Gold and International Liquidity: the Flow of Credit in Relation to Gold in the International Monetary System* (Johannesburg: South African Institute of International Affairs, 1961); Peter A. Abken, 'The Economics of Gold Price Movements', *Economic Review of the Federal Reserve Bank of Richmond*, March-April 1980; W. C. Butterman, 'Gold', in the United States Department of the Interior, Bureau of Mines, *Minerals Yearbook 1978-79* (Washington: US Government Printing Office, 1979); *Hearings Before the Senate Committee on Banking, Housing and Urban Affairs, 96th Congress*, S. 2704, 29-30 May 1980 (Washington: US Government Printing Office, 1980), pp. 466 *et seq.*; estimates used by Edward M. Bernstein in the *EMB Reports* and kindly put at my disposal; Phillip Cagan, *Determinants and Effects of Changes in the Stock of Money, 1875-1960*, Studies in Business Cycles No. 13 (New York and London: Columbia University Press, for the National Bureau of Economic Research, 1965); Joseph Kitchin, 'Gold', in *Encyclopaedia of the Social Sciences* Vol. VI, (New York: Macmillan, 1931), pp. 689-93; and *International Financial Statistics Yearbook 1979* (Washington: International Monetary Fund, 1980). Abken and Bernstein, as well as myself, have made substantial use *inter alia* of the estimates of Consolidated Gold Fields Ltd, London.

3. Herbert Giersch, *Allgemeine Wirtschaftspolitik*, Vol. 2: *Konjunktur- und Wachstumspolitik in der offenen Wirtschaft*, Die Wirtschaftswissenschaften, Reihe B: Volkswirtschaftslehre, Beitrag Nr 10 (Wiesbaden: Gabler, 1977), pp. 177 *et seq.*

4. Robert J. Barro belongs among these contributors. See, in addition to his paper cited in note 1, Barro, 'Money and the Price Level under the Gold Standard', *The Economic Journal*, Cambridge, March 1979.

5. This is not to say that in respects other than those stressed in the text the 'gold exchange' variety of gold-standard-type systems is not worth being distinguished from other varieties. Even as concerns the ability of the

authorities to hold the price of gold at a fixed level—that is, even in the context of the discussion in this essay—it is to be noted that all gold-saving devices have an effect on the proportion of the gold output available for satisfying the private demand. This is a point to which I shall return. Further, the adjustment mechanism under the gold-exchange variety of the system must satisfy specific conditions: whenever the manageability of the system requires a gradual increase in the gold-convertible reserves of participating countries, the countries whose money is held by others as a gold-convertible reserve must have a sum of current-account transactions and private capital exports or imports to which (jointly) a negative sign attaches. That is, they must have a balance-of-payments deficit in this sense. I am, of course, not opposed to distinguishing such special characteristics of the gold-exchange standard, but for the purpose of the analysis in this essay it is a variety of the gold standard.

6.   It must always be remembered that 'expected' gain or loss in this sense means an expected value derived from a personal probability distribution which is known also to involve possible outcomes very different from the 'expected' value, and this 'variance' plays a different role for different assets. Depending on the preferences (the 'utility function') of the owner, an asset with a somewhat negative expected rate and with small variance may have a legitimate place in a portfolio, particularly if the assets with a positive expected rate have a large variance.

7.   The present total stock, including the component owned by the monetary authorities, is estimated at 2,800 million ounces. From the 1930s on, the monetary gold stock is unequivocally the stock owned by the monetary authorities. Up to World War I, monetary gold included a considerable proportion consisting of gold money in circulation which became a small component after World War I and has played no role since the 1930s. The present privately-owned stock is comparable with the non-monetary part of the privately-owned stock of the era prior to the 1930s.

8.   A small part of the portfolio-mix incentive would, however, continue to play a role after the completion of the stock adjustment, since somewhat more of the current increase of the asset holdings of each period will have a gold-price-raising effect.

6 Interest Payments on Commercial Bank Reserves to Curb Euro-money Markets

Herbert Grubel

This essay begins with a brief summary of the economic costs and benefits of Euro-currency markets which provide the rationale for proposals to control them. Several of these proposals are then discussed and shown to be deficient on several grounds. There follows a description of how Euro-currency market growth can be curtailed through the payment of interest on required reserves and a discussion of the added benefits of the policy for domestic monetary management. The money and real economic costs of the proposed policy are analysed in the perspective of Federal Reserve profits and United States government spending. The final section contains a summary of the analysis and conclusions for policy.[1]

EURO-CURRENCY MARKET BENEFITS AND COSTS

Since 1965 there has been an enormous growth in Euro-currency banking, which consists of taking deposits and making loans in currencies other than that of the country which hosts the bank. It has been estimated that bank liabilities of this type have grown from a very small amount in 1965 to about $1 million million by the end of 1980, of which 80-90 per cent consists of interbank obligations so that only about $100,000 to $200,000 million of the Euro-currency business involves intermediation between ultimate borrowers and lenders in the private sector.[2] For the purposes of analysis in this essay it is important to put these figures into perspective with regard to overall United States banking. Thus, since Euro-banks have practically no deposits payable on demand, if they were included in surveys measuring the United States money stock, their dollar liabilities would contribute only 10 to 15 per cent to this M_4 measure, which consists of demand plus time deposits.[3]

Analysts are in widespread agreement that Euro-currency banking has raised the efficiency of the global capital markets, has

117

forced national capital markets to become more efficient and has provided an effective vehicle for intermediation between oil-surplus and oil-deficit nations. Not all of the growth of the Euro-currency markets reflects real economic gains, since the true cost of producing money is very low and banks are motivated to save on institutionally determined private costs that are in excess of this social cost. Nevertheless, it is difficult to find analysts who claim that Euro-currency markets have had zero economic benefits. The real controversy involves the costs of Euro-currency banking and whether they are greater or smaller than these benefits.[4]

Externality Costs

Euro-currency markets are alleged to have resulted in economic costs largely in the form of externalities. Thus, they are considered to have contributed significantly to inflation, exchange-rate instabilities, default risks of banks, difficulties in managing United States monetary aggregates and inefficiencies due to the diversion of trade. The theoretical arguments and empirical evidence concerning the magnitude of these costs briefly are as follows.

Euro-currency banking has contributed to increased world liquidity, the velocity of circulation of liquidity, or both. The expansion of liquidity is due to the fact that some domestic bank liabilities subject to central bank reserve requirements have been shifted abroad where there are no such requirements. Consequently, the credit multiplier can be larger and can lead to an increase in the total bank liabilities based on a given stock of high-powered reserves. The velocity of circulation of global money supplies is increased by Euro-currency banking because excess reserves of national banking systems that used to be idle have been put to use throughout the world, often on terms that simply take advantage of the world's different time zones and business days. Similarly, the general public has been induced to lend out funds that would have remained idle at the marginally lower yields available in purely domestic credit markets.

There is little doubt about the nature and direction of these influences on global liquidity and velocity caused by Euro-currency banking. The magnitude of these effects, however, is highly uncertain. The measurement of Euro-currency multipliers has been attempted with very inadequate data and the estimates reached by different researchers cover a wide range. Velocity has not been measured directly. Some of the best informed students of the market, though, believe multipliers to be very small because of large leakages from the system which take place wherever dollars, for example, enter the portfolios of central banks and of United States residents.[5]

Indirect measures of the effects in a sense have been most successful and revealing. Thus, monetarist equations of global price increases and aggregate national money stocks have yielded excellent statistical results that were not improved by the adding of Euro-currency balances. These results suggest that most Euro-currency deposits are already counted in national money supply data and that changes in circulation velocity have not been great.[6]

These findings of the relatively small effects of Euro-currency banking on world inflation do not mean, of course, that conditions may not change in the future. There is a risk and the basic issue is the cost of the policies by which it can be reduced or eliminated.

Exchange-rate Instability

During the 1970s the exchange rates of all countries were more unstable than at any time since the 1930s, the basic causes of this instability being disturbances in the real sector and differences in national inflation rates.[7] Euro-currency banks have contributed to this instability through the integration of national capital markets into one global market at low transactions and information costs, which encourages wealthholders to switch more funds between countries at lower interest-rate differentials than they would have in the absence of this market integration. As a result of the greater capital mobility, individual countries have lost some of their national monetary sovereignty; there are externalities costs from exchange-rate instability in the real sector; more reserves are required to stabilise exchange rates and the private sector spends more resources in forward-exchange markets and other institutions to reduce exchange-rate uncertainty. These costs are mitigated somewhat by the greater ability of countries to use interest-rate policies to attract private capital to finance payments imbalances or avoid otherwise necessary exchange-rate changes. Analysts who distrust the ability of policy makers to fine-tune economies might even argue that the increased capital mobility has put desirable constraints on the freedom of action of national policy activism.

Any qualitative evaluation of the effects of Euro-currency banking on exchange-rate stability and national monetary sovereignty must deal with the question of what the integration of global capital markets and the elasticity of short-term capital flows would have been if these Euro-banks had not existed. Given that the advances in communications technology in recent years have been exogenous, they probably would have been used by the financial community to achieve nearly the same degree of international capital-market efficiency that is presently attributed to Euro-currency banking. From this reasoning it follows that Euro-currency banks have contributed only marginally to the high elasticity of international capital movements and that therefore the control of Euro-banks would do little to stabilise exchange rates and raise national monetary sovereignty.

Bank-default Risks

Euro-currency banks in most countries are outside the regulatory and supervisory control of national monetary authorities. This means that, by and large, these banks' lending policies and capital structures are determined solely by the profit-maximisation motive. Some analysts therefore believe that these banks have entered into lending and capital-exposure risks which may be consistent with private welfare-maximisation criteria, but which are too great from a social point of view, given the possibly serious externalities that accompany large-scale international bank failures. These externalities from failures would be especially great, since these banks typically are not members of national deposit insurance schemes. Furthermore, because Euro-currency banks are normally not members of national banking systems, they do not have access to the rediscount facilities of central banks to bail them out of liquidity crises.[8]

It is very difficult to arrive at objective and reliable judgments about the privately and socially optimal risks in Euro-currency banking, especially since there are no historic precedents and no experience with lending to national governments and quasi-government agencies, which dominates the loan portfolios of these banks. There is, however, increased awareness among Euro-currency banks about the 'country risk' of such loans, so they pursue diligently the diversification of risks and there have been indications that the total resources of the large banks in the business would be available to deal with bankruptcy of legally separate foreign branches of these banks. The very efficiency of the global capital market would assure that liquidity crises can be solved by central banks through rediscounting at any point of entry into the market.

The preceding analysis suggests that bank failures and serious general financial instabilities are not very likely to occur. Nevertheless, since the externalities from such failures may represent a very large cost to the world, even small levels of such default risks should concern policy makers and the real policy issue is again the cost of policies that can reduce the risk of failures.

Economic Inefficiencies

Most analysts agree that the growth of Euro-currency banking is due to the partial de-regulation of a special type of banking activity that is implicit in the absence of reserve requirements on foreign-currency deposits. This partial movement towards free and de-regulated trade does not necessarily lead to increased efficiency in the allocation of real resources internationally, for reasons well known from the theory of economic integration. In the case of Euro-currency banking such a situation can arise when a bank is induced to move abroad by the partial de-regulation and, under completely free trade or uniform regulation, the bank's true least-cost location is at home. The move abroad under these conditions is privately profitable, but from a social point of view involves the wasteful expenditure of extra resources in the non-optimal location.[9]

The inefficiency cost of such trade diversion, as it may be called, may or may not be offset by the efficiency gains from increased business activity, or trade creation, following the partial de-regulation which was discussed above. The overall merit of Euro-currency banking due to partial de-regulation therefore is an empirical question for which there exists no answer at present. The preceding argument suggests, though, that any economic policy which can remove the distortionary wedge of cost differences implicit in the partial de-regulation, *ceteris paribus*, reduces the social cost of trade diversion.

United States Money-supply Management Difficulties

Given the aim of United States monetary policy to regulate the country's money-supply growth, any unforeseeable influences on the high-powered money base make this task more difficult. Euro-currency banking results in such influences on the base through the increased capital mobility it has created and through the shifts of funds between United States banks and their Euro-currency

F

branches abroad that are undertaken by the banks themselves or by their customers.[10]

The United States monetary authorities have never quantified the difficulties which Euro-currency banking has created for domestic monetary policy, especially in the light of the argument made above that even if there were no Euro-currency banks, international capital mobility would be very high. Nevertheless, the preceding argument suggests that there may be some social cost from increased difficulties of monetary control that should be considered in any rational analyses of the costs and benefits of Euro-currency banking.

Policy Issue Stated

The preceding analysis of the costs and benefits of Euro-currency banking has shown how tentative and unreliable existing knowledge of the subject is. For this reason alone it has been difficult to reach international agreement just on the basic question whether there is any need at all for some policy action to control Euro-currency banking. In addition, two other important issues have complicated the process of reaching agreement on the basic question. First, the benefits and costs of Euro-currency banking have been distributed unevenly among countries. For example, the financial communities of London, Singapore and Panama probably have enjoyed substantial benefits in the form of economic rent to their residents with special skills and to land housing banks. These gains have been to a considerable degree at the expense of United States and German banking, from which much of the business in these centres may have been diverted.[11] The gains also came at the cost of potential externalities for the world as a whole.

Second, there exists considerable uncertainty about the efficacy and costs of policies designed to deal with either the general growth of Euro-currency banking or the potential problems that would follow default of banks. The basic issue, noted briefly above in connection with some of the alleged costs of Euro-currency banking, is the cost of any policy relative to the benefits expected from it. Put another way, if it were possible to design a policy that resulted in very few costs directly and which reduced benefits from Euro-currency banking only slightly, then it would be worthwhile initiating this policy even if there were only small costs and risks associated with Euro-currency banking. The case for such policies for the control of Euro-currency banking would be even stronger if they did not result in costs, but yielded additional benefits. The proposed policy for the payment of interest on required reserves has exactly these properties, as will be seen below. But before analysing this proposal, it will be useful to review briefly the policies for Euro-banking control that have been proposed and in some instances acted upon.

POSSIBLE POLICIES FOR CONTROL OF EURO-BANKING

The policies to be discussed fall into two distinct categories. First, there are those which attempt to reduce the externalities which would accompany the widespread default of Euro-currency banks. Second, there are those which would curb the general growth of Euro-currency banking and thus reduce the level or growth of all the costs and risks noted in the preceding section.

Curbing Externalities from Default

One attempt to limit the potential problems from Euro-currency bank defaults was carried out successfully by the Bank of England when it succeeded in obtaining the informal consent of the major international banks to come to the rescue of their branches participating in the Euro-currency markets in London, even though they are not legally required to do so.[12] While such gentlemen's agreements may have worked in Britain successfully throughout the history of the Bank of England, it is not entirely certain that they will work in dealings with foreign banks.

The ex-Governor of the Bank of Greece, Xenophon Zolotas, has suggested the establishment of an international loan-insurance scheme, which would prevent bank failures if some borrowers defaulted on their loans.[13] The author has suggested the creation of an international deposit-insurance corporation to protect depositors from the consequences of loan defaults and bank failures and to limit the spread of the financial difficulties into other sectors which resulted from such bank-failures in the past, before national deposit-insurance programmes were widely adopted.[14]

The advantages of these insurance schemes are that they are self-supporting and that they involve the efficient and private internalisation of the externalities. An existing international organisation such as the International Monetary Fund (IMF) or the Bank for International Settlements (BIS) would have to guarantee the insurance agencies' potential obligations initially, but in the longer run premiums would build up an adequate contingency reserve. The insurance premiums paid by the banks would raise the cost of doing business and reduce somewhat the level of intermediation by Euro-banks, but these costs would reflect correctly the true economic costs of the business, including the prevention of the externalities from bank failure and would, therefore, move the economy towards optimal efficiency.

The insurance schemes are not without difficulties and costs. Fundamentally, there are the problems raised by moral hazard, which accompany all insurance schemes.[15] These can be dealt with only imperfectly through appropriate design of the insurance policies and the inclusion of provisions for co-insurance. The insurance schemes would be most efficient if all countries required banks in their jurisdiction to join them. Failure to do so would not destroy the competitiveness of insured banks, however, because rational depositors would be willing to accept the lower yields caused by the banks' insurance costs. The problem is that risk preferences of depositors might make them choose to deal in large enough numbers with non-insured banks that most of the default risks remain and, with them, the global problem of externalities. Analogous arguments can be made about the need for international agreement in the loan insurance scheme.

Since the insurance schemes have been proposed, no policy initiatives appear to have been taken. This fact suggests that the costs of putting in place and operating such schemes appear to be too high relative to the expected benefits in the views of officials in governments and international agencies which have to initiate negotiations, establish the institutions and retain an interest in their operation.

Curbing the Growth of Euro-banking
Curbing the growth of Euro-banking can be achieved by eliminating the main source of the competitive advantage which banks in their business enjoy over normal banks. This elimination could be achieved through the imposition of uniform reserve requirements on bank deposits of all currency denominations in all countries. These uniform required reserves can be either zero or equal to those of regular banks in each country.

As was argued above, there is widespread agreement among analysts that the zero reserve requirements of Euro-currency banks have provided the most important stimulus for their growth. There is little doubt, therefore, that if this source of competitive advantage were eliminated, the growth of the Euro-banks would be curbed.

The problem with this approach is that the *elimination* of reserve requirements on domestic banks would result in the loss of the key instrument for the conduct of monetary policy. For this reason it has never been contemplated seriously as a general policy. In the New York Free Banking Zone, however, the American banks may maintain deposits free from reserve requirements if the deposits are owned by foreigners and meet some other requirements to make them imperfect substitutes for regular United States demand deposits.[16] This zone is clearly an attempt to permit some American banks to compete directly with Euro-currency banks abroad while the basic domestic system remains unchanged. Other American cities may establish such zones and it remains to be seen whether they succeed in returning substantial proportions of the business to the United States. Clearly, the effect of this partial de-regulation will be to lower the United States cost of trade diversion, but it will not reduce and may increase the overall level of Euro-currency banking through the diversion from regular domestic financial intermediaries in the United States and other countries.

In 1979 legislation was introduced into the United States Congress which proposed that reserve requirements be imposed on all Euro-currency deposits by American banks in the United States and abroad.[17] The Congressional initiators of the legislation made it clear during the hearings on the bill that they would not recommend its passage if it imposed a discriminatory burden on the American banks alone. In other words, the passage of the bill was made dependent upon reaching international agreement that other countries would impose analogous reserve requirements on Euro-banks within their jurisdiction or on their home country banks operating Euro-bank branches abroad.

Attempts by the United States Government to get the major industrialised countries to agree to the simultaneous imposition of reserve requirements on foreign currency deposits were without success, although it should be noted that West Germany had imposed such requirements unilaterally during the 1970s and Canada did so early in 1981. There are three basic reasons for this failure of the United States policy initiative.

First, if all major industrial countries were to agree to the proposed imposition of reserve requirements, there is a very high probability that semi-industrial and developing countries would become hosts for newly founded or displaced banks that would carry on with the Euro-currency business, although there might be some overall reduction in global Euro-banking. There would be extra real economic costs as customers in industrial countries shift their business abroad in a classical example of wasteful trade diversion. Since there are very great returns to individual countries which do not impose the recommended reserve requirements, there is virtually no chance that agreements to include all countries of the world can be reached.

Second, the distribution of the costs and benefits from the imposition of the reserve requirements on foreign-currency deposits would vary greatly for individual countries. The United States and Canada would be the main beneficiaries, as domestic banks would regain some of the business Euro-banks had diverted abroad, although the benefits might in fact be quite small, depending on the growth of substitute business in other countries noted above. The losers, on the other hand, would be the countries now hosting most of the Euro-currency banks, such as Britain and Luxembourg and, to a lesser degree, France, Switzerland and Italy. For these countries the costs of imposing reserve requirements on foreign-currency deposits would be extremely high relative to benefits and it is not surprising that they refused to accept the United States policy recommendations.

Third, as will be shown in the next section, existing reserve requirements involve an inefficient method of taxing an economic activity, which Euro-banking in effect is avoiding. There exist, therefore, strong arguments in support of an approach which does not lead to an extension of the inefficient taxation, but which causes it to be removed. It may well be that the United States' proposals for reserve requirements were rejected because of the availability of a superior method for dealing with the problems of Euro-banking, namely, the payment of interest on banks' required reserves. There have been informal stories, but no published reports, about the fact that proposals for the adoption of this approach were developed in research departments of some major countries' central banks and in international organisations, which found some support among politicians, but which were rejected by top-level policy makers. The next section of this essay analyses the proposal and concludes with some arguments supporting it on grounds of efficiency.

PAYING INTEREST ON DOMESTIC
REQUIRED RESERVES

The basic rationale for the payment of interest on the required reserves of financial intermediaries on deposit with central banks is that under existing conditions of zero interest, the reserve requirements involve an excise tax on banking that has been the primary cause of the development of Euro-currency banking. In support of this proposition it is useful to consider the effective taxation rate[18] of the financial intermediation business that is implicit in the reserve requirements. For this purpose consider a simplified model of banking which assumes that banks' only business consists of accepting deposits D on which they pay interest at the rate r and out of which they make loans L at an interest i. Under competition, value added of banks V yields only normal returns to investment. In the absence of required reserves in equilibrium

$$V = Li - Dr. \tag{1}$$

If there is a reserve requirement of q per cent on deposits, the amount of loans the banks can make is reduced to

$$L = D(1-q), \tag{2}$$

and value added with reserve requirements V' in equilibrium is

$$V' = D(1-q)i - Dr = D(i-qi-r). \tag{3}$$

Let us now assume that the interest rates i and r are determined in domestic markets where reserve requirements are positive and competition within the existing legal framework regulating the financial industry has resulted in only normal returns being earned by banks. These assumptions describe quite realistically conditions in the United States and Canada in the early 1960s. Now consider the development of a low-cost means of communication which makes it possible to assure effective control over foreign bank subsidiaries and suppose that those subsidiaries engage only in the sale of dollar deposits and loans which are not subject to reserve requirements. What is the percentage increase in value added that can be earned by these foreign subsidiaries of United States banks, using the domestic value added as a base and assuming that the lending and borrowing rates of the foreign subsidiaries are the same as those of the domestic banks?

The percentage increase is:

$$b = (V - V')/V' \tag{4}$$

which, after substitution and simplification, becomes:

$$b = qi/(i - qi - r). \tag{5}$$

The interpretation of this equation is facilitated through the use of a numerical example. Thus, consider i = .10, r = .08 and q = .15. Under these conditions, b = 3.00, which implies that the value added of the foreign subsidiaries of banks free from reserve requirements is three times as large as the value added of domestic banks required to keep interest-free reserves against deposits.[19]

The equation underlying this calculation shows clearly that the competitive advantage of shifting the business abroad is an increasing function of the required reserve ratio and the levels of the interest rates and a decreasing function of the size of the spread. A set of numerical examples can provide some insights into the elasticity of the benefits with respect to these variables, assuming the spread between lending and borrowing rates is 2 per cent.

TABLE 6.1
Excess Value Added of Foreign Banking[a]

| Values of i | Values of q | | |
	q=0.05	q=0.10	q=0.15
0.03	0.080	0.17	0.29
0.06	0.176	0.43	0.82
0.09	0.290	0.82	2.07
0.12	0.429	1.50	9.00
0.15	0.600	3.00	——[b]
0.18	0.818	9.00	——[b]

[a]Calculated from $b = qi/(i-qi-r)$ where,
b = excess value added
q = reserve requirement
i = bank lending rate
r = bank deposit rate
and $i-r = 0.02$.
[b]The equation underlying these calculations becomes economically meaningless when $qi > 0.02$, that is, when the cost of maintaining the reserves exceeds the size of the assumed spread. In the real world this is not possible because the implicit tax of reserve requirements determines the size of the spread.

The preceding, simple model shows the strength of the profit incentives[20] that underlie banks' move abroad and into the business free from required reserves, especially when interest rates are high and banking is efficient and results in small spreads between lending and borrowing rates. The simple model could readily be amended to consider the existence of liabilities other than deposits and the fact that foreign subsidiaries have to offer marginally higher deposit rates in compensation for greater risks and charge marginally lower rates on loans to attract borrowers away from their usual sources and compensate them for extra costs of dealing abroad. But these refinements would not alter the basic conclusions reached with the simple model.[21]

Advantages of Interest on Required
Reserves

The analysis of the preceding section showed clearly that the maintenance of required reserves imposes heavy taxes on domestic financial intermediation, which banks can avoid by shifting business into the Euro-currency market. From this fact it follows that if this tax on financial intermediation were eliminated, incentives for Euro-currency banking would be sharply reduced. The elimination of this tax could be achieved simply through the payment of interest on required reserves by central banks. In the framework of the above model, if interest is paid on required reserves, equation (1) determines the value added of domestic *and* foreign currency banks since $D = L$, equation (2) is irrelevant, $V = V'$ and b is always zero.

The proposed solution to the problems raised by Euro-currency banking has three main advantages over all the others discussed above. First, the payment of interest on domestic required bank reserves can be implemented by unilateral action of national governments. Foreign countries can counter the effects of this policy only through the payment of subsidies to foreign currency banking, which, in all likelihood, they would not do since it would be very costly.

Second, the interest payment on required reserves increases the efficiency of financial intermediation by eliminating the tax-induced wedge between the private returns on the activity in different geographic locations or different currencies. As was noted above, this wedge has induced a privately profitable, but socially costly, diversion of trade and constitutes the most fundamental efficiency cost of Euro-currency banking.

In this context it is important to note that Euro-currency banking is really only one of a class of competitive market responses to this tax incentive. In domestic markets financial intermediaries are constantly at work to develop financial instruments that can serve as substitutes for demand deposits, but which are not subject to required reserves. Certificates of Deposit and Negotiable Orders of Withdrawal (NOW) accounts in the United States markets were such developments. In addition, new financial intermediaries such as cooperative savings banks are created or grow in response to differential rates of taxation. The magnitude of such substitutes would be even greater if regulatory authorities did not always curtail their growth after they have been developed. The costs of development, the trade diversion during the period before they are controlled through regulation and the cost of operating the regulatory authorities are all avoided by the proposed elimination of the tax.

Third, because the interest payments on required reserves would eliminate incentives for the development of new financial instruments, the velocity of circulation of money and the growth of monetary aggregates would be more stable through time. As a result, monetary authorities would find it easier to attain stable and non-inflationary growth in liquidity.[22] In the United States, interest payments on reserves would remove one of the primary motives for banks to leave or not to join the Federal Reserve system. Greater and more stable Federal Reserve membership would facilitate the conduct of monetary policy and avoid the need for regulatory procedures to assure adequate membership.

The Cost of Interest on Required Reserves

The most important reason why the governments of the United States, Canada and other major industrial countries have in the past opposed the payment of interest on required reserves is that it represents a large drain on the central government's tax revenue. A minor objection related to this expenditure is that it tends to favour high-income owners of bankshares and therefore is inequitable.

The gross figures on required expenditures are, indeed, quite impressive. In December 1979 the required reserves in the form of deposits with Federal Reserve Banks (that is, excluding vault cash) for all United States commercial banking institutions, were $29,000 million.[23] During that period, short-term interest rates were about 10 per cent. These figures suggest that the cost of paying interest on required reserves at competitive short-term money-market rates would have been about $3,000 million. In Canada, at the end of 1979, Bank of Canada deposits serving as required reserves were $4,600 million, so that with interest rates at around 10 per cent, the cost would have been about $500 million.[24]

These gross figures have to be put into several perspectives. First, the initial excess profits of banks resulting from the interest payments would lead immediately to a return of one-half of the costs to the governments of the two countries through the payment of corporate income taxes at 50 per cent. To the extent that the higher bank profits would result in greater dividends, wealthy private owners would pay in personal income taxes one-half of the dividends received, lowering the net cost of the policy to possibly only one-quarter of the gross figures.

In the longer run, competition among financial intermediaries at home and abroad would result in the elimination of excess profits through a narrowing of the spread between lending and borrowing rates. At this point, tax revenues from excess profits would be zero, but the overall tax revenue would be increased in ways which are known generally, but impossible to estimate. Thus, the return of business from abroad raises revenues, as specialised resources employed in the industry earn higher rents and banking personnel previously employed abroad return to broaden the tax base.

Second, the above figures on tax-revenue losses are inflated by extremely high (by historic standards) short-term money-market rates. In the future, when interest together with inflation return to more normal levels, costs will be considerably lower. If short-term money-market rates were at 5 per cent, these costs would be one-half of those noted above.

Third, even the gross tax-revenue losses calculated above are very small fractions of central government expenditures and deficits. Thus, for the United States, the $3,000 million projected decline in 1979 revenue would have been only about .5 per cent of total expenditures and 5 per cent of the deficit. For Canada, the projected tax reduction of $500 million represents about 1.0 per cent of central government expenditures and 4 per cent of the deficit.[25] These figures imply that the losses could readily be absorbed through the natural growth in revenue accompanying increases in real and nominal income in the presence of progressive income taxes,[26] or they could be overshadowed by cyclical changes in revenues.

Fourth, the fact noted above that the initial excess profits of banks raise corporate and personal income-tax revenues and that competition eventually eliminates these excess profits implies that the net revenue losses from interest payments on required reserve deposits have a time profile which permits absorption in the government budgets without requiring drastic adjustments in other taxes and expenditure.

Fifth, governments can avail themselves of well known policies to reduce the initial impact effects of the proposed interest payments. Thus, they might pay interest initially at only one-half the money market rate and move to the full rate over a period of years. Alternatively, interest payments at the full market rate may be accompanied by temporary surcharges on bank profits that capture a part of the windfall profits in a politically expedient manner without eliminating the favourable effects of the basic policy noted above. Undoubtedly, legislators and bureaucrats can devise other methods for lowering the budgetary impact and political costs of paying interest on required bank reserve deposits.

CONCLUSION

Euro-currency banking has been shown, in this essay, to have resulted in a mixture of economically beneficial and harmful effects, all of which are difficult to assess empirically. Of the harmful effects, the most important one, with regard to efficiency, is the trade diversion implicit in the operation of banking in foreign locations and currencies which would not take place if taxation of banking were uniform. An analysis of the rate of taxation implicit in the maintenance of required reserves showed the strength of the incentives for Euro-banks to escape the taxes.

The proposed and widely discussed methods for dealing with the costs of Euro-banking were analysed and shown to be deficient on several grounds. Only the payment of interest on domestic required bank deposits was seen to be efficient in eliminating the cost of trade diversion and not requiring international agreements which would be difficult to achieve. The policy would, in addition, improve the efficiency of domestic financial intermediation and the efficacy of monetary policy. In relation to these important benefits, the budget implications of the interest payment on required deposits are very small, especially if the policy is instituted gradually. The net social rate of return from the payment of interest on required bank reserve deposits would be very high.

NOTES AND REFERENCES

1. The work on this essay was supported by a grant from the British Columbia Programs for Excellence project.

2. The basic source for information on Euro-currency banking is provided by the *Bank for International Settlements Annual Reports* (Bank for

International Settlements, Basle, various issues). For some data on United States conditions and their relative importance, see Hearings before the Subcommittee on Domestic Monetary Policy and the Subcommittee on International Trade, Investment and Monetary Policy, *Eurocurrency Market Control Act of 1979*, Serial No. 96-23 (Washington: US Government Printing Office, for the Committee on Banking, Finance and Urban Affairs, United States House of Representatives, 1979).

3.   See the testimony by Jeffrey Nichols in *ibid.*, pp. 15-16.

4.   For institutional and analytical backgrounds relevant to the discussion in this section, see Paul Einzig and Brian S. Quinn, *The Euro-Dollar System*, 6th ed. (New York: St Martin's Press, 1977); Jane S. Little, *Euro-Dollars: The Money Market Gypsies* (New York: Harper and Row, 1979); Adrian Throop, 'Eurobanking and World Inflation', *Voice of the Federal Reserve Bank of Dallas*, August 1979; and John R. Karlik, 'Some Questions and Brief Answers about the Euro-dollar Market', in John Adams (ed.), *The Contemporary International Economy: a Reader* (New York: St Martin's Press, 1979), pp. 310-29.

5.   This is the view taken and backed by persuasive reasoning by Helmut W. Mayer, *Credit and Liquidity Creation in the International Banking Sector*, BIS Economic Paper No. 1 (Basel: Bank for International Settlements, 1979).

6.   See Throop, *loc. cit.*, for one such study.

7.   For an analysis of the facts and speculation about causes, see John R. Artus and John H. Young, 'Fixed and Flexible Exchange Rates: A Renewal of the Debate', *International Monetary Fund Staff Papers*, Washington, December 1979; and Jacob A. Frenkel, 'Flexible Exchange Rates in the 1970s', in Murray Weidenbaum (ed.), *Stabilization Policy: Lessons from the 1970s and Implications for the 1980s* (St Louis: Center for the Study of American Business at Washington University, 1980).

8.   For analysis of these issues, see Federal Reserve Bank of Boston, *Key Issues in International Banking*, Conference Series No. 18 (Boston: Federal Reserve Bank, 1977).

9.   For a more complete analysis of this point, see Herbert G. Grubel, 'Towards a Theory of Free Economic Zones', *Weltwirtschaftliches Archiv*, Kiel, No. 1, 1982.

10.   These arguments underlie United States policy initiatives to impose reserve requirements on Euro-banking. See *Eurocurrency Market Control Act of 1979, op. cit.*, for expression of these views.

11.   West Germany unilaterally imposed reserve requirements on Euro-banking deposits during the 1970s.

12.   Christopher W. McMahon, 'Central Banks as Regulators and Lenders of Last Resort in an International Context: A View from the United Kingdom' in *Key Issues in International Banking, op. cit.*, pp. 102-10.

13.   Xenophon Zolotas, *An International Loan Insurance Scheme: a Proposal*, Bank of Greece Papers and Lectures No. 39 (Athens: Bank of Greece, 1978).

14.   Grubel, *A Proposal for the Establishment of an International Deposit Insurance Corporation*, Princeton Essays in International Finance No. 133 (Princeton: International Finance Section of Princeton University, 1979).

15.   Franklin Edwards (ed.), *Issues in Financial Regulation* (New York:

McGraw-Hill, 1979). This book is based on a series of faculty seminars held during the 1976-77 academic year by Columbia University's Center for Law and Economic Studies.

16.   See Hang-Sheng Cheng, 'From the Caymans', *Federal Reserve Bank of San Francisco Weekly Letter*, 13 February 1981.

17.   See *Eurocurrency Market Control Act of 1979, op. cit.*

18.   The approach used here is based on the theory of effective protection, which is presented most authoritatively in W. M. Corden, *The Theory of Protection* (London: Oxford University Press, 1971).

19.   Using the values in the text, a bank subject to reserve requirements would earn, on a $100 deposit, $8.50 from loans and have a cost of $8.00 due to the interest paid on the deposits, leaving a value added of $0.50. The de-regulated bank can earn $10.00 and has a cost of $8.00, for a value added of $2.00. The advantage of operating the de-regulated business therefore is $1.50, or 300 per cent of $0.50.

If the 'free trade' or de-regulated value added is used as a base to measure the effect of reserve requirements, the implicit rate of taxation is defined as $t = (V - V')/V$, which comes to $(2.00 - 0.50)/.50 = .75$ under the assumed conditions.

20.   If 10 per cent of value added is profits, and if primary factor costs and production functions are the same in regulated domestic banking and Euro-currency banking, then the effective profit advantage of escaping the regulation is 3,000 per cent in the above example.

21.   Federal Deposit Insurance premiums in the United States also are much like a tax on value added that can be escaped by shifting business to Euro-markets. Since depositors receive a benefit from the domestic banks' membership in the insurance scheme, though, domestic banks' deposit rates can be lower than those of the foreign banks, whose cost advantage therefore is not equal to the savings in the premiums and required reserves. The analysis is complicated by the existence of size limits on insured deposits and investors' different attitudes towards risk, but space limitations prevent a full treatment of these issues. We may conclude, however, that compulsory deposit insurance membership can be equivalent to a tax on value added in regulated banking.

22.   The academic literature concerned with interest payments on required reserve deposits mostly considers the impact of financial intermediation on the effectiveness of monetary policy, relying on the same argument made here that the taxes implicit in required reserves encourage the growth of competitive substitutes for banks. Anthony M. Santomero and Jeremy J. Siegel, 'Bank Regulation and Macro-Economic Stability', *The American Economic Review*, Menasha, March 1981, use a stochastic model of banking to expand on the arguments made by James Tobin, 'A General Equilibrium Approach to Monetary Theory', *Journal of Money, Credit and Banking*, Columbus, February 1969; and by James Tobin and William C. Brainard, 'Financial Intermediaries and the Effectiveness of Monetary Controls', *The American Economic Review*, Evanston, May 1963.

23.   *Bank of Canada Review* (Ottawa: Bank of Canada, 1980), Table 5, Series B404.

24.   *Federal Reserve Bulletin* (Washington: Board of Governors of the

Federal Reserve System, 1980), Table A16, line 33.

25. Government expenditure (net of social security) and deficit data are from *Government Finance Statistics Yearbook 1980* (Washington: International Monetary Fund, 1980).

26. This argument is not applicable to Canada, where the income tax schedule is indexed.

Part III

Payments and Exchange-rate Policies

7 Autonomous and Induced Items in the Balance of Payments

Fritz Machlup

One would think that after decades, nay, centuries of discussion economists would have reached some sort of agreement about the 'forces' that determine the balance of international payments. Unfortunately, we are far from a common understanding, and different schools of thought offer different explanations. Some of the differences are merely terminological and can be reconciled by appropriate adjustments of language or jargon. Other differences, however, are substantive: they reflect different views about the working of the economy. One may try to reconcile some of these differences too, for example, by saying that the divergent findings are 'merely' due to different choices of assumptions. This is true enough, but judgments about the appropriateness of assumptions in the interpretation and explanation of observed phenomena are crucial in economic analysis; it is not just a matter of taste.

In this essay I shall undertake a restatement of conflicting positions. I am choosing a strictly verbal form of argument. I am aware that this exposes me to the charge of being old-fashioned or perhaps inept in mathematical argumentation. So be it, but I am sticking to verbal reasoning chiefly because I have found that many readers of algebraic expositions are less critical of implicit assumptions.

In the first section of this essay I shall make a brief statement about pertinent conceptual and terminological questions, in the hope that this will reduce the danger of misunderstanding what follows. In the second section I shall speak of the statistical balance of payments and the usually misguided attempts to read cause-and-effect relations into (or out of) accounting statements. Any economist deserving of the appellation ought to be immune to the confusion between definitional identities and behavioural tendencies. Yet, if one wished to spend some time unproductively, one could compile a long register of unguarded or obviously wrong statements in the literature, claiming causal connections among identities. Hence, a brief discussion of these issues seems to be in order.

In the third section, conflicting views about causal relationships among different kinds of international transactions will be contrasted, and five of these views will be examined. Some of the positions on 'what causes what' are related to monetary, monetarist and portfolio-theoretic approaches to the balance of payments and the determination of foreign-exchange rates, and will invite observations of a more general nature. Different regimes regarding foreign-exchange rates—fixed, managed, freely flexible—will be seen to require more divergent applications of our theoretical instrumentarium than many analysts have been willing to concede.

INDEPENDENT AND DEPENDENT VARIABLES

A discussion of approaches to the determination of the balance of international payments—asking 'what causes what'—presumes some measure of agreement about conceptual and terminological questions and about methodological notions such as dependent and interdependent variables, static and dynamic equilibrium, its disturbance and restoration.

The discussion of causal sequences in international trade and finance, as in many other economic areas, has been carried on with the help of a large variety of terms and phrases. Cause and effect, disturbance and adjustment, disequilibration and equilibration are equivalent pairs of nouns. Even more popular are combinations of adjectives and nouns, such as independent and dependent variables, exogenous and endogenous factors, disturbing and adjusting transactions, disequilibrating and equilibrating changes, autonomous and induced items. More sophisticated than these pairs is the triadic distinction of spontaneous disturbance, subsequent repercussions and ultimate effects. All these terms are acceptable. What is not acceptable is to attach any of them to selected items or accounts in the statistical balance of payments on the assumption that these items or accounts are 'by nature' autonomous or induced, or 'as a rule' cause other magnitudes to change or, contrariwise, result from changes in other magnitudes. Alas, precisely this is done by alternative approaches to the 'explanation' of the balance of payments.

Mutual Interdependence

We should guard against the conclusion that, because the variables in a general-equilibrium system are assumed to be inter-dependent, this mutual dependence forbids us to single out particular changes of some variables as independent and others as dependent. Interdependence may involve 'feedback loops', recursive dependences, or cross-influences, but this does not rule out that a chain of causal relations starts at some point and ends with the magnitudes of most variables, including the one that changed first, being different from what they were at the outset and in the early stages of the process of adjustment.

Interdependence between two variables, say A and B, means that the magnitude of A at the time t is influenced by the magnitude of B at the time $t - 1$ (or earlier), and is influencing the magnitude which B will reach at the time $t + 1$ (or later); likewise, the magnitude of B at the time t is influenced by the magnitude of A at the time $t - 1$ (or earlier), and is influencing the magnitude which A will reach at the time $t + 1$ (or later). Thus, A_t and B_t are, strictly speaking, independent of each other. The disregard of time in static analysis has sometimes confused readers exposed to 'simultaneous' equations.

Interdependence between A and B is perfectly compatible with one of the two changing first—as a result of an explained or unexplained primary disturbance—causing the other to vary, which in turn makes the first react, effecting another change in the second, and so on until their magnitudes are again compatible with each other. Most economic problems call for far more than two variables. The inclusion of large numbers of variables in our models would cause no serious difficulties were it not for the need to provide all of them with unambiguous assumptions about how they depend on one another and how long the reaction times are. Unfortunately, experience does not warrant a strong belief that estimated or chosen coefficients of relation and the time coefficients are stable over time.

Primary Disturbances and Stereotyped Effects

Assume a primary disturbance is seen in an increase in the imports of a particular good; if one looks for the *cause* of this increase, it may be found in all sorts of changes 'exogenous' to the model constructed for explaining the *effects*. For example, tastes in the importing countries may have shifted in favour of that good; prices of competing domestic products may have increased, or prices of complementary goods may have declined; domestic incomes may have increased; import tariffs may have been lowered; foreign price reductions or quality improvements may have made these imports more attractive; credits from foreign suppliers may have become more liberal; and so forth. If we do not care to explore the cause of the increases in imports, we may start the causal chain with the increase in imports as the primary, autonomous, spontaneous 'disequilibration'.

The changes induced by the primary disturbance—by the increase in particular imports—need not, as many writers have assumed, consist chiefly of movements of monetary reserves, although this is one of several possibilities. If reserves are actually changed, this will surely not be the end of the causal chain, because consequent monetary changes are likely to affect all sorts of variables, including liquidity, interest rates, inventories, commodity prices, investments, incomes, employment, with effects upon all kinds of imports, exports and capital movements. Thus, one has to accept the notion of induced, equilibrating changes in exports and imports. In other words, changes in merchandise trade may be autonomous or induced, disequilibrating or equilibrating, exogenous or endogenous: only by virtue of an arbitrary assumption can we insist that things started from an equilibrium that was disturbed by a change characterised as 'primary'.

The trouble is that some writers have formed stereotypes of international transactions and international accounts—stereotypes that may prevent a real understanding of the essential inter-relationships. To expose the stereotypes is one of the chief purposes of this essay.

THE ACCOUNTING BALANCE

The presentation of the statistics of a nation's international transactions has often changed and is not uniform now. Yet, the arrangement of major accounts and sub-accounts as shown below is rather typical:

    (1) Balance on current account

Goods

Services

Investment income

Unrequited transfers

    (2) Balance on capital account, exclusive of official reserves

Direct investment

Portfolio investment
Other long-term capital
Other short-term capital
   (3) Balance of official-reserve transactions
Monetary gold
Special drawing rights
Reserve position in the Fund
Foreign-exchange assets
   (4) Errors and omissions (statistical discrepancy)

The Major Accounts

This scheme of only four major accounts and twelve sub-accounts (line items) is selected for purposes of the didactic exercise undertaken in this section. The 'detailed presentation' in the latest *Balance of Payments Yearbook* of the International Monetary Fund (IMF) has 112 line items.[1] The reasons for distinguishing the current, capital and reserve accounts are related to basic economic concepts and theories. The current account collects transactions that pertain to *income* accounting, the other two to *capital* accounting. For example, exported goods and services are produced by productive factors that derive their incomes from the production and sale of the respective outputs; investment income is part of national income; and unrequited (or unilateral) transfers are grants, gifts, donations and other remittances without promise of future repayment, hence not constituting changes in foreign claims or other foreign assets in the capital account.

The separation of capital movements into one account that excludes official-reserve transactions and another that exhibits nothing but these transactions is related to the notion that changes in official reserves often, or ordinarily, have particular monetary effects. The balance of non-reserve-capital movements is usually subdivided into long-term and short-term capital, and the latter should for purposes of analysis be further subdivided into not-perfectly liquid and perfectly liquid funds (bank balances). Both statistical divisions, however, are questionable, because the observable (operational) criteria do not fit the theoretical constructs. Statisticians classify bonds as long-term capital assets on the basis of their original maturity at the time of their issuance—not on the basis of the time remaining till their redemption—so that their purchase or sale constitutes a long-term capital movement even if the bonds fall due within a few months. Moreover, long-term securities are frequently held for only such short periods that acquisition and disposal in effect function like movements of short-term funds. (Indeed, short-term loans, renewed or 'rolled over', and bank deposits are often more nearly 'long-term' than portfolio investments for short-term capital gains or other reasons. For purposes of analysis, both had better be treated as short-term capital.)[2] The separation between perfectly and not-perfectly liquid claims is questionable because large balances on bank deposits payable on demand are in effect frozen as collateral for outstanding loans or other commitments. Obligations to keep minimum balances or 'compensating balances' on checking accounts contradict the convention of treating all demand deposits as liquid. If there were some way of separating movements of transient capital from transfers of capital funds with good prospects of staying in the host country for a long time, the distinction between short-term and long-term capital would be eminently sound and significant.

The Zero-sum Game among the Accounts

Balance-of-payments accounting is designed like double-entry book-keeping: there must be no credit entry without a corresponding debit entry in an equal amount. Only because the data reported to the recording accountants come from different sources without advice of the appropriate counter-item can there be a discrepancy between the sum of credit entries and the sum of debit entries. The statistical discrepancy is sometimes very large; it is recorded, often under the traditional heading 'errors and omissions', in such an amount as to make the total balance equal to zero. Thus, the accounts, some showing credit balances (positive signs), others debit balances (negative signs), must add up to zero. Confining ourselves to the four major balances of the scheme presented, we may write:

$$\text{Current} + \text{Capital} + \text{Reserves} + \text{Omissions} = 0.$$

Of the three accounts that are composed of reported data, the official-reserve account is probably the most accurate in most countries, with a few, possibly important, exceptions. Some central banks, for reasons of their own, prefer to conceal substantial changes in their reserves; they do this by swap arrangements with their own commercial banks—for example, selling foreign exchange to them with re-purchase agreements attractive to the banks that provide a temporary home to the foreign balances taken from the official reserves. This constitutes a switch from the reserve account to the 'capital account exclusive of official-reserve movements'. Other, sometimes large, discrepancies in the statistical accounts of official-reserve movements have to do with placements in the Xeno-currency markets. These deliberate substitutions, however, affect only the balances in which the transactions in question will be entered, but do not result in net statistical discrepancies. Thus, 'errors and omissions' are likely to occur only in the current account and the private capital account, and it is widely agreed that in most countries the omissions are chiefly unreported—and therefore unrecorded—capital movements.[3]

Let us assume that all errors and omissions are detected and correctly distributed to the appropriate accounts; we then can arrange all items in the three major accounts:

$$\text{Current} + \text{Capital} + \text{Reserves} = 0.$$

It follows logically that the balance on any one of these accounts must be equal to the sum, with signs reversed, of the two other balances:

(1) Current $= -$ Capital $-$ Reserves
(2) Capital $= -$ Current $-$ Reserves
(3) Reserves $= -$ Current $-$ Capital

These identities do not express any causal relationships, but only truisms, definitional relationships. They are not, for that reason, devoid of significance. The first identity says that any surplus on current account must equal, every day, month, or year, the combined deficit on capital and reserve accounts, that is, net capital exports and reserve accumulations during the same period. The second identity says that any surplus on capital account, a net capital import, must equal the combined deficit on current account and official-reserve account, for example, import surpluses and reserve accumulations. The third identity says that any surplus on official-reserve account (which means a loss of foreign reserves or an increase in net foreign borrowing by the monetary authorities) must equal the combined deficit on current account and capital account, for example, an import surplus and/or a capital outflow.

Let us repeat, for emphasis and reinforcement, that these are not cause-and-effect statements. A surplus on current account, for example, a trade surplus, does not *cause* an export of capital (a deficit on capital account), but *is* an export of capital, either an increase in claims against foreigners or a decrease in liabilities to foreigners. Such claims may be against the foreign buyers of the exported merchandise or against the foreign banks on which they drew their cheques to pay. If the cheques were drawn on banks in the exporting country, the capital export would be in the form of a decrease in the banks' liabilities to foreign (bank or non-bank) depositors.

Truism v. Causal Connection

It is sometimes difficult to see clearly the difference between definitional (tautological) and causal statements. If the capital balance and the official-reserve balance are merged, so that all international transactions are either capital movements or current-account transactions, it is a mere truism to state that a surplus on current account *is* a deficit on capital account and that a surplus on capital account *is* a deficit on current account. From this definitional identity no statement on cause and effect can logically be inferred. Whether an increase in the supply of foreign capital leads to an increased demand for imported products, or whether an increase in the demand for imports leads to an increased supply of foreign capital; whether larger capital exports by some persons (individuals or firms) induce capital imports by other persons or rather increased exports or reduced imports of merchandise; whether a reduction in imports of merchandise leads to reduced exports or to reductions in capital inflows or to increases in capital outflows—none of these possibilities is either excluded or ordained by the zero-sum game among the accounts in the balance of payments. 'What causes what' is an entirely different question.

How easy it is to confuse causation and mere truism is illustrated by countless official statements and 'expert' pronouncements in journals and newspapers about the consequences of an increase in the price of oil for poor oil-importing countries. The virtually unanimous conclusions are that an oil-price increase 'necessitates' *deficits on current account* and that these deficits 'cause' problems of financing, that is, of finding the funds—capital imports—to cover the deficits. This—unless one refers to the 'programme balance of payments' (not the accounting balance)—is wrong. The higher price of oil does not necessitate a deficit on current account, but it raises problems of finding funds with which to buy the more expensive oil. If such funds cannot be obtained, the country concerned may have to make more of its products available for export, perhaps at ruinous prices, or it may have to do without other urgently needed imports, or it may have to reduce its oil imports so drastically that operations in whatever industry it has will be curtailed, essential services cut or eliminated—and unemployment may rise to catastrophic levels, with starvation becoming even more widespread than before. The country, in other words, cannot have a current-account deficit as long as it cannot obtain the loans to finance it. Only when such finance, allowing a surplus on capital account, is obtained can a deficit on current account arise or continue.

In other words, a higher price of oil may have a variety of possible effects: reduction in oil imports, reduction in other imports, increase in exports, receipt of grants, use of scarce monetary reserves, or receipt of larger foreign loans and investments. Only in the last two cases—use of existing foreign-exchange reserves and receipt of larger foreign loans and investments—can a deficit on current account arise, continue, or increase. That is to say, only if it is possible to finance a deficit can there be a deficit on current account. The existence, or continued existence, of such a deficit *implies* the existence, or continued existence, of a surplus on capital account. The current-account deficit *neither causes nor is caused by* the capital-account surplus. The two imbalances are logical correlatives.

CAUSES AND EFFECTS

We may now proceed from accounting to economics, that is, to principles helpful in understanding 'what causes what'. These principles may be seen in terms of partial equilibrium, which disregards many potentially relevant variables on the ground that they are probably of minor influence (so that their repercussions can be left out of the explanatory model). More often, however, the principles will be seen in terms of general equilibrium with many more mutually interdependent variables. Even a system of general equilibrium can be made relatively simple by including only a few products, still fewer productive factors, only a few individual countries and only a small choice of financial assets; by excluding such spoilsports as increasing returns to scale or non-convex preferences and by assuming relatively stable propensities, elasticities and reaction times. Of course, a proof that equilibrium 'exists' reassures us only that its conditions are mutually consistent, not that any observable situation in the real world can properly be characterised as an equilibrium. Equilibrium exists only in the analyst's imagination and refers to a never-reached endpoint of an imaginary causal chain extending into the future. Equilibrium serves as a mental aid in explaining certain changes as likely adaptations to a change that is assumed to be a primary disturbance.

Proceeding from accounting to economics, we ought to point to a significant change in expression: no longer should we speak of a *balance* of one account *implying* a change in the balance of another account. Instead, we should speak of *types of particular transactions that tend to induce* other kinds of transactions by causing, through market signals, certain economic agents to change their minds and decide on a different course of action. We will not stress this point on every page, but it would be helpful to the reader if he never forgot that sound economic reasoning about effects should include the interventions of human minds in the process of receiving information and deciding on action.

Autonomous and Induced Items

Unfortunately, much of the discourse on the balance of payments is characterised by unhelpful stereotypes. Using again the schematic balance of payments arranged in three major accounts, we find different schools of thought inclined to argue that transactions on one or two of the accounts should be regarded as autonomous, causing transactions on the other accounts to adjust. Some of the protagonists of these schools provide theoretical descriptions of the processes of equilibration by which changes in the induced items are brought about. The following alternative, or rival, approaches can be found in the literature:

(1) Current transactions are autonomous and compel capital and reserve transactions to adjust.

(2) Current transactions and capital transactions (especially long-term capital) together are autonomous and compel reserve transactions to adjust.

(3) Capital transactions (especially long-term capital) are autonomous and compel current and (temporarily) reserve transactions to adjust.

(4) Reserve transactions, together with other determinants of national monetary aggregates, are autonomous and compel

current and capital transactions (long- and short-term) to adjust.

(5) Reserve transactions and non-reserve short-term capital transactions involving near-money assets, together with other determinants of national monetary aggregates, are autonomous and compel current transactions and non-liquid-capital transactions to adjust.

This is not a complete round-robin: logically, six combinations are possible for three factors, in pairs or singly, to influence the other one or two. But no one has taken the missing approach, at least not to my knowledge: no theorists have been tempted to argue that current- and reserve-account transactions combined would compel the non-reserve capital transactions to adjust.[4]

The literature offers few clear instances in which unambiguous claims of *exclusivity* are made on behalf of one of the five approaches or theories. Yet, many expositors of the causal relationships among different categories of international transactions have presented strong arguments in support of the *prevalence* or *dominance* of one of the positions. These positions will be referred to here as:

(1) the theory of the autonomy of current-account transactions,

(2) the theory of the autonomy of either the basic balance or the 'overall' non-reserve balance,

(3) the theory of the autonomy of long-term capital movements,

(4) the theory of the autonomy of monetary movements, and

(5) the theory of the pervasive influence of money and near-money items, or all financial assets.

Some writers single out one of these theories as the 'traditional' position; this designation may be confusing, because it has happened that two or three different traditions existed side by side.

Autonomy of the Current Account

The position that transactions on current account—chiefly flows of goods and services—are independent of other international transactions implicitly denies that these flows are influenced, let alone determined, by movements of capital and/or money. This anti-monetarism was most vigorously expounded by the English 'anti-bullionists' between 1797, when specie payments were suspended, and 1825, after the Bank of England had restored the convertibility of its banknotes into gold coins. The bullionists had explained the high price of gold bullion, along with higher prices of commodities and foreign currencies, by an excess supply of paper money; the anti-bullionists reversed the direction of the causal sequence and pointed to the needs for large imports and, particularly, for heavy remittances to foreign countries as the prime causes of the depreciation of the paper money. The state of the current account was, in this 'anti-monetarist' view, not a consequence of monetary expansion but, instead, the autonomous cause of the depreciation of English banknotes in terms of gold and foreign exchange.[5]

Similar views were expressed occasionally during the rest of the nineteenth century; but in the twentieth century the autonomy of the current account became the fervent creed of fanatic anti-monetarists during the German hyper-inflation after World War I. In their view, the depreciation of the German mark in the foreign-exchange markets was not, as the 'inflation theorists' said, the consequence of the huge expansion of the money stock; instead, it was to be attributed to the needs for large imports. This 'naive balance-of-payments theory' of the external depreciation of the mark became the official theory of the German central bank in justifying its expansionary policy: the 'autonomous' trade deficit of the balance of payments caused higher prices of foreign currencies, which in turn caused higher prices of imported goods and, in consequence, also of domestic goods, which reduced the real value of the domestic money stock, which compelled the central bank to replenish the 'real' money supply by printing more and more paper currency.[6]

'The fallacy of the autonomy or independence of the balance of trade' re-emerged during the debate about German reparations payments.[7] The solution to the transfer problem depends, obviously, on the working of the adjustment mechanism. The levying of taxes on the people in the paying country and the use of the transferred purchasing power in the receiving country are supposed to change incomes and prices in such ways as to increase exports and reduce imports in the paying country. John Maynard Keynes, the renowned British economist, however, held that trade flows were insensitive:

> 'My own view is that at a given time the economic structure of a country, in relation to the economic structures of its neighbours, permits of a certain "natural" level of exports, and that arbitrarily to effect a material alteration of this level by

deliberate devices is extremely difficult. Historically, the volume of foreign investment has tended, I think, to adjust itself—at least to a certain extent—to the balance of trade, rather than the other way round, the former being the sensitive and the latter the insensitive factor. In the case of German Reparations, on the other hand, we are trying to fix the volume of foreign remittance and compel the balance of trade to adjust itself thereto. Those who see no difficulty in this . . . are applying the theory of liquids to what is, if not a solid, at least a sticky mass with strong internal resistances.'[8]

In claiming that the trade balance is insensitive to the flows of funds—reparations payments as well as capital movements—Keynes cast his vote in favour of the theory of the autonomy of the trade flows. In the cited context this autonomy is anchored in the belief in 'the economic structure of a country, in relation to the economic structures of its neighbours'. In his opposition to the theory of the autonomy of capital movements Keynes later fell back on other arguments. These will be discussed in connection with theory number '3'.

Autonomy of the Basic Balance or the Overall
Non-reserve Balance

A survey of balance-of-payments theories, not long ago, contained the statement that 'there is no widely accepted theory incorporating both current and capital account items'.[9] This judgment may have presupposed a restrictive definition of the term 'theory', since there is no scarcity of interpretations that merge the current account and long-term capital into a 'basic' balance of payments, which is supposed to determine movements of short-term capital and official reserves. And the more comprehensive merger of all non-reserve transactions into one overall balance of payments offset by 'compensatory financing' has had wide currency.[10]

Walter R. Gardner defined 'autonomous transactions' as 'the miscellany of merchandise, service, and capital transactions undertaken because of the profit to be made or because of political or other ends that are sought for reasons of their own'.[11] By 'reasons of their own' he evidently meant to exclude only one reason: to accommodate an excess supply or excess demand in the foreign-exchange market. He went on to say that:

'we have autonomous transactions above the line matched by

compensatory financing below the line. The compensatory financing may take the form of a movement of reserves, or a drawing on the International Monetary Fund, or the use of ad hoc loans or other financing for the purpose. It is only as we draw a line of this sort and group above it the autonomous transactions, and group below it the compensatory financing that comes into play only because the autonomous transactions fail to balance, that we see what it is that is pushing the country's international exchange rate up or down and creating an exchange-market problem.'[12]

Mr Gardner distinguished an intermediate type of transaction between the basic balance and compensatory financing, namely, net movements of 'open-market capital'. The transactions recorded in the basic balance 'include most of the fundamental and persistent elements in the balance of payments'. Under the heading 'open-market capital' Mr Gardner 'gathered . . . all those forms of capital movement that can easily shift from market to market—a sort of footloose capital'. This sub-category of the capital account includes portfolio investment in stocks and bonds and private short-term balances, besides errors and omissions. It is in the open-market-capital balance that 'wide swings back and forth' will be found; this is why it is not admitted into the basic balance, but is regarded as a part of the autonomous balance that requires offsetting by compensatory financing.[13]

I have found serious fault with the conception of compensatory financing.[14] This may be surprising to some who know that I coined a rather similar phrase: accommodating capital movements.[15] The difference between the two concepts is that one is designed for balance-of-payments statistics, the other for theoretical analysis. I deny the possibility of identifying *ex post* the mass of transactions, or even worse, any net balance of transactions spread over several months up to a year, as autonomous or not autonomous; yet, precisely this identification is attempted by some analysts of the accounting balance of payments.[16] On the other hand, I consider accommodating capital movements, such as interventions of the central bank in the foreign-exchange market, to be causally significant in an analysis of changes in the market balance of payments.[17] This significance is related to the pervasive influence of changes in monetary aggregates. The accommodating capital movements in the form of obligatory sales and purchases of foreign exchange (or gold) by monetary authorities under a true gold or gold-exchange standard, or under any other tight regime of fixed exchange rates, can be regarded as automatic and, therefore, as truly induced or caused by excess demand or excess supply in the foreign-exchange market. In this case, all transactions on official-reserve account can be regarded as induced. This does not, however, make all transactions on current and private-capital account autonomous. Many of these transactions will be induced by the monetary effects of the movements of official reserves. Repercussions must not be confused with spontaneous disturbances.

Mr Gardner's theory of the autonomy of the 'exchange-market balance', that is, the basic balance combined with the open-market-capital balance, has entered several textbooks. Thus, in the text of Paul T. Ellsworth, autonomous transactions are defined as those 'that are undertaken for their own sake, for the profit they entail or the satisfaction they give', and 'induced transactions' as those that result from 'autonomous transactions'.[18]

The 'balance on basic transactions' is recognised as the one 'to focus on long-run trends and deep-seated economic forces that change only slowly'. It 'supposedly divides transactions affected by enduring from those affected by transitory influences'.[19] The inclusion of short-term capital movements among autonomous transactions is said to be justified in so far as they are 'motivated by the desire to earn a higher return, to make a speculative gain' or as they are 'made for their own sake'. This reasoning overlooks the fact that the higher return on funds placed abroad, or expected capital gains from such placements, may well be a consequence of (that is, induced by) transactions on trade account, current account, or in the basic balance, or (perhaps most importantly) in the official-reserve balance.

There can be no serious objection to separating, in the statistical tables, balances on official-reserve account from other capital balances. What is objectionable is the designation of all items other than reserve movements as autonomous, that is, not dependent on other international transactions. A large part of the non-reserve transactions is probably induced by the consequences of reserve transactions. That is to say, many transactions on the merchandise account, in other parts of the current account and on the private-capital account, would not exist or would be of different magnitudes were it not for certain changes in liquidity, interest rates, effective demand, income, employment, output and prices, that are consequences of changes in official reserves and in the associated money

G

aggregates brought about by official operations in the foreign-exchange market. There is no conceivable way to trace such causal relationships and to identify the individual 'induced' transactions. But to designate transactions as autonomous merely because they are not official-reserve transactions is utterly unreasonable.

Autonomy of Long-term Capital Movements

One of the most absorbing controversies in this area has centred on the rival claims of autonomy of the trade balance and of the long-term capital balance. Keynes was quoted above as a protagonist of the autonomy of trade flows. Gottfried Haberler considers this as the 'modern' approach, in contradistinction to 'classical' analysis or 'traditional' theory, according to which 'capital movements are usually regarded as an active, autonomous, factor which induces a change in the trade balances'.[20] Likewise, Jacob Viner, after citing Keynes as having 'maintained that historically the international movement of long-term capital has adjusted itself to the trade balance rather than the trade balance to capital movements', referred to the support of 'the opposite, and traditional, view' of the American economist, F. W. Taussig.[21] I have referred to the two views as 'neo-classical' and 'neo-mercantilist', respectively.[22]

In Keynes' statement quoted in support of his claim for the autonomy of the trade balance, the argument was based on the structural determination of the movements of goods and their insensitiveness to influences from the side of money and demand. In his later denial of the autonomy of capital movements, the argument was different. Keynes no longer disregarded the effects of changes in income—he had discovered the marginal propensities to consume and to import—but he had decided to merge long-term capital, short-term capital and official reserves into one all-embracing capital account. The receipt of foreign long-term loans and investments would be offset by a holding of liquid foreign balances, so that for the time being no net capital movement would take place. Only after net imports of goods had been received would, through the payments for this trade deficit, a net flow of capital (usually in the form of reserve balances) be recorded. In this sense, it is the trade balance that 'dictates' changes in the capital account.[23]

This is no longer a real controversy in theoretical analysis. There is, on the one hand, the theory that movements of long-term capital are ordinarily autonomous, that is, not induced by trade imbalances, and that these movements are likely to affect international trade, either through associated reserve movements, expansions or contractions in money stocks, changes in interest rates, effective demand, incomes and prices, or through associated changes in foreign-exchange rates and relative prices. This is a theory about causes and their probable effects. On the other hand, there is the statement that movements of long-term capital, as long as they are not matched by changes in commodity trade, are 'necessarily' offset by counter-movements of short-term capital, usually in the form of official reserves; and that a *net* capital movement cannot be registered before a *net* change in the current account is registered. This is a truism; the identity of the two net changes is a matter of accounting definitions. Since the difference between autonomous and induced events is a matter of causal probability and not of definitional tautology, attempts to deny the autonomy of long-term capital movements by taking recourse to definitional resolutions cannot be sustained.

This does not mean that there cannot be historical situations in which a trade deficit occurs first (financed by accommodating capital imports in the form of a depletion of the official foreign reserves or borrowing rights of the importing country) and is followed by long-term foreign loans sought and received for the purpose of replenishing the official reserves. Indeed, such situations have been well publicised in the recent years of drastic oil-price troubles. These situations, however, are exceptional. An economic historian would have a difficult time trying to explain large international flows of direct investment or long-term loans as consequences of preceding trade deficits of the receiving countries and of trade surpluses of the lending and investing countries.[24] The idea that capitalists and financiers, in selecting the places to make direct investments, or the governments and business firms whose long-term bonds they wish to purchase, should favour countries with existing trade deficits is too funny to be accepted. The classical idea that countries that were able to attract foreign investors and to obtain long-term loans from abroad were using the funds received to purchase imports and incur trade deficits is plausible, indeed, cogent.[25]

Endogenous Monetary Movements: Fixed
Exchange Rates

The balance of official-reserve transactions can be regarded as a *dependent* variable if, but only if, the monetary authorities are committed to purchase, at a fixed price, all the foreign exchange that is offered and to sell, at the same (or slightly higher) price, all the foreign exchange that is demanded. Under these conditions, changes in official reserves may be regarded as *induced* by, or an automatic result of, all transactions that make up supply and demand in the foreign-exchange market. (Note, however, that quarterly or annual net balances reported in balance-of-payments statistics do not show transactions or excess supply or demand on any market day. Annual net data may mask successions of large net inflows and net outflows of reserves.)

Under a regime of absolutely fixed exchange rates (pegged by unrestricted purchases and sales of reserve assets by the monetary authorities) and of fixed links between official reserves and the total stock of money, both reserve movements and money supply are dependent on all international transactions on current and capital account. The dependence in this case runs both ways, since there are repercussions from monetary changes on flows of goods, services and private capital funds. This interdependence is precisely what was implied in the classical theory of the specie-flow mechanism and the self-regulation of the balance of payments. The specie flow or, more generally, the flow of reserve assets, was entirely dependent on international transactions in goods, services and transfers: on the other hand, foreign trade and private-capital movements could be either autonomous or induced by the changes in money supply that resulted from the movements of official reserves.

If no fixed link is maintained between changes in reserves and changes in the stock of domestic money, the money supply may, in the short run, change independently of reserve movements. Domestic credit creation may then be regarded as autonomous (spontaneous, exogenous) and will affect international flows of goods, services and funds: however, these flows will in turn induce automatic movements of official reserves with associated adjustments of the domestic money supply. This dependence of reserve movements had led many analysts to assert that a gold-standard, or fixed-exchange-rate regime, makes total money stocks an endogenous variable, not subject to arbitrary management by the monetary authorities, at least not in the long run.[26] Domestic credit expansion (proceeding at a faster rate than expansion abroad) will induce outflows of private capital and imports of foreign goods and services, which results in a loss of reserve assets and pares down the domestic money supply, perhaps to its initial level. Another influence from the side of money may come from changes in the demand for money balances; this separate force in the determination of the balance of payments has in recent years engaged the analysts' interest with increasing intensity and will call for comment later on.

The above propositions about induced, or even automatic, changes in official reserves applied to a regime of permanently fixed exchange rates. They are not valid under a system of managed flexibility of rates. When there are no definite and binding obligations for the monetary authorities to purchase and to sell foreign exchange at fixed prices, it is easier and more appropriate to regard all their interventions and, therefore, all changes in foreign-reserve holdings as autonomous transactions.

Autonomy of Monetary Movements: Managed Exchange Rates

Changes in official reserves are of strategic importance because they influence directly and indirectly the supply of money. The *direct* influence is through the creation or destruction of both central-bank money (monetary base, high-powered money) and commercial-bank money in the process of buying or selling foreign exchange. One *indirect* influence is through the positive or negative effect on domestic credit creation by the central bank, another through the effect on deposit liabilities of banks whose money-creating capacity depends on the size of the monetary base. Some theorists express this in an equation that states the stock of domestic money as a function of the sum of the foreign and domestic assets acquired by the central bank, multiplied by a coefficient named the 'money multiplier'. Besides interest rates, the consequent changes in the money stock affect total spending, employment, prices, production and income and, thereby, imports and exports of goods and services as well as sales and purchases of assets to and from foreign residents. It is through these processes that the 'autonomous' movements in official reserves induce changes in other international transactions on current and non-reserve-capital accounts.

The balance of official-reserve transactions, also called the balance of official settlements, is not a perfect proxy for what some writers of the modern monetarist school have named the 'monetary-base-effect balance'. One difference between the two may be due to the fact that the official-settlements account of the United States 'includes changes in foreign official holdings of US Treasury

securities and of commercial-bank deposits in the United States'.[27]
These are official transactions that do not change the monetary
base in the countries whose central banks acquire or dispose of some
of their foreign-exchange reserves in these forms. (Institutions and
practices are not the same in different countries. Too many generalisations are made on the basis of conditions specific to the United
States.)

Where central banks manage the exchange rates by means of
operations in the foreign-exchange markets and, in the process,
change the size of the monetary base as they change their reserve
position, it is reasonable to regard these changes as autonomous
causes of all sorts of private transactions on current and capital
accounts. The trouble is that one cannot be sure just what will
happen as a result of a particular monetary change, say, an increase
in reserves:

(1) The central bank may reinforce the effects of the reserve
increase by increasing its domestic assets as well.

(2) The central bank may offset the reserve increase by reducing its domestic assets.

(3) Commercial banks may, through their lending activities,
increase or reduce the ratio of deposit liabilities to their own
reserves.

(4) Non-banks may increase or reduce the ratio of their
average cash balances to their total transactions.

(5) Individuals and firms may use their surplus cash balances
for the purchase of domestic goods and services.

(6) They may purchase more imported goods.

(7) They may acquire domestic securities.

(8) They may acquire foreign long-term assets.

(9) They may acquire foreign short-term assets.

Economists are prone to consider assumptions as almost perfect
substitutes for knowledge, or perfect antidotes for ignorance.
Thus, instead of wavering between the diametrically opposite
possibilities regarding the first two reactions of the central bank, one
'simply' assumes that the bank would follow a fixed rule, at least
in the intermediate run, of adjusting domestic credit to reserve
holdings. In order to deal with the uncertain reactions of the commercial banks—see '3' above—one assumes a constant 'money
multiplier', making the total of *M1* a definite multiple of the
monetary base. In order to get rid of the bothersome uncertainty
regarding the possible reactions of non-banks—see '4' above—one

assumes a given demand for money (or a given velocity of circulation of money), stable over time, although perhaps not from week to week. In order to cope with the several possibilities mentioned under the numbers '5' to '9' above, one assumes given marginal propensities to buy this or that (or given income elasticities of demand for this or that) and given asset-preference maps for portfolio selections and so forth. With all these coefficients, given, fixed, constant, or stable, all outcomes are determinate and predictable. The question, however, is whether we have any right, earned by empirical evidence, to assume that any of the mentioned (plus some unmentioned) coefficients are stable enough and knowable enough to allow a human economist—aided by artificial intelligence—to engage in predictions.

One can make the forecasters' lives easier by forgetting the distribution of additional purchasing power among different things to purchase. One need not pretend to know just how people will spend their extra cash, but may be satisfied with stating the probability that some indefinite portions of it will go for the acquisition of imported goods, for direct and portfolio investment abroad and, perhaps, for some deposit balances in foreign currency. In any case, there will be induced changes in the current account, long-term capital account and short-term capital account, all resulting from the increased acquisition of foreign-reserve assets by the central bank. If this is all that the monetary approach to the balance of payments is intended to convey, one cannot see why anybody should object to its findings. What it essentially says, although in a more convoluted way of speaking, is that a country that accelerates its money creation beyond the pace chosen by its major trading partners will soon find either its current and private-capital accounts getting into deficit—if there are monetary reserves to finance deficits—or its currency getting depreciated, if there are no official reserve transactions which permit such deficits.

Flows and Stocks and Equilibria

Monetarists and other portfolio theorists, on the one hand, and non-monetarists, on the other, usually approach problems from different angles. It used to be commonplace to think and speak about transactions within some (short or long) period of time, that is, about flows per period: about *flows* of goods and services, incomes and transfers, private funds and official reserves; and about disturbances of the equilibrium among the different sorts of flows and the adjustments needed to restore 'flow equilibrium'. Monetarists and portfolio theorists, however, prefer to think and speak about *stocks* of moneys, domestic and foreign, and stocks of other financial assets of various sorts (including claims and debts) and about disturbances of the equilibrium among different kinds of stocks and the adjustments needed to restore 'stock equilibrium'. The difference between these two interpretations has implications that need to be explored.

At first blush, the difference between stocks and flows seems quite straightforward. There exists at any moment in time a stock of the assets regarded as money; this stock can be increased or reduced, and the creation and destruction of money can be seen as flows within some period of time. Money is always held by *somebody*, so that the money holdings of all individuals, firms and agencies add up to the total stock. Each holder, however, can add to his stock by disbursing less than he receives, or reduce his stock by disbursing more than he receives. These inflows and outflows are sometimes called hoarding (autonomous or induced) and dishoarding (autonomous or induced), which definitely constitute flows over periods of time. They need not affect the total stock of money of the entire community, but merely its distribution among different holders. Analysts have occasionally been snared by the ambiguous notions of 'net hoarding' or 'net dishoarding' with the total money stock remaining unchanged; they have failed to see that autonomous hoardings, or autonomous increases of money holdings by some holders, impose on others instantaneous reductions of receipts and thus of money holdings and eventually induce others—through market adjustments of prices of goods, services and assets (interest rates and all sorts of incomes)—to increase their disbursements relatively to receipts and be satisfied with smaller money balances. This is a rather complicated process to visualise and its essentials were capsuled in a model of the demand for 'money to hold', depicted by a curve showing the nominal quantity of money demanded (by all members of the nation in question) as a function of prices of goods, services and/or securities.[28]

The real purpose of models featuring a demand for holding stocks of a certain type of asset is to explain *flows* as stock adjustments 'dictated' to holders by some 'disturbance' that has made their stocks excessive or insufficient relative to their preferences. Disturbance and restoration of 'stock equilibrium' is a mental device for the explanation of a supply or demand in the market for a particular type of asset during one or more periods of time. It should be clear that this device is helpful only in connection with markets in which an overwhelming share of the trade is attributable to stock-shifts, that is, to redistributions in the holdings of existing stock. The device is inappropriate in connection with markets in which the larger part of the flow comes from new production and goes into use for processing and consumption.

Probably the most typical of the markets serving chiefly the redistribution of existing stock is the 'stock market' or 'stock exchange', that is, the market for shares of corporate stock. The bond market is similarly constituted as a place in which existing securities are traded, with relatively few new issues being floated and even fewer redeemed. The largest part of the turnover in both these markets consists of flows due to stock readjustments by particular holders. Only a tiny fraction of the annual turnover of securities—shares and bonds—relates to new issues. When we ask, however, what economic purposes the securities markets are ultimately to serve, we learn that they are designed to channel a flow of funds derived from new saving into presumably productive investment. We know, of course, that not all new funds used for purchasing securities will actually go to sellers of new securities issued by corporations or agencies that plan new productive investments. Some flows of new saving may result only in capital gains used by the sellers for increased consumption, so that the new saving is offset by new dissaving. Traditional theory says that enlarged inflows of funds are likely to raise prices of securities and thereby attract offers of new issues and consequently enlarged outflows of funds into uses that include real investment. In a way, therefore, the tiny fraction of the flows of new saving and new securities may matter more than the redistribution of existing assets through continual stock readjustments realised in the markets. (What 'matters more' is, of course, a judgment founded on positive and evaluative economics.)

International Capital Movements: the Role of Stock Adjustment

If 'stock adjustment' and 'stock equilibrium' are regarded as fundamental in the explanation of both the flows of money balances from one holder to another and the flows of securities and other financial assets from one holder to another, the question arises whether international capital movements should be seen essentially as flows of investible funds from residents of one country to residents of another country or merely as a redistribution of possession or ownership of existing stocks of financial assets. Perhaps what was said about domestic stock markets and bond markets is valid also for international capital transactions, namely, that the *bulk* of transactions during any period, short or long, is nothing but the redistribution of existing stocks of assets. But *what matters*, especially in the long run, is an international flow of investible funds from savers and disinvestors in one country channelled into new real investments in another country. The older literature, in the nineteenth century and in the first half of the twentieth, looked at international capital movements largely in this way, that is, as flows of investible funds; more recent writers have found it more helpful, perhaps more realistic, to regard international capital movements almost entirely as portfolio adjustments.

I submit that the two points of view are not mutually exclusive (but, instead, complementary) and that the length of the period involved is the major criterion for choosing between them. Within a short period the flow of new saving into new real investment counts for too small a portion of the total stocks of assets to be accorded first place in the analyst's attention; he will prefer to reason in terms of portfolio preferences and stock adjustments. Within a long period, however, with stocks of assets increasing and total holdings abroad growing substantially, stock equilibrium, confined to the optimal distribution of *given* amounts of wealth, will appear less relevant. Not that the model of stock adjustment could not be serviceable under conditions of growth, but the older models of flow equilibrium seem easier to handle.

In short-run analysis, attention to stock adjustment is of the essence. To some extent this is so because the stocks of financial assets ordinarily include near-money and liquid foreign assets. If the monetary authorities are not the only source of supply of domestic and foreign money, but if financial intermediaries, private dealers and transnational corporations can disgorge previously inactive stocks of domestic and foreign assets that are money, quasi-money, or money substitutes, suitable to satisfy a demand for holding (if not also a demand for money to pay out), then it is clear that stock adjustment with regard to financial assets can be disregarded only at the peril of inadequate comprehension.

The Pervasive Influence of Money Stocks and Other Financial Assets

To recognise the explanatory power of new theories that emphasise the pervasive influence of the supply of, and demand for, stocks of financial assets including money and near-money is not to accept all the contentions of their proponents. Indeed, in as much as they contradict one another, acceptance would be impossible; and an attempt at a general criticism would be unfair to some. Sometimes it is difficult to compare different expositions because they focus on different assumptions: fixed exchange rates, managed exchange rates, or freely flexible exchange rates. A portfolio approach to the balance of payments at fixed exchange rates is in several respects different from a portfolio approach to the determination of exchange rates in the absence of official pegging.

For an adequate examination of some of the essential constructs and models of the monetary, monetarist and portfolio-theoretic approaches to the determination of the balance of payments and exchange rates, I would have to engage first in a methodological and conceptual discourse. I must defer such an undertaking for another occasion. But there is some unfinished business that should not be deferred. Having discussed the cases of fixed and of managed exchange rates, we have still to deal with the case of freely flexible rates.

Absence of Reserve Movements: Freely Flexible Exchange Rates

Under a regime of exchange-rate management, the monetary authorities decide on buying or selling foreign currency for or from their reserves, and in this way they increase or reduce the stock of national money except when they completely offset these changes by opposite changes in their portfolio of domestic loans and securities. The deliberate changes in the money stock engender changes in transactions on current account and private-capital account. Thus, many changes in transactions on current and private-capital account are seen as induced items.

Things are altogether different when the assumption of *managed* flexibility is changed to one of *free* flexibility of exchange rates. Free flexibility implies non-intervention by the monetary authorities, thus no official purchases or sales of foreign exchange and, hence, no effects on the national stock of money. The balance of official settlements or official-reserve transactions is now stuck at zero, and zero-changes cannot exert any influences on other international transactions, at least not in ways envisioned by models of money-stock equilibrium. The zero balance in the official-reserve account makes variations of foreign-exchange rates all but inevitable and these variations cause transactions on current and private-capital accounts to adjust.

The absence of change on official-reserve account need not eliminate or reduce the role of the monetary approach. But instead of an approach to the balance of payments it will now largely be an approach to exchange-rate determination. Two possible influences from the side of money remain: one is exerted by the domestic part of monetary policy, that is, expansion or contraction of domestic bank credit; the other is exerted by the non-official part of international movements of short-term capital, that is, the movement of private money assets, especially deposit liabilities of commercial banks.

Monetary policy in the form of expanding or contracting domestic bank credit is, in the analysis of changes in the balance of payments under a regime of freely floating exchange rates, definitely an *exogenous* factor. Through its effects on interest rates and securities prices it tends to change international capital movements; through its effects on money supply, aggregate spending, demand for imports, product prices and supply of exports it tends to change transactions on current account. These tendencies, since accommodating movements of reserve balance are excluded, will push foreign-exchange rates (up or down) to such levels as will compel the sum of the balances on current and capital account to *remain at zero*. The containment of these two accounts to the zero-sum state is not just the (tautological) implication of identities in the *ex post* accounting-balance of payments, but also an implication of behavioural assumptions regarding market reactions to offers and bids in the foreign-exchange market.

In the case of an expansion of domestic bank credit, the domestic currency will fall in the exchange market. At the changed exchange rate—and this change cannot help being almost instantaneous—the mentioned tendencies will be partly attenuated and partly offset by countervailing transactions. For example, although the demand for imports will surely increase as a result of the monetary expansion, the quantity of actual imports or their total value in terms of foreign currency need not increase. Why not? Because the higher price of foreign currency raises the domestic price of importable goods so that the right-shift of the demand curve for imports may be offset by an upward movement along the (negatively inclined) demand curve. Analogous counter-forces may operate on the tendency towards reduced exports. Even the tendency of private capital funds to move out of the country that has expanded domestic credit, and thereby created a relative surfeit of money, may be offset by its external depreciation if this depreciation is expected to be only temporary (so that the promise of capital gains may even attract foreign capital), or if the monetary expansion promotes an industrial expansion that attracts foreign capital funds. These possibilities are mentioned here only to avoid the suspicion of dogmatism; still, the *most likely consequence* of domestic credit expansion remains a *tendency* towards deficits in current and capital transactions, *counteracted* by a depreciation of the currency, as long as no official support of the exchange rate is forthcoming.

Immediate, Fast, Slow or Never

The questions of the speed with which currency depreciation follows the expansion of domestic bank credit and the speed with which international transactions on current and private-capital account equilibrate after the currency depreciation have sometimes been discussed with astounding black-outs of logic.

The role of logic lies in inferences from explicit assumptions. How quickly incremental bank credits lead to increased demand and increased spending, including demand and spending for imports, is sometimes, but surely not always, implied in stated assumptions. Whether the increase in bank lending actually leads to a *reduction* in interest rates or, perhaps because of fears of accelerated inflation of prices and incomes, to an *increase* in interest rates, and whether this will or will not attract capital funds from abroad, cannot be inferred from the traditional set of assumptions. On the other hand, if demand for imports and/or foreign financial assets does increase as a result of domestic credit expansion, then the *immediate and fully effective depreciation* of the currency in the foreign-exchange market is a logical implication of the assumption that this market is free from restrictions as well as interventions by the authorities. Movements of official reserves, and therefore official sales of foreign exchange, are excluded by the assumption of freely floating exchange rates: since nobody can buy what nobody sells, any increase in the demand for foreign currency can be met only by increased supply and/or at the expense of would-be purchasers squeezed out of the market by higher prices of foreign currency. If new supply (say, through increased exports) is slow in coming and if it takes time to squeeze out persistent bidders in the foreign-exchange market, this does not retard the currency depreciation in becoming effective; it merely makes it more drastic. Should an increase in the prices of foreign currencies by 10 or 20 per cent not be enough to do the job, the increase may be 50 or 100 per cent—or whatever percentage is required to keep imports down, get capital funds in and perhaps push exports up. What in actual fact will most likely balance the accounts—not eventually, but immediately—are enhanced capital imports through the liquidation of foreign financial assets which private holders will be induced to sell at what they think are extraordinarily good prices.

The point is logically quite simple: if no foreign exchange is donated, lent, or sold by official agencies, then imports of commodities and exports of capital can be paid for (and hence take place) only to the extent that the buyers of foreign goods, services and financial assets can acquire foreign exchange from exporters of goods, services and financial assets. Offers of high prices for the foreign exchange may be required to induce the transactions that yield the exchange or to suppress the demand on the part of would-be buyers. The result, however, the zero-sum of the balances of current and private-capital transactions, is 'certain' because it follows from the stated assumptions.

Experience is said to contradict these conclusions: substantial variations in exchange rates have been observed and yet imbalances on current and private-capital accounts have not compensated each other to yield a net balance of zero. The explanation is that exchange rates were not freely flexible, but were managed, so that net deficits (or net surpluses) on current and private-capital account could exist thanks to financing from official reserves. This need not mean that the world would be a better place if authorities were not interfering with the balancing acts of free economic agents and free economic forces. The interventions by official agencies have the very purpose of slowing down the adjustments and equilibrations described in the economists' models because it is widely felt that fast adjustments are too painful. If it hurts too much to have things done in a hurry, one can well understand an effort at slowing them down. But then one should not complain that 'theory' is 'wrong' in as much as it 'promised' quick restoration of equilibrium after disturbance.

NOTES AND REFERENCES

1. *Balance of Payments Yearbook*, Vol. 31, International Monetary Fund, Washington, 1980, p.v.

2. The holdings of long-term United States Treasury securities (bonds and notes) by international financial institutions vary from quarter to quarter: they increased by \$939 million in the second quarter of 1978, fell by \$1,307 million in the third quarter, increased by \$735 million in the fourth quarter and fell by \$524 million in the first quarter of 1979, to fall by another \$556 million in the second quarter. Demand deposits in American banks held by foreign commercial banks fell by \$446 million in the third quarter of 1978, rose by \$1,538 million in the fourth quarter, fell again by \$1,892 million in the first quarter of 1979, to rise again by \$1,798 million in the second quarter. The figures have been taken from *Survey of Current Business*, US Department of Commerce, Washington, June 1980, p. 54, Table 9.

3. In some countries the statistical discrepancies are especially large in years when the capital account undergoes large changes, including changes in signs that indicate a reversal in the direction of capital flows. In 1971, when outflows of American capital jumped from \$9,300 million in the previous year to \$12,500 million, and inflows of foreign capital jumped from \$6,400 million to \$23,000 million, omissions were \$9,800 million, which could have been unrecorded outflows. In 1976, when recorded outflows jumped from \$39,700 million the year before to \$51,300 million, and inflows jumped from \$15,700 million to \$36,500 million, the statistical discrepancy was plus \$10,400 million, which could be under-reported capital inflows. Errors and omissions in the United States statistics reached a record in 1979 with plus \$23,800 million; recorded capital inflows in that year had gone down from \$64,100 million to \$37,600 million.

4. These formulations of alternative positions seem to leave no place for the 'portfolio approach' to the balance of payments. This will not keep me from alluding to it in connection with the 'monetary approach' accommodated by positions '4' and '5'.

5. For a scholarly and fascinating history of these ideas, see Jacob Viner, *Studies in the Theory of International Trade* (New York: Harper, 1937), pp. 119-217.

6. I combatted the naïve balance-of-payments theory in my first book, *Die Goldkernwährung: Eine währungsgeschichtliche und währungstheoretische Untersuchung* (Halberstadt: Meyer, 1925). See my comments on this controversy in my article 'My Early Work on International Monetary Problems', *Banca Nazionale del Lavoro Quarterly Review*, Rome, June 1980, especially pp. 118-20.

7. The quoted phrase is from my article 'Währung und Auslandsverschuldung: Bemerkungen zur Diskussion zwischen Schacht und seinen Kritikern', *Mitteilungen des Verbandes Österreichischer Banken und Bankiers*, Vienna, September 1928, p. 202. English translation, as 'Foreign Debts, Reparations, and the Transfer Problem', in Fritz Machlup, *International Payments, Debts, and Gold: Collected Essays* (New York: Charles Scribner's Sons, 1964; reprinted New York: New York University Press, 1976) p. 408.

8. John Maynard Keynes, 'The German Transfer Problem', *The*

Economic Journal, London, March 1929, p. 6.

9. Anne O. Krueger, 'Balance-of-Payments Theory', *The Journal of Economic Literature*, Menasha, Wisconsin, March 1969, p. 2.

10. The concept 'compensatory official financing' was developed by the staff of the IMF under the leadership of Walter R. Gardner. The 'new concept' was designed to cover 'the financing undertaken by the monetary authorities [not only the central bank] to provide exchange to cover a surplus or deficit in the rest of the balance of payments' (possibly including some flows of short-term capital). See *Balance of Payments Yearbook 1938, 1946, 1947* (Washington: International Monetary Fund, 1949), p. 5.

11. Walter R. Gardner, *An Exchange-Market Analysis of the U.S. Balance of Payments*, Staff Papers (Washington: International Monetary Fund, 1961), p. 196.

12. *Ibid.*, Gardner's illusion is that we can 'see' what happens in the market. We cannot even guess what is 'autonomous' and what is 'induced'. Of course, we can 'see' where a statistician has been moved to draw his 'line' between different categories of items.

13. *Ibid.*, pp. 198-99.

14. Machlup, 'Three Concepts of the Balance of Payments and the So-Called Dollar Shortage', *The Economic Journal*, March 1950, especially pp. 62-67. Also in *idem, International Payments, Debts, and Gold: Collected Essays, op. cit.*, pp. 84-88.

15. Machlup, *International Trade and the National Income Multiplier* (Philadelphia: Blakiston, 1943; reprinted New York: Kelley, 1961), pp. 130-35, especially pp. 134 and 135.

16. 'In an analysis of the foreign-exchange market it is essential to distinguish, for example, between imports which give rise to additional demand for foreign exchange, and imports which are induced by additional supply of foreign exchange. The accounting balance of payments, regardless of the way the accounts are selected, cannot say anything about such problems. All imports are considered as representing a demand for foreign exchange.' See Machlup, 'Three Concepts of the Balance of Payments and the So-Called Dollar Shortage' *loc. cit.*, p. 62, footnote 1, and *ibid.*, in Machlup, *International Payments, Debts, and Gold: Collected Essays, op. cit.*, p. 84, footnote 21.

17. James E. Meade adopted my phrase. He divided the 'accommodating payments' into those made by private persons, like foreign-exchange dealers, and those by public authorities, like governments and central banks; and he also distinguished between 'automatic, i.e. unplanned and unforeseen', and 'discretionary, i.e. planned and foreseen'; and he held that the 'true' balance-of-payments surplus or deficit was the 'balance of autonomous trade and transfers', a 'sum which must be matched by what we have called accommodating finance'. See James E. Meade, *The Balance of Payments* (London: Oxford University Press, 1951), pp. 11 and 13. I criticised Meade's often contradictory usage of his terms in my article 'Equilibrium and Disequilibrium: Misplaced Concreteness and Disguised Politics', *The Economic Journal*, March 1958, pp. 18-24; reprinted in Machlup, *International Payments, Debts, and Gold: Collected Essays, op. cit.*, pp. 128-32.

18. Paul T. Ellsworth with J. Clark Leith, *The International Economy*, 4th ed. (London: Macmillan, 1969), p. 314.

19. *Ibid.*, p. 316. I wonder why such myths continue to be taught when they are clearly contradicted by statistical records. These presumed slow-moving changes can be contradicted by the fact that the balance on the current and long-term capital accounts (the 'basic balance') moved from a surplus of 4 thousand million in 1967 to a deficit of 4 thousand million in 1972, back to a surplus of 27 million in 1973 and then to deficits of 3.8 thousand million in 1974, 754 million in 1975 13 thousand million in 1976 and 27 thousand million in 1978. See *Statistical Abstract of the United States 1981* (Washington, U.S. Bureau of the Census, Department of Commerce, 1981).

20. Gottfried Haberler, *Prosperity and Depression*, 3rd ed. (Geneva: League of Nations, 1946), p. 472.

21. Viner, *op. cit.*, p. 364.

22. Machlup, *International Trade and the National Income Multiplier*, *op. cit.*, p. 40. The classical writers, regarding capital flows as autonomous and trade flows as induced by them, include Hume, Thornton, Wheatley, Ricardo, Longfield, Torrens, Joplin, J. S. Mill, Cairnes, Bastable and Nicholson; the neo-classical economists, endorsing this view, include Taussig, Wicksell, Mises, Cassel, Angell, Haberler, Ohlin, Iversen and many others. See Machlup, *ibid.*, p. 136, footnote 1.

23. Machlup, *International Trade and the National Income Multiplier*, *op. cit.*, pp. 130-48, especially the sections on 'Net Capital Exports' and 'Cause or Effect', pp. 139-43.

24. The findings of Viner's study of the Canadian experience in the period 1900-13 were consistent with the 'classical' theory: '. . . the Canadian experience does show that the growth of the import surplus was preceded by a growth in the amount of means of payment in Canada, that this growth . . . was both primary [inflows] and secondary [domestic], that the primary fluctuations in the amount of means of payment were relatively more marked than the secondary fluctuations, and that there was a variable time-lag between borrowings abroad and economic transfer [imports], with the recorded, or long-term, borrowings usually but not always preceding the economic transfer chronologically'. See Viner, *op. cit.*, p. 431.

25. I admit ignorance of the relevant research in the history of the United States foreign trade, but am curious how historians have explained the following records: from 1855-63, eight export surpluses, only one import surplus; 1864-73, only one export surplus, but nine import surpluses; 1874-88, thirteen export surpluses, one even balance and one import surplus; 1889-1933, forty-five export surpluses without interruption; 1934-40, seven import surpluses; 1941-70, thirty export surpluses; 1971-79, two export surpluses, seven import surpluses. If I had to engage in this research, my hypotheses would make me examine data on long-term capital movements, changes in official foreign reserves, changes in domestic money supply, changes in exchange rates and various changes in analogous magnitudes in the countries with which the United States had substantial trade relations.

26. This is the strongest argument of advocates of a return to the gold

standard, but in fact it is the reason why countries will not return to a system that reduces their freedom to inflate the currency.

27.   Mordechai E. Kreinin and Lawrence H. Officer, *The Monetary Approach to the Balance of Payments: a Survey*, Princeton Studies in International Finance No. 43 (Princeton: International Finance Section, 1978), p. 3.

28.   This 'stock demand for money' (or, in more intelligible English, the demand for money balances to hold) is often simplified by singling out one variable as the essential one. Marshall selected prices of commodities—Keynes, prices of securities. In order to draw a normal-looking demand curve, Marshall showed the commodity value of a unit of money (expressed by the inverse of some specific index of the price level) on the vertical axis of his diagram; Keynes showed the bond value of a unit of money (expressed by the representative rate of interest) and called his curve the 'liquidity preference' curve. Which of these two models of the demand for liquid money balances is more helpful in economic analysis depends on what problems one wishes to explore and what time spans are of interest. Emphasis on interest rates seems more appropriate for short-run analyses; emphasis on prices of goods and services appears to be more attuned to longer-run analyses. Is it necessary, however, to make a choice of one to the exclusion of the other? Should diagrammatical limitations compel us to disregard variables that cannot be accommodated in more than two dimensions? To relate the demand curves for 'money to hold' to the concepts of hoarding and dishoarding, one should understand that *autonomous* hoarding (dishoarding) is depicted by a right-shift (left-shift) of the curves, and *induced* hoarding (dishoarding) by a downward movement (upward movement) *along* the curves.

8   Exchange-rate Intervention: Arbitrage and Market Efficiency

Robert Z. Aliber

Under the Bretton Woods system of pegged rates of exchange between currencies, intervention by the United States in the currency market was redundant, since the monetary authorities abroad determined the foreign-exchange rate of the dollar as they bought and sold their own currencies within the support limits around their parities. With the breakdown of the Bretton Woods system, the authorities in the United States faced a new problem— should they intervene in the foreign-exchange market or should they instead follow a policy of benign neglect, so that the value of the American dollar, in terms of various other currencies, would be determined by some combination of market forces and the inter- vention policies of foreign monetary authorities? Prior to the breakdown, it was generally believed that official intervention would be far less extensive with a floating exchange-rate regime; the irony, however, is that official transactions in reserve assets have been substantially larger under the floating exchange-rate system than under the pegged exchange-rate system.

The sharp fluctuations in the foreign-exchange value of the dollar since 1973—much sharper than the differences between changes in the American and foreign price levels—have led to proposals for a more systematic intervention policy in the United States.[1] Yet numerous arguments have been raised against intervention. One is that official intervention would be ineffective; another, that private investors have a better view of the appropriate foreign-exchange value of the dollar than the monetary authorities have; a third, that intervention by the authorities in the United States would be costly; and a fourth, that official transactions in the exchange market would be redundant because foreign monetary authorities already intervene extensively in the market for dollars.

The authorities in the United States have intervened in the exchange market on an occasional basis, especially when the dollar

171

was weak.[2] The decision to intervene appears to have been pragmatic and was not based on a systematic view of whether intervention would be effective—or how intervention could be managed
to maximise its effectiveness.[3] Most intervention by the American
authorities has involved sales of German marks and, to a much
lesser extent, Swiss francs.

Intervention in the foreign-exchange market by the American
authorities entails the Treasury or the Federal Reserve buying
dollar demand deposits and selling demand deposits denominated
in a foreign currency, almost certainly in transactions with major
commercial banks. Since the authorities in the United States hold
only modest amounts of deposits and other liquid assets denominated
in foreign currencies, they must obtain demand deposits denominated in foreign currencies either by a sale of bonds—or other debts
denominated in the foreign currency—to the foreign monetary
authority or to private investors. Hence at least three separate
transactions are associated with exchange-market intervention in
the United States. The first transaction involves the sale of Government debts denominated in a foreign currency (perhaps in the
context of a central bank swap), while the second transaction
involves the sale of the United States-owned demand deposits
denominated in the foreign currency in exchange for dollar-
denominated demand deposits. The third transaction involves open-
market purchases of dollar debts using the dollars acquired in
exchange-market transactions. Hence the first and third transactions are mirror images of each other; the open-market sales of
debts denominated in the foreign currency enable the American
authorities to obtain dollars (through the intermediate transaction
in the foreign-exchange market) to use in the open-market purchases of dollar debts. Depending on the extent to which the
authorities in the United States vary their holdings of demand
deposits denominated in dollars and in the foreign currency, these
various transactions may occur at different times.

The sale of debts denominated in the foreign currency would
tend to raise interest rates on debts denominated in this currency,
while American interest rates would tend to fall when the American
authorities purchased dollar debts. This change in the interest-rate
differential would lead to a weaker dollar; by contrast, the sale of
United States-owned deposits denominated in the foreign currency
(and the counterpart purchase of dollars) in the foreign-exchange
market would lead to a stronger dollar. The increase in the interest

rates on debts denominated in the foreign currency is virtually unavoidable if the authorities in the United States sell foreign currency debts; the decrease in interest rates on dollar debts is also unavoidable once the same authorities buy American dollar securities with the dollars obtained in the foreign-exchange market. Even if the authorities in the United States obtain the foreign currency under a credit swap with the foreign central bank, interest rates on debts denominated in the foreign currency will increase, unless foreign monetary policy is accommodating and the impact of the open-market sale of foreign-currency debts by the United States is fully sterilised. Similarly, the impact of the American authorities' purchase of dollar securities will lead to a decline in interest rates on dollar debts unless this transaction is fully sterilised.

The greater the sterilisation of these open-market transactions in the United States, the smaller the decline in interest rates on dollar debts relative to the interest rates on debts denominated in the foreign currency. By contrast, if the foreign monetary authorities sterilise while the authorities in the United States do not, the greater will be the decline in interest rates on dollar debts relative to interest rates on debts denominated in the foreign currency. Moreover, the greater the decline in interest rates on dollar debts associated with exchange-market intervention, the less likely it is that exchange-market intervention will have the desired impact on the foreign-exchange value of the dollar. Hence, the greater the extent of the sterilisation of the open-market transactions associated with exchange-market intervention, the more likely it is that intervention will achieve its objectives.

Thus, the effectiveness of intervention in dampening the rate of depreciation of the foreign-exchange value of the dollar requires that the impact of the foreign-exchange transactions dominate the impact of the open-market transactions. Official intervention may not be effective in altering the level or range of movement in the exchange rate and may thus be redundant, perhaps because the interest-rate impact of the open-market transactions off-sets the exchange-rate impact. Intervention by the United States might be redundant if foreign monetary authorities already buy and sell dollars in support of their currencies. If, however, the authorities in the United States decide to intervene in support of the dollar, they might do so in the market for only one foreign currency and permit market forces to set the foreign-exchange value for the dollar in terms of other currencies; under certain assumptions, the currency in which the American authorities intervene might be a matter of indifference. Similarly, the choice between intervention in the spot market and the forward market might also be a matter of indifference if arbitragers link the spot exchange rate and the forward exchange rate in a perfectly costless way.

This essay discusses the following four questions related to intervention policies in the United States: (i) Should the authorities in the United States intervene in the foreign-exchange market? (ii) If the authorities intervene in the foreign-exchange market, should they not follow the practice of foreign monetary authorities and buy and sell only one foreign currency and permit market forces to set the rates for other currencies? (iii) Should the authorities refrain from intervention in the foreign-exchange market if the monetary authorities in other countries support their currencies by buying and selling dollars? And (iv) should the authorities be indifferent between buying and selling the dollar in the spot exchange market and in the forward exchange market?

The premise of this essay is that the answer to each question depends on characteristics of the financial and goods markets. The answer to each question is *no* if certain 'perfect market-type' assumptions are valid. The purpose of the essay is to suggest an answer to each question by discussing the reasonableness of the assumptions central to each question.

INTERVENTION POLICY . . .

. . . Should the authorities in the United States intervene in the foreign-exchange market?

A number of arguments can be advanced for official intervention in the foreign-exchange market under a floating exchange-rate regime. A generation ago, it was argued that speculation in the exchange market had a destabilising effect and amplified the variability of the exchange rates around their equilibrium values and, perhaps, through feedback to the domestic money supplies, affected the level and changes in the level of the equilibrium exchange rates.[4] A derivative argument is that the excessive depreciation in the foreign-exchange rate of the dollar may have a significant or measurable upward impact on the price level in the United States; this argument is sometimes linked with the 'vicious and virtuous circle' and the 'ratchet effect'. A third argument for intervention is that the level of the foreign-exchange value of the dollar (or changes in the level) may have an impact on the current account balance in the United States and hence on employment and profits in tradeables or in manufacturing or even in individual industries. A more traditional argument for intervention is that the variability of the exchange rate and uncertainty about its future values retards international trade and investment; in this case the argument for intervention is similar to the argument for pegging the currency.

These arguments for official exchange-rate intervention in the foreign-exchange market involve the impact of changes in the foreign-exchange value of the dollar or domestic economic variables such as prices, incomes and profits and the international levels of trade and investment. The underlying assumption is that from time to time the value for the exchange rate differs significantly from an equilibrium value. Adjustments of financial markets, such as those for long-term debts and for equity, and of markets for both primary products and manufactures to this transient disequilibrium value, incur welfare costs which exceed the costs of intervention.

A major response is that official intervention in the foreign-exchange market will prove ineffective and hence redundant unless there are counterpart changes in domestic monetary policy and domestic interest rates; the underlying assumption is that the foreign-exchange value of the dollar is determined by the differential between interest rates on dollar assets and interest rates on comparable assets denominated in foreign currencies. Even if this argument is rejected and the view accepted that official intervention might have an impact on the exchange rate, intervention is frequently considered redundant because international investors and traders set the 'right value' for the exchange rate.[5] A third argument is that official intervention will be 'too expensive' because if the authorities 'lean against the wind', the market participants will 'lean against the authorities' and will profit as the authorities permit the currency to depreciate or appreciate under pressure.

Evidence that official intervention may be redundant has been inferred from data on exchange-rate movements and especially from tests of 'exchange-market efficiency'. Thus, if the changes in exchange rates follow a random path and forward exchange rates are—on average—unbiased predictors of future spot exchange rates, the exchange market can be considered efficient.[6]

A frequent *sequitur* is that intervention would be redundant if the exchange market were efficient. A rejoinder that the evidence shows that the foreign-exchange market is not inefficient is not conclusive—such evidence would satisfy the necessary condition for concluding that intervention is redundant but not the sufficient condition.[7] Thus, the case for intervention is based primarily on evidence that large and sudden movements in exchange rates, sometimes reversed after two or three quarters, have disruptive impacts on goods markets or long-term financial markets; the sufficient condition for concluding that intervention is redundant is that these large, sudden movements are not associated with changes in 'real exchange rates'. According to this view, the case for official intervention in the exchange market is based on deviations from 'goods market efficiency'. In effect, there is an apparent deviation from purchasing power parity and from its counterpart for the long-term debt and the equity market that cannot be explained by changes in the terms of trade or by the differences among countries in the phasing of business cycles.

The case for official intervention in the foreign-exchange market becomes stronger, the more the data lead to the conclusion that neither the goods market nor the money market satisfies the test of efficiency. Conversely, if the data from both markets fail to lead to the conclusion that the efficiency tests are not satisfied, the case for intervention is not likely to be convincing, even though there are large sudden movements in the nominal exchange rate. There are two intermediate cases where the inferences about market efficiency from the goods market and the foreign-exchange market differ. In one of these intermediate cases, the inference from the goods market data might suggest market inefficiency, while the inference from the foreign-exchange market data might not. The argument for official intervention is stronger, the more extensive is the evidence for goods market efficiency. By contrast, if the evidence suggests that the foreign-exchange market does not satisfy the efficiency test while the data from the goods market do not suggest an inefficiency, the case for intervention is weaker.

The discrepancy between the seemingly efficient behaviour of the international money market and the apparently 'inefficient' behaviour in goods markets when viewed internationally—deviations from the Law of One Price and from purchasing power parity—is already explained. The current exchange rates are set by anticipations of values for exchange rates. By contrast, the goods markets, especially in brand-name manufactures (as opposed to non-brand-name primary products) and in services, are set by historic costs; these prices and wages change much more slowly than the exchange rates. Prices in the goods market therefore appear 'frozen', relative to prices in the money market; yet it is the lethargic quality of these prices which limits the movements of the exchange rate. That is, the goods markets and long-term capital market 'stabilise' the foreign-exchange market, because the sharp depreciation of a country's currency results in plentiful bargains in its goods and real assets.

The observed movements in exchange rates in the last several years have led to various attempts to explain 'over-shooting'. The foreign-exchange value of the dollar has varied sharply and the changes in the exchange rates have been very large relative to the changes in real exchange rates. At any moment the exchange rate may be the anticipated nominal rate discounted to the present by the money market interest-rate differential. Various hypotheses have been advanced to explain the determinants of the anticipated exchange rates, including changes in monetary policy, the extrapolation of recent changes in exchange rates and the extrapolation of both recent changes in monetary policies and recent price-level developments. The tests are inconclusive in that no hypothesis appears to have explanatory power over a range of currencies, in part because the anticipated exchange rates are not readily observable. Nevertheless, the fact that the direction of the movements in the spot exchange rates in relation to the long-term trend value are reversed suggests that the factors that determine the anticipated spot exchange rates are also eventually reversed. One possible explanation is that policies are eventually reversed. The movements in the real exchange rates, while less extensive than the movements in the nominal exchange rates, are nevertheless much larger than the movements in the real exchange rates under a pegged exchange-rate system. Moreover, since these movements in the real exchange rates are reversed, in that the real rates move away from and then back towards a 'trend real rate', the key question is whether economic welfare would be enhanced if the movements in the real exchange rates away from the equilibrium value were dampened or limited.

The intervention activity almost always involves dampening the movement of the spot exchange rate (either by official transactions in the spot exchange market or in the forward market—see below) away from the real exchange rate. The presumption which appears to be supported by extensive data is that real exchange rates change slowly—rarely by more than 3 or 4 per cent a year. The probability is high that when the real exchange rate changes by more than 3 or 4 per cent away from its trend value in the course of a year, the direction of movement in the nominal value of the spot rate will be subsequently reversed.

Most of the changes in the real exchange rates result from disturbances in the financial markets. In some cases, however, these changes in the real rate may result from the differences in the phasing of the business cycle in the United States and its major trading partners. At that time the authorities would reverse the pattern of their intervention transactions, although most intervention would be delayed until the nominal rate moved through and beyond the real exchange rate. Just as with the pegged rate, official intervention should prove profitable, at least as judged by the difference between the price the authorities pay for a currency and the price at which they subsequently sell. If intervention profits are viewed more comprehensively and compared with the interest-rate differential, one country may incur losses in that the interest-rate differential is large relative to the exchange profits; such evidence was pervasive under the pegged exchange-rate system.[8] In general, given interest rates on assets in those foreign currencies in which the American authorities would intervene, intervention is likely to be profitable. Even if this projection proved incorrect, the effective comparison is between the costs and the welfare gains from limiting foreign-exchange rate movements.

The argument for official intervention rests on the premise that the monetary authorities have a longer time horizon than the private investors. Private investors 'run with the exchange rate', regardless of their views about the equilibrium rates; altering the currency mix of their foreign-exchange exposure to profit from the departures of the nominal rate from its equilibrium values can be very costly. These investors are almost exclusively concerned with how to minimise their net borrowing costs or maximise their net interest income over the next three to six months, where a major term in borrowing costs and investment returns is the anticipated change in the exchange rate during this interval. In many cases, the value for the exchange-rate term is substantially larger than the interest-rate differential. As each of their short-term investments approaches maturity, the private investors repeat the same question about how to minimise borrowing costs or maximise interest returns over the next three to six months. They may hold or reverse their currency exposure. The change in their currency exposure may be triggered by changes in the interest-rate differential or changes in monetary policy or changes in some political events or by the anticipation of changes in these or other variables. The monetary authorities have a significantly longer time horizon and should recognise that the exchange rates cannot depart for long from the equilibrium real rates.

There are alternative ways for the authorities to stem the sharp movements in the exchange rates. Exchange controls might be applied to short-term capital movements or even more broadly to international transactions. Foreign-exchange transactions might be taxed. Interest rates might be managed with a view towards limiting exchange-rate movements, which implies an increased burden on fiscal policy to maintain domestic targets—a reversal of the traditional association of these instruments and targets with floating exchange-rate regimes. These alternatives are administratively much more complex than intervention policy. Moreover, foregoing intervention policy involves the loss of a degree of freedom, for the number of policy instruments is reduced without a corresponding reduction in the number of policy targets.

Even if the argument that official intervention would be desirable for limiting the deviations in the real exchange rate from its trend value is accepted, such intervention would be redundant unless it had a significant impact on the exchange rate. It might be argued that intervention would not be affected unless the right combination of the appropriate sterilisation policies were adopted; and that if these policies were adopted, intervention would be redundant. Yet both points ignore the fact that the changes in nominal exchange rates reflect much more than one-to-one changes in the interest-rate differential. To the extent that changes in the nominal exchange rate reflect only changes in the interest-rate differential, there will be a multiple effect; a 1 per cent change in the interest-rate differential will be associated with a larger percentage change in the exchange rate. Indeed, unless this assumption is accepted, intervention will affect the exchange rate and the impact of different combinations of sterilisation actions by the United States and foreign authorities will modify the impact of intervention on the exchange rate.

Official intervention is effective in several ways. Intervention may alter the view of private investors about the anticipated spot exchange rates; indeed, one of the reasons why the pegged exchange-rate system worked in the 1950s and 1960s was that the expectations about spot exchange rates were strongly influenced by the official commitments to the parities and the credibility of such commitments. If, in the absence of intervention, there is serial correlation on the exchange-rate movements, then intervention may be effective in forestalling the efforts of investors to run their positions. Even in the absence of evidence of serial correlation, intervention may limit or dampen the movements in real exchange rates because investors have a very imprecise or inexact view of the anticipated exchange rate. In this case, firmness in official intervention would obviously enhance its effectiveness.

If the case for intervention is accepted, the question then arises of how specific the rules of the intervention system should be. Specificity has two advantages. One is to limit or constrain the choices of the intervention manager, primarily to avoid 'beggar-thy-neighbour' policies, a problem discussed below. The second is to provide signals to the market participants about the strategy and tactics of intervention. The moot issue is whether the value of such signals exceeds the cost of the constraint imposed on the authorities.

The case against intervention must rest on evidence that intervention will increase the variations in the real exchange rate, or that the welfare gain from limiting these variations will be smaller than the cost associated with intervention, or that intervention is not profitable, or that intervention is likely to be mismanaged. The available evidence suggests that intervention has been profitable. There is limited evidence that intervention has increased the variability of the exchange rate. Intervention policy, like other government policies, may be mismanaged, but the implication is to change the policies or to change the managers.

INTERVENTION IN THE FOREIGN-EXCHANGE MARKET ...

... *If the authorities in the United States intervene in the foreign-exchange market, should they not follow the practice of foreign monetary authorities and buy and sell only one foreign currency?*

The authorities in the United States face a decision which no other national monetary authority has to face—which currency or currencies should they buy and sell when they intervene in the foreign-exchange market? For all other countries the choice of intervention currency is almost automatic: they intervene in the currency in which their commercial banks hold their inventories of foreign exchange; for many countries the dollar is the currency for intervention in foreign-exchange markets. Indeed, the dollar is used for intervention in foreign-exchange markets by countries which are not part of the dollar-currency area and by countries which hold only a small part of their reserves in dollars. Virtually all of these countries intervene in only one foreign-exchange market.[9] Once they intervene and set the price for their currency in terms of the dollar, market forces will automatically 'arbitrage' the exchange rates with every other currency.

One possible answer to the question posed above is that the authorities in the United States should intervene in the market for only one currency and allow arbitragers to arrange the exchange rates in all other currencies; they might be indifferent about the currency chosen for intervention. This argument rests on the assumption that there is perfect arbitrage among the various foreign currencies so that intervention does not alter 'real' cross rates. Thus, any success that the authorities might have in altering the foreign-exchange value of the currency in which they intervened would soon be reflected in changes in the foreign-exchange values of numerous other currencies; arbitrage would prevent or limit any change in the cross rates. The lack of correlation in the movement of real exchange rates for the dollar relative to the currencies of the major trading partners of the United States indicates that arbitrage is less than perfect.

Once the argument that arbitrage among various real exchange rates is perfect has been rejected, the authorities in the United States must decide in which foreign-exchange markets and in how many foreign currencies they will intervene. One necessary condition for intervention is that the foreign currency be that of a country which is an important partner in trade and financial transactions; probably no more than six or seven countries meet this criterion. The currencies might be the five currencies, other than the dollar, now used to calculate the value of the Special Drawing Right (SDR). A second condition is that intervention be undertaken only if there appears to be a substantial change in the real exchange rate in one of these currencies relative to the dollar.

It might be argued that just as some currencies are pegged to the SDR, so the authorities in the United States should intervene in the exchange rate for SDRs. In a narrow sense, intervention in the SDR is not feasible, since it is not traded in the foreign-exchange market. The authorities might, however, intervene in several different national currencies at the same time, with the amounts of intervention geared to the importance of each currency to the SDR. The consequence of intervention in a 'currency bouquet' to support the dollar is that the authorities might, at a time when the dollar is unusually weak, sell a particular foreign currency even though that currency is also weak in terms of most other foreign currencies. Alternatively, the authorities might buy and sell individual foreign currencies with SDRs to alter the foreign-exchange value of these currencies relative to the dollar.

The authorities in the United States face a particular problem relative to the currencies participating in the European Monetary System (EMS). The changes in the value of many of these currencies in terms of the dollar are strongly correlated to changes in the German mark price for the dollar. The authorities should intervene in markets for each of these currencies, perhaps on a weighted basis. (The authorities in the United States construct their own bouquet of EMS currencies.) Intervention in the market for the Dutch guilder or the Belgian franc might have a major impact on the value of these currencies in terms of the mark and only a minor impact on the value of the dollar in terms of the mark. Consequently, the effectiveness of intervention by the United States will be greater the more directly it is concentrated on those currencies which are at the centre of currency zones.

FOREIGN MONETARY POLICY . . .

. . . Should the authorities in the United States refrain from intervention in the foreign-exchange market if the monetary authorities in other countries support their currencies by buying and selling dollars?

Once the case is accepted that the characteristics of the foreign-exchange market suggest official intervention might be both desirable and effective, the question remains whether the authorities in the United States should intervene if foreign monetary authorities also intervene in the foreign-exchange market. Intervention may appear to be redundant since there is one less independent exchange rate than there are currencies. The case for intervention is based on one of two premises. One is that the authorities in the United States and the foreign monetary authorities share a view on the appropriate level or range for the relevant exchange rate and thus have a shared interest in dampening the movement of the real exchange rate away from its equilibrium value. Since the foreign monetary authority has a budget constraint, intervention on the part of the United States would add substantially to the resources available for intervention. 'Currency bouquets' involving American and foreign-owned funds might be used at the same time.

The second premise for intervention is that the level or range for the exchange rate deemed optimal by the foreign monetary authority may differ from that deemed optimal by the authorities in the United States. Thus, some countries which place considerable emphasis on domestic employment might dampen the appreciation of their currencies, while other countries which place considerable emphasis on a low inflation rate might intervene to prevent their currencies from depreciating as rapidly as might be deemed preferable in terms of the American interest.

Once the case is accepted that the foreign monetary authority has a national interest in the level and rate of change in the foreign-exchange value of its currency, the American authorities cannot permit the foreign monetary authority to 'monopolise' the intervention in the foreign-exchange market. In the 1930s, attention was given to the 'beggar-thy-neighbour' policies; supposedly countries preferred weak currencies to enhance domestic employment. By contrast, over the last few years, countries have tended to prefer strong currencies because of the favourable anti-inflationary impulse experienced when their currencies appreciate. Yet the dollar and the currencies of the United States' major trading partners cannot both appreciate relative to one another—the foreign monetary authorites, therefore, prefer a weaker dollar than the authorities in the United States.

Intervention by the authorities in the United States at the same time as foreign intervention would provide tremendous profit opportunities. Intervention might be coordinated in various ways. One approach would be to establish a jointly-owned exchange stabilisation fund managed by technicians from both countries which might intervene with 'bouquets' of American and foreign-owned funds.

FORWARD AND SPOT EXCHANGE MARKETS . . .

. . . Should the authorities in the United States be indifferent between buying and selling the dollar in the spot exchange market and the forward exchange market?

Traditionally, central banks have intervened in the spot exchange market, a practice which goes back to the gold standard, when central banks supported their currencies by selling gold to private parties at the mint parities. Subsequently the Articles of Agreement of the International Monetary Fund (IMF) provided that member countries were obliged to maintain the foreign-exchange value of their currencies in spot transactions within a range or band around their parities—one quarter of 1 per cent on either side of their parities. This band was widened to 1 per cent and then to 2.25 per cent on either side of the parities. Most intervention by central banks under the Bretton Woods system was with transactions in the spot exchange market, although they occasionally intervened in the forward market. Central banks have intervened in the forward market far less extensively than in the spot exchange market. One possible reason is the large revaluation loss incurred by the Bank of England on its forward transactions undertaken prior to the 1967 devaluation of sterling. Another possible reason is that, under the system of pegged exchange rates, it might have seemed less uncertain to maintain the spot rate within the support limits by intervention in the spot exchange market rather than in the forward exchange market.

Most foreign-exchange trading occurs in the forward market and changes in the spot rate are linked to changes in the forward rate by arbitragers. Hence, intervention in the forward market provides a more effective way to 'lean against the wind' than spot market intervention. With the move to floating exchange rates, central banks are no longer constrained to hold the spot exchange rate to a particular value or range of values. Hence, they might equally as well intervene in the forward market as in the spot exchange market. Whether forward intervention or spot intervention is more efficient depends on the efficiency of the arbitrage process. If arbitrage is riskless and costless, then the authorities might be indifferent between intervention in the spot market and in the forward market.[10] If arbitrage is less than completely riskless and costless, then official intervention in the forward market might be associated with a somewhat smaller spread in the differential between the forward rate and the spot exchange rate than would occur with intervention in the spot market when the dollar is unusually weak and a somewhat larger spread when the dollar is unusually strong. The larger-than-average spread when the dollar is unusually weak, which is a forward discount larger than predicted by the interest-rate differential, could readily lead to increased private sales of the dollar in the spot market. If the authorities had engaged in a volume of purchases of the dollar in the forward market comparable with the volume of purchases they might otherwise have made in the spot market, the forward discount would be substantially smaller. Indeed, some investors who sold the dollar forward might also buy the dollar spot to profit from the return on covered arbitrage, whereas with spot intervention these investors might have sold the dollar spot and bought it forward.

The evidence is that arbitrage is neither riskless nor costless and so the authorities cannot remain indifferent between intervention in the two markets. Consequently, forward market intervention is more efficient than intervention in the spot market.

One other important advantage in forward intervention by the authorities is that they are not obliged to engage in open-market transactions in the foreign currency in order to gain the funds needed to support the dollar in the spot exchange market. In effect, if the authorities in the United States bought the dollar forward they would be selling the foreign currency short. Under the current arrangements, before the authorities buy dollars in the spot market they also sell the foreign currency short by selling liabilities denominated in the foreign currency. If the authorities intervene in the forward market, the issue of the sterilisation of their open-market transactions in the United States and abroad becomes irrelevant. When the forward contracts mature, the authorities would be obliged to deliver foreign currencies, but these currencies might be readily obtainable by selling dollars in the spot market. Moreover, the authorities would not be obliged to report immediately their spot exchange position.

CONCLUSION

This essay has evaluated four questions central to a policy of intervention in foreign-exchange markets by the United States authorities. The approach of the essay involves considering the assumptions necessary to reach the following conclusions: (i) that welfare in the United States would not be enhanced by official intervention, (ii) that the authorities should be indifferent towards the currency they buy and sell relative to the dollar, (iii) that the authorities should be indifferent between intervention in the spot exchange market and intervention in the forward market, and (iv) that the authorities should forgo intervention because the foreign monetary authority is already buying and selling the dollar. In each case, the structure of markets leads to the conclusion that the

H

authorities cannot remain indifferent towards these questions.

The dominant point is that evidence of the efficiency of the foreign-exchange market—that forward rates are on average unbiased predictors of future spot exchange rates and that period-to-period changes in exchange rates are not serially correlated—is irrelevant in denying the net welfare gains from intervention. Instead, the case for intervention rests on deviations from 'goods market efficiency'—departures of real exchange rates from the long-run trend value—and the counterpart equilibrium observation for both long-term debt and equity. Moreover, intervention will almost certainly be effective, regardless of whether the open-market transactions in the United States and abroad are sterilised, although the effectiveness of intervention is enhanced if it is accompanied by the appropriate sterilisation policies.

Since changes in real exchange rates across currencies are not perfectly correlated, the authorities in the United States cannot remain indifferent towards the currencies in which they may choose to intervene. Intervention should be directed at those currency markets which involve the United States' five or six major trading partners—and then only if there are significant deviations from the estimated real equilibrium exchange rate. Moreover, intervention in the dollar-SDR market—when and if possible and against a fixed bouquet of currencies in the interim—is inferior to selective intervention. The authorities in the United States cannot be indifferent to the intervention policies of monetary authorities abroad, since the foreign-exchange values for the dollar that complement American monetary and fiscal policy may differ from the values which best complement the foreign monetary authorities' policies, perhaps by a substantial amount. Finally, intervention in the forward exchange market has substantial economic, operational and cosmetic advantages relative to spot market intervention.

NOTES AND REFERENCES

1. Tom de Vries, 'In Search of an Exchange Rate for the Dollar', *Banca Nazionale del Lavoro Quarterly Review*, Rome, June 1978.

2. Scott E. Pardee, 'Treasury and Federal Reserve Foreign Exchange Operations: Interim Report', *Federal Reserve Bulletin*, Washington, December 1980. See, also, earlier issues.

3. Henry C. Wallich, 'Foreign Exchange: New Tactics Needed?', *Journal of Commerce*, New York, December 1980.

4. Ragnar Nurkse, *International Currency Experience: Lessons of the Inter-war Period* (Princeton: League of Nations, 1944).

5. Milton Friedman, 'The Case for Floating Exchange Rates' in his *Essays in Positive Economics* (Chicago: University of Chicago Press, 1953).

6. Steven Kohlhagen, *The Behavior of Foreign Exchange Markets—a Critical Survey of the Economic Literature* (New York: New York University Press, 1978); and Richard M. Levich, *The International Money Market: Tests of Forecasting Models and Market Efficiency* (Greenwich, Conn.: JAI Press, 1979).

7. David King, 'Exchange Market Efficiency and the Risk-Taker of Last Resort', *Columbia Journal of World Business*, New York, Winter, 1979.

8. Robert Z. Aliber, *Exchange Risk and Corporate International Finance* (London: Macmillan, 1978).

9. Members of the EMS may intervene in the currency of some other member.

10. Aliber, 'A Strategy for Central Bank Intervention', in Aliber (ed.), *The International Market for Foreign Exchange* (New York, Praeger, in co-operation with the Graduate School of Business of the University of Chicago, 1969).

9   Disillusionment in the Conduct of Exchange-rate Policies

Olaf Sievert

Anyone reflecting on the events of the 1960s and the early 1970s undoubtedly will reach the conclusion that economists are just as dissatisfied with the world exchange-rate situation now as they were then. At that time criticism was levelled, in particular, at exchange-rate changes which failed to take place: nowadays it is aimed at changes which have taken place. Within the space of a few months, exchange rates between important currencies may move by between 20 and 30 per cent. The central banks are affected by what happens abroad as much as they ever were. An important difference, however, is that devaluation is viewed in a far less favourable light by those concerned with economic policy than ever before.

Economists' knowledge of international monetary theory is always improving: we are continually finding better explanations for recent events on the foreign-exchange markets. For example, most of the work in preparing the theoretical ground for the move from fixed to flexible exchange rates had to be carried out using only the instruments of flow analysis. Soon after that came the monetarist approach and the more adequate theory of stock equilibria. The predominance of the goods markets faded. Economists saw the need for real changes in exchange rates, both short-term and permanent, in a new light. They learned that wealth effects can play a role in this connection and that a wide band of massive exchange-rate variations becomes plausible if, purely on the basis of the theory of portfolio optimisation, one takes into account the simple fact that assets in different currencies are not perfect substitutes and that estimates of risks relating to such assets can change rapidly and greatly.

But economists learned, too, that they are still unable, though, to forecast exchange-rate movements with any certainty. Forward rates ceased to be regarded as reliable indicators of future spot rates in spite of the fact that they are the best indicators available. It became clear that interest-rate differentials, reflecting permanent differences in inflation rates and cyclical influences, were still good indicators of corresponding changes in exchange-rates. But allowances had to be made for actual exchange-rate changes diverging quite considerably from the predicted values implicit in the differential for unforseeable reasons; and this not only exceptionally, but in most cases.

Economists have an explanation in terms of monetary and exchange-rate theory for the fact that (i) for years a shortage of German marks resulted from the interaction of a high demand for more assets and a large supply of government bonds (arising from greatly increasing public-sector debts) as long as there was a large surplus in the West German balance of payments on current account and (ii) the picture changed completely when the surplus position was replaced by large current-account deficits. This explanation is contained within the risk-premium model. But can this really be called an explanation? By giving things a name are we really doing anything more than classifying processes and helping to dispel the fear of an environment we have not understood?

Laying down a code of conduct for economic policy on monetary and exchange-rate matters entails the ability to make quantitative statements, with the help of monetary and exchange-rate theory, on the inter-relationships between them (for example conditional, but not too meaningless, exchange-rate prognoses). At the moment, this obviously is not possible. Alternatively, we would have to be able to make reasonably reliable statements as to the nature and direction of the effects of exogenous or controllable variables on the movements of the money supply and exchange rates—but this has become debatable in too many cases. The final alternative is that we would have to be able to predict that everything would run smoothly without any economic measures. Under present conditions, this may well be regarded as absurd.

What William H. Branson, of Princeton University, New Jersey, says on the point is probably true: 'I think economists have come a long way in analyzing and understanding what is happening in international money and exchange rates, in the sense of positive economics. But policy prescription in the new environment is just beginning.'[1]

Of course the adventure of flexible exchange rates was not embarked upon completely naively. It is, however, presumably correct to say that all those who advocated the abolition rather than the reform of the ailing Bretton Woods system envisaged a world where exchange rates changed steadily rather than abruptly. The experience of recent years is, in that respect, in marked contrast to expectations. Nobody, however, actually gave a guarantee against strong exchange-rate fluctuations. In 1966 twenty-two economists from all over the world called for the abandonment of fixed exchange rates and advised the adoption of the crawling peg, rather than the system of freely fluctuating exchange rates. They did this not only out of respect for the fears of the many who were opposed to fluctuating exchange rates but also because they were aware of the possibility of excessive fluctuations in the rates of exchange. Herbert Giersch was among those Germans who signed the appeal. For a time Professor Giersch even considered a guaranteed increase in the parity of the German mark to be a sufficient policy response to the continuing stability of the mark in excess of the stability of other currencies in the 1960s, thus retaining the necessity of intervention by the central banks at completely predictable, if constantly changing, intervention points.[2]

Nor did the apologists of flexible exchange rates promise that adjustment to monetary or real external disturbances would be painless. Egon Sohmen and Professor Giersch were the two most important German advocates of flexible exchange rates in the early period of the fight against Bretton Woods. From the very beginning Sohmen admitted that real external disturbances, for example, cyclical disturbances of the world economy, could, in principle, affect an economy under flexible exchange rates.[3] Professor Giersch believed even less in the simple idea that disturbances in the external equilibrium could be eliminated, without problems, merely by exchange-rate movements. He was much more concerned with how a revaluation could be made cyclically neutral by means of domestic economic measures and with how a devaluation could be prevented from increasing inflation.[4] Thus, there was awareness that the change in flexible exchange rates would not solve problems, but only transform them, thus making them, however, partially soluble. There is scarcely a sentence of exchange-rate theory which lends itself more easily to misunderstanding than that which states that there are no balance-of-payments problems under flexible exchange rates. The classical conflict between external and internal equilibrium does not disappear without trace under flexible exchange rates: it reappears as a conflict between the two domestic economic goals of price-level stability and a high rate of employment. Even the Federal Republic of Germany, in 1981, was a case in point. But no promise was made of a perfect world and therefore there is no reason for disappointment. An important genuine reason for disappointment, however, is that there is far less certainty as to the trend in the long-term development of exchange rates than had been hoped for. More stability in the development of spot rates had been expected from the assumed stability of medium-term exchange-rate expectations. Sohmen, in particular, also thought that functioning forward markets could be created for the longer term.[5] The hope for stable medium-term expectations was misplaced and it appears that this was not just an unfortunate accident.

So-called 'dirty' floating has been apparent ever since the change to flexible exchange rates was effected. In the first few years, it was possible to use this fact as a partial explanation for the continuing disorientation of longer-term expectations and the delays in the formation of longer-term forward markets. Up to the present day there still remain doubts as to the 'smoothing' effect of intervention by central banks. But surely it is not possible that this intervention should account for a large part of the instability of exchange rates which has been experienced since 1973.

There are better reasons for the fact that stable exchange-rate expectations over the longer term have not been formed. In particular, differences in inflation rates have not been stable and, too, the purchasing-power-parity argument has proved far less accurate beyond the short term than had been widely assumed.

When the propaganda for flexible exchange rates began in the 1960s, it was generally thought that it was intended to take into account permanent—but, by today's standards, rather small—international differences in the tendency to inflation and differences in the Phillips Curve. The idea proved to be unfounded. Economics historians will fight long and in vain about whether the gradual abandonment of the Bretton Woods system itself contributed greatly to the fact that international differences in inflation rates became larger and more variable. It is, however, apparent that medium-term exchange-rate expectations did not receive any clear guidance from the differences in inflation rates. But even if this had not been the case, there would still remain the failure of the parity of purchasing-power hypothesis. It is not intended to discuss here in detail the many reasons why the parity of purchasing-power hypothesis is questionable even for longer than short-term periods.[6] What is important is that it can be relied upon for, at best, such an uncertain period that no unambiguous exchange-rate expectations can be formed.

None of this means that in the past differences in inflation, changes in the differences in inflation and expected changes in the differences in inflation have exerted no influence on the formation of exchange rates. On the contrary, the fact that the parity-of-purchasing-power argument does come into play sooner or later doubtlessly has a great effect on positions taken in the foreign-currency markets. It is not necessarily a stabilising effect, however.

The evidence suggests that exchange rates which for some time diverge substantially from purchasing-power-parity exert more than a marginal influence on the purchasing-power-parity itself. This does not affect the validity of the parity of purchasing-power hypothesis, but it does affect the core of thinking on exchange-rate policy matters.

CURRENT AND 'CORRECT' EXCHANGE RATES

The philosophy of the flexible exchange-rate system is based on the idea that the market is the best means of finding and realising the equilibrium exchange rate. Cautious economists, for example, Fritz Machlup, of New York and Princeton Universities, have always warned against imagining that the equilibrium exchange rate is anything other than the rate which is actually realised on the open market.[7] The discussion on disruptive factors—for example, distorted expectations, cyclical influences, changes in monetary policy—which cause great variations in exchange rates, seems, however, to be influenced more by the idea that alongside or behind the current exchange rate there exists the 'correct' exchange rate, the 'underlying equilibrium exchange rate' or the 'medium-term equilibrium exchange rate'. Jürg Niehans, of the University of Bern, refers to the 'permanent exchange rate'.[8] The fundamental factors which are often not expressed in the current exchange rate are brought into focus here. Such split thinking on 'refined' and 'less refined' exchange rates may be useful for certain analytical purposes. It does suggest, however, a rationality in the formation of exchange rates, at least in the long term, which does not really exist. Under conditions of flexible exchange rates the economy adjusts to the exchange rate (thus making what was initially an 'incorrect' exchange rate into a 'correct' exchange rate) and the exchange rate also adjusts to the economy. The concept of a 'correct' exchange rate, the 'underlying equilibrium exchange rate', *et cetera*, is therefore meaningless when considering the question of the stability of medium-term exchange-rate expectations: an exchange rate which has been determined by distorted expectations is not always subsequently corrected. The problem of determining the exchange rate is no longer merely, or perhaps not even primarily, a problem of information processing for which the market is allegedly the most appropriate mechanism.

This point is vitally important to the theory of an efficient market and also to all advocates of flexible exchange rates. If an exchange rate resulting more or less arbitrarily is supposed to be effective, why, then, should it not be a rate or a movement in the rate determined by the monetary authorities?

The theory that foreign-exchange markets are determined to a large extent by arbitrary factors is virtually completely unacceptable to monetarists. In the long term, at least, the parity-of-purchasing-power argument is quite convincing, except when special circumstances create a permanent need for a significant real change in exchange rates. There is also evidence that in the long term the money supply and the price level are highly correlated. If one adhered to the axiom that the money supply is determined exogenously, this evidence would, indeed, justify a firm monetarist position.

Experience has shown, however, that even in countries where the central bank attempts, in principle, to pursue a policy of a steady medium-term-orientated expansion of the money supply (for instance, in the Federal Republic of Germany) the targets for the future money supply are determined *inter alia* as a function of the most recent inflation rates. This is done in the belief that inflation cannot be brought under control rapidly without unacceptable effects on employment. It means, however, that, despite flexible exchange rates, there is no defence against imported inflation if there is a sharp real devaluation of the currency. Moreover, no initially accommodating monetary policy has been assumed! The elasticity of the monetary system ensures that it is sufficient if the central bank engages in accommodating transactions, as is usual, *post hoc*. Of course, a genuine monetarist will not consider even such subsequent accommodation to be necessary, which may explain why cases of self-fulfilling disequilibrium exchange rates are typically encountered only as appendices in much of the literature on monetary economics, unless exceptional examples of vicious circles are under discussion. But, in practice, it seems to be a regular rather than an exceptional occurrence that monetary policy encounters this problem. It is the present situation in the Federal Republic of Germany. The well-founded fear of its own future weakness prevents the Bundesbank from allowing the exchange rate to find its own level.

THE ROLE OF BALANCE-OF-TRADE DISEQUILIBRIA

The fact that the foreign-exchange markets almost continuously confront the central banks with large and mysterious movements of the real exchange rate may be due to factors other than uncertainty about changing differences in inflation rates. Besides the many factors outside the field of economics, which can be very important for portfolio decisions,[9] the increasing number of problems arising from the balance of current transactions seems to have been the main contributing factor. This happens because the foreign-exchange markets are without information and therefore without a real sense of orientation regarding the question of how much and for how long a country's currency should be revalued or devalued, if current-account surpluses or deficits occur which are considered to be too high. The phrase 'considered to be too high' is a problem in itself, as it is by no means evident that the current-account disequilibria must disappear at all. Nevertheless, the idea that these surpluses or deficits cannot simply be allowed to accumulate without limit seems, rightly or wrongly, to influence the markets. Yet what changes in exchange rates are considered to be 'correct'?

The daily reports of events on the foreign-exchange markets give a rather depressing picture of the key motives of dealers. Someone who has been an observer for many years once said that 'there seem to be psychological switches that go off and on in people's heads. My idea is that the market is always focussing on a particular psychological variable. For a while, it's interest rates. If they go up, in the case of the dollar, then the dollar should probably go up. But now the big factor seems to be trade balances.'[10] Monetary theory seems to have been lagging behind developments rather than taking the lead. But theory has now reached the point where, as Marina von N. Whitman, of the University of Pittsburgh, said recently, it has come full circle. This circle started with the Keynesian emphasis on transfer problems, went on to the monetarist theory of the neutrality of the exchange rate in the long run (which fitted so well with the excessive fixation on the need for nominal exchange-rate changes in the discussion before the demise of the Bretton Woods system) and returned to the old concern with the importance of real variables, current-account balances and the terms of trade.[11] Yet the size of the exchange-rate changes which are considered necessary in the case of real disturbances seems to be arbitrary.

We have to ask ourselves whether it is a process of trial and error in which the possibility of expectations becoming self-fulfilling is a relief or an additional burden. Moreover, it may well be indisputable that, since 1973, exchange rates have been much more unstable than was predicted by the proponents of flexible exchange rates— but was this instability as intolerable as had been predicted by the opponents of flexible exchange rates?

EXCHANGE-RATE CHANGES AND DOMESTIC POLICIES

Members of the private sector do not complain much about the flexible exchange-rate system. It must be considered today an outcome of pure pessimism that, before 1973, numerous dangers for international trade were predicted. The private sector has learned to live with the new system and hence was not a proponent of the foundation of the European Monetary System (EMS).

As expected, the economy has become accustomed to the fact that the contents of business deals already concluded are subject to exchange-rate risks. Forward markets offering protection against exchange-rate fluctuations on reasonable terms are still not as strongly developed as might have been thought. Private firms, however, have found other ways of minimising their open foreign-exchange positions, either by keeping their own balance of trade in equilibrium, or by hedging their foreign trade transactions through financial transactions.

The rapid change in exchange-rate conditions may raise the costs of negotiating new business deals. Yet, in the years since 1973, there have been such enormous international upheavals in variables other than exchange rates—the great change in inflation rates, the oil-price shocks, excesses in the prices of other raw materials, world recession—that a longing for a return to the Bretton Woods system seemed unrealistic and, probably for that very reason, did not emerge.

The makers of economic policy had greater cause for complaint than the private sector of the economy. The large real changes in exchange rates produced by the foreign-exchange markets made life difficult for domestic economic policymakers and certainly did not foster the conditions necessary for harmonising policy on an international level. The greatest difficulties have been in the field of monetary policy—precisely the sphere where it had been hoped that the change to flexible exchange rates would bring about complete autonomy. The liberation from the chains of the Bretton Woods system was followed in a number of countries by attempts to establish stricter rules for control of the money supply. But large real changes in exchange rates created unexpected problems—even new conceptual problems. The monetarist credo, inherent in the new monetary policy, requires a steady increase in the money supply, either at a constant rate or at least at a rate based on the growth of the productive capacity of the whole economy, which changes only gradually. This raises the question of whether large real changes in the exchange rate should continue to be regarded as insignificant when setting targets for money-supply control. Real changes in exchange rates may be a reflection of shifts in the required holdings of a particular currency as an international reserve currency. In such cases an accommodating policy is advisable, even though it seems almost impossible to specify the correct amount.

It is much more difficult, on a conceptual level, to give the correct monetary-policy response to real changes in exchange rates caused by other factors. Their effect on the price level and/or employment may well be undesirable. Nonetheless, a monetary policy based on constant growth is not allowed to combat these effects actively: it dispenses with anti-cyclical measures on principle. Among the advantages of the monetarist concept are its clarity and the unambiguity of the instructions it gives in the field of monetary policy, which provides clarity in the definition of the roles of monetary policy, fiscal policy and incomes policy. The monetarist approach and its inherent advantages must not be cast aside thoughtlessly, simply because external economic problems happen to arise. We would then slip back into the arbitrariness of a discretionary policy which lacks quantitative direction. But when there are massive real changes in exchange rates one cannot simply sit back on one's principles and trust to God that the world will not come to an end as it is, after all, held together by a stable demand-for-money function. The only people who might do so are those who are convinced that a 'distorted' exchange rate cannot exist for more than a short time. In past years, the Bundesbank has encountered such external economic limits to the efficiency of money-supply control several times. In 1978, a period of massive revaluation of the mark, and in 1980, a period of massive real devaluation, it abandoned the policy of controlling the money supply on the basis of the growth of the economy's productive capacity and, subsequently, it attempted to counteract the prevailing trend of the exchange rate through large-scale intervention ('leaning against the wind'). The Bundesbank took this course because it wanted to avoid the inflationary or deflationary consequences of the trend of exchange-rate movements.

In an analysis of the intervention policy of the central banks of numerous countries, Rüdiger Dornbusch, of the Massachusetts Institute of Technology, established that the intervention policy of the Bundesbank contains an element of a 'beggar-thy-neighbour' attitude[12] in that its inclination towards intervention is noticeably dependent on the requirements of domestic stability and employment policies. This view could only be endorsed, however, (i) if one ascribed to intervention on foreign-exchange markets a far greater effect on the exchange rate than to all other measures of money-supply control and (ii) if the need for domestic stabilisation and employment policies had not itself been the consequence of real changes in the exchange rate.

There are good grounds on which to dispute point (i) as, for example, Professor Niehans has suggested.[13] But we cannot talk of a central bank having a beggar-thy-neighbour attitude to intervention if exchange-rate effects are only a by-product of overall monetary policy. They are then merely a way in which the effects of monetary policy are transmitted from the domestic economic sector to the external economic sector (exchange-rate effects as the external equivalent of interest-rate changes).

The latter point has proved to be a problem on several occasions and was, at least according to the Bundesbank's own commentaries, a decisive factor in determining the extent of its intervention. Admittedly, the Bundesbank always has very good reasons for its interpretation of events.

Let us return, however, to the question of the domestic auto-

nomy of monetary policy under flexible exchange rates. As mentioned earlier, it is the concept of money-*supply* control which has
created the clear impression that, in spite of predictions to the
contrary, domestic monetary policy continues to be greatly affected
by events abroad, even when exchange rates are flexible. Everything that compels us to depart from domestic money-supply
targets (generally external economic shocks) seems to indicate that
autonomy in the field of monetary policy is restricted. But is this
not too narrow a definition of autonomy?—for the ability to pursue
a monetary policy to stabilise the price level is not questioned.

When, in the 1950s, economists like Sohmen began to enlist
support for flexible exchange rates by arguing that they would give
domestic monetary policy greater autonomy, they were not thinking
of a concept of money-supply control, but rather of interest-rate
policy. More particularly, they still considered monetary policy to
be a useful instrument for controlling the business cycle. While
admitting that a 'conflict' situation might well arise as a result of
disturbances originating abroad, this possibility was not explained in
any more detail. What was emphasised was the—correct—prediction that purely monetary disturbances from abroad could be
absorbed without conflicts between policy goals. This gave rise to
the temptation to over-emphasise the formally quite correct proposition that, in the strict sense, there are no balance-of-payments
problems and therefore no balance-of-payments imperatives in
monetary policy under flexible exchange rates. This is not wrong,
but what is important in the final analysis is that we cannot be
indifferent to the answer to the question: at which exchange rate are
demand and supply brought into equilibrium? For this reason, the
possibility of a conflict in aims exists.

Is it then true that 'restricted autonomy of domestic monetary
policy' and 'monetary policy in a conflict of aims' are one and the
same thing? From experience of the dangers of excessively large
real changes in exchange rates some people draw the conclusion
that it is illusory to think that monetary policy affects only the value
of money and not the employment level. This, they claim, is true,
in any event, if the exchange rate takes on a dominant inflationary
or deflationary role. It will assume this leading role, they say,
when, under a neutral money-supply policy, neither any reasonable
fiscal policy nor any acceptable incomes policy could cope with
disruptive impulses which emanate from the exchange rate without
affecting either inflation or employment. Then, according to this

view, decisions on monetary policy must be taken which cannot avoid the conflict of aims. One does not have to draw this conclusion: it is possible to retreat to the position that an anticyclical monetary policy does not help even in such circumstances. But there is no compelling evidence for that position.

Not only national autonomy of monetary policy is under discussion here. We are also concerned with national autonomy with regard to the level of real wages in the economy. If a country's exchange rate is a function of change in average wage rates, and if such a functional relationship is not counteracted by monetary policy, then the country cannot increase its level of employment by means of an incomes policy designed to improve the international competitiveness of the firms in its export sector. All that can then be done is to increase employment in the domestic economic sector—which is admittedly easier in this case (see below). One might have gained the impression from past experience in the Federal Republic of Germany that every attempt to create new opportunities for employment through a cautious wages policy turned out to be in vain, since it induced even greater confidence in the stability of the mark, thereby forcing the exchange rate to ever-higher levels. A country in this position certainly has no overall cause for complaint. The opposite is rather the case. (Nowadays the lack of the beneficial effects of such confidence in the mark is rather regretted in West Germany.) Nevertheless, an international monetary system which influences the effectiveness of a country's incomes policy in this way greatly reduces the credibility of the assignment of roles to the different types of domestic economic policies. If monetary policy is supposed only to be used to determine the value of money, and fiscal policy to control efficiency and growth, while incomes policy regulates the level of employment, then incomes policy ought at least to have a fair chance of being effective.

With regard to fiscal policy, hopes of improved efficiency were not great when flexible rates were instituted. On the other hand, deterioration was not expected. The conception was that an expansionary fiscal policy financed by borrowing would attract foreign capital through its interest-rate effects. Thus, the monetary side of the chain of effects would in itself tend towards a revaluation of the currency. This conception was, however, mistaken. An increase in the supply of domestically issued bonds constitutes an impulse in the direction of currency devaluation. Devaluation of a currency and/or higher interest rates are the two ways of placing the increased supply of bonds in the portfolios of residents and non-residents. If such borrowing causes expectations regarding the stability of the currency to deteriorate, a massive devaluation or a massive rise in interest rates may be required. The belief that an expansionary fiscal policy can be financed by an increase in government debt without a pronounced rise in interest rates therefore must have been weakened under flexible exchange rates. The level of interest rates is determined less by confidence in the debtors than by confidence in the currency and, in the case of flexible exchange rates, a greater weight is attached to the confidence of foreigners in the external value of the currency.

EXCHANGE RATES AND STRUCTURAL IMBALANCES

Last but not least, it is one of the most regrettable consequences of unwanted real exchange-rate changes that structural distortions are caused in the economies affected.

In the Federal Republic of Germany, the Bundesbank, in 1980-81, was attempting to counteract a massive tendency towards a real devaluation of the mark, which would create a strong expansive impulse for export industries and those sectors of the economy which compete with imports. Such an expansive impetus was, in itself, quite desirable in the state of the economy at that time. Nevertheless, it was considered too strong because of its possible inflationary consequences. Its initial positive effect was therefore dampened by rising interest rates: the long-term real rate of interest was for a while above five per cent. For the external sector, a surplus gained from the expansionary impulse from the changed exchange rate may well have outweighed the contractionary impulse from the restrictive monetary policy. But for the domestic economic sector, especially residential construction which is sensitive to interest rates, there was nothing but restriction.

In view of West Germany's enormous balance-of-payments deficit on current account in 1980, it was inevitable that the external sector expanded at the cost of the domestic economic sector. An arbitrarily large change in relative prices in favour of the external sector cannot continue, though. Experience has shown that it disappears, at least partially, in an increase in the general price level. The degree of effectiveness of a devaluation (initial real devaluation in relation to the real devaluation remaining after a certain period) may well decrease very rapidly as the rate of the devaluation increases.

An excessively high rate of interest for a brief period is not, however, necessarily the correct criterion for selecting those sectors of the economy which must reduce their capacity. This task really should be carried out by changes in relative prices. A drop in wage costs would also work in the right direction from the structural point of view. One might even wish to have a low rate of interest to accelerate the process of adjustment in the economy to changed external conditions—for example, a move away from oil—on the ground that the adjustment requires huge extra investment. In fact, though, we had an exceptionally high rate of interest forced upon us by the exchange-rate situation. It is true that our low rate of inflation should allow fairly low interest rates without a fall in the exchange rate, even in a situation of high current-account deficits, but the required international confidence cannot be obtained by force. There is, on the other hand, no need to praise an international monetary system in which minor fluctuations in international confidence make the problems of adjustment of an open economy so difficult. After all, there are hardly any reasons for a large loss of confidence. Why should anybody in the world doubt that during the next few years the Federal Republic of Germany will be able to pay its bills without having to stage a closing-down sale?

At this point we must return to the question of the autonomy of monetary policy. The Bundesbank was forced not only to follow the restrictive course of monetary policy in other countries (although the domestic economic situation provided us with reasons to do so), but also even to outdo it, simply to keep in check an exchange rate which had gone out of control. Are we now even less autonomous with regard to the real rate of interest than at the time of Bretton Woods because of unrestrained movements in exchange rates?

It is not only the question of the autonomy of domestic economic policy under conditions of flexible exchange rates which, in most cases, is generally seen more rationally these days than ten years ago. There has also been a great change in the way the opportunities and risks inherent in exchange-rate changes are assessed. There are at least two reasons for this, which, however, are not independent of each other. One reason is the change in attitude to the problem of inflation in the world. The second is the greater awareness of the problems on the supply side of the economy.

Inflation is nowadays regarded all over the world as Public

Enemy No. 1. It is unfashionable to hope for permanent advantages in the sphere of employment by accepting inflation. It has proved to be a mistake to reduce excessive demands on aggregate output by inflation. But this certainly does not abolish excessive demand. Thus economic policy must refer back to the supply side: voluntary reductions of wage claims, increasing the scope for high claims by encouraging innovation and increases in productivity, lowering the risk premium required of entrepreneurs by lowering risks and increasing the supply of risk-bearing willingness—these are the themes of economic policy after the demise of the Keynesian illusions. A money-supply policy aimed consistently at achieving stability is a vital part of this, but it is certainly not a cure for all evils.

REVALUATION AND THE ADJUSTMENT PROBLEM

Changes in exchange rates are also seen differently today. It is now considered outdated to believe either that changes in exchange rates are a neutral correlate of international differences in inflation rates or that they affect aggregate demand via a change in relative prices—expansively in the case of a devaluation of the domestic currency, contractively in the case of a revaluation. In the field of employment policy, interest was previously focussed primarily on the effects of devaluations, even though under fixed exchange rates countries were not exactly anxious to devalue their own currency, but preferred a revaluation of foreign currencies. This interest has, to a great extent, disappeared, since it has become clear how difficult it is to give the real *quid pro quo* necessary for lasting effects on employment—the 'acceptance' of a deterioration in the terms of trade—by merely manipulating the exchange rate. Experience has shown too often that a country experiencing stability problems adjusts more quickly to more expensive imports via increases in its price and wage levels than it does to better export opportunities via changes in production and employment.

Apart from the fact that there is a far greater fear of inflation nowadays, the reversal of the old exchange-rate argument as a theoretical basis for employment changes usefully fits the ubiquitous aversion to devaluations. In fiscal policy an increase in public expenditure is received as expansionary from the point of view of demand, whereas a cut in public expenditure is considered as expansionary from the point of view of supply; similarly, a (real) devaluation is expansionary on the demand side, whereas a (real) revaluation is expansionary on the supply side. To be more precise: real revaluation is a proof of an expansionary impulse on the supply side. That a drop in interest rates prescribed by monetary policy cannot be regarded as a real improvement in the investment conditions of an economy is just as true as the same proposition for the case of a revaluation of the currency staged by economic policy. Only if the market places a higher (real) value on the currency, can the revaluation be considered as indicating an improvement in the supply conditions of the economy.

The main reasons for a real revaluation are either one, or all, of the following: it enables one to buy foreign products at a lower real price than previously, one can sell one's own products abroad at a higher price, and one can borrow capital at lower interest rates. It is evident that this is equivalent to an increase in productivity in the whole economy. It is becoming increasingly obvious that international confidence in a currency is as good as cash itself.

An excessive amount of confidence can, however, cause irksome difficulties. For example, if an economy experiences an inflow of capital from abroad, which forces its exchange rate upwards, it is, for the reasons mentioned above, wrong immediately to interpret this whole process as having a contractionary effect on the economy in that it causes a reduction in exports and an increase in imports. The change in the exchange rate is not the first link in the chain of events. If the inflow of capital is an expression of increased international confidence in the economy and its currency, that is, an expression of willingness to hold domestic assets with a lower risk premium, then the revaluation and the real transfer it initiates is, in principle, only a by-product of a process in which the beneficial effect of the increase in wealth resulting from the increased confidence is realised. It is, however, uncertain whether the overall effect on the level of employment will be positive or negative. This will be decided by the way in which the economy uses the increase in wealth. If there were complaints about the improved terms of trade from trading partners, this would mean that the economy would not be able to use the increase in wealth adequately. Using it adequately means making sure that the opportunities to share in the benefits from the improvement in the terms of trade offered to the economy are distributed in such a way that the adjustment, according to market-economy principles, is eventually divided up in a purposive way between greater consumption (from domestic and foreign production) and higher or perhaps lower domestic production (and employment).

If, as in capital theory, we start from the assumption of the liquidity-preference theory of the rate of interest, then the adjustment to the increase in wealth must be controlled by the development of (real) wages and interest rates, with wages being the dominant factor. Greater consumption and more capital-intensive domestic production (possibly higher exports, too) are therefore achieved by means of a real wage, which is higher than it would have been without the increase in wealth, but certainly not so much higher that it completely absorbs the terms-of-trade gain. Some of the gain must remain to make an increase in domestic production profitable. The interest rate on capital would then fall because of a shift to the right of the IS *and* the LM curve, with the latter, however, in this case dominating. On its own the capital inflow does, in principle, mean a shift of the LM curve to the right. This shift must, however, be backed up domestically. Moreover, the danger must be averted of an ultimate shift to the left caused by the induced real transfer and the resulting domestic burden of adjustment. It is therefore only by means of an 'adequate use' of the increase in wealth arising from the gain in confidence that the greater confidence, which is actually confidence granted in advance, will, so to speak, be safeguarded.

The task of adjustment may be difficult. But a country like the Federal Republic of Germany, which faced this task in 1978, today appreciates how much greater are the opportunities contained in such a situation when compared with the present one, where a loss of confidence in the mark has become apparent.

THE INTERNATIONAL MONETARY SYSTEM TODAY

The international monetary system is beset by problems on all sides. Even its advantages cannot be taken up without first overcoming difficulties. Can, or should, this system survive?

If one were in the same situation now as in the second half of the 1960s, armed with all the experience of hindsight, I am sure that one would fight with all one's might to keep to the rules of the Bretton Woods system instead of watching the destruction of the system by an excess of infringements of the rules. But this is not the situation. No one has the chance to make the same mistake twice.

Apart from returning to the Bretton Woods system there are a number of other possibilities which are equally unattainable.

(a) There is no question of a monetary policy aimed at stabilising real exchange rates. Even though there are many—even too many—unwanted changes in real exchange rates, this does not mean that they can be dispensed with. We know as little about the 'correct' exchange-rate trends as we do about the changes needed in case of current-account disequilibria. Moreover, monetary policy is not able to achieve this.

(b) Neither is there any question, as a worldwide solution, of everyone pursuing a monetary policy completely determined by the balance of payments with the proviso that they should keep to a particular path with regard to the movement in nominal exchange rates. The international differences in inflation rates are not (yet) stable enough for this.

(c) There is no question of pursuing a monetary policy which does not take into account the balance of payments and the exchange rate. No central bank would be well advised to underrate the danger of a vicious circle, not even the Bundesbank with its long reputation of keeping inflation at bay. Confidence can easily disappear where money is concerned.

(d) There is no question of levying the Tobin tax on every international exchange of money ('to throw some sand in the wheels of our excessively efficient international money market')[14] or any other similar capitulation to the problems of the international movement of capital. In most cases efficiency of international money markets is particularly welcome. Why should we obstruct them on a global level?

As all of these solutions cannot seriously be considered, we are left with the necessity of muddling through, which is hardly a precise concept.

With the foundation of the EMS a number of European countries have tried to give the fascinating idea of a fixed exchange-rate system a new lease of life, on a regional basis at least. Its main aim is to provide the monetary framework for an international division of labour by requiring each country to cope with the unforeseen disturbances which constantly occur in such a way that the external value of its currency remains constant, and by each country agreeing to grant credit to other member countries. Stabilisation of the domestic value of money is based on the same wisdom. That the

EMS was founded in spite of the large differences in inflation rates between members can be understood only against the background of the re-evaluation of the importance which the fight against inflation was supposed to have in the future. The problem of inflation in Europe has not diminished since the EMS was established in 1980. In fact, the opposite has been true. Nevertheless the EMS is underrated by those on the academic scene. One cannot criticise the EMS in 1982 for not achieving its aims as one did in the case of Bretton Woods in 1973. After all, not many of the dreams associated with flexible exchange rates have been realised.

On the other hand, the exchange rates of the currencies involved in the EMS have been unexpectedly stable during the first years. It is a stability which is admittedly inexplicable. It is inexplicable that there have not yet been any serious crises caused by speculation. The obvious aversion of all countries to devaluation is not a sufficient explanation; it certainly was not sufficient before 1973. At this point, I might mention that it would have been better if the United Kingdom had joined the EMS at the very beginning. The unpopular revaluation of the pound sterling in 1980 might possibly have been avoided or would at least have been considerably smaller.

Unfortunately the EMS does not yet have any regulatory mechanism which takes into account the desire for stability expressed in the aversion to devaluations and which simultaneously provides for timely changes in exchange rates even when they are not enforced by the market. National economies must have the courage to give the market instructions. But such action has to be realistic. If this is done energetically, the process of adjustment should be under control.

No satisfactory middle way has yet been found between a system of fixed exchange rates and a system of 'clean' floating. Academic discussion of this problem is also weak, much weaker than at the time when the crawling peg was under discussion. It must be hoped that those eminent economists who have in the last fifteen years distinguished themselves by explaining to the world, both in advance and at the time, what life would be like under a system of flexible exchange rates, will participate more strongly in this discussion and that they will not consider it beneath themselves to question the purity of their strict concept.

I see only one alternative to the attempts to find acceptable middle ways in international monetary policy. This is that we should prolong the experiment with flexible exchange rates for another few years. During this time we should, however, adopt a rigorous policy of stabilising the price levels of the most important economies. Such stabilisation should not have the vague aim of 'relative' stability of the value of money, but should aim at a zero inflation rate. At the end of this path it could be seen whether fewer unforeseeable real changes in exchange rates had occurred or not. We would then have to decide whether to retain flexible exchange rates or to re-establish a new system of fixed exchange rates on a worldwide basis.[15]

NOTES AND REFERENCES

1. Rüdiger Dornbusch, 'Exchange Rate Economics: Where Do We Stand?', *Brookings Papers on Economic Activity*, Washington, No. 1, 1980, pp. 143-85; and 'Comments' by William H. Branson, *ibid.*, p. 194.

2. See Sachverständigenrat zur Begutachtung der gesamtwirtschaftlichen Entwicklung, *Expansion und Stabilität—Jahresgutachten 1966/67* (Stuttgart and Mainz: W. Kohlhammer GmbH, 1966), paragraph 274.

3. See Egon Sohmen, *Flexible Exchange Rates: Theory and Controversy* (Chicago and London: University of Chicago Press, 1961), pp. 132 *et seq.*

4. See, for instance, Herbert Giersch, 'On the Desirable Degree of Flexibility of Exchange Rates', *Weltwirtschaftliches Archiv*, Kiel, Vol. 109, 1973, pp. 191-209.

5. See Sohmen, *op. cit.*, pp. 111 *et seq.*

6. See, for instance, Peter Isard, *Exchange-Rate Determination: a Survey of Popular Views and Recent Models*, Princeton Studies in International Finance No. 42 (Princeton: Princeton University Press, 1978) and Dornbusch, *op. cit.*, pp. 145 *et seq.*

7. See Fritz Machlup, 'On Terms, Concepts, Theories and Strategies in the Discussion of Greater Flexibility of Exchange Rates', *Banca Nazionale del Lavoro Quarterly Review*, Rome, No. 92, March 1970.

8. Jürg Niehans, 'Stabilisierung in einer offenen Volkswirtschaft', in Hans K. Schneider, Waldemar Wittmann and Hans Würgler (eds), *Stabilisierungspolitik in der Marktwirtschaft*, Schriften des Vereins für Socialpolitik, N.F., Vol. 85 (Berlin: Duncker & Humblot, 1979).

9. See Paul Einzig, *Foreign Exchange Crises: an Essay in Economic Pathology*, 2nd ed. (London: Macmillan and New York: St Martin's Press, 1970), p. 113.

10. J. Barnett, Vice-President of Citibank, quoted in Jacque Artus, 'Methods of Assessing the Long-Run Equilibrium Value of an Exchange Rate', *Journal of International Economics*, Amsterdam, No. 1, pp. 277-293, 1978.

11. See Marina von N. Whitman, 'Comments' on Dornbusch's paper, *op. cit.*, pp. 195-202.

12. See Dornbusch, *op. cit.*, pp. 173-76.

208   *Reflections on a Troubled World Economy*

13. See Niehans, 'Volkswirtschaftliche Wirkungen alternativer geld-politischer Instrumente in einer kleinen offenen Volkswirtschaft', 1980, mimeograph.

14. James Tobin, *A Proposal for International Monetary Reform*, Cowles Foundation Discussion Paper 506 (New Haven: Yale University Press, 1978), p. 3.

15. This article was translated, from the German, by Stephen F. Frowen and Bruce Gibbons.

Part IV

General Economic Policies

10 Economic Malaise and a Positive Programme for a Benevolent and Enlightened Dictator

Gottfried Haberler

In a paper written in 1979,[1] I analysed the economic malaise that in the 1970s had gripped the United States and other Western industrial countries after a long period of rapid growth, optimism and euphoria in the 1950s and early 1960s. The malaise continued and became more intense in 1980. All recent reports on the state of the world economy and the prospects for the coming years from national and international agencies—the International Monetary Fund (IMF), the Organisation for Economic Cooperation and Development (OECD), the Bank for International Settlements (BIS), the Commission of the European Community, the Institut für Weltwirtschaft in Kiel, *et cetera*[2]—are tinged with pessimism and gloom, predicting more inflation, near-zero or negative productivity growth, stagnating or declining gross national product (GNP) and high unemployment. The Reagan Administration in the United States has been warned of the danger of an 'economic Dunkirk', requiring the declaration of an economic emergency. And even some of those who, rightly in my opinion, reject the idea of declaring an economic emergency, call the present outlook frightening.

In my 1979 paper [3] I traced the malaise to two related developments: a seemingly intractable chronic inflation in its modern vicious form of stagflation; and low or near-zero productivity growth and GNP stagnation. I argued that these twin afflictions are not due to a basic flaw in the free-market and free-enterprise capitalist system; on the contrary, they are the result of the Western industrial economies having moved too far away from the competitive ideal.

In this essay I discuss how a benevolent and enlightened dictator would deal with the problem. This approach permits me to concentrate on the economics of the problem and to bypass the, admittedly important, question of the political feasibility of such a programme in a democracy.

211

A benevolent dictator is one who respects consumer sovereignty, who does not, as actual dictators usually do, impose on the people his own views of what is good for them. An enlightened dictator is one who realises that to get the best results, to achieve rapid growth, full employment and price stability, he has to rely on free and competitive markets, with real competition, private property, the means of production and respect for adequate profit margins. In other words, an enlightened dictator does not try to substitute central planning for free markets and recognises the theories of democratic, competitive socialism *à la* Oscar Lange and H. D. Dickinson[4] as what they are—unrealistic utopias.

HOW MUCH POWER TO THE DICTATOR?

The power of the enlightened dictator must be circumscribed in a reasonable way. Simply to endow him with omniscience and omnipotence would beg too many questions and stamp the approach as an irrelevant and utopian exercise.

It is not unreasonable, however, to assume that the dictator would be in full control of monetary and fiscal policies. That would make it possible for him to solve the credibility problem. It would exclude political interference by a recalcitrant parliament swayed by pressures of special interest groups. Thus the public could be persuaded that the announced policies would be carried out consistently.

Monetary Restraint

The central bank would be instructed to reduce monetary growth to approximately the rate of potential real GNP growth. That leaves open technical questions such as the choice of the monetary aggregates, the speed of the reduction of monetary growth and occasional deviations from the norm. These decisions can be left to the monetary experts, who would be freed from political interference and the pressures of special interest groups.

Need for Fiscal Restraint

The enlightened dictator would realise, however, that for optimum results monetary policy needs to be supported by fiscal policy. Specifically, large government deficits must be scaled down. True, sufficiently tight money could bring down the rate of inflation irrespective of the size of the budget deficit. But the side effects on productivity and investment of tight money and an easy budget (large deficits) would be serious. This policy mix would drive up interest rates and crowd out productive private investment, thus slowing down the growth of productivity and GNP. This in turn would make the fight against inflation more difficult, for in a stagnating economy it is much harder than in a growing one to accommodate rising claims on the national product and to shift resources from obsolescent and declining industries to new growth industries.

But the importance of a tight fiscal policy, as a supplement to monetary restraint, goes far beyond balancing the budget. The size of the budget and the tax structure are equally important for productivity growth and thus indirectly for the fight against inflation. Thus our enlightened dictator would do his best to reduce government expenditures, expenditures on goods and services as well as transfer payments, in order to free resources for productive investment and to lighten the tax burden. The magnitude of the tax burden and the tax structure have become a major impediment for the attainment of maximum growth. The tax structure has been greatly distorted by inflation. Inflation has pushed taxpayers into higher and higher tax brackets, has led to the taxation of inflationary phantom profits and of negative interests—thereby discouraging saving and investment. A radical reform of the tax system to eliminate the existing distortions would be a high priority task. Reducing the progressivity and indexation of the income tax and realistic allowances would go a long way to reforming the tax structure. [5]

The beneficial effects of such reform measures on the flow of savings and investment and on productivity and GNP growth would be substantial and thus can be expected eventually to result in an increase in tax revenues. But our enlightened dictator would realise that these beneficial effects are likely to emerge only slowly. He therefore would carefully watch the impact on the budget. In the short run, tax revenues will decline and the budget deficit will increase. In order to avoid inflationary effects, tax reductions and tax reform should therefore go hand in hand with expenditure cuts.

Monetarists who, rightly, stress the monetary nature of inflation and the primary responsibility of monetary policy for winding down inflation, usually add that it is imperative that tight money be supplemented by a tight fiscal policy. They concede that in order to avoid side effects of monetary restraint on output, employment and investment, and to improve the growth performance of the economy, budget deficits must be scaled down, the size of the government reduced and the tax structure reformed.

Role of Wage and Price Rigidity

This qualification of pure monetarism has very important implications. It raises the question: are there no factors other than a soft fiscal policy that also aggravate the side effects of an anti-inflationary tight-money policy on output, employment and productivity? The answer is: there are, indeed, such factors which, in a sense that will become clear presently, are even more basic and important than the budgetary and fiscal policy problem. Our enlightened dictator would understand that the fight against inflation would not be so difficult, in fact he would understand that stagflation on the present scale would be impossible, if our economy had not moved so far away from the competitive ideal. He would realise that changing that trend, making the economy more competitive and flexible, is of great importance for curbing inflation and promoting growth.

Let us compare how the problem of unemployment would be solved in an ideally, or even a moderately, competitive economy with the actual situation. If monetary-fiscal restraint initially causes unemployment, in a fully competitive economy, money wages and labour cost would decline, so that the level of employment could be quickly restored. In a moderately competitive economy, money wages would at least stop rising, so that wage costs could decline gradually parallel to the rise in labour productivity. Actually, money wages have become almost totally rigid downwards, both in the aggregate and in particular industries. Striking examples are provided by the American automobile and steel industries. These industries pay the highest union wages in the economy although they are in deep trouble and suffer from high unemployment and slack. This would be impossible in a competitive economy. Furthermore, real wages, too, have become increasingly rigid downwards, through formal and *de facto* indexation, and unions often push up real wages in the face of substantial unemployment.

Labour unions are not the only culprits. Other pressure groups often force the government through political pressure to do for their members what unions do for workers. Organised agriculture is the most conspicuous and important example. Monetarists in general have neglected, ignored, downplayed or even denied the importance of this development for the fight against inflation. But there is one exception. The great monetarist Harry G. Johnson, in one of his last papers before his death in 1977, wrote:

'Over the period since World War II governments have been assuming wider and wider responsibilities. In particular, their commitment to full employment has been carried to absurd lengths, well beyond the limits of feasibility. In some countries, there now appears to be a commitment not only for every man to be employed, but for him to be employed in the occupation of his choice, in the location of his choice and, it would sometimes seem, at the income of his choice.'

In a footnote to the second sentence of this passage Johnson added: 'This has been a significant factor in the inflationary tendencies that have developed in a number of industrialised countries— especially in the United Kingdom.'[6]

Typical of the neglect of the problem of institutional rigidities by most monetarists and rational expectations theorists is a paper by Karl Brunner, of the Graduate School of Management, University of Rochester, and Alex Cukierman and Allan H. Meltzer, both of Carnegie-Mellon University, Pittsburgh.[7] The gist of the paper can be told and evaluated without wading through the flood of mathematical formulae with which the argument is presented. According to the authors, 'persistent unemployment' and stagflation 'can occur in a neo-classical framework[8]. . . in which all expectations are rational and all markets clear instantaneously'.[9] In other words, perfect competition is compatible with unemployment and stagflation.

For the problem at hand the relevant part of the authors' theory is the supply function of labour. It goes like this: to determine the amount of labour they are willing to supply, 'workers compare the currently prevailing wage to the wage they currently perceive as permanent'.[10] If the prevailing wage is equal to the perceived permanent wage, there is full employment. Now suppose the economy is subjected to a 'shock'—the authors usually speak of a 'change in productivity'. If productivity goes up, the actual real wage is raised 'on impact'. But the workers cannot know immediately whether the change is permanent. Therefore 'the currently perceived permanent wage' will for some time be below the actually ruling wage. This will induce workers to supply more labour, that means 'to work now and substitute future for current leisure', resulting in 'negative unemployment'.[11] Negative unemployment is what is usually called overfull employment.

If the shock is unfavourable (negative), the real wage will be reduced 'on impact'. But again the workers cannot be sure what the permanent wage will be. Therefore the actual wage will for some time be below the currently perceived permanent wage. This will induce 'part of the labor force which looks for work [to] abstain from accepting current employment. This group is counted as unemployed in the official statistics'.[12] If 'negative unemployment' means 'substitution of future leisure for current leisure' then positive unemployment means 'substitution of present leisure for future leisure'.

To describe unemployment as leisure is rather odd. At any rate, it is voluntary unemployment, workers being on the margin of indifference between working and non-working (leisure). But the authors do not even mention the indispensable distinction between voluntary and involuntary unemployment.

That the authors are a little uneasy about their definition of unemployment is suggested by the fact that, while they speak repeatedly of *persistent* unemployment, in a footnote[13] they suddenly say: 'Since the focus of the paper is on cyclical unemployment, we do not discuss types of unemployment that arise for other reasons.' What the other types of unemployment are is not explained. A rational interpretation, I suggest, would be that despite the talk about *persistent* unemployment, the authors had the comparatively mild postwar recessions in mind all along. It is true that in these recessions, due to generous unemployment benefits and welfare payments, the official unemployment figures contain a significant amount of spurious, that is voluntary, unemployment. It is also well known that generous unemployment benefits have increased frictional unemployment (workers who have lost their jobs taking more time to look for suitable new jobs) and have reduced the hardship of unemployment. But it is surely an exaggeration to say, as the authors seem to imply, that all or the great bulk of registered unemployment is of the voluntary kind and that unemployment no longer involves great hardship.[14]

How to Make the Economy More Competitive

Since government policies are to a large extent responsible for the power of the various pressure groups to push up wages and prices, our enlightened dictator should be able to reduce the pressure on wages and prices considerably without taking such drastic steps as prohibiting collective, industry-wide bargaining, outlawing indexation of wages, abrogating existing union wage contracts and the like. Merely withdrawing privileges, protective measures and subsidies that are now accorded lavishly to numerous pressure groups would go a long way towards taking some of the burden of fighting inflation off the shoulders of the monetary authorities, towards producing price stability and towards reducing the transitional unemployment resulting from monetary-fiscal restraint.

As far as industrial monopolies and oligopolies are concerned, freer trade is the most powerful and administratively easiest method to restore and maintain competition. Given the enormous growth of world trade, especially in manufactured goods during the postwar period, and the fact that numerous new industrial centres have emerged in developed and less developed countries, few significant monopolies or oligopolies could survive under free trade (outside the public utility area where prices are controlled anyway). Needless to say that, in addition to ensuring competition, freer trade would also increase GNP through more extended international division of labour. The increased flow of goods would have an anti-inflationary effect. Since high tariffs, import quotas and other non-tariff measures affecting trade are still widespread, in spite of the liberalisation of international trade that has taken place under the aegis of the General Agreement on Tariffs and Trade (GATT), there is a rich field here for our enlightened dictator to move the economy closer to the competitive ideal. The concept of non-tariff measures should be interpreted broadly to include subsidies to non-competitive firms and industries, also in the form of taking over non-competitive firms and operating them with great losses at the expense of the taxpayer.

Curbing the power of labour unions is probably the most difficult part of a policy for liberalising the economy. But opening up the economy to foreign competition would go a long way towards reducing the power of unions. Unions know, or find out quickly, that striking against world markets is risky. This is the reason why in small countries where international trade is a large fraction of the economy, labour unions are usually much more reasonable than in large countries.

Specific measures in the United States to reduce the power of unions to push up wages are the abolition of the Davis-Bacon Act which forces the government to buy exclusively from industries

J

paying the highest union wages, eliminating minimum wage laws, prohibiting closed-shop agreements, restricting the right to picket and withdrawing unemployment benefits from striking workers.

Doing all these things would reduce monopolistic wage and price pressure, promote labour mobility, enlarge the international division of labour, stimulate growth and reduce government expenditures by eliminating the vast bureaucracies that are now needed to administer the existing restrictions, privileges and subsidies. It is needless to add that de-regulation of industries will rank high on the list of urgent tasks. The regulatory explosion of the 1970s, and earlier, should be stopped and rolled back a good distance.

The question arises: is that all there is to it? Are there not other causes of inflation that have not been mentioned so far? Does our dictator not need additional powers to deal with those factors?

The Oil-price Rise

What comes to mind first is the Organisation of Petroleum Exporting Countries (OPEC) and the recent and prospective oil-price rises. In the United States and lately also in West Germany the second oil shock of 1979-80 is frequently mentioned as the major if not decisive cause of inflation and stagnation.

That the oil-price rise as such was not decisive is demonstrated by the fact that some countries that depend much more on imported oil than the United States, for example West Germany, Switzerland and Japan, have managed to reduce the rate of inflation way below the American level despite the oil-price rise. Furthermore, there are several energy-rich and oil-exporting countries, for example, Canada and Venezuela, that had even more inflation than the United States.

According to the OECD, 'the quadrupling in 1973, and the more than doubling of the oil price between the end of 1978 and early 1980 represents a shock on the OECD economies equivalent to roughly 2 per cent of GNP on each occasion'.[15] After the first oil shock in 1973, the burden was lightened by inflation because the dollar price of oil was kept stable for several years; this is not likely to happen after the second oil shock.[16]

A 2 per cent reduction in real GNP is a shock, but it is not a crushing burden. In an ideal, fully competitive economy, if the monetary authorities keep the price level constant, prices of commodities other than oil would decline slightly and there would be a once-and-for-all roughly 2 per cent decline of money wages (or more generally money incomes). In a growing economy a short pause in wage growth would take care of the problem. In a perfectly competitive economy there would be no unemployment or, if we relax our assumption and assume some stickiness of wages, there would be some transitional unemployment.

Now suppose money wages are rigid downwards while real wages are not (the Keynesian assumption). In this case, to maintain full employment, a small once-and-for-all increase in the price level, a slight extra spurt of inflation, would be necessary to accomplish the unavoidable once-and-for-all reduction in real wages.

At the other extreme, if real wages are rigid downwards through indexation, the only remedy—that is to say the only way to maintain equilibrium in the balance of payments—would be unemployment and slack in aggregate demand which would reduce the demand for oil.

In the real world the outcome will probably be somewhere in the middle, with some, hopefully merely transitional, unemployment and some inflation.

This analysis, rough and simple though it is, permits us to draw an important conclusion: if, and to the extent to which, our enlightened dictator is able to bring the economy close to the competitive ideal, he will also solve *ipso facto* the problem of the oil shock. No additional powers are needed.

Secular Stagnation?

Another factor that is often mentioned as a cause of low productivity growth is somewhat reminiscent of the theory of secular stagnation that flourished in the 1930s. Today, no one would argue, as the proponents of secular stagnation in the 1930s did, that we are suffering from over-saving, that is an excess of saving over investment with deflationary consequences. But it is said, as in the 1930s, that investment has declined because of a lack of entrepreneurship, or the absence of a technological breakthrough or the slowing down of technological progress. Symptoms or aspects of this broad development are a declining trend in expenditures on research and development and an increasing share of lawyers and accountants among corporate executives reflecting a decreasing share of business-men.

The enlightened dictator would strongly doubt that there is a lack of entrepreneurial talents and a decrease in the flow of usable inventions as distinguished from actual innovations.[17] But he would

recognise that innovating investments by Schumpeterian entrepreneurs have been seriously impeded and reduced by the growing
web of government controls and regulations, by the low level of
profits due to chronic inflation and stifling taxation and the growth
of government expenditures. This is the reason for the decline of
expenditures on research and development and the tendency of
lawyers and accountants to replace businessmen as directors of
corporations.[18] These are the same factors that are responsible for
stagflation and low productivity. Our dictator would, therefore,
redouble his efforts to reduce the size of the public sector, cut
government expenditures, de-regulate industry, *et cetera* and thus
make the economy more competitive and flexible.

The enlightened dictator would understand that the job of
introducing creative innovations, of 'revitalising industry' as the
modern phrase goes, is best done by private entrepreneurs, large
and small. Our dictator would resist the temptation of trying to
speed up the process by government interventions, government
commissions or bureaucrats trying to identify growth industries as
candidates for special subsidies, tax rebates and other privileges.
Such attempts almost always lead to the creation of white elephants
and a waste of resources. The dictator would also understand that
the widespread practice of propping up uncompetitive, obsolescent
firms and industries with subsidies and import restrictions is the very
opposite of a rational growth policy.

The proper method for stimulating growth is to provide a
favourable climate for private innovators through cutting government expenditures, lowering taxes, curbing inflation and dis-
mantling controls and regulations.

CONCLUSION

Inflation has been at the centre and at the bottom of the economic
malaise in recent years—*fons et origo malorum*. That does not mean,
however, that the *real* economy, growth and employment are not
intrinsically more important than price stability. But we have learned
that the attainment of maximum growth, full employment and
price stability are inextricably interrelated. Whatever is true in the
short run, in the long run inflation is incompatible with satisfactory
growth. And the longer inflation lasts, the less can be achieved even
in the short run by sudden spurts of inflation. In technical terms,
even the short-run Phillips curve tends to become vertical. More-

over, as we have seen, it is largely the same type of policies that are indicated for bringing down inflation and for promoting growth.

The statement that inflation, along with the associated low productivity growth, is the major problem confronting the industrial countries will be questioned by the many people who have become greatly alarmed by what is now called the North-South dialogue or confrontation allegedly resulting from a growing income gap between the developed industrial countries, the 'North', and the less developed countries, the 'South'. This problem has recently been dramatised by the report of a prestigious 'independent commission on development issues' under the chairmanship of Willy Brandt. The title of the report is *North-South: a Programme for Survival*.[19] The sub-title indicates the alarmist, not to say hysterical, tone of the report. No one can fail to be appalled by the stark poverty in some less developed countries. But to say, as the Brandt Commission does, that poverty in less developed countries and the great inequality between the 'North' and the 'South' is responsible for wars, violence and tensions in the world cannot be taken seriously. None of the recent wars had anything whatsoever to do with the North-South income gap—not the two world wars, nor any of the many local postwar conflicts, the wars in Korea and Vietnam, the Israel-Arab wars, the Persian Gulf war between Iran and Iraq, the conflicts between Greece and Turkey, Ethiopia and Somalia. The *East-West* tensions and confrontations are a real global threat compared with which the *North-South* skirmishes are of minor importance.[20]

The so-called 'South', or Third World, is a very heterogeneous group. It comprises many countries (Argentina, Brazil, Taiwan *et cetera*) that are well on the way to joining the industrial 'North'. The really poor countries, sometimes called the Fourth World, are but a fraction of the 'South'.

Here is not the place to discuss the commonly proposed policies to deal with that problem ('resource transfer' from the rich to the poor countries, foreign aid and international charity, commodity price stabilisation *et cetera, et cetera*).[21] I confine myself to saying that if the industrial countries put their economic houses in order, curb inflation, resume normal growth and liberalise trade, they will make a great contribution to the development of the less developed countries, including the very poor, by providing markets for the Third World's exports. World Bank statistics show that the less developed countries, as a group, have made excellent progress during the prosperous period after World War II.

NOTES AND REFERENCES

1. This is an abbreviated version of my paper, 'The Economic Malaise', which appeared in *Contemporary Economic Problems, 1981-1982 Edition* (Washington: American Enterprise Institute, 1982).

2. A lame duck economic report is an exception. An outgoing administration likes to depart on an at least moderately cheerful outlook, leaving the blame for future troubles and disappointments squarely on the shoulders of its successor. Of course, the incoming party has the opposite bias.

3. Haberler, 'The Economic Malaise', *op. cit.*

4. H. D. Dickinson, *The Economics of Socialism* (London: Oxford University Press, 1939) and Oscar Lange, 'On the Economic Theory of Socialism', in Benjamin E. Lippincott (ed.), *On the Economic Theory of Socialism* (Minneapolis: University of Minnesota Press, 1939), pp. 57-143. For a critical discussion see Herbert Giersch, *Allgemeine Wirtschaftspolitik, Vol. 1: Grundlagen*, Die Wirtschaftswissenschaften, Reihe B: Volkswirtschaftslehre, Beitrag Nr 9 (Wiesbaden: Gabler, 1977), pp. 165-68.

5. A related measure that might be considered would be to offer the public purchasing power government bonds, indexed for the rise in the price level, to enable the small saver to protect his savings from the ravages of inflation. The interest on indexed bonds, determined by demand and supply in a free market, would, of course, be much lower than on non-indexed bonds. See also Giersch, 'Index Clauses and the Fight against Inflation', in *Essays on Inflation and Indexation*, Domestic Affairs Study 24 (Washington: American Enterprise Institute, 1974), pp. 1-23.

6. Harry G. Johnson, 'Foreword', in Geoffrey Denton, Seamus O'Cleireacain and Sally Ash, *Trade Effects of Public Subsidies to Private Enterprise* (London: Macmillan, for the Trade Policy Research Centre, 1975; and New York: Holmes and Meier, 1975), pp. xiii and xxxviii. See also Giersch, 'Beschäftigungspolitik ohne Geldillusion', *Die Weltwirtschaft*, Tübingen, No. 2, 1972, pp. 127-35.

7. Karl Brunner, Alex Cukierman and Allan H. Meltzer, 'Stagflation, Persistent Unemployment and the Permanence of Economic Shocks', *Journal of Monetary Economics*, Amsterdam, October 1980, pp. 467-92.

8. *Ibid.*, p. 483.

9. *Ibid.*, p. 490.

10. *Ibid.*, p. 470.

11. *Ibid.*, p. 470.

12. *Ibid.*, p. 470.

13. *Ibid.*, p. 470, footnote 12.

14. For a careful analysis of how to separate voluntary from involuntary unemployment, see Giersch, *Allgemeine Wirtschaftspolitik, Vol. 2: Konjunktur- und Wachstumspolitik in der offenen Wirtschaft*, Die Wirtschaftswissenschaften, Reihe B: Volkswirtschaftslehre, Beitrag Nr 10 (Wiesbaden: Gabler, 1977), pp. 254-57.

15. *Economic Outlook*, OECD, Paris, July 1980, p. 114. For the United States it is less than 2 per cent.

16. I ignore another factor which postponed and potentially lightened the burden for some countries, such as for the United States, namely the fact that they received a large share of the 'petro-dollars', in other words, that they could run a balance-of-payments deficit corresponding to the OPEC surplus.

17. It will be recalled that since Joseph S. Schumpeter, economists distinguish between inventions, that is, discoveries of new or improved products or methods of production from theoretical work or laboratory experimentation on the one hand, and the actual production of new products or the use of new methods of production or marketing by innovating, risk-taking entrepreneurs on the other hand. (J. S. Schumpeter, *The Theory of Economic Development*, translated by Redvers Opie [Cambridge, Mass.: Harvard University Press, 1934, first German edition 1912].) See also Giersch, 'Aspects of Growth, Structural Change, and Employment— A Schumpeterian Perspective', *Weltwirtschaftliches Archiv*, Kiel, No. 4, 1979, *passim*.

18. Since business management has to spend more and more time and effort to cope with the rising flood of government regulations and to find ways to reduce the tax burden, it is quite natural that lawyers and accountants play an increasing role in corporate boardrooms. These basically unproductive activities drain scarce human resources away from the creative and productive entrepreneurial activities.

19. The Report of the Independent Commission on International Development Issues under the Chairmanship of Willy Brandt, *North-South: a Programme for Survival* (Cambridge, Mass.: MIT Press, 1980; and London and Sydney: Pan Books, 1980).

20. On recent United States and other Western policy statements (especially but not only before the invasion of Afghanistan) that present the opposite view, see the article by the great historian and Soviet expert, Adam B. Ulam, 'How to Restrain the Soviets', *Commentary*, New York, December 1980, pp. 38-41.

21. The largely dubious policy proposals of the Brandt Commission have been critically analysed by P. T. Bauer and B. S. Yamey, 'East-West/North-South: Peace and Prosperity?', *Commentary*, September 1980, pp. 57-63; and P. D. Henderson, 'Survival, Development and the Report of the Brandt Commission', *The World Economy*, London, June 1980, pp. 87-117. For a thorough discussion of the so-called New International Economic Order (NIEO), see Ryan C. Amacher, Haberler and Thomas D. Willett (eds), *Challenges to a Liberal Economic Institute* (Washington: American Enterprise Institute, 1979).

11 The Supply-side Approach to Macro-economic Policy: the West German Experience

Gerhard Fels

There is a growing awareness that the current economic difficulties of most industrial countries can be ascribed to unsolved structural problems. Governments of most countries have shifted their attention to supply rigidities and their causes. As a consequence thereof, the magnitude and composition of productive potential, rather than its current rate of utilisation, become a matter of economic policy. The drastic oil-price increase in 1973-74 intensified competition from newly industrialising countries of the Third World and the disincentives caused by the expansion of the public sector have revealed structural weaknesses in the mature economies. A large part of unemployment and inflation is interpreted as resulting from rigidities on the supply side. Supply-oriented policy can be seen as an attempt to restore and enlarge adjustment capacity, which was eroded during an era dominated by the belief that demand management is an answer to all serious economic problems. Disenchantment with this policy in the course of subsequent inflation has redirected the attention of policy makers to the supply side of the economy.

The second oil-price shock in 1979, and the adjustment pressures created by it, have challenged most countries so strongly that they have embarked on a policy which aims at an improvement of supply conditions in domestic and international markets. In many countries this involves an abstention from short-term action against unemployment and a strong stand against inflation.

Japan has managed to transform a sharp devaluation into a rapid expansion of exports, thereby penetrating the traditional markets of North American and West European suppliers with considerable success. The fact that the drastic devaluation of the yen in 1979 did not create a wave of inflation indicates the high adjustment capacity of the Japanese economy. Subsequently, foreign-exchange markets have credited the Japanese success with a revaluation of the yen.

224

A spectacular shift towards supply policy has taken place in the United States. The Reagan Administration is trying to revitalise the economy by deregulation, tax cuts and reductions in public spending in those areas where it discourages private activity. The incentives provided by this policy, however, are currently being countered by the discouraging effects of high interest rates which emerge from anti-inflationary monetary policy in combination with high and increasing public deficits.

The United Kingdom has burdened itself with painful monetary restrictions, with the intention of breaking inflation, of lowering wage pressures and improving industrial structure. Whether the deep recession generated by this kind of policy will in fact set free dynamic forces in the economy is still an unanswered question.

For several years France has been undertaking the restructuring of her industrial sector and the liberalisation of her domestic markets. An ambitious nuclear energy programme was started to reduce dependency on oil and to improve conditions for industrial activity. The political change which occurred in May 1981 led to the reformulation of economic policy, but only partly brought about a return to demand orientation.

In West Germany, a high degree of supply orientation has characterised economic policy since the recession of 1975. Supply-oriented measures contributed to the recovery during the second half of the 1970s, although, in practical implementation, supply policy has never gathered such momentum as at present in the United States. From a supply-side-oriented approach, the main task of the 1980s is to establish a more favourable framework for private investment, including a removal of political and bureau-cratic impediments to investment in sectors like energy, communications, construction and transportation. It is now widely recognised that further steps within the framework of supply policy are necessary, but severe budget constraints narrow the scope for policy action.

While the departure from Keynesian demand policy is common to most major countries, it is obvious that the design of supply-oriented policy differs from country to country. Except in the case of the Federal Republic of Germany, this is too recent a shift in economic policy to allow an evaluation of its effects. Supply-oriented efforts are presently also overshadowed by the short-term effects of anti-inflationary policies. In most countries, combating inflation is so urgent a task that any efforts aiming at faster supply growth have to be postponed or are counteracted by the restrictive effects of high interest rates. In such a situation supply policy can hardly be expected to produce early results. While in principle, of course, faster supply growth is conducive to bringing down the rate of inflation, initiation of such faster growth may be hindered by restrictive monetary policies aimed at fighting inflation in the short run.

West Germany has had the longest experience with a supply-oriented policy. After the recession of 1975 it became more and more evident that much of the recession and the sluggishness of the recovery thereafter was mainly caused by unsolved structural adjustment problems. An upward jump in the real rate of exchange, the first oil-price increase, and increased competition from newly industrialising countries confronted the West German economy with significant changes in relative prices. A wide range of activities, especially in the international sector of the economy, lost its competitiveness. New activities which would have been in line with the new relative prices emerged only slowly. A structural weakness of the West German economy became visible. Adjustment to the new situation generated frictions, the consequence of which were stubborn unemployment problems after 1975. A balance-of-payments problem emerged as the current account ran into a high deficit in the course of the second oil-price shock.

CHALLENGE POSED BY ENERGY
PROBLEM

The energy problem has created an additional challenge for supply-oriented policies. Higher energy prices reduce the equilibrium price for other factors of production. This is, however, not the whole story. The oil-producing countries, especially some of the Arab countries, are currently not only the major oil suppliers but also important lenders in the international financial markets. Their expectations as to the future development of the oil price determine their interest-rate expectations. This is because they have the power to restrict the oil supply if the returns on their assets fall short of the value increase which they expect for their oil deposits. Of course there are limits to a supply cut which normally leads to an increase in the oil price. As recent developments have shown, the world economy may slow down and the incentives for the development of oil substitutes may become too strong. But experience has also shown that the oil-producing countries have scope enough for bringing the oil-importing countries into severe trouble. This strategic weapon makes the capital surplus of oil-producing countries a powerful partner in the financial markets. The rate-of-return expectations of the oil-producing countries create a lower limit for real interest rates. On the demand side, the necessity of oil substitution alters the need for capital in the world. The present high level of real rates of interest can be interpreted as a structural and thus a more or less permanent phenomenon. In view of structurally higher capital costs and, if the level of real total costs is to remain unchanged, the income aspirations of other factors of production, especially labour, must be reduced.

One way to bring down the real rates of interest would be to make the oil producers less certain with regard to the realisation of their oil-price expectations. Exploration for, and exploitation of, energy sources other than oil would be the basic means to achieve this goal. Recent experience has shown that this is not easily done, either because the costs are high or because there is vociferous resistance to a faster use of nuclear energy and coal. To levy higher taxes on oil consumption can be an instrument for limiting the scope for future oil-price increases. There is, however, a danger evolving from such a policy, namely that the oil producers might react with further price increases if they suspect that the oil-consuming countries are attempting to participate in the scarcity rent of oil. This is, of course, a strategic game. The oil-importing countries should not surrender before that point in time which they might consider to be risky with respect to influencing the oil price. Nevertheless, their possibilities for reversing the expected upward price trend of oil producers are no doubt limited. It is reasonable, therefore, to assume that labour income and other factor incomes will have to be reduced in response to higher prices of oil and capital. The crucial task lies with the unions, which exert the main influence on the price for labour, and with the enterprises, which influence the efficiency of labour, capital and energy. Supply-oriented economic policy can also be used to facilitate the adjustment burden.

GERMAN AND AMERICAN APPROACHES

The German move to a supply-oriented policy, after the recession of 1975, resembled a stepwise approach rather than a spectacular shift in economic policy. What seemed to be necessary in Germany after 1975 was the encouragement of new activities rather than the creation of demand for old activities. The high level of wage costs was widely considered to be an obstacle to the emergence of a spontaneous wave of job-creating investment and innovation. Public expenditure programmes which had been instituted during the recession were revealed as insufficient instruments for overcoming this obstacle. As a matter of fact, the financing of the resulting deficits even seemed to have adverse effects on private investment, since it absorbed funds at interest rates detrimental to many investment projects. Since the flexibility of real wages is limited—if one rules out the exploitation of money illusion—it was the German Council of Experts' idea that supply-oriented policy measures could complement the attempts to moderate wage pressure and to reduce the public budget deficit. The term 'supply-oriented policy' appeared for the first time in the Council's annual report of 1976 as the common denominator of these three components.[1] Since then the Council's policy proposals have centred on these components, alternately emphasising one of the three, this depending upon the Council's judgment as to the necessity for, and possibility of, taking various policy actions.

In the United States supply-oriented policy has recently, since the Reagan Administration bought the ideas of some of the American supply-side economists, emerged as a political movement. Although the basic ideas of the German and the American concepts are very similar, there are significant differences:

(i) The German concept aims mainly at revitalisation of the economy, for example, structural adjustment, new investment and innovation. The underlying hope is that such a policy will also be more conducive to job creation than demand policy, which may have only a temporary impact. While this is also an important element in the American concept of supply policy, the emphasis there lies also on combating inflation, an assignment which has never been made in West Germany.

(ii) In the German concept the main emphasis is on wage policy. Government action plays only a complementary role. In the United States, government policy is the predominant instrument since the possibilities of influencing union behaviour through moral suasion are more limited.

(iii) Crowding-out effects which may go along with supply-oriented budget policies play a dominant role in the German concept. In the United States, at least one influential faction of the advocates of supply-oriented policy—Arthur Laffer and his group—ignores the repercussion in the financial markets.

The philosophy behind the German concept was not original in the sense that there were no precedents in the economic history of the Federal Republic. On the contrary, West German economic policy during the 1950s and for longer periods during the 1960s can easily be classified as supply-oriented. It aimed at restoring the functioning of competition through deregulation and anti-cartel legislation and at encouraging private activity through investment-oriented tax laws and a rather small public sector. Anti-cyclical demand management was unknown as an obligation of government. This policy design was significantly changed during and after the recession of 1967 when there was a growing belief that Keynesian instruments could free the economy from recession and inflation, a paradigm which was manifested in the Stability and Growth Law of 1968. But this philosophy predominated only a couple of years. The recovery after the 1967 recession can be ascribed in some part to incentives from demand management. During the 1970s, however, it became increasingly clear that policies of this type were not conducive to solving the overall economic problems. The acceleration of German inflation in the early 1970s was mainly due to insufficiently adjusted exchange rates and the significant increase in domestic wage pressure. The oil-price increase of 1973-74 was an additional factor. The sluggishness of the recovery after 1975 was the consequence of an excessively high cost level and an unmastered structural change. The insight into these causes led to a reconsideration of classical adjustment needs.

CONTRIBUTION OF THE GERMAN COUNCIL OF EXPERTS

The German Council of Economic Experts, in which Herbert Giersch played a dominant role in the initial period following its creation in 1964, never centred its analysis on a demand-oriented approach. Although the Council encouraged the government to go ahead with public demand expansion, in the recession of 1967 its paradigm was of a more neo-classical nature. The Council's key plea was for flexible exchange rates in order to combat imported inflation, for a wage policy neutral *vis-à-vis* the overall cost level in order to avoid unemployment and for a public budget neutral *vis-à-vis* capacity utilisation in order to prevent cyclical disturbances from the public sector. There was also a clear preference for a medium-term orientation of economic policy. Anti-cyclical policy was only considered as an emergency action. This kind of concept can more easily be classified as supply-oriented than as demand-oriented. Of course, it would not fully fit the problems of today. In those days the rate of economic growth was felt to be adequate and structural change could be mastered without major friction. Therefore there was no need to consider the question of how to promote the dynamics of the economy. But Professor Giersch's *Rentabilitätspolitik*, which circumscribes all policy measures aiming at an improvement of investment profitability, already anticipated much of what is now called supply-oriented policy.[2]

Against this background, the German Council's supply-oriented approach after 1975 was more an amendment to the older concept than a fundamental change in paradigm. The situation then differed from that of the 1960s. Exchange rates had become flexible, with the consequence of a drastic revaluation of the German mark not only in nominal but also in real terms. Competition from abroad had increased sharply, both from traditional trading partners and from newly industrialising countries. Increased competition, along with rapidly rising labour and energy costs, had burdened private business with a sharp profit squeeze. Investors' confidence in an investment climate, undisturbed by income distribution struggles, had been shaken. Additional investment risks emerged from the fact that the technological level of the West German economy had reached that of its Western partners, so that the scope for technology import and imitation from abroad had been narrowed. The public sector, at the same time, had expanded rapidly, thereby absorbing more and more capital resources for deficit financing. What was demanded of economic policy in this situation was a concept conducive to improving the environment for private investment.

As far as direct promotion of private activity was concerned the Council's supply concept emphasised measures which aimed at improving the entrepreneurs' capability to bear the risks of forward-looking adjustment. The 1976 and 1977 catalogues of proposed policy measures covered in particular:

(a) an accelerated depreciation;
(b) a shift from direct towards indirect taxation;
(c) assistance for new firms; and
(d) more incentives for occupational mobility.

The ultimate aim of these proposals was to generate favourable conditions for autonomous investment, based on innovations in processing and on new products. One may also say that Schumpeterian investment was seen as a solution, rather than Keynesian investment which could, indeed, be expected of a reflation of the economy, but could easily be jeopardised by newly emerging inflation.

The methods which the Council used, in order to evaluate the supply situation of the economy, were of an approximate and selective nature. A unique variable which indicates the supply situation can hardly be identified. In the Council's concept, real wage costs as well as the real rate of exchange are key variables. The readiness of entrepreneurs to commit venture capital and to innovate is another important factor. Not only do these basic conditions matter, but so does the social and institutional environment in which an economy can operate, for example, labour-market organisation, social consensus, the degree of competition in goods markets, government intervention, incentives and disincentives of taxation and bureaucratic impediments.

It was also in 1976 that the Federal Government commissioned the five major economic research institutes in West Germany to undertake a comprehensive research project, the purpose of which is to shed light on the process of structural change and its implications for overall economic development (the so-called *Struktur-berichterstattung*). The project was planned as a periodic, scientific review of the whole issue of structural change, comparable to the well-established reports on business-cycle conditions.[3]

At the end of 1980 the five institutes submitted their first reports on structural change in the West German economy to the Federal Government. The competitive approach led to a certain amount of heterogeneity in topics, methods and results. But there was a wide field of common ground on the crucial issues of the economy. All five institutes observed employment problems as a result of un-mastered structural change, a strong challenge from the world economy to adjust industrial patterns, a decline in the international competitiveness of key industries and a substantial degree of government interference with private business. These are more or less the common denominators of the reports. If one tries to be more precise one would also have to depict the different views of the institutes.

Since 1977, several of the supply measures proposed by the Council have been implemented by the Government, but only piecemeal and without the announcement that a fundamental change in economic policy was to take place. Nevertheless, it would

not be an exaggeration to state that the investment climate improved considerably after 1977. There were clear signs that entrepreneurs had taken up the challenge of structural change. Private
capital spending accelerated, more firms were founded, a higher
share of investment than in previous years was undertaken to
introduce new products and processes, to enter new markets and
to create new jobs. Overall employment was nearly 4 per cent
higher in 1980 than in 1977. In 1980 the recovery was interrupted
by the restrictive effects of the second oil-price shock and of the
monetary policy which the Bundesbank was bound to pursue in
response to accelerated inflation and the current-account deficit.
Despite high interest rates, private investment revealed itself as
rather robust during this phase of economic weakness, which indicates that autonomous investment was of great importance.

ROLE OF SUPPLY POLICY IN
   ADJUSTMENT

It would be too simple an explanation to ascribe the post-1977
recovery of private investment to the supply-oriented policy alone.
The recovery must also be seen in the context of general fiscal policy
and of monetary developments, which were both strongly influenced by the international monetary scene. This leads to the
question of how supply policy fits into the general assignment of
goals and instruments in economic policy.

Structural adjustment problems have to do mainly with the
complex nature of price and wage adjustment. Put more bluntly:
they originate from distorted relative prices. An example may
illustrate this. In the case of a drastic oil-price increase in an oil-
poor country like West Germany, either a depreciation of the
currency or a reduction of domestic wages and other cost factors is
necessary to bring about a real transfer to the suppliers of oil. In
other words, in order to avoid creating unemployment the real rate
of exchange and the terms of trade have to fall until full employment
is realised. The first method of real devaluation—currency depreciation—involves the risk of countervailing reactions because those
who fear a real deterioration in their real income position will try
to defend it. The outcome would be more inflation in the first
place and more unemployment in the second. The *malaise* thus
created is nothing other than an expression of resistance to necessary
adjustment. This method of terms-of-trade adjustment may be
especially unacceptable in countries which are highly sensitive to

inflation. The second method—domestic supply price reduction—
is as difficult as the first is dangerous. It requires a high degree of
consensus in an economy in order to achieve its goal without
setting off a recession. But a sharp recession will inevitably occur
if monetary policy does not accommodate inflationary pressure and
if a consensus solution is also impossible.

If an economy is drawing near to achieving terms of trade which
are compatible with full employment, supply-policy-induced
reduction of the domestic cost level is a superior alternative to
nominal depreciation. Unlike depreciation, such a reduction is not
burdened with the risk of additional inflationary pressure and
interest rates set so high that they prevent the exchange rate from
overshooting. Adjustment can occur without the uncertainties
which normally accompany inflation. One could also expect this type
of adjustment to produce a lower unemployment rate.

Even in an economy like West Germany, a wage-adjustment
strategy can only be realised in small steps, as the experience after
1976 indicates. The Council's main emphasis in its supply concept
was on advocating a moderate wage policy in view of the fact that
profits had been squeezed to the extreme in previous years and
investment risks had increased to a certain degree. The unions'
representatives strongly resisted recommendations of this type in
most of the following years. In practice, however, the real wage
increase did not fully exhaust the scope created by growth in
productivity and terms-of-trade changes, so that real wage costs
did decline slightly after all. Government supply policy came to the
fore as a means of easing the adjustment burden of wage earners by
strengthening the ability of firms to take the risks of innovation and
new investment.

The problem is that a kind of moral hazard can arise, since there
is the danger of governmental participation in investment risks
giving unions free rein to claim higher wages, the burden of which
will ultimately have to be shouldered by the tax payer. Thus some
coordination between government and unions seems necessary in
order to prevent such additional wage increases from thwarting
the desired effects of supply policy. In the years after 1975, such
coordination did not take place. On the contrary, the so-called
concerted action, a round table of representatives of government,
union organisations and entrepreneurs' organisations was phased
out in 1977. In spite of this, the unions did not take action to

thwart supply-policy measures. An informal mutual understanding had at least been achieved.

The supply potential is not only influenced by the wage level and by supply-oriented measures themselves, but also by the impact which the public sector deficit has on private activity. An increase in the public sector deficit—for whatever reason—would normally have some kind of crowding-out effect in the private sector, resulting from changes in interest rates, exchange rates and output prices. It is likely that all these changes and the expectations they generate would result in a lower volume of profitable private investment. The strength of this crowding-out effect would of course vary, depending on the interest elasticity of supply of domestic or foreign capital and of goods and services and on the general confidence in the government's capability to deal with overall economic problems. Any approach to supply policy which overlooks this effect would be incomplete. Additional public spending, which does not improve supply conditions, may stimulate effective demand but may easily cause general supply conditions to deteriorate so that the net effect of the economy's performance may be negative. Moreover, supply-oriented measures which lead to an increase in public sector debt must also be weighed against possible crowding-out effects. There is, of course, a wide scope for empirical judgment and controversy here. For instance, judging the matter from a monetarist view, those who expect strong crowding-out effects would advocate supply-oriented tax cuts, parallel with reductions in public spending. Those who emphasise crowding-out less are more confident that tax cuts will finance themselves through incremental tax revenues resulting from a faster growth of productive potential.

GERMAN EXPERIENCE AFTER 1976

As to the German economy's situation in recent years, there may also be doubt whether the supply-oriented steps were not cancelled out by the rapid increase in the public sector deficit which occurred at the same time. This increase in the deficit resulted only to a minor extent from the supply-oriented measures themselves. It was primarily the consequence of increased consumption-oriented public spending and across-the-board cuts in income tax, the intention and effect of which was a strengthening of the purchasing power of tax payers. Marginal tax rates were thus lowered only slightly, so that the incentive character of the tax reduction was not at the centre of the policy.[4] The greater part of the mounting public sector deficit must, therefore, be ascribed to demand rather than supply promotion.

Nevertheless, there is reason to believe that supply-oriented steps in combination with a moderate wage increase were an important source of recovery from 1978 to 1979, since they created the scope for an acceleration of private investment during that period. Of great significance, however, was the strong support for supply-oriented policy resulting from a revaluation of the German mark. In 1977 the mark was allowed to appreciate again. Declining interest rates together with an appreciating mark accompanied the recovery of private investment and created rather more favourable conditions for innovation and positive structural adjustment. The Bundesbank had allowed an acceleration of monetary growth, arguing that positive domestic price effects resulting from exchange-rate appreciation would keep down inflationary pressure. One may suspect that the excessive monetary expansion in 1977 and 1978 was the cause of higher inflation and higher interest rates in the following year. But it is difficult to be decisive here due to the influence of the second oil-price increase. It is the Council's opinion that the frictions generated by the oil shock have hindered the West German economy from reaping the full benefits of the supply policy pursued previously.[5]

SUPPLY POLICY AND THE EXCHANGE RATE

A crucial question remains: how does supply policy influence real exchange rates or the international standing of an economy? In the first place, there seems to be no doubt that a lowering of the cost level and an improvement of other cost conditions would lead both to more competitive supply prices in international markets and to a higher return on domestic investment. Consequently, the current account would improve and foreign capital would be attracted, thus causing the domestic currency to be revalued. While this is a positive result, it is often argued that it actually conflicts with supply policy.

In the German discussion on negative feedback via the exchange rate, this argument was employed against the proposal for wage restraint. Representatives of trade unions were afraid that in an open economy with flexible exchange rates there would be no chance of increasing employment through nominal wage restraint since the revaluation generated thereby would tend to raise real wages.

Indeed, during the period from 1977 to 1979, when wage increases were rather moderate, the mark became more and more attractive as an international currency for private business and central banks. But it is hardly possible to establish a close relationship between this revaluation and the development of the domestic cost level. Of course, the revaluation can be interpreted as a positive evaluation of the economy's capability to cope with adjustment problems, one element of which is union behaviour towards wage policy. To that degree a link between the change in supply conditions and in the exchange rate certainly exists. It should also be noted that the forces which tend to raise the exchange rate—more exports, less imports, more investment from abroad than usual—tend to increase employment at the same time. Even if the competitive advantage generated originally is offset by the appreciation of the exchange rate, the employment level will be higher than it was before.

Another important reason for the strength of the German mark at that time was, however, the weakness of the dollar due to accelerating inflation in the United States. Moreover, the appreciation of the mark had positive supply effects in the form of low and declining import prices for intermediate goods and low and declining interest rates. The domestic sector of the economy improved its terms of trade compared with those of the international sector. The bulk of employment creation after 1977 took place in the service and construction sectors.

Thus the criticism often made by supporters of demand policy that supply policy leads first to a revaluation of the currency, then to an increase in real wage costs and ultimately to a fall in employment, is not supported by experience in the Federal Republic of Germany.

NOTES AND REFERENCES

1. See Sachverständigenrat zur Begutachtung der gesamtwirtschaftlichen Entwicklung, *Zeit zum Investieren—Jahresgutachten 1976/77* (Stuttgart and Mainz: W. Kohlhammer, 1976), pp. 123 *et seq.*

2. See Herbert Giersch, 'Strategien der Wachstumspolitik', *Zeitschrift für die gesamte Staatswissenschaft*, Tübingen, No. 2, 1963; *idem, Allgemeine Wirtschaftspolitik, Vol 2: Konjunktur- und Wachstumspolitik in der offenen Wirtschaft*, Die Wirtschaftswissenschaften, Reihe B: Volkswirtschaftslehre, Beitrag Nr 10 (Wiesbaden: Gabler, 1977), pp. 123 *et seq.*

3. The five institutes were committed to work in competition with each other. Only a general framework, covering relevant research topics and the minimum statistical requirements, was fixed by the Ministry of Economics. The Federal Statistical Office was asked to provide the institutes with

hitherto missing data. The individual institutes are free to choose their own topics, except for those research topics which have to be covered by all five institutes.

4. See Sachverständigenrat zur Begutachtung der gesamtwirtschaftlichen Entwicklung, *Wachstum und Währung—Jahresgutachten 1978/79* (Stuttgart and Mainz: W. Kohlhammer, 1978), p. 118.

5. See *idem, Unter Anpassungszwang—Jahresgutachten 1980/81* (Stuttgart and Mainz, W. Kohlhammer, 1980), p. 140.

12 Welfare Economics, Public Finance and Selective Aid Policies

Alan Peacock

In his justly renowned book on *Wirtschaftspolitik*, Herbert Giersch develops not only a logic of economic policy, but a perceptive analysis of the problems inherent in any attempt to devise efficient linkages of policy instruments to the range of relevant policy objectives.[1] The theme recurs in much of his later writing, but by now, no doubt, deeply influenced by long, hard experience as one of West Germany's most distinguished economic advisers. This contribution offers a modest complement to his work, concentrating on an analysis of a policy experience which we share—the problem of preventing government measures designed to correct so-called 'market failure' from being characterised by the very sources of failure that they are designed to correct. My thesis is exemplified by selective aid policies which frequently have been justified by economists as suitable instruments for promoting a better allocation of resources than is assumed possible if their allocation is left to the market.

The subject is introduced by a re-examination of the claims of welfare economics to identify the budgetary measures appropriate to correct 'market failure'. It has become increasingly recognised that the theory of social goods, as a branch of welfare economics, largely ignores the imperfections in collective provision, other than in the problem of devising an analogue to the market in the system by which political choices are made. This recognition has taken the form of an examination of the allocational effects of bureaucracies in charge of public production of non-marketed output. While certain features of this analysis are relevant to the examination of selective aid policies, the conventional model has to be extended considerably in order to contain additional features, notably the 'interface' between bureaucracies and companies in the private sector which has not been incorporated in the standard economic analysis of bureaucracy, which concentrates on the strategy of

238

bureaucratic managers in their dealings with the government or legislature. Subsequent sections of this contribution employ economic analysis in order to explain why the allocative and technical inefficiencies endemic in the reactions of companies which negotiate claims for selective aid are difficult, if not impossible, to eradicate.

MARKET FAILURE AND COLLECTIVE FAILURE

In standard texts on the economics of public finance and, indeed, in many articles in which the phenomenon is discussed, 'market failure' is attributable to a number of standard causes:

(1) the existence of 'publicness' in goods (non-rivalness and non-excludability) normally of a consumption nature;

(2) the existence of 'mixed' goods of a consumption or production nature which generate benefit and cost externalities which are not 'internalised' (case '1' is sometimes regarded as a polar case of '2') and

(3) the existence of market imperfections resulting from both a 'technical' (decreasing costs) and an institutional (restrictive practices) character.

While it is not denied that 'market failure' problems may be solved by voluntary agreement, it is generally considered to be the case that such agreements can only be reached if bargaining costs are relatively small and if free-riding opportunities are restricted, that is, where small numbers of transactors obtain. Removing market failure therefore justifies a whole range of policy measures designed, as far as possible, to improve allocative efficiency. Such measures range from compulsory levies to finance public provision of 'pure' social goods (defence is the usual example given) and sophisticated tax and subsidy measures of a selective kind in order to 'internalise' costs and benefits associated with externalities, to controls such as anti-monopoly measures or nationalisation designed to force firms to adopt marginal cost pricing, and which may also require the use of subsidy and tax measures.

Latterly this approach to the identification of the tasks of the system of public finance has become the subject of increasing criticism. As a prelude to the particular concerns of this essay these criticisms may be listed briefly:

(1) The empirical suppositions of the analysis have been

challenged on the grounds that in very few cases do goods embody the characteristics of 'publicness', that is, that they are 'non-excludable' and 'non-rival'.[2]

(2) The normative criteria of Paretian welfare economics are too circumscribed, even if individual preferences are to be regarded as paramount. Thus, it is generally found that supporters of these criteria either contract out altogether of discussion of distributional objectives, or are in dispute with one another about the appropriateness of 'solving' the distributional problem by the introduction of interdependent utility functions along Hochman/Rodgers lines.

(3) The empirical suppositions mean that the wrong questions are frequently asked when a positive analysis of the functions of the public sector is undertaken. The emphasis on a 'public goods' explanation of the growth of the public sector places undue emphasis on the shifts in consumer preferences through time. This ignores the importance of the growth both of transfers to persons and of subsidies to industry as factors in public sector growth, a fact which suggests that the 'taste for redistribution' is ignored[3] and that supply influences (for example, the assets and preferences of bureaucrats) are ignored.[4]

Supporters of Paretian welfare economics have not been unaware of these difficulties, but have tended to concentrate on arguing with one another about 'fiscal politics'. Some, following Kenneth J. Arrow, of Harvard University, have taken refuge in the idea of the 'ethical observer' who 'solves' the basic problem of market failure by devising means to reveal the 'true preferences' of the community.[5] Others, notably James M. Buchanan, Gordon Tullock and latterly H. Geoffrey Brennan in his joint publication with Professor Buchanan—all of the Virginia Polytechnic Institute and State University, Blacksburg—fear that the 'ethical observer' will turn into a dictatorial Leviathan.[6] They have sought to define public choice arrangements which stimulate choice conditions in competitive markets, following the Wicksell tradition. It is not my purpose to resolve this debate, but it is relevant to this contribution to emphasise that it is carried on within a very narrow context. Even if it were possible to achieve some approximation of the choice conditions in the market by suitable voting arrangements, so that individual preferences received their full expression for both public and private goods, this would not automatically guarantee that public goods and public policies (using budgetary instruments to influence private sector production) will be supplied in a fashion which would promote optimal allocation of resources.

We are now in a position to go to the heart of the problem created by government action to reduce the incidence of market failure, namely that measures designed to reduce its incidence may be 'counter-productive'. In short, 'market failure' may be matched by 'collective' or 'non-market' failure, *even if we assign a role to the public sector which is strictly derivable from Paretian welfare propositions.*[7] In illustrating the phenomenon of collective failure, however, I shall not regard myself as necessarily bound by strict Paretian welfare criteria, particularly in appraisal of selective aid measures.

PUBLIC 'OUTPUT' AND COLLECTIVE FAILURE

The first area in which collective failure is frequently identified is in government bureaux, whose function is to produce non-marketed output financed by compulsory levies, for pricing of output is considered impossible even in approximate form.

Following William A. Niskanen, of Ford Motor Company World Headquarters, an influential economic theory of bureaucracy has been constructed in which the analytical expression usually takes the form of simple comparative statics.[8] Using 'maximising the bureau's budget' as (often) the sole argument in the bureaucrat manager's welfare function, and assuming that the manager operates in a market environment similar to that facing a discriminating monopolist, it is demonstrated that the bureau will 'over-produce' and will therefore be allocatively inefficient.

Within this framework there are many games which can be played in order to improve the explanatory power of the original model. It is now common practice to introduce a 'labour preference variable' in the welfare function of the bureaucrat to represent a desire for power, in which case, as labour is also an input, allocative inefficiency—as is shown by William P. Orzechowski, of Oglethorpe University, Atlanta—will be accompanied by X-inefficiency (that is, technical inefficiency reflected in a bureau cost curve lying about the minimum cost curve in the conventional diagrammatic representation).[9] I consider that these models ignore an essential feature of bureaucracy—the desire for a 'quiet life' which infects executive-level decision making in bureaucracies where there is security of tenure. Adding 'on-the-job leisure', as I call it, as an argument in the bureaucrat's welfare function does not, however, substantially alter Professor Orzechowski's results.[10]

This model and its variants do tell us a good deal about the prospect of collective failure within a transactions framework in which politicians are 'customers' and bureaucrats suppliers of services; and there is a good deal of empirical information suggesting that both allocational and X-inefficiency can be detected in cases where the government provides services not sold in the market. In applying such a model to other methods of correcting market failure such as when the government transfers money to persons or to firms, much more attention has to be paid to transactions between bureaucrats and households or firms, that is directly with the public, rather than indirectly through the political process. Another way of looking at this problem is to regard transfer receivers (such as pensioners) or aid beneficiaries (such as companies) as factors of production who are 'paid' (not always a positive amount in the latter case) to adjust their actions in a way which conforms to the objective of optimal allocation and efficiency. This, however, requires us to examine much more explicitly than is found in the 'standard' bureaucratic model, the question of what the economic relations between bureaucrats and these factors of production are.

The conventional method of illustrating how externalities emanating from the activities of firms may be internalised is to use what may be called the 'Pavlovian dog' model, in which companies react to 'stimuli' such as taxes and subsidies in a particular way. The analysis makes some very strong assumptions:

(1) The bureaucrat has perfect information of the cost and demand structure of the individual firm(s) so that he is aware of the price and output effects of any quantum of subsidy.

(2) The bureaucrat has clear instructions on the relation between the changes in prices and output and the externality change.

(3) The sole change in the constraints on the firm(s) desiring to maximise their objective function is represented by the subsidy measure. (In other words, the firm derives no benefit from any attempt to adopt strategic behaviour in respect of its dealings with government.)

If we relax these assumptions in order to embody major real world factors that could influence the result, it can be shown that a subsidy policy designed to promote allocative efficiency may not promote that objective and that we may be faced with the further

problem that the policy itself encourages X-inefficiency. The problem is created not only by the opportunities for strategic behaviour
by firms, but also by the reactions of 'suppliers' of such policies to
that behaviour.

Consider the following situation commonly encountered in making
policy decisions.[11] Assume that a large firm expects to make substantial losses over some given planning period and establishes a
case, on externality grounds, for subsidy. The government decides
that it will negotiate an output subsidy and is willing to meet losses
up to the point where the (subsidised) marginal cost of the product
equals its price. The initial position is illustrated in Figure 12.1.
TC is the planned cost curve (for simplicity assume only one
input—labour—and that marginal cost = average cost), TR is the
estimated total revenue curve for product X, and $(TC - S)$ is the
subsidised cost curve, where S varies in proportion to output. Let
us assume now that the subsidising authorities decide that, on
grounds of allocative efficiency, the optimal level of output is OC.
If it were presented with TC as the cost curve, it would then offer
a total subsidy of AB or per unit subsidy of AB/OC. This is the end
of the story so far as the textbook is concerned.

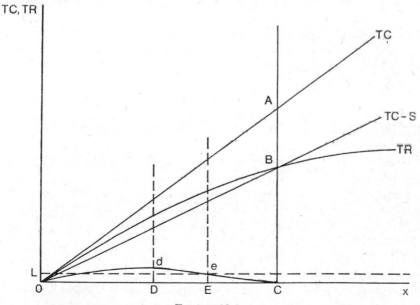

FIGURE 12.1

Note: O-d-e-C is the total net profit curve if the output is variable.

Obviously, the managers of a firm choosing to remain in business with subsidy, rather than to go into liquidation, could 'satisfice' (to use Simonian terminology) and accept both the subsidy per unit and output constraint. It is unlikely, once the unit subsidy had been decided upon, that the firm could bargain over the output level. Clearly, if the firm were a profit maximiser, it would prefer to produce where the difference between planned total revenue and planned total cost would be maximised, that is, at output level OD; or, if a sales maximiser (subject to a minimum profit constraint [OL > 0]), at output level OE. While the firm could argue that the *total* cost of the subsidy to the government would be less than at OC, whichever objective function of the firm is relevant, it is unlikely, even if the government is uncertain about the optimal level of output, that it will countenance a situation where part of the subsidy would 'disappear' into profits over and above those which would be necessary to keep the firm in business. The firm's managers have to bear in mind that, were it to emerge that it was likely to make net profits, the government has several weapons at its disposal associated with other ways in which it may affect the fortunes of the firms, for example, denial of government contracts and of benefits from making the subsidy payment depend on some rule concerning profit-taking.

There is one strategy open to the firm if, as may often be the case, it is the sole source of information on its prospective costs of production. It can inflate its estimate of costs. If profits can be 'disguised', the profit maximiser will attempt to inflate costs so that the difference between 'true' costs and 'revealed' costs is maximised. The revealed cost curve would then be TC′ instead of TC in Figure 12.2. Similarly, if the firm maximised sales, subject to a minimum profit constraint, it would inflate costs by the amount of the minimum profit constraint. The revealed cost curve would then become TC″. The success of the strategy will depend on whether the government authorities will accept cost estimates which would mean offering a unit subsidy of GB/OC in the case of the profit maximiser and of FB/OC in the case of the sales maximiser, where GB/OC > FB/OC > AB/OC.

The example is perhaps a little artificial, for it assumes that managers have an incentive to maximise profits or meet a profit constraint in circumstances where shareholders could not receive money profits. Only if the managers are the shareholders will they endeavour to obtain an amount of subsidy compatible with the

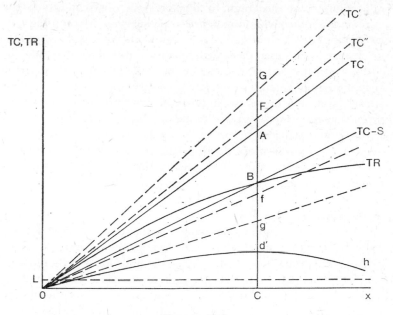

FIGURE 12.2
Notes: 1. O-d′-h is the total 'disguised' profit curve.
2. Bf = AF = OL; Bg = AG = Cd′.

assumed objective functions, for 'disguised' profits redound to their
benefit. Nevertheless, the incentive to inflate costs remains. If
managers are sales maximisers they are constrained by the government output target, but they will not be averse to inflating costs
which will permit 'slackness' in the firm and reduce the costs to
them of policing employees' actions. If managers are revenue
maximisers, then clearly they will endeavour, at a given target
output, to maximise the amount of subsidy per unit of output. Thus
any perceived improvement in allocative efficiency resulting from
the government's action may be counterbalanced by an increase in
X-inefficiency.

The analysis raises an important question about policy formulation and execution in the area of selective aid. Officials will know
perfectly well that firms will endeavour to bargain with them. They
are likely to be constrained in the amount of technical information,
for example, from accountants and economists, that they can
acquire in order to check on firms' estimates of costs. Even if they
have such resources, the process of bargaining is tedious and the

opportunity costs are high, if our previous observations on the bureaucrats' objective function are to be believed. Maximising that function, particularly if one of the arguments is the loss of 'on-the-job leisure', may offer them little incentive to pursue their investigations with the zeal and efficiency that may be called for in order to minimise the amount of subsidy necessary to produce the desired output level. It is not possible, however, within the confines of this simple exposition to do justice to major features of the operation of selective aid policies. In order to reinforce our argument, it is necessary to look in more detail at the policy-making process and how it may defeat attempts to relate those policies to standard economic criteria.

THE SELECTIVE AID CASE

One of the most significant changes in the composition of government expenditure in recent years has been the growth in the relative importance of cash payments and loans to industrial concerns, including nationalised industries. This change reflects both short- and long-term policies. The latter are associated with the perceived policy objective of industrial countries, that if they are to retain their growth potential they must develop 'supply-oriented', rather than 'demand-oriented', policies. It is no longer simply a question of maintaining the growth in domestic aggregate monetary demand and of seeking agreement (for example, through the Organisation for Economic Cooperation and Development [OECD]) about maintaining aggregate demand in Western industrialised nations as a stimulus to growth. There must be, so it is claimed, measures introduced in order to improve the 'balance' in factor inputs and greater efficiency in factor use, coupled with structural changes in output which promote economies of scale. The short-term set of policies reflects the fears that the long-term process of adjustment may mean heavy immediate sacrifices for the labour force. Sometimes there is an obvious conflict between short- and long-term policies, as in cases where governments subsidise output or inputs (notably by the use of employment subsidies) of declining industries, in response to these fears. One of the most challenging tasks for contemporary economists is how to reconcile these long- and short-term aims, for example, by 'active' labour market policies encouraging labour mobility and re-training. These schemes all require some form of selective aid from the public budget.

There are two preliminary points to be made about the analysis of these policies. The first is how little of their content can be made to fit with the welfare economics framework which dominates much contemporary public finance. The best that can be done to maintain the relevance of Paretian analysis is to abandon attempts to seek optimal solutions within a static framework and to identify whether or not particular 'structural' policies requiring selective aid measures produce potential Paretian improvements. Inevitably this involves us in the difficulties associated with the distributional changes wrought by such policies and how far Paretian solutions can be devised to solve them. The second point concerns the mode of analysis of subsidy measures commonly found in standard literature. As I have demonstrated, economic analysis is applied in a particularly narrow context. Usually considered sufficient is the 'Pavlovian dog' model, by which firms, individually or in aggregate, are subject to stimuli and, maximising subject to constraints, change their output or input in the desired direction. More sophisticated analyses may rank alternative measures designed to achieve the same result, within a budget constraint and, in rare cases, consider the opportunity cost dimension presented by the financing of aid programmes. Remaining problems of implementing particular measures are the concern of others: the scientists engaged in technological forecasting, the politicians engaged in 'selling' policies and the bureaucrats having to administer them.

Our knowledge of economic analysis should itself indicate why the 'standard' approach of the economist to selective aid policies so often fails to have the influence which economists claim it should have. There is a parallel here to some of the contemporary discussion, particularly in the United States, about the extent to which economists' proposals to regulate business may finish up benefiting only the regulated.[12]

Let us imagine that a government decides that there is a *prima facie* case for offering investment aid to a firm or group of firms because the perceived benefits might exceed the perceived costs. For simplicity, let us assume that the decision rule can be represented by a simplified cost-benefit analysis formula:

$$\left(\sum_{i=1}^{N} \frac{B_i^x - C_i^x}{(1 + r)^i} \right) - (a.K^x) \geqslant 0$$

where B_i^x = gross benefits accruing from project x in the i-th period
C_i^x = gross current costs of producing the benefits in the i-th period

r = the social time preference rate (STP)

K^x = capital cost of project x (assumed here to be incurred at once)

N = amortisation period

a = 'shadow price' of capital.

My purpose in reproducing the formula is to demonstrate that what is normally regarded by economists as a technical device is not likely to become operational without reference to the interests and expertise of others.[13] Briefly stated, in whatever context cost-benefit analysis is used, the measurement of benefits (B_i^x) involves judgments (for example, externalities) which cannot be resolved by economic analysis, the amortisation period (N) depends on subjective attitudes to risk and therefore on policy makers' attitudes, as does the STP (r); and, as the shadow price of capital (a) entails discounting the yield of marginal private investments by the STP, it, too, is not immune from political judgment.

Further complications arise, however, when cost-benefit analysis is applied not to government projects, but to projects in the private sector financed by governments:

(1) The policy is being implemented, so to speak, 'at arm's length', and any *ex ante* assessment of returns and costs involves taking into account the reaction of individual firms participating in the projects.

(2) As a consequence of (1), data-gathering problems may be formidable and, if, as with 'rescue operations', decisions have to be taken quickly, the exercise may be very crude. A further difficulty encountered by project evaluators is that of analysing the quality of these data which may be 'massaged' to maximise the chances of receiving aid.

(3) The treatment of risk and uncertainty is further complicated by the fact that the attitude of subsidised firms to risk and uncertainty may be conditioned by the form and amount of the aid on offer.

(4) The appraisal process may have to be more 'open', with the greater prospect of political 'feedback'.

Let us now go a stage further and assume that an economic appraisal of a selective aid scheme has been carried out and that the result is that the decision rule produces a negative answer, that is, the economist's view is that, *ceteris paribus*, the 'policy' should not be 'supplied', at least in that form. I am sure that nobody with a knowledge of policy will believe that this is the end of the story, but it is interesting to enquire why this is frequently not the case:

(1) Even if the decision rule and methods of calculation are accepted and understood, the results may not be regarded as credible. The economist may be challenged on his own ground if large margins of error in calculation are unavoidable. Therefore, those involved in policy making whose objective function differs from that implicit in economic calculation may exploit technical disagreements among economists.

(2) Others involved in the decision-making process have a much more direct interest in stressing the 'intangible' benefits which economists are not competent (or are not supposed to be competent) to evaluate. Thus there is often considerable disagreement between natural scientists and economists in government about the mode of evaluation of aid directed at supporting high-technology projects. Scientific advice is frequently more acceptable to administrators and politicians, for the dramatic element in scientific innovation and the precision in scientific experimentation have a positive quality which contrasts with the rather negative results of the cautious economist who is hampered by difficulties in conducting economic experiments. Scientists whose career prospects in government and whose professional reputation rest on producing and exploiting new areas of research are therefore rather prone to go along with the argument that intangible benefits of aid projects (for example, 'the national interest') must overshadow narrowly defined economic benefits.[14] It is paradoxical that the precision, characteristic of scientific investigation of the effects of innovation on production technology, seems to desert natural scientists engaged in policy when it comes to their evaluation of benefits.

(3) The attraction of selective aid projects to utility-maximising administrators (bureaucrats) and politicians is clear. They more effectively dramatise their actions and put them in a more favourable light than 'negative' measures (such as tax measures, or regulation) which only consolidate their personal power. For politicians, in particular, this may improve their chances within the political hierarchy as well as provide the possibility of catching votes if the 'feedback effects' of a project are carefully 'orchestrated', for example, by concentrating projects in marginal constituencies. As projects may have uncertain outcomes, however, the risk of 'failure' to administrators and

K

politicians has to be considered. An important way of reducing this risk is to 'obfuscate the objective function'. This may be done by resisting clear definition of the 'arguments' in the objective function and trade-offs between them and by concealing, if necessary, the nature of the calculations of the relation between costs and benefits. In short, the economic analysis of utility maximisation of those involved in the decision-making process regarding selective aid itself offers a quite convincing explanation as to why economic analysis of aid projects applying Paretian-type decision rules have so often little influence on eventual outcomes.

I suppose I should apologise for the oracular nature of these observations, more so because the production of empirical backing that would satisfy the rigorous standards of quantitative analysis would be difficult.[15] The reader has, therefore, to take a good deal on trust. Fortunately, one very dramatic case of selective aid policy in the United Kingdom has been carefully documented by David Henderson, of University College, London, from published sources.[16] Professor Henderson was Chief Economist of the then Ministry of Aviation and was responsible for economic appraisal of the *Concorde* project in its initial stages, whereas I (as Chief Economic Adviser of the Departments of Trade and Industry in 1974) was responsible for similar appraisal when a decision had to be taken on whether to build the last three *Concordes*. Both of us are unable to complete the story of that astonishing project because access to unpublished sources is not possible, under British government rules, until 1992! The published information is, however, sufficiently revealing so that neither of us need risk landing up in the Tower of London.

Professor Henderson produces a careful and detailed calculation of the total cost of the *Concorde* Programme financed by government from its inception in 1962 to mid-1976, expressed in 1975 prices. It is interesting to note how sensitive the calculations are to the choice of a social rate of discount. If the official so-called 'test rate of discount' of 10 per cent is used, the total costs amounted to £2,150 million, whereas a possibly more realistic and lower rate of 4.5 per cent (suggested to Professor Henderson by Maurice Scott, of Nuffield College, Oxford), produces a figure of £1,480 million. It is perhaps of interest to record that in the appraisal work undertaken under my supervision in 1974 the first challenge to the estimates made by my political masters was aimed at the 'too high' rate of discount applied to future benefits! In any event the total costs were astronomical.

Professor Henderson then estimated that the net returns from *Concorde* operations from 1975-76 onwards—that is from the period when *Concorde* became (at last) airborne—were likely to be substantially negative! There would be substantial outgoings on further development and production costs and British Airways' net returns from flying *Concorde* would be negative. The only positive item would be revenue from overseas sales of the aircraft. Thus, at a rate of discount of 10 per cent, net returns would be minus £140 million and, at 4.5 per cent, net returns would be minus £120 million. Thus, the total estimated programme loss ranged from £2,290 million to £1,640 million, discounting estimates at any rate from 10 to 4.5 per cent. Nothing that has happened since these calculations were made makes it likely that the *Concorde* project could conceivably survive the test of economic viability, particularly as no *Concordes* have been sold overseas. (Professor Henderson quotes the Chairman of Lufthansa as saying 'I wouldn't take it [a *Concorde*] if it was given to me'.)[17]

One can rule out altogether any suggestion that successive governments of different political complexion deliberately incurred such losses with the intention of justifying them by an appeal to a valuation of the external benefits which would equal or exceed the losses. This is not to say that externality arguments were not deployed both within and outside government, but it must be noted that 'positive' factors, such as technological spin-off, national prestige derived from technical achievement, *et cetera*, were counterbalanced by 'negative' ones, such as, for example, social and environmental damage, sonic boom, engine noise and even effects on the ozone layer. Within the framework of Paretian welfare analysis, it is well known that devising methods for revealing true preferences for the public goods element in any project is extremely difficult and that the results are questionable. One can sympathise with Professor Henderson's reliance on his informed, although subjective, judgment in such matters and I for one would find it difficult to disagree with his conclusion that the net valuation of external benefits would yield a figure close to zero.

How such mismanagement of policy, leading to a massive misallocation of resources, can happen, should be clear from the analysis which preceded its discussion. It may be summed up in the obvious proposition enunciated long ago by Adam Smith that in circumstances in which the individuals responsible for the decisions incur no financial penalties if they miscalculate, as would happen in competitive markets, then these individuals will be less mindful of the consequences of failure and uninhibited by the prospect that resources may be misallocated. In the British context this conclusion is reinforced by the traditional anonymity and secrecy characteristic of the bureaucratic process. Few individuals know who is responsible for what and even the resurgence of parliamentary probing in the United Kingdom in recent years has not changed the situation to any marked degree. As Professor Henderson puts it: '[Secrecy] obscures and distorts the recent past, so that the lessons of experience become even harder to learn; and it both narrows and restricts in number the channels bearing information and ideas which might illuminate future choices'.[18]

Much of the traditional welfare analysis applied to problems in public finance has to rely on an artificial construction—such as an 'ethical observer'—or abstracts altogether from the problem of how to resolve the conflict between the power and motivation of interest groups in policy making not subject to market forces, and the aim of improving allocative and technical (X) efficiency. It is only by understanding the process by which 'market failure' is corrected by fiscal measures and the concomitant 'failures' which are embodied in that process that economists can 'recover their wind' and suggest suitable institutional devices by which collective failure might be reduced. Designing such devices is an important and difficult task, but, fortunately for the author, is outside the scope of this contribution!

NOTES AND REFERENCES

1. Herbert Giersch, *Allgemeine Wirtschaftspolitik, Vol. 1: Grundlagen*, Die Wirtschaftswissenschaften, Reihe B: Volkswirtschaftslehre, Beitrag Nr 9 (Wiesbaden: Gabler, 1960).

2. For a study of a range of cases, see Kenneth D. Goldin, 'Equal Access vs. Selective Access: A Critique of Public Goods Theory', *Public Choice*, Blacksburg, Virginia, No. 1, 1977.

3. *Cf.* Sam Peltzman, 'Toward a More General Theory of Regulation', with comments by Gary Becker and Joe Hirshleifer, *The Journal of Law and Economics*, Chicago, No. 2, 1976 and 'Economics of Politics and Regulation', Proceedings of a Conference Held in Honor of Professor George Stigler on His Sixty-Fifth Birthday on 17 January 1976 at the University of Chicago Law School.

4. *Cf.* Alan T. Peacock and Jack Wiseman, 'Approaches to the Analysis of Government Expenditure Growth', *Public Finance Quarterly*, Beverley Hills

and London, No. 1, 1979.

5.   Kenneth J. Arrow, 'The Organization of Economic Activity: Issues Pertinent to the Choice of Market versus Nonmarket Allocation', in Robert H. Haveman and Julius Margolis (eds), *Public Expenditures and Policy Analysis*, Markham Economics Series (Chicago: Markham, 1970).

6.   Geoffrey Brennan and James M. Buchanan, 'Towards a Tax Constitution for Leviathan', *Journal of Public Economics*, Amsterdam, No. 3, 1977.

7.   For further discussion of the methodology and typology of collective failure, see the pioneering article by Charles Wolf Jr, 'A Theory of Nonmarket Failure: Framework for Implementation Analysis', *The Journal of Law and Economics*, No. 1, 1979, and commentary by Peacock, 'The Anatomy of Collective Failure', *Public Finance*, The Hague, No. 1, 1980: *Festschrift* Paul Senf.

8.   William A. Niskanen, *Bureaucracy and Representative Government* (Chicago and New York: Aldine-Atherton, 1971) and *idem*, 'Bureaucrats between Self-interest and Public Interest', International Symposium on Anatomy of Government Deficiencies, 1980, mimeograph.

9.   See William Orzechowski, 'Economic Models of Bureaucracy: Survey, Extensions, and Evidence', in Thomas E. Borcherding (ed.), *Budgets and Bureaucrats: the Sources of Government Growth* (Durham, North Carolina: Duke University Press, 1977).

10.   See Peacock, 'Public X-Inefficiency: Informational and Institutional Constraints', unpublished article.

11.   The analysis is a development of that found in Peacock, 'The Anatomy of Collective Failure', *loc. cit.*

12.   *Cf.* George J. Stigler, 'The Theory of Economic Regulation', in *idem*, *The Citizen and the State: Essays on Regulation* (Chicago and London: University of Chicago Press, 1975); Peltzman, *loc. cit.*, and Murray L. Weidenbaum, 'The Changing Nature of Government Regulation of Business', *Journal of Post-Keynesian Economics*, White Plains, New York, No. 3, 1980.

13.   For an earlier discussion of this matter see Peacock, 'Cost-Benefit Analysis and the Political Control of Public Investment', in James N. Wolfe (ed.), *Cost Benefit and Cost Effectiveness: Studies and Analysis* (London: Allen & Unwin, 1973).

14.   For an enlightening analysis of the British case, see N. K. A. Gardner, 'The Economics of Launching Aid', in Alan Whiting (ed.), *The Economics of Industrial Subsidies*, Papers and Proceedings of the Conference on the Economics of Industrial Subsidies, held at the Civil Service College, Sunningdale, February 1975 (London: HMSO, for the Department of Industry, 1976).

15.   For further discussion of this point, see Peacock *et al.*, *Structural Economic Policies in West Germany and the United Kingdom* (London: Anglo-German Foundation for the Study of Industrial Society, 1980).

16.   P. D. Henderson, 'Two British Errors: Their Probable Size and Some Possible Lessons', *Oxford Economic Papers*, Oxford, No. 2, 1977.

17.   *Ibid.*, p. 171.

18.   *Ibid.*, p. 191.

Part V

Policies for Industrial Development

13 Industrial Prospects and Policies in the Developed Countries

Bela Balassa

The growth of the developed countries' imports of manufactured goods from the developing countries has received much attention in recent years. It has been alleged that increases in imports have adversely affected the industrial sector of the developed countries and that the continuation of this trend bodes ill for the future of the sector.[1] In turn, it has been claimed that growing protectionism in the developed countries has compromised the prospects for an outward-oriented industrial strategy in the developing countries and makes it necessary for these countries to turn to domestic markets or to trade among themselves.

This essay will subject these conflicting claims to scrutiny. It will examine recent changes in the pattern of international specialisation in manufactured goods and consider their impact on the industrial sector of the developed countries. The protectionist measures applied by these countries and their effects on international trade flows will also be analysed. It will then further review the prospects for manufacturing trade and for industrial growth in the developed countries. This will be followed by a discussion of the possibilities for intra-industry trade between developed and developing countries and of the implications this trade has for the process of adjustment in the developed countries. Finally, desirable policy changes in the developed countries will be considered briefly.

CHANGING PATTERNS OF TRADE IN MANUFACTURES

The 1963-73 period was characterised by rapid industrial expansion in the developed countries. Manufacturing output rose at an average annual rate of 5.4 per cent, exceeding the gross domestic product (GDP) growth rate of 4.6 per cent. The volume of manufactured imports from the developing countries grew even faster, averaging 16 per cent a year in volume terms. Starting from a low base, these imports reached $15,000 million in 1973, accounting for 19 per cent of the total exports of the developing countries, with fuel included in the total exports, and 32 per cent, with fuel excluded.[2] Nevertheless, they barely exceeded 1 per cent of the value of manufacturing production in the developed countries.

With slow recovery following the world recession of 1974-75, the rate of growth of GDP in the industrial countries averaged 2.5 per cent, and that of manufacturing output 2.2 per cent, between 1973 and 1978. At the same time, imports of manufactured goods from the developing countries continued to increase rapidly, with their rate of growth averaging 10.2 per cent a year.

These figures should not be interpreted, however, as evidence that trade in manufactured goods with the developing countries had adverse effects on developed-country industries. This is because their increased export earnings permitted the developing countries to increase their purchases of manufactured goods from the developed countries. In fact, financed in part by foreign borrowing, the exports of manufactured goods from the developed countries to the developing countries grew more than their imports. The dollar value of these exports more than tripled, from $52,000 million in 1973 to $159,000 million in 1978, while imports increased from $16,000 million to $44,000 million. As a result, the export surplus of the developed countries in trade in manufactured goods with the developing countries rose from $36,000 million to $115,000 million, accounting for 3.7 per cent of manufacturing output in the developed countries in 1978. In the same year, the share of manufactured exports to, and imports from, the developing countries in domestic output was 5.1 per cent and 1.4 per cent, respectively.[3]

One can thus reject the contention that trade in manufactured goods with the developing countries would have adversely affected industrial growth in the developed countries. Rather, given the existence of unused capacity in these countries during the period under consideration, their rising export surplus in trade in manufactured goods raised the level of their industrial output, both directly and indirectly through its multiplier effects. And developed countries further enjoyed the benefits of increased specialisation according to comparative advantage which provided gains to both groups of countries.

The explanation for the slow growth of industrial output in the developed countries lies elsewhere. To begin with, the adverse effects of the quadrupling of oil prices aggravated the recession that was to follow the 1972-73 boom. The parallel application of deflationary policies by countries further deepened the recession and slowed the subsequent recovery.[4] Finally, the growth of the public sector, the increased scope of government regulations, as well as fiscal and social measures that tend to discourage work effort, risk taking, savings and investment, adversely affected the growth of their manufacturing output.

Protectionist Actions by the Developed Countries

The question needs further to be answered whether increased protectionism in the developed countries has adversely affected the imports of manufactured goods from the developing countries. In fact, in the wake of the oil crisis and the world recession, protectionist actions multiplied and assumed new forms, including non-tariff measures, such as import quotas, orderly marketing arrangements, 'voluntary' export restraints and countervailing actions, as well as government aids and efforts made to establish international cartels. Government aids might have been provided purportedly for adjustment assistance but, more often than not, they in effect supported the industry against import competition.[5]

Protectionist actions against developing countries culminated in 1977, when European countries again experienced a recession and the United States balance of payments deteriorated as a result. The process has not continued and, in some respects, it has even been reversed in subsequent years. This will be apparent if we consider changes in tariff and non-tariff measures, government aids and cartel-type arrangements.

To begin with, the Tokyo Round of multilateral trade negotiations has been brought to completion. It has involved an average one-third tariff reduction on industrial products of interest to the developing countries as well as agreement on several codes on non-tariff measures, with the significant exception of a code on safeguards, elaborating on the provision in the General Agreement on Tariffs and Trade (GATT) for emergency protection against a sudden surge of imports of a particular product. Of particular importance is the introduction of an injury test in the United States legislation on countervailing action against imports which benefit from subsidies either for their production or for their export; previously, countervailing duties were irrespective of whether there had been injury to domestic industry.

The developing countries have further benefited from more liberal treatment in the application of escape clauses in the United States and the increased use of tariffs in the place of import restrictions in the few cases when escape-clause actions have been taken against them. Also, since 1977, there have been fewer instances of safeguard measures being used by Western Europe against the developing countries. Last but not least, Japan has liberalised imports, favourably affecting in particular the imports of manufactured goods from the developing countries.

Following the proliferation of government aids to industry in the years following the oil crisis, some changes in the opposite direction have occurred in this respect also. After the spring 1978 parliamentary elections, the Government of Raymond Barre announced its intention to reduce the scope of government aids to industry in France and the Government of Margaret Thatcher has subsequently introduced a similar programme in Britain. It also appears that government intervention is on the decline in Japan, and the Reagan Administration is not likely to pursue the interventionist strategy proposed under the heading 're-industrialisation' by Jimmy Carter.

At the same time, France has ceased to promote her earlier proposal for worldwide organised trade; and the defeat of Commissioner Etienne Davignon's scheme for the establishment of a synthetic fibre cartel in the European Community has discouraged attempts to set up cartels in other industries, although the cartel went ahead anyway without official approval. Finally, efforts made to establish shipbuilding and steel cartels in the framework of the Organisation for Economic Cooperation and Development (OECD) have met with little success.

The easing of protectionist pressures since 1977 has helped to accelerate the growth of the developed countries' imports of manufactured goods from the developing countries. While the volume of these imports grew by only 7.6 per cent in 1977, the increase was 15.5 per cent in 1978. A further increase of 26 per cent in terms of dollar value occurred in 1979 which may be translated into a volume increase of about 16 per cent.

Furthermore, the imports of textiles and clothing from the developing countries have risen again after stagnating in 1977, although the more restrictive rules on textiles and clothing imports from the developing countries which were adopted in the course of the 1977 revision of the Multi-fibre Arrangement (MFA) have remained in effect. The increase was 25 per cent in 1978 and 23 per cent in 1979 in terms of dollar value, corresponding to a rise of 8-9 per cent and 7-8 per cent, respectively, in volume terms.

These conclusions should not give rise to undue optimism, since protectionist forces in the developed countries remain strong. Nevertheless, it is noteworthy that the 1980 recession has not brought on an aggravation of protectionist tendencies against the developing countries as had been feared. Rather, the fire of the protectionists has been directed against other developed countries that can better defend their interests than the developing countries.

Once economic expansion in the developed countries is again under way, the time may be propitious for a further assault on protectionism. Suggestions to this effect will be made in the concluding section of this essay. In the following, prospective trends in trade in manufactured goods will be examined on the assumption that the trade policies presently applied in the developed countries will continue during the period under consideration.

Projections for 1978-90

The author has projected the developed countries' imports of manufactured goods from the developing countries for the 1978-90 period for the case that present trade policies, including the MFA, continue.[6] It has further been assumed that the gross national product (GNP) of the developed countries would rise at an average annual rate of 3.9 per cent between 1978 and 1990 and that their income elasticity of import demand for manufactured goods originating in the developing countries would be 3.2 per cent during this period. This elasticity is lower than the estimated income elasticity of 4.1 per cent in the 1973-78 period, reflecting the view that developing countries would obtain smaller relative gains from the higher absolute level of exports reached in 1978.

In turn, it has been assumed that income elasticities of import demand for manufactured goods originating in the developed countries would be 2.0 per cent in the area of the Organisation of Petroleum Exporting Countries (OPEC) and 1.5 in non-OPEC developing countries, representing a decline from the observed income elasticities of 3.0 per cent and 1.8 per cent, respectively, in the 1973-78 period. With projected GNP growth rates of 6.0 per cent and 5.5 per cent, averaging 5.6 per cent, the exports of manufactured goods from the developed countries to the developing countries would rise at an average annual rate of 9.7 per cent between 1978 and 1990, as compared with projected increases of 12.5 per cent in their imports.

Notwithstanding the higher rate of import growth, the projections would entail an increase in the export surplus of the developed countries in their trade in manufactured goods with the developing countries from $115,000 million in 1978 to $374,000 million in 1990, expressed in terms of 1978 prices. This increase would contribute to industrial growth in the developed countries, raising the rate of growth of production (3.9 per cent) above that of consumption (3.6 per cent) of manufactured goods.

At the same time, the developing countries would become increasingly important markets for the manufactured products of the developed countries, accounting for 18 per cent of the increment in production, and for 59 per cent of the increment in exports to non-partner countries between 1978 and 1990. In the same period, the developing countries would provide 9 per cent of the increment in the developed countries' consumption of manufactured goods and 45 per cent of the increment of their imports from non-partner countries.[7]

The developed countries would benefit from the growth of international trade in manufactured goods with the developing countries through specialisation according to comparative advantage, entailing the expansion of industries embodying sophisticated technology, high-level manpower and physical capital. Still, this pattern of specialisation would not involve a decline in output in any of the eight industrial categories for which separate projections have been made.

In particular, the growth rates of the imports of textiles and clothing of 6 per cent and 7 per cent, projected under the assumption of the continued operation of the MFA, would permit production in these industries of the developed countries to continue to rise. For the 1978-90 period, production in the developed countries is projected to increase at average annual rates of growth of 2.2 per cent for textiles and 2.5 per cent for clothing.

INTRA-INDUSTRY TRADE IN
MANUFACTURED GOODS

Following the traditional discourse on the effects of trade between developed and developing countries, the above discussion has been couched in terms of inter-industry specialisation that concerns the allocation of resources among industries. In this section, the possibilities for intra-industry specialisation in trade in manufactured goods between developed and developing countries are considered.

Following a paper by the author on the effects of trade liberalisation in the European Community,[8] considerable attention was given to intra-industry trade among the developed countries. This trade may involve horizontal specialisation through the exchange of differentiated products, as well as vertical specialisation through trade in parts, components and accessories of a particular product.

Intra-industry trade was said to occur among countries at similar levels of development that have similar relative factor prices. Empirical research also dealt with intra-industry trade among such countries, first in developed areas and subsequently in developing regions. This orientation of theoretical and empirical research was confirmed by contributions to a recent symposium on intra-industry trade.[9]

At the symposium, the author further addressed himself to intra-industry trade between developed and developing countries. He suggested that 'horizontal specialisation will also occur among countries at different levels of development, when the product varieties traded will incorporate attributes that correspond to the factor endowments of the countries concerned'.[10] Drawing on earlier work on sub-contracting, he also noted the existence of vertical specialisation between developed and developing countries in the framework of the international division of the production process.[11] In the following, empirical evidence will be provided on the extent of horizontal and vertical specialisation between the two groups of countries, further indicating its implications for the process of adjustment in the developed countries.

Horizontal Specialisation

The United States' textiles and clothing industry provides a case study of horizontal (product) specialisation.[12] As an introduction to the discussion, reference may be made to the employment effects of productivity growth and of changes in trade flows since 1977, the year when the industry mounted a protectionist campaign.

The data of Table 13.1 indicate that, in their impact on employment, the growth of labour productivity far outweighed changes in trade flows; whereas productivity growth was responsible for the loss of 71,000 jobs in textiles and 105,000 jobs in clothing between 1977 and 1979, changes in trade flows led to a gain of 14,000 jobs in textiles and to a loss of 17,000 jobs in clothing.

TABLE 13.1

Textiles and Textile Products: United States Domestic Production, Apparent Consumption, Imports, Exports and Employment, 1977-79

	Textile mill products (22)[a]			Apparel and other textile products (23)[a]			Textiles and textile products (22+23)[a]		
	1977	1978	1979	1977	1978	1979	1977	1978	1979
Current values ($m)									
Domestic production	40,823	43,888	46,900	40,079	43,215	46,690	80,902	87,103	93,590
Total imports	1,765	2,212	2,190	3,650	4,833	5,075	5,415	7,045	7,265
Total exports	1,857	2,073	3,027	524	551	819	2,381	2,624	3,846
Net imports	-92	139	-837	3,126	4,282	4,256	3,034	4,421	3,419
Apparent consumption	40,731	44,027	46,063	43,205	47,497	50,946	83,936	91,524	97,009
Total imports/apparent consumption	4.33	5.02	4.75	8.45	10.18	9.96	6.45	7.69	7.49
Net imports/apparent consumption	-0.23	0.32	-1.82	7.24	9.02	8.35	3.61	5.08	3.52
Employment, production, prices									
Employment ('000)	867.1	864.5	855.9	1,331.6	1,334.3	1,313.1	2,198.7	2,198.8	2,169.0
Output per man ($'000)	47.1	50.8	54.8	30.1	32.4	35.6	36.8	39.6	43.1
Price index (1977 = 100)	100.0	103.0	107.4	100.0	104.0	109.3	100.0	103.5	108.3
Values in 1977 prices ($m)									
Domestic production	40,823	42,610	43,668	40,079	41,553	42,717	80,902	84,163	86,385
Apparent consumption	40,731	42,745	42,889	43,205	45,670	46,611	83,936	88,415	89,500
Actual net imports[b]	-92	135	-779	3,126	4,117	3,894	3,034	4,252	3,115
Expected net imports[c]	-92	-98	-99	3,126	3,307	3,375	3,034	3,209	3,276
Excess of net imports[d]	0	233	-680	0	810	519	0	1,043	-161

Employment effects ('000)

Hypothetical employment[e]	867.1	904.7	927.2	1,331.6	1,380.5	1,419.2	2,198.7	2,285.7	2,346.4
Actual employment	867.1	864.5	855.9	1,331.6	1,334.3	1,313.1	2,198.7	2,198.8	2,169.0

Employment loss due to

Productivity increase[f]	0	40.2	71.3	0	46.2	106.1	0	86.4	177.4
Excess of net imports[g]	0	4.9	-14.4	0	26.9	17.2	0	31.8	2.8

SOURCE: United States Department of Commerce, *1980 U.S. Industrial Outlook* (Washington: US Government Printing Office, 1980) chapter 34, 'Textiles', p. 357 and chapter 35, 'Apparel', p. 368.

[a] Classification number according to the Standard Industrial Classification (SIC) system used by all United States Federal statistical agencies.

[b] Domestic price increase was assumed to apply to imports and exports.

[c] Expected net imports were calculated on the assumption that their 1975 share in apparent consumption remained unchanged in subsequent years.

[d] Differences between actual and expected net imports.

[e] Hypothetical employment was calculated on the assumption that 1975 levels of output per man remained unchanged in subsequent years.

[f] Employment loss due to productivity increases equals the difference between hypothetical and actual employment.

[g] Employment loss due to excess of net imports is calculated by dividing the excess of net imports by the 1977 level of output per man. The employment effects of change in the net imports of man-made fibre have been calculated in the same way.

The results do not confirm the fears expressed as to the adverse effects of imports on employment in the United States' textiles and clothing industry. At the same time, the aggregate data do not permit gauging the welfare gains obtained through product specialisation in the industry. Evidence on the existence of these gains is provided by differences in unit values in domestic production and in imports.

In 1979, average unit values calculated per pound of fibre equivalent were $7.47 in United States production and $4.70 in imports.[13] These figures represent the outcome of a process in which the shift of domestic industry to more sophisticated products with higher value added is accompanied by the growth of imports of relatively simple products that have low value added.

The process of upgrading may involve shifts between products made from different materials or between products made from the same material. To begin with, man-made fibres have increasingly gained at the expense of cotton in the United States. Expressed in terms of linear yards, the production of cotton broadwoven fabrics fell from 6,300 million in 1970 to 4,400 million in 1977 and to 3,900 million in 1979; in the same period, the production of man-made fibre fabrics rose from 4,900 million to 6,300 million and, again, to 6,600 million.[14]

Furthermore, among cotton broadwoven fabrics, shifts have occurred from lower value-added sheeting, duck and print cloth to higher value-added cotton fabrics and, in particular, to corded coloured yarn fabrics. As a result of these shifts, the former group's share of the total declined from 70.5 per cent in 1970 to 57.0 per cent in 1977 and it stabilised at that level afterwards.

Finally, within the duck, sheeting and print cloth category, there has been a shift towards finer fabrics in the United States industry. The existence of this shift is indicated by the higher unit values of United States production and, in particular, exports as compared with imports. In 1979, export and import unit values, respectively, were $0.73 and $0.39 for cotton sheeting; $0.90 and $0.68 for cotton duck; and $0.80 and $0.34 for cotton print cloth. Average unit values for the three categories, taken together, were $0.53 for domestic production, $0.80 for exports and $0.38 for imports.[15]

In explaining these differences, use may be made of information provided in a recent report of the United States International Trade Commission on cotton textiles imported from Pakistan—which account for one-third of the United States' imports of cotton sheeting, cotton duck and cotton print cloth. According to the report, 'the types of cotton fabric which are produced in the largest quantity by the Pakistani textile industry include heavy coarse fabrics, which consume large quantities of raw cotton and can be manufactured by less sophisticated machinery with relatively lower skilled labor'.[16] Thus, while 'imports of sheeting from Pakistan are heavily concentrated in the coarse osnaburg and classes A and B sheeting . . . the finer class C sheeting accounted for more than two-thirds of domestic production'.[17] Also, imports of single-warp ducks from Pakistan 'were concentrated in the lighter weight single fillings of average yarn numbers 10 to 15 [whereas] the domestic production of ply-warp ducks [a more sophisticated product] had very little competition from Pakistani imports'.[18] Finally, imports of print cloth from Pakistan were concentrated in types of fabric having average yarn numbers from twenty to thirty-nine, as compared with a usual range of twenty-seven to forty-four.[19]

Men's and boys' cotton T-shirts provide another example of differences in product composition in United States production, exports and imports. In 1979, unit values per dozen were $14.35 in domestic production, $20.70 in exports and $9.45 in imports.[20] These differences reflect the fact that men's and boys' T-shirts have increasingly become fashion items, with American producers offering brand names that have particular consumer appeal.

The described cases provide evidence of an upgrading process in the United States' textiles and clothing industry, with imports taking the place of domestic production which has shifted to higher value-added items that are more profitable and use more skilled labour. Value added per unit is even higher for exports, indicating the comparative advantages of the United States in relatively sophisticated products.

Product specialisation, then, provides advantages to the United States' textile and clothing industry and to the national economy in general which are not reflected by the industry averages. In this connection, it should be added that the process of upgrading in the American textile industry continues, with the shift from woven to knitted fabrics and, most recently, to stretch fabrics.

Vertical Specialisation

Because of its prominence in discussions on the effects of imports from developing countries, the textiles and clothing industry has been chosen as a case study in this essay. But welfare gains may be obtained through horizontal or product specialisation in other industries as well.[21] Further gains can be derived from vertical specialisation through the international division of the production process.

A well known example of vertical specialisation is importation into the United States under tariff items 807.00 and 806.30, when duties apply only to value added abroad, but not to the United States inputs used in foreign production. The total value of such imports rose from $1,000 million in 1966 to $2,200 million in 1970, $7,200 million in 1977, $9,700 million in 1978 and $11,900 million in 1979. In recent years, on the average, 72-73 per cent of the total represented value added abroad.[22]

About 45 per cent of all imports entering under tariff items 807.00 and 806.30 originate in developing countries, with imports from Mexico ($2,100 million), Malaysia ($700 million) and Singapore ($600 million) being the most important. But value added abroad amounts to only 51 per cent of the value of such imports originating in the developing countries.[23]

In the trade literature, much attention has been given to imports under tariff items 807.00 and 806.30 into the United States and to imports under similar provisions into European countries.[24] These forms of offshore procurement, however, represent only part of the trade that occurs within the framework of the international division of the production process. Thus, while American imports from developing countries under tariff items 807.00 and 806.30 are dominated by television apparatus and semi-conductors, there are rising imports of parts, components and accessories of machinery and transport equipment from the developing countries.

Parts, components and accessories figure prominently in United States imports originating in Hong Kong, Korea and Taiwan. Each of these countries ships several times more manufactured goods to the United States than Mexico and Malaysia which, in turn, surpass them in terms of United States imports under tariff items 807.00 and 806.30. There is, furthermore, a reverse flow of parts, components and accessories from the developed countries for assembly in the developing countries. For example, Taiwanese firms buy technologically sophisticated—as well as capital-intensive—parts, components and accessories from the United States and Japan for assembly in Taiwan. This is the converse of the pattern observed in the developed countries which purchase simple, labour-intensive parts, components and accessories from the developing countries.

Note, finally, that the end products of the international division of the production process may also be sold in third countries. A case in point is worldwide sourcing in the automobile industry by General Motors and Ford which have established plants producing particular parts, components and accessories in some two dozen countries. At the same time, practically no automobiles and auto-mobile parts are imported into the United States from developing countries under tariff items 807.00 and 806.30.

Changing Scope of Intra-industry Trade

The preceding considerations point to the increasing importance of intra-industry specialisation in manufactured trade between developed and developing countries. This proposition is supported by the results of empirical studies by Joseph M. Finger and Morde-chai E. Kreinin, of the World Bank and Michigan State University, respectively, by Frank Wolter, of the Institut für Weltwirtschaft in Kiel, and by the present author. The studies show that the extent of intra-industry specialisation increased over time in trade with the newly industrialising or semi-industrial developing countries, as well as with countries at lower levels of development.

Using an index of export similarity, Dr Finger and Professor Kreinin have concluded that 'the [manufactured] export pattern of the Semi-Industrial LDC [less developed country] has become markedly more similar to the export patterns of the old EEC [that is, the Community of the Six] and the United States, and slightly more similar to the export pattern of Japan'.[26] Changes in the same direction have been observed in countries at lower levels of develop-ment, although the export structure of these countries has remained more dissimilar to that of the developed countries.

The increased similarity of the export structure of developed and developing countries is indicative of the growing importance of intra-industry specialisation between developed and developing countries. This conclusion is confirmed by Dr Wolter, who examined changes over time in the extent of intra-industry specialisation in West Germany's trade in manufactured goods with various groups of countries.

Dr Wolter has found that, between 1969 and 1977, the extent of intra-industry specialisation increased substantially in Germany's trade with the newly industrialising developing countries and other developing countries, while it increased far less in trade with the developed countries and declined in trade with the centrally-planned economies. Nevertheless, the extent of intra-industry specialisation continued to be the highest in trade with the developed countries, followed by the newly industrialising developing countries, the centrally planned economies and the other developing countries.[27]

Dr Wolter's calculations have been made using the three-digit breakdown of the United Nations' Standard International Trade Classification (SITC). The present author has employed a ninety-one-industry classification scheme, consisting of three- and four-digit SITC items and their combinations, which defines an industry to include commodities with high substitution elasticities in production.[28] The author has made estimates for the United States, West Germany, the United Kingdom and Japan for the years 1969 and 1979;[29] these results are shown in Table 13.2.

TABLE 13.2

Extent of Intra-industry Specialisation in the United States, West Germany, the United Kingdom and Japan in Trade with Various Country Groups[a]

		DC^b	CPE^b	NIC^b	LDC^b	$OPEC^b$	World
United States	1969	0.602	0.215	0.341	0.137	0.013	0.568
	1979	0.672	0.269	0.407	0.250	0.011	0.611
	Ratio	1.12	1.25	1.19	1.82	0.85	1.08
West Germany	1969	0.699	0.289	0.208	0.069	0.009	0.605
	1979	0.772	0.280	0.376	0.169	0.014	0.666
	Ratio	1.10	0.97	1.81	2.45	1.56	1.10
United Kingdom	1969	0.556	0.283	0.263	0.152	0.027	0.617
	1979	0.797	0.243	0.386	0.432	0.093	0.763
	Ratio	1.43	0.86	1.40	2.84	3.44	1.24
Japan	1969	0.378	0.142	0.174	0.045	0.007	0.333
	1979	0.393	0.137	0.313	0.087	0.004	0.275
	Ratio	1.04	0.96	1.80	1.93	0.57	0.83

[a]Indicated on a scale from 0 to 1. For an explanation of the formulae used to obtain these figures, see the Appendix.
[b]Countries are grouped as follows: DC = developed countries; CPE = centrally-planned economies; NIC = newly industrialising developing countries; LDC = oil-importing less developed countries; OPEC = oil-exporting developing countries.

In 1979, the extent of intra-industry specialisation in manu-factured trade with developed countries was the highest in the United Kingdom and Germany: they were followed by the United States, with Japan far behind. The greater degree of intra-industry specialisation in the first two countries is explained by their partici-pation in the European Community, where the elimination of tariffs has been conducive to such trade.[30] Also, its entry into the Community in the early 1970s explains the fact that between 1969 and 1979 the extent of intra-industry specialisation increased the most in the United Kingdom, where the ratio of the 1979 to the 1969 results was 1.43 as compared with 1.12 in the United States, 1.10 in Germany and 1.04 in Japan.

In turn, Japan's long history of protectionism contributed to the low level of intra-industry specialisation in her trade with developed countries, as well as to the small increase shown between 1969 and 1979. This conclusion also applies to trade with developing coun-tries, where Japan exhibits a substantially lower degree of intra-industry specialisation than do the other three countries.

At the same time, in all four countries, the 1969-79 period saw a rapid increase in the extent of intra-industry specialisation in trade with both the newly industrialising developing countries and the group of oil-importing less developed countries.[31] The ratios of the 1979 to the 1969 results in trade with the two groups of countries respectively, were 1.19 and 1.82 in the United States, 1.81 and 2.45 in Germany, 1.40 and 2.48 in the United Kingdom and 1.80 and 1.93 in Japan.

The extent of intra-industry specialisation in trade with develop-ing countries was already high in 1969 in the United Kingdom and the United States, reflecting the effects of relatively liberal policies towards the manufactured exports of the developing countries and, in the case of the United Kingdom, Commonwealth preference. In turn, the extent of intra-industry specialisation in trade with the two groups of developing countries remained at a level far below that of the three other countries in Japan, where protection was the strongest.

With the exception of the United Kingdom, the extent of intra-industry specialisation was considerably higher in trade with the newly industrialising developing countries than with the oil-importing less developed countries, indicating the increased importance of intra-industry specialisation in countries at higher levels of development. In the case of the United Kingdom, the results are explained by the effects of Commonwealth preference that benefited several large less developed countries, but did not affect the newly industrialising developing countries other than Hong Kong.

At the same time, apart from the United States, the extent of intra-industry specialisation in trade with the centrally planned economies declined between 1969 and 1979 to a level far below that in trade with the newly industrialising developing countries. Finally, trade with the OPEC countries is characterised by inter-industry specialisation.

CONCLUSIONS AND POLICY IMPLICATIONS

The increasing importance of intra-industry trade between developed and developing countries points to the conclusion that the adverse effects of imports from the developing countries on particular industries of the developed countries have been much exaggerated. As Dr Wolter notes, 'With the increase in intra-industry trade, adjustment can often take the form of reorganizing production within existing firms by changing the product mix, product differentiation, upgrading, and so forth, at their original location'.[32] Thus, horizontal specialisation entails a shift to higher value-added products in the developed countries as simple lower value-added products are imported from the developing countries. In turn, vertical specialisation involves the exchange of parts, components and accessories requiring skilled and technical labour, more sophisticated technology, and physical capital.

The importation of inputs that use largely unskilled labour also lowers the cost of production in the developed countries, thereby increasing export possibilities and/or leading to more effective import competition. This is the case, for example, in the textiles industry where grey fabrics imported from developing countries are transformed into higher value products.

At the same time, intra-industry trade involves little adjustment cost in the developed countries. This is the situation, in particular, in the case of horizontal specialisation, since firms can change their product composition and workers can be redirected within the firm. In fact, the rise of imports may benefit the firm and its workers through shifts to more profitable lines of production and the upgrading of the labour force. And, reducing product variety may provide further gains through the use of specialised machinery and learning by doing.

Adjustment costs associated with vertical specialisation will also be relatively low. In cases where the same firm produces several parts or components, the shift can be accomplished within the firm. And even if this is not the case, the skills used in the production of particular parts, components and accessories are likely to be transferable to the production of others.

Exploiting comparative advantage through inter-industry specialisation, however, involves adjustment costs. At the same time, these costs decline with the length of the period of adjustment. In this connection, the experience of New England in the United States is of particular interest.

New England provides an example of successful adjustment. With the relocation of the textiles and shoe industries to the south of the United States, New England has shifted to the production of high-technology products such as computers, electronic equipment and instruments. Following the near-exhaustion of the labour supply, these industries have recently expanded from the state of Massachusetts northwards, where they utilise the skills of workers in declining industries. It has been reported, for example, that 'because they had done stitching in the old shoe factory . . . Littletown [New Hampshire] workers were adept at learning the wiring, assembling and other hand work required for an electronic subcontractor'.[33] Also, in Berlin, New Hampshire, 'a converse sneaker factory closed in 1979, primarily because of the area's strength in computers and electronics'.[34]

The case of the shoe workers conflicts with the claim as to the practical impossibility of moving workers from one industry to another.[35] The transferability of skills is also indicated by a study of 120 occupational categories in 58 industries which cover all the major developed countries.[36] And in cases where skills are not directly transferable, retraining programmes may be employed and the normal attrition of the labour force may be reinforced by the application of early retirement provisions.[37]

Such provisions, together with normal attrition and retraining, will determine the speed at which decreases in the production of a particular industry may be acceptable to the developed countries. At the same time, it should be emphasised that, apart from the push emanating from technological change and imports, there is a pull from other industries, as indicated by the example of the sneaker factory. 'Pull' and 'push' factors also operate within individual industries as imports in part take the place of the abandoned home production of low value-added products of low domestic profitability and in part prompt the upgrading of home production for domestic use, as well as for exports.

These considerations indicate the benefits developed countries would derive from increasing the exchange of manufactured goods with the developing countries at rates exceeding the projections made for the period 1978–90. Increased imports would be desirable, in particular, in textiles and clothing, where the MFA may serve as a vehicle for this purpose. The aim should be to reach the maximum growth of imports compatible with an acceptable speed of adjustment in the developed countries.

In this way, one could transform the MFA from an instrument of protection to one of adjustment. The opportunity for such a transformation was provided by the 1981 renegotiation of the Arrangement. Apart from allowing for a satisfactory overall growth of imports from traditional sources, it would be necessary to ensure markets for newly emerging exporters and to modify the provisions of the 1977 Arrangement which increased the discretion of developed countries for unilateral action and reduced the flexibility of the developing countries to shift products among individual categories.[38] The opportunity mentioned above passed unrecognised.

Rather than *ex ante* quantitative limitations as under the MFA, *ex post* safeguards should be utilised in the event that a sudden surge of imports causes serious injury in other industries of the developed countries. This, in turn, would require rectifying the failure of the Tokyo Round of multilateral trade negotiations to reach agreement on an international safeguards code. The newly established code should provide for the surveillance of national practices, as well as for the resolution of conflicts in cases where safeguard measures have been employed.

One may envisage a two-stage procedure, under which national authorities could impose safeguard measures unilaterally, subject to certain conditions.[39] These conditions would include the provisions that the share of imports from the developing countries in the domestic consumption is not reduced, that the safeguards are not invoked against the least developed countries and that the application of the safeguard measures remains temporary. The temporary nature of the safeguard measures would be expressed by their limited duration, the progressive liberalisation of import restrictions during the period of their application and the requirement that the re-imposition of safeguards be countenanced by an international forum.

The application of these provisions would allow for speedy action on the part of the developed countries without the need for agreement on the international level. Developing countries could, however, bring complaints under the safeguards code to an international forum if the provisions are not respected and this forum would countenance an extension of the period of application of safeguards only if appropriate adjustment measures have been taken. The provision of the code should also apply to the safeguard measures presently employed that would be subject to review under the code.

NOTES AND REFERENCES

1. The original version of this essay was prepared for the symposium on 'De-industrialisation', organised by the Austrian Institute of Economic Research, held in Vienna on 8-9 January 1981. The author is indebted to the participants of the symposium as well as to Michael Finger, Isaiah Frank and Martin Wolf for helpful comments.

The author is Professor of Political Economy at the Johns Hopkins University and Consultant to the World Bank. The opinions expressed in the essay are the author's alone and should not be construed to represent the views of the World Bank.

A recent example is provided by Paul Samuelson, 'Economist Paul Samuelson Charts Global Shifts', *World Business Weekly*, New York, 1 December 1980. In Samuelson's view 'manufacturing industry is trying to leave North America and Western Europe. The basic comparative advantage is moving to the "Gang of Four": South Korea, Taiwan, Hong Kong and Singapore'.

2. Unless otherwise noted, data on the gross domestic product and manufacturing output are taken from the *United Nations Yearbook of National Account Statistics* (New York: United Nations, Department of Economic and Social Affairs, 1978), while the trade figures are derived from *International Trade 1978/79* (Geneva: GATT Secretariat, 1979) and *idem, International Trade 1979/80*. Both developed and developing countries have been defined to exclude southern Europe.

3. Bela Balassa, 'Trade in Manufactured Goods: Patterns of Change', *World Development*, Oxford, March 1981.

4. Balassa, 'Resolving Policy Conflicts for Rapid Growth in the World Economy', *Banca Nazionale del Lavoro Quarterly Review*, Rome, September 1978.

5. Balassa, 'The "New Protectionism" and the International Economy', *Journal of World Trade Law*, Twickenham, September-October 1978. For a discussion of subsequent events, discussed in the next paragraph, see the author's 'The Tokyo Round and the Developing Countries', *ibid.*, March-April 1980.

6.   This section relies on Balassa, 'Prospects for Trade in Manufactured Goods between Industrial and Developing Countries', *Journal of Policy Modeling*, New York, October 1980.

7.   Trade with non-partner countries excludes United States-Canada trade which takes place largely in the framework of multinational corporations (one-third of which is not subject to duty under the North American Automotive Agreement), as well as trade among the member countries of the European Free Trade Association in manufactured goods.

8.   Balassa, 'Tariff Reductions and Trade in Manufactures among Industrial Countries', *The American Economic Review*, Evanston, Illinois, June 1966.

9.   Herbert Giersch (ed.), *On the Economics of Intra-Industry Trade: Symposium 1978* (Tübingen: J. C. B. Mohr [Paul Siebeck] for the Institut für Weltwirtschaft an der Universität Kiel, 1979).

10.   Balassa, 'Intra-Industry Trade and the Integration of Developing Countries in the World Economy', *ibid.*

11.   In this connection, reference may be made to the ongoing research project directed by Joseph Grunwald of the Brookings Institution, 'North-South Complementary Intra-Industry Trade', which examines various forms of vertical specialisation and the economic effects of international sub-contracting in selected Latin American countries.

12.   This section draws on the author's submission to the United States International Trade Commission for its publication *Textiles and Textile Products of Cotton from Pakistan* (Washington: US Government Printing Office, 1980).

13.   Table 13.1 and United States Department of Commerce, International Trade Administration, *United States Import and Import/Production Ratios for Cotton, Wool and Man-Made Fiber Textiles and Apparel* (Washington: US Government Printing Office, 1980), pp. 3-11.

14.   United States Department of Commerce, Bureau of the Census, *Broadwoven Fabrics (Gray)*, Current Industrial Reports, Summary for 1979 (Washington: US Government Printing Office, 1980), Table 2.

15.   United States International Trade Commission, *op. cit.*, pp. A-22–A-32. All figures are per square yard; unit values for United States production of the individual fabric types are not available.

16.   *Ibid.*, p. A-14.

17.   *Ibid.*, p. A-15.

18.   *Ibid.*, p. A-16.

19.   *Ibid.*

20.   *Ibid.*, pp. A-79–A-82.

21.   This is the case, for example, in the shoe industry, where an upgrading of domestic production occurred *pari passu* with increased imports from the developing countries.

22.   United States International Trade Commission, *Tariff Items 807.00 and 806.30 U.S. Items for Consumption*, Specified Years 1966-79 (Washington: US Government Printing Office, 1980), Table 1.

23.   *Ibid.*, Tables 13 and 26.

24.   Compare, for example, Joseph M. Finger, 'Tariff Provisions for

Offshore Assembly and the Exports of Developing Countries', *The Economic Journal*, Cambridge, June 1975.

25. In the following, the expressions 'intra-industry trade' and 'intra-industry specialisation' will be used inter-changeably.

26. Finger and Mordechai E. Kreinin, 'A Measure of "Export Similarity" and its Possible Uses', *The Economic Journal*, December 1979, p. 909.

27. Frank Wolter, 'Restructuring for Import Competition from Developing Countries, II: The Case of the Federal Republic of Germany', *Journal of Policy Modeling*, May 1980, Table 9. The results further show that the extent of intra-industry specialisation is greater with the countries of North America and Western Europe than with Japan and it is greater in trade with the oil-importing than the oil-exporting developing countries.

28. The same classification scheme was used in the author's earlier studies referred to above.

29. The extent of intra-industry trade has been estimated by utilising a formula developed by Antonio Aquino in the modified form earlier used by the author. Aquino's original formula has been used by Wolter in the article cited above. For the formula used in making estimates, see the Appendix.

30. Balassa, 'Tariff Reductions and Trade in Manufactures among Industrial Countries', *loc. cit.*

31. Newly industrialising countries have been defined as countries that had per capita incomes between $1,400 and $3,500 in 1977 and where the share of manufacturing in the GDP was 20 per cent or higher in 1977. The group includes Argentina, Brazil, Chile, Mexico, Uruguay, Greece, Portugal, Spain, Turkey, Yugoslavia, Israel, Hong Kong, Korea, Singapore and Taiwan. (Following the usual practice, Israel, with per capita incomes of $4,120, has been included in the group that excludes Ireland, with per capita incomes of $3,476.) The data are taken from the *1977 World Bank Atlas* (Washington: World Bank, 1980) and the *World Development Report, 1979* (Washington: World Bank, 1979).

32. *Ibid.*, p. 192.

33. *The New York Times*, New York, 20 October 1980.

34. *Ibid.*

35. The author recalls a statement made at a World Bank seminar on 'Industrialization and Trade Policies in the 1970s', held in October 1972, by Nat Goldfinger, a senior adviser to the American Federation of Labor and Congress of Industrial Organizations. According to Mr Goldfinger, the period of adjustment in the shoe industry was fifty years!

36. Manuel Zymelman, *Occupational Structure of Industries* (Washington: World Bank, 1980).

37. This point is made by Giersch, who eloquently argues the need for adjustment in the developed countries to imports from the developing countries. Giersch, *A European Look at the World Economy*, Kieler Sonderdruck No. 60 (Kiel: Institut für Weltwirtschaft, 1978). The publication is the text of the twelfth Annual William K. McInnally Memorial Lecture, delivered by Giersch at the University of Michigan on 7 April 1978, Ann Arbor, Graduate School of Business Administration, University of Michigan, 1978.

38.   For a detailed discussion, see Donald M. Keesing and Martin Wolf, *Textile Quotas against Developing Countries*, Thames Essay No. 23 (London: Trade Policy Research Centre, 1980).

39.   The following discussion draws on Balassa, 'The "New Protectionism" and the International Economy, *loc. cit.*, and 'The Tokyo Round and the Developing Countries', *loc. cit.*

40.   Balassa, 'Tariff Reductions and Trade in Manufactures among Industrial Countries', *loc. cit.*

41.   Herbert G. Grubel and Peter J. Lloyd, *Intra-Industry Trade* (London: Macmillan, 1975).

42.   Antonio Aquino, 'Intra-Industry Trade and Inter-Industry Specialization as Concurrent Sources of International Trade in Manufactures', *Weltwirtschaftliches Archiv*, Kiel, No. 2, 1978.

43.   Balassa, 'Intra-Industry Trade and the Integration of Developing Countries in the World Economy', *op. cit.*

APPENDIX

The author originally estimated the extent of intra-industry specialisation as an unweighted average of 'representative ratios', defined as the ratio of the absolute difference between exports and imports to the sum of the exports and imports in each industry.[40] The formula is shown in equation (1).

$$\frac{1}{n} \sum \frac{|X_i - M_i|}{(X_i + M_i)} \qquad (1)$$

Herbert G. Grubel, of Simon Fraser University, Burnaby, and Peter J. Lloyd, of the Australian National University, Canberra, subsequently calculated trade-weighted, rather than unweighted, averages of these ratios and attempted to adjust for the extent of trade imbalance.[41] In turn, Antonio Aquino, of the University of Calabria, showed that the Grubel-Lloyd adjustment for trade imbalance does not provide consistent results and proposed an alternative for consistent measurement.[42] The present author made use of Professor Aquino's formulation, but made adjustment for the imbalance in total trade, rather than in trade in manufactured goods as Professor Aquino had done, so as to take account of inter-industry specialisation between primary and manufactured goods.[43] The same procedure has been applied in the present essay except that, following Professors Grubel and Lloyd and Professor Aquino, the results obtained have been deducted from (1). This formulation has the advantage that changes over time in the extent of intra-industry trade are more directly observable from the results.

The relevant formula is shown in equation (2) where X_t and M_t refer to total exports and imports, respectively.

$$1 - \frac{\sum |X_i^e - M_i^e|}{\sum (X_i^e - M_i^e)} \quad , \qquad (2)$$

where $X_i^e = X_i \dfrac{\frac{1}{2} \sum (X_i + M_i)}{X_t}$ and $M_i^e = M_i \dfrac{\frac{1}{2} \sum (X_i + M_i)}{M_t}$.

14 Re-appraisal of Foreign Trade Strategies for Industrial Development

Juergen B. Donges

One of the recurring themes in thought and opinion about the process of economic development is the appropriate foreign trade strategy for less developed countries (LDCs) to apply in pursuit of rapid and sustained industrialisation. Most academic economists and economic policy makers share the view that foreign trade policies, while certainly not sufficient to achieve specific industrialisation objectives, do matter. It is still controversial, however, whether these policies should be protectionist or liberal, that is, whether the industrial development efforts should include a little or much trade in order to be successful.

That this controversy goes on is a remarkable fact in itself. Not only have we witnessed over the past forty years the application of a great variety of foreign trade policies as part of the development strategies followed by LDCs, we have also seen economic research build a systematic body of knowledge about how these policies affect the development process. Most prominent are the comparative country studies conducted under the auspices of the Development Centre of the Organisation for Economic Cooperation and Development (OECD), the World Bank, the National Bureau of Economic Research (NBER) and the Institut für Weltwirtschaft in Kiel, altogether covering (a partly-overlapping group of) twenty-four countries, most of which are relatively industrialised by now (and therefore called 'newly industrialising countries' or NICs), and several of which are quite populous.[1] It seems that a number of misconceptions and misunderstandings about the role of trade policies in the development process, frequently resulting from a deep mistrust about the working of the market mechanism, still prevail.

As the LDCs are determined to accelerate their process of industrialisation ('Lima target'),[2] it is in their own interests to take care that the fulfilment of this objective is not impaired by in-

279

appropriate policies towards foreign trade at national level. It is the purpose of this essay to trace the advances in our understanding of the relationship between trade policies and industrial development. The development experience in LDCs under import-substitution and export-promotion policies will be reviewed first. Subsequently, it will be argued that the internal government policies improve and the behaviour of economic actors becomes more efficient, in the economic sense, in a framework of (more) open markets. The question of how far world trade conditions should affect the LDCs' foreign trade policies will be discussed after that. A concluding section summarises the main points and re-confirms the relevance of the comparative-costs approach for shaping promising industrialisation strategies.

STRAIGHTFORWARD EVIDENCE

Pure trade theory has a long tradition of rigorously showing that foreign trade can make a country better off in welfare terms as compared with autarky and that, if the country does not possess a monopoly of monopsony power, gains from free trade are potentially larger than those from restricted or no trade. In spite of the pervasiveness of this proposition, most LDCs (including present-day NICs) relied on heavily protectionist foreign-trade policies for promoting industrialisation until the 1960s (and many still do).[3] Their governments encouraged import-substituting activities wherever this seemed technically feasible, frequently starting with the domestic production of finished consumer goods and often moving into 'modern' intermediate- and capital-goods activities. Comparative-costs criteria were deliberately neglected, due to the belief that a rapid and sustained rate of growth would otherwise not be possible. A very common optimism among policy makers as to the existence of great external economies seemed to 'justify' the indiscriminate promotion of a wide range of industries. Although the countries applied different sets of instruments and techniques, involving severe tariff and quantitative restrictions on imports as well as exchange controls, the import-substitution strategy has turned out to be a serious *impasse* in the industrialisation process almost everywhere.[4]

One way of recalling the weakness of this strategy is to compare its outcome with what the governments expected. Generally, they expected the following results:

(1) That import-substitution would be a dynamic engine of

growth. There was in fact an acceleration of (economic and industrial) growth in numerous (not all) countries, but only for a limited time span (around ten years) during which simple consumer-goods imports could easily be replaced by domestic products requiring relatively little labour skills, physical capital and indivisible equipment. But growth rates slowed down markedly when domestic market saturation in this area was reached, and advances in productivity of both capital and labour, as well as of material inputs, remained relatively small during the whole process.

(2) That import substitution activities would be a forceful absorber of indigenous labour. They were not, for various reasons, one being the pursuit of policies unsuitable to the existing factor endowment, which raised industrial labour costs above their scarcity value and simultaneously kept the price of capital artificially low. Both domestic and foreign entrepreneurs reacted to these factors by adopting more capital-intensive methods of production and running less working shifts than they otherwise would have, and by creating additional productive capacity instead of utilising more fully the capital stock already in existence.

(3) That import substitution would make the national economy independent from the world economy. This certainly happened in the short run, when foreign trade became predictably smaller relative to the gross domestic product (GDP), but dependence on essential raw materials, spare parts, capital goods and technology from abroad deepened as industrialisation continued; and import-substituting industrialisation paradoxically came up against balance-of-payments constraints at various times, because the increasing import requirements were, in most instances, not accompanied by rising foreign-exchange proceeds from exports.

Added to this unsuccessful outcome is a great variety of distortions which import-substitution policies imposed on the economy. For instance, these policies improved excessively the inter-sectoral terms of trade for the manufacturing industry and indiscriminately discouraged the development of non-industrial activities, agriculture in particular. Moreover, the protected domestic market permitted firms to produce at high costs and low quality and it allowed monopolists or oligopolists to flourish, with profits growing stronger and domestic consumers paying substantially more than

L

would have been the case within the framework of a less closed economy. Furthermore, the protection-induced over-valuation of the domestic currency penalised export activities and thus impaired the country's ability to fully exploit whatever export potential it possessed at any given time. And no less important was the move towards a complex system of administrative import and exchange controls on which the policy package rested and which had four serious negative consequences: first, to divert the efforts of business-men away from productive activities towards frequently exhausting efforts (including bribery) which assured the continuance or improvement of protection; secondly, to contribute to substantial arbitrariness on the part of the bureaucracy when applying in-centives, with the concomitant increased uncertainty for investors; thirdly, to generate 'rents' accruing to those in possession of crucial economic rights such as import licences or foreign-exchange quotas; and fourthly, to lead to the creation of black markets and to en-courage smuggling and capital flight, which included the over-invoicing of imports and under-invoicing of exports in intra-firm trade.[5] The real social cost of all these factors can hardly be ignored.

In short, the import-substitution environment which emerged in practice, was not conducive to sustained growth, or to high levels of employment and capacity utilisation, or to reduced 'dependence' on foreign supplies (including official development aid). Whatever the initial gains associated with import substitution might have been, they tended to be outweighed over time as the costs of distortions increased, particularly in countries which persevered in across-the-board import substitution. The policies served to favour, more or less systematically, the comparatively less efficient and less essential industries. And they left the economy just as incapable of adjusting quickly and easily to internal or external unpredictable opportunities and setbacks as it had been before starting industrialisation. Even strong supporters of import-substitution policies must admit that these views do not stem from stubborn adherence to orthodox international trade theory, but reflect the plain historical reality recorded for almost all industrialis-ing LDCs, including the forerunners among them, such as Argentina, Brazil or India.[6] Although one important source of the observed troubles might be traced to intrinsic institutional rigidities and political instabilities and another to cyclical macro-economic disturbances, the neglect of the ordinary operation of the com-parative-costs principle also appears to be responsible, to a large degree, for the deplorable results. Where comparative-costs considerations were not neglected in shaping import-substituting policies, as in South Korea and Taiwan during the 1950s and in Malaysia and Singapore during the 1960s, the achievements were noticably greater.[7] The same holds in cases in which industrialisation was export-oriented from the beginning, most notably in Hong Kong.

The proposition, that comparative advantages do matter, has received impressive support from the experience of an increasing number of present-day NICs which gradually opened their markets during the 1960s and early 1970s and also oriented their industrial production towards the world market. A corrected and more sensible tariff-subsidy policy, combined with more realistically valued exchange rates and more rational factor pricing have constituted the pillars of the new strategy (more about this later). This has caused manufactured exports from the Third World to increase spectacularly, outpacing both world trade expansion and domestic industrial output growth. As Table 14.1 shows, these exports expanded at an average annual rate of 14.5 per cent in real terms during the period 1965-79 and they gained relative weight with regard to both total non-oil LDCs' exports and world manufactured exports. Although the bulk of manufactured export expansion came from the sixteen countries mentioned in Table 14.1 (together they supplied about 85 per cent of the absolute increment of the LDCs' total), the advance has spread more widely throughout the Third World.[8] Anyone who had forecast such a performance in the mid-1960s would most likely have met only with scepticism.[9]

The upsurge of manufactured exports from industrialising LDCs contradicts two popular views held by the critics of the operationality of the comparative-costs principle. One is that contemporary latecomers to the process of world industrial development cannot compete successfully with established manufacturers from the highly advanced countries. This they can do, by simply applying policies which induce, or compel, local industries to do well what they can do best. Increased competitive pressure will then be put on workers and firms in the industrial countries which continue producing in manufacturing lines in which LDCs have actually or potentially a comparative advantage (predominantly those involving products of a high labour content). A second popular belief is that the potential benefits of participating in the system of international division of labour can be reaped only by 'powerful' countries which

TABLE 14.1
Manufactured Exports of Developing Countries,[a] 1965-79

	Export value (US $ million)				Real average annual growth[b]	
	1965	*1970*	*1973*	*1979*	*1965-79*	*1973-79*
All developing countries						
Export value (US $ million)	4,480.0	9,550.0	24,100.0	83,000.0	14.5	9.6
Share in LDC total non-oil exports (%)	17.8	25.7	36.0	39.0		
Share in world manufactured exports (%)	4.4	5.0	6.9	8.8		
Leading countries	*US $ million*					
Argentina	81.4	245.8	730.1	1,737.0	15.7	3.0
Brazil	111.0	362.5	1,216.8	5,733.2	23.2	15.4
Chile	15.0	50.6	44.5	758.0	23.0	43.0
Colombia	33.8	58.3	307.3	850.0	17.0	5.6
Egypt	122.9	206.6	283.4	372.6	0.6	−6.7
Hong Kong[c]	867.0	1,949.4	3,636.8	10,702.3	11.2	6.7
India	809.0	1,051.2	1,560.7	4,958.5	5.8	8.1
Israel	276.3	539.9	1,108.8	3,650.3	11.8	8.7
Republic of Korea	103.8	640.5	2,709.8	13,281.0	31.4	16.2
Malaysia	67.8	151.7	346.5	2,085.4	18.7	20.2
Mexico[c]	165.8	408.2	1,102.9	1,785.2	10.1	−3.4
Pakistan	190.2	425.0	592.9	1,147.4	5.7	−0.5
Philippines	65.8	78.4	219.6	783.8	10.9	10.2
Singapore[c]	72.1	238.4	1,143.1	6,389.1	28.0	18.8
Taiwan	186.6	1,139.7	3,674.3	14,561.0	26.9	12.1
Thailand	12.1	38.6	255.4	1,213.4	29.2	15.6

SOURCES: *Yearbook of International Trade Statistics*, recorded years, supplemented by *Commodity Trade Statistics*, and *Monthly Bulletin of Statistics*, United Nations, New York, various issues, *Handbook of International Trade and Development Statistics*, UNCTAD Secretariat, Geneva, various issues, *International Trade 1979-80* (Geneva: GATT Secretariat, 1980) and national trade statistics.
[a]Manufactures are defined in terms of the standard international trade classification (SITC) 5 to 8 minus 68 (non-ferrous metals). The south European newly industrialising countries are excluded.
[b]For lack of price indices, export values are deflated by dollar unit value indices of total manufactured exports of developed countries.
[c]Excluding re-exports.

can negotiate preferential terms for access to the highly absorptive markets in the industrial world. This is incorrect. World trade conditions have, to a large extent, been uniform (equally good or equally bad) for the Third World as a whole. Whenever the trade policies of the industrial countries have attempted to discriminate **against** particular LDCs, those chiefly affected have been South

Korea, Taiwan and Hong Kong. These three countries have nonetheless been the forerunners of export-led industrial development in the Third World and, in terms of export earnings, they have clearly out-distanced industrially advanced (and politically influential) India, which ranked second (very close to Hong Kong) in the list of LDCs exporting manufactured goods in 1965. If we substitute enterprises for countries, because enterprises rather than countries are competing on the world markets, we may better understand these events. Firms and individuals are simply more flexible than nation-states.

Comparing economic performance under export-oriented industrialisation with that under import substitution, the evidence points to a superiority of the former (Table 14.2).[10] Country-specific peculiarities apart, it is safe to state that the more open framework in which the economies (now) had to operate:

(1) has provided for fast rates of growth of GDP on a sustained basis as well as for a fresh acceleration of industrial development, as export expansion was pulling production upwards and economies of scale could be taken advantage of;

(2) has enlarged the opportunities for an increasing number of job-seekers to obtain employment (with accompanying increases in remuneration), since the exploitation of comparative advantage was bringing about a higher labour intensity in manufacturing (due either to the choice of indigenous and/or foreign technology or to the selection of products); and

(3) has eased the typical balance-of-payments constraint on economic development in spite of rapidly rising imports, as more foreign exchange from exports was becoming available and thereby, stronger international credit standing was attained.

INDICATIONS OF MICRO- AND MACRO-ECONOMIC RATIONALITY

The empirical evidence also sheds some light on the crucial question of why outward-looking foreign trade policies have brought about such encouraging results. Basically, the answer revolves around two aspects: one is the improvement of trade (and trade-related) policy making as such; the other is a policy-induced change in the behaviour of economic agents. Both aspects will be considered briefly below.[11]

The improvement of the policy framework has taken place in

TABLE 14.2
Summary of (Actual) Effects of LDCs' Foreign Trade Policies

Selected Targets	Policies built around	
	Import substitution	Export expansion
Output		
Initiation of economic growth	+	+
Initiation of industrial growth	+	+
Sustained output growth	—	+
Resources		
Employment creation	—	+
Up-grading of skills	—	+
Allocative efficiency	—	+
External Financing		
Attraction of foreign direct investment	+	+
Access to international capital markets	—	+
Relief from foreign-exchange constraints	—	+
Equity		
'Basic' human needs	m	m
Personal income distribution	m	m
Regional balance	m	m

+ impact is, as a rule, positive.
— impact is, as a rule, negative.
m impact is rather complex and not attributable to one or the other strategy.

SOURCE: Empirical evidence documented in numerous country studies. The various investigations have focussed on five African countries (Egypt, the Ivory Coast, Ghana, Kenya and Tunisia); ten Asian countries (Hong Kong, India, Indonesia, Israel, Korea, Malaysia, Pakistan, the Philippines, Singapore and Taiwan); six Latin American countries (Argentina, Brazil, Chile, Colombia, Mexico and Uruguay); and three south European countries (Spain, Turkey and Yugoslavia). See Ian Little, Tibor Scitovsky and Maurice FG. Scott, *Industry and Trade in Some Developing Countries: a Comparative Study* (London, New York and Toronto: Oxford University Press, for the OECD, 1970); Bela Balassa and Associates, *The Structure of Protection in Developing Countries* (Baltimore and London: Johns Hopkins Press, for the International Bank for Reconstruction and Development and the Inter-American Development Bank, 1971); Balassa and Associates, *Development Strategies in Semi-industrial Countries* (Baltimore and London: Johns Hopkins Press, for the World Bank, 1982); Jagdish Bhagwati, *Foreign Trade Regimes and Economic Development: Anatomy and Consequences* (Cambridge, Mass.: Ballinger, for the NBER, 1978); Anne O. Krueger, *Foreign Trade Regimes and Economic Development: Liberalization Attempts and Consequences* (Cambridge, Mass.: Ballinger, for the NBER, 1978); Krueger *et al.* (eds), *Trade and Employment in Developing Countries: Individual Studies* (Chicago: Chicago University Press, for the NBER,

various areas. To begin with, exchange-rate policy has become more rational in the sense that provisions were made to prevent chronic over-valuation of the domestic currency, as it is typically observed under import substitution. This was done in some instances by applying flexible exchange rates or by resorting to sliding parity adjustments in a downward direction, in order to keep the currency valuation abreast of domestic, relative to world, inflation. More realistic (although not necessarily true equilibrium) real exchange rates have not only contributed to an expansion of manufactured exports along with import substitution—they have also helped to bring otherwise under-utilised local resources into the production of tradeable and (indirectly) of non-tradeable goods. Hence, real exchange-rate adjustments have not been ineffective, as the monetarist believers in the so-called 'law of one price' would have contended.

Concomitant to the exchange-rate policy, have been serious attempts to reduce distortions (i) in capital markets (by means of upward adjustments of ceilings on both savings-deposit interest rates and bank lending rates and by decelerating inflation and allowing some indexing of financial assets); (ii) in labour markets (by making job-tenure regulations more flexible and by allowing the structure of real wages to reflect better the structure of skills in the domestic labour force) and (iii) in public utility markets (by charging the consumers of public utilities higher prices, that are more compatible with the social marginal costs incurred in their production). These reforms have acted as a powerful stimulus to industries with a high potential for labour absorption and productivity growth.

The greatest improvements have been made with regard to trade policies as such. Numerous quantitative import restrictions were eased or replaced by import tariffs and other price measures; the tariff structures have generally been rescheduled, thereby reducing both the overall level and the inter-industry dispersion of the rates of effective protection. Direct and indirect cost disadvantages to export industries arising from the continuing import protection have been substantially corrected or even neutralised by granting these firms duty-free access to imported inputs as well as compensating

---

1981); Juergen B. Donges and Lotte Müller-Ohlsen, *Aussenwirtschaftsstrategien und Industrialisierung in Entwicklungsländern*, Kieler Studien, 157 (Tübingen: J. C. B. Mohr, for the Institut für Weltwirtschaft an der Universität Kiel, 1978).

subsidies and, in some cases (such as Malaysia, Mexico, South Korea and Taiwan), by establishing free trade export processing zones (as are Hong Kong and Singapore, essentially). Exports thus have become much more profitable than they were during the import substitution era and, depending on the extent and the efficiency of the trade policy reforms, the profitability of exports has equalled or even surpassed that of domestic sales. Moreover, the greater uniformity of incentives has contributed to a specialisation closer to comparative advantage and, thereby, to relatively lower capital requirements of the output growth.

A less visible, but not unimportant fact is that the outward-looking approach has imposed limitations on governments' scope to provide excessively generous incentives to manufacturing enterprises. In using subsidies, for instance, governments had to take into account the possibility of retaliation by trading partners and have therefore exercised moderation. Furthermore, although trade (and trade-related) policies did not in any case become optimal, the danger of their hindering growth is now much less. If, for example, export diversification is extended to include products bearing high marginal domestic resource costs per unit of foreign-exchange earnings (as happened in Brazil, India, Israel and several other NICs with regard to highly capital-intensive goods), then evidently a resource misallocation, analogous to that observed under excessive import substitution, will emerge. The crucial difference, however, is that now the country's industrialisation process need not come up against a balance-of-payments constraint as a result of internal distortions—which is almost inevitable under an import-substitution approach.

Let us now turn to the second argument explaining the performance superiority of outward-looking policies—the one which points to changes in individual behaviour. Here, too, various strands of evidence are involved, all of which have in common a considerable responsiveness of economic agents to price signals. First, the widening of the relevant market has induced firms which were operating on downward-sloped scale curves to expand production, replacing imports and increasing exports; and it has enabled newly established enterprises to make better use of the opportunities for introducing larger-scale production. Secondly, it became apparent that among the many high-cost producers inherited from the previous import-substitution phase, there were not only those who were inherently inefficient and therefore unable to compete with imports, but also those who could actually compete —were it a matter of survival—by reducing costs, upgrading skills and improving the quality of their products. 'X-inefficiency' at the firm level, although difficult to measure from outside, has presumably decreased, particularly in those activities in which entrenched monopolistic or oligopolistic structures have been broken by new entrants (both from within the country and abroad).

Of particular interest in this context is a third strand of evidence: the changed behaviour of foreign firms. Under the unduly protectionist import-substitution regimes, direct foreign investment (DFI) in manufacturing was oriented as much towards the domestic market and skewed towards capital-intensive production as was investment by indigenous firms. Not only were sales to the world market rather exceptional because of the anti-export bias inherent in the system of protection; in many cases, the investment was subjected to the condition that exports must not take place. When trade policies were altered, however, an increasing number of formerly inward-looking foreign firms, taking advantage of their marketing expertise, embarked upon export activities on a significant scale:[12] and the outward-looking countries have attracted more and more export-oriented DFI from industrial countries, where manufacturing firms were adjusting to their loss of international competitiveness by transferring production to industrialising, labour-abundant LDCs. All this has had a positive impact on employment and on the balance of payments of various host countries, Taiwan being again an outstanding case in point.[13]

INTERNATIONAL ENVIRONMENT IN TRANSITION

The previous analysis has stressed that the main forces determining the success of export-oriented industrialisation are to be found on the supply side. But, in order to get a more complete picture, one has to enter the external factors which evidently also matter (and which are explicitly incorporated in the received trade theory). In doing so, it could be (and in fact has been) argued that the evidence in support of the superiority of export-oriented industrialisation refers to past experience and that, therefore, the arguments based on it can only hold as long as world market conditions are favourable and do not change significantly—once the conditions change and deteriorate, the operative significance of the comparative-costs principle could be called in question.

This argument emerges from a number of major events which have deeply affected the world economy since the early 1970s: the quadrupling of oil prices in 1973-74 and the subsequent rounds of price rises; the deep economic recession in the industrial countries in 1974-75, followed by a rather slow recovery; and the recent waves of protectionism in world trade. Because the international environment is now in sharp contrast to what it was in the 1950s, 1960s and early 1970s (when energy was cheap, the world economy grew fast and the OECD countries liberalised trade to a large extent) doubts seem warranted as to the feasibility for NICs to continue with, or for other LDCs to embark upon, export-oriented industrialisation in the future. More concretely, if the capability of the industrial countries to adjust their production structures to the new conditions is deemed to be small, if the advanced economies are therefore predicted to go into a serious long-term downturn, and if world trade in manufactures is projected to expand only slowly or not at all under these circumstances, then effective world demand for manufactured exports from LDCs would naturally be very weak and worldwide resort to quantitative import restrictions would be most likely—comparative advantage would almost cease to be of any practical advantage. Such a diagnosis of the present state and the prospects of the world economy would be similar to the one which prevailed in many LDCs (particularly in Latin America) a quarter of a century ago in the aftermath of the Great Depression (foreign demand decreases) and of World War II (foreign supply cuts). The therapeutic consequences could also be similar. For the present, they would consist of (re-) shaping industrialisation policies (again) in an anti-trade manner towards further import substitution. All in all, however, the omens do not seem to be that bad.

Recent experience reveals that although all LDCs were suddenly confronted with the need to overcome increasing balance-of-payments pressures in order to preserve the momentum of their development process, the capability of effectively meeting this need differed widely among them. In general, it was greater in countries which had been pursuing more outward-looking policies than in the countries which had been relying mainly upon import substitution as their means of industrialisation.[14] There are various explanations for this: one is that the more outward-looking economies, by their very nature, have a business community capable of quickly discovering and then actively exploiting sales opportunities even in sluggish world markets. Although less orders were coming in, those which did could be satisfied; and although protectionism in industrial countries was becoming more selective, it could be circumvented by changing the export-mix. Secondly, these countries generally have had an import-to-GDP ratio high enough to allow, eventually, some import curtailment without severely curbing long-term industrial growth. Thirdly, they have enjoyed considerable international creditworthiness, which has helped to mitigate growth-restricting foreign-exchange stringencies. All these circumstances reinforce the case of pro-trade policies.

The point then is that LDCs (like the industrial countries) cannot do without policies which effectively stimulate the adjustment of the domestic industrial structures to new world market circumstances, if their economies are to continue growing at a reasonable rate. However difficult the structural adjustment process may be (particularly if it is to come about quickly), it will definitely require more efficiency in production—not less. An outward-looking framework provides a strong incentive for adjusting through efficient import substitution and export diversification, while the danger is great that the adjustment is pushed far away from comparative-advantage patterns, or even postponed, if governments resort to protectionist practices. And efficient (pro-trade) policies will strengthen the capability of the country to attract a growing volume of new DFI needed to support the adjustment and to keep sufficient creditworthiness and borrowing ability for the financing of oil-price-induced balance-of-payments deficits on current account, even if the country's foreign indebtedness is already high. Should LDCs' manufactured exports increase in years to come at lower rates than in the past, due to unfavourable external conditions, their importance as an (direct and indirect) engine of industrial growth remains just as crucial[15]—export proceeds which are harder to get obviously become more valuable from a social point of view.

A continuation (or initiation) of export-oriented industrialisation policies presupposes reasonably liberal access to import markets, not only in the Western industrial countries and in the centrally-planned economies (CPEs) of Eastern Europe, but also within the Third World itself. In order for the inter-LDC trade in manufactures to increase significantly over the next decades, the still prevailing high protectionist barriers will have to be reduced to moderate levels gradually and predictably. That this is, for economic and political reasons, a difficult task to perform, has been shown in the past: neither have the various regional economic integration schemes—which many LDCs joined—been very successful, nor have LDCs from different regions made significant progress in liberalising mutual trade on preferential terms along the lines of a respective Protocol within the General Agreement on Tariffs and Trade (GATT), which entered into force in 1973.[16] More open access to the CPEs' markets may be even harder to accomplish in the aggregate because these countries regulate foreign trade flows bilaterally, according to their own plan criteria or foreign-policy considerations.[17] Hence, the LDCs' manufacturers must, presumably, continue to rely heavily on access to OECD markets.

It is still a matter of conjecture whether the reappearance of protectionist sentiments and policies in Western Europe, the United States and Japan can be abated effectively. The results of the Tokyo Round of multilateral trade negotiations, conducted under the auspices of the GATT during 1973-79, do not provide a clear answer. The agreed tariff cuts are smaller for manufactured exports from LDCs than on average (about 25 as compared with 35 per cent) and will be distributed over eight years, so that their incidence will be very limited. More important, however, is the fact that no removal of quantitative import restrictions and subsidies to domestic industries has been accomplished and that the European Community seems determined to penalise eventually the LDCs' most efficient producers of specific goods by discriminating against imports which are growing too fast and which originate in countries whose retaliation it fears the least. And finally, the new so-called 'Codes of Conduct'[18] will only counter the adverse effects of the non-tariff barriers if their rather vague drafting does not, perhaps, tempt governments to apply them in a restrictive manner. That LDCs have been granted special and differential treatment within the amended GATT rules, in order to take into account their trade and development needs, may be an advantage for actual and would-be exporters in the Third World; this should not obscure the danger, however, that this new principle also allows discrimination among LDCs by industrial countries making trade policy concessions, if they wish to do so.[19]

In spite of this uncertainty, the governments of the LDCs should recognise that there is no need to sink into despair and that it would be counterproductive if they were to use protectionism in industrial

countries as an excuse for not pursuing pro-trade policies themselves. After all, the 1970s have revealed that shifts in product
quality and the composition of exports are a promising avenue for
circumventing even selective import barriers.[20] If LDCs now
subscribe to the Tokyo Round agreements (however incomplete
these still may be), they have the chance of influencing international
trade policy actions in the future. Any expectation about the
possibility of obtaining better conditions for market access by
rejecting the agreements does not rest upon a solid basis and might
therefore be illusory.

The LDCs themselves can contribute to the re-establishment of
the principles of non-discrimination and irrevocability of import
concessions if they permit the comparative-costs principle to serve
as a basis for structuring production and guiding trade flows. The
NICs are in a position to diversify further out of the simple labour-
intensive items (the main target of protectionist devices abroad)
and to include in their export assortment higher-technology
products, including those which belong to the more mature segments
of the product cycle within a given industrial branch. The micro-
electronic technology, as soon as it becomes accessible to these
countries, may also provide them with the opportunity to make
significant gains in productivity of both capital and labour and to
achieve greater product differentiation. Thereby, the laggards
within the industrialising Third World obtain room for exporting
the traditional labour-intensive goods, which need not then lead to
excess supplies on the world markets and a concomitant fall in
export prices.[21] These trends of trading and catching up are rooted
in the past, as Table 14.3 shows. It obviously is a misconception to
think of LDCs' manufactured exports only in terms of textiles and
clothing—engineering products have become almost as important.
Hence, the industrial countries need not fear that competitive
pressures originating in the LDCs' export potential will necessarily
exceed manageable orders of magnitude and must therefore be
checked by protective devices.

THE COMPARATIVE-COSTS APPROACH
REASSURED

It has been argued so far, on the basis of available real-world
evidence and logic, that LDCs are likely to gain more from foreign
trade policies which facilitate export expansion (and, incidentally,
contribute to a better national integration of product and factors

TABLE 14.3

Commodity Composition of LDCs' Manufactured Exports[a]

(%)

SITC	Commodity Group	1965	1970	1973	1979
65	Textile yarn and fabrics	25.1	19.8	17.5	13.0
84	Clothing	3.0	13.8	16.7	15.2
5	Chemicals	11.3	9.1	7.4	8.1
67	Iron and steel	4.7	5.9	4.4	5.0
7	Machinery, transport equipment and electronics	8.9	14.7	19.9	25.9
65+67 +68+84	Other manufactures	47.0	36.7	34.1	32.8

SOURCES: *Monthly Bulletin of Statistics*, United Nations, New York, various issues; and *Handbook of International Trade and Development Statistics*, UNCTAD Secretariat, Geneva, various years.
[a]Manufactures are defined in terms of SITC 5 to 8 minus 68 (non-ferrous metals).

markets), than from foreign trade policies which exclusively encourage import substitution (and become a source of national economic fragmentation). The comparative-costs principle can, in fact, be interpreted in an operational way and provides some basic and dependable guides for shaping industrialisation policies.

Even so, critics have usually charged that the comparative-costs argument is made in terms of static optimality and that the assumptions on which it rests lack reality.[22] The concerns about the restrictiveness of the assumptions are largely artificial. What seems to be a restriction is just a means of presenting rigorously (and mathematically) the theorem and its implications.

Moreover, there is nothing in the comparative-costs argument which excludes dynamic considerations, particularly with reference to economies of scale and externalities typically associated with industrialisation. On the contrary, these factors enhance the potential static gains from free or freer trade, whereas linkage and multiplier-accelerator effects of trade increases give rise to the rate of economic growth. Thus the proposition that comparative costs do count amounts to saying that the relative abundance of one or several factors of production is a source of international competitiveness (provided realistic exchange rates prevail). It is, in fact, reasonable from a development point of view that resource-rich countries engage in agricultural or metal processing and extend such operations downstream as industrialisation proceeds; it also makes much sense to use up whatever efficiency-wage-cost advantage exists in LDCs due to a high elasticity of labour supply; and it is probably advisable that LDCs build up technologically sophisticated industrial activities once unskilled-labour surpluses run out and physical, as well as human, capital becomes more readily available.

What the comparative-costs argument (whether in its static or in its dynamic version) does not tell, *ex ante*, is where the most promising investment opportunities at the firm level will lie. In economic systems which leave reasonable scope for decentralised decision-taking, every private firm or public enterprise has to find out the details and assume the risk on his investment. Consumer acceptance or refusal of goods offered on competitive markets is the ultimate test of whether the investment is a success (yielding a profit), or a failure (leaving a loss). In the absence of certainty about the future, governments are in no better a position than the market to guide particular, privately and socially beneficial, investments— a trivial fact which many critics of the comparative-costs argument are in the habit of ignoring. Negative sanctions through the workings of international competition are then a powerful stimulus for the investor to examine as carefully as possible the prospects of a particular project, to correct eventual mistakes, and not to rely on having the losses 'socialised'.

Finally, it is not always recognised that the comparative-costs argument neither excludes import substitution, nor does it give priority to export expansion. Rather, it treats both activities symmetrically. Under free trade conditions there will always be a 'natural' import substitution as the real income increases, its extent depending on the income elasticity of demand and on changes in relative prices. By the same token, there is a process of 'natural' export expansion when growing firms reach a size at which the production capacity exceeds the absorptive capacity of the domestic market. In the presence of externalities which are not corrected by the market through appropriate institutional arrangements ('Coase theorem'), government incentives to the manufacturing industry would be warranted ('infant-industry argument'). But such encouragement should be neutral between producing for home and foreign markets, especially as dynamic external economies are not necessarily specific to the market-orientation of production.[23] The country would then experience, in terms of domestic resource costs, both efficient import substitution and efficient export expansion.

CONCLUSION

To sum up, the relevance of the comparative-costs argument for LDCs ought not to be underrated. Policy makers may not be expected to secure formal Pareto-optimality in the course of development. But they can be expected to provide for a proper trade policy framework which allows the mechanism of relative prices to operate and which encourages investors to exploit comparative advantages and, altogether, generate a product-mix which on average faces an income elasticity of world demand as high as possible. Ultimately, it is not necessary in order for the net benefits of pro-trade attitudes to be significant that each industrialising country achieves growth rates and levels of manufactured exports comparable with the South Korean or Taiwanese paths: it suffices if exports rise, year after year, rapidly and steadily enough to ensure the greatest possible headway in industrialisation.

It has not been argued in this essay that pro-trade policies are sufficient to deal with the complexities of the industrial development problem, or that they can initiate a take-off in the least developed countries—a claim which critics of the comparative-costs principle often wrongly impute to the adherents of a better integration of LDCs into the world economy. An outward-looking approach is only a pillar of the wider strategy of economic development. While there is no guarantee of industrialisation miracles, persistent departures from the comparative-costs principle may suddenly frustrate sensible industrialisation objectives.

Nor was it the intention of this essay to give the impression that we already know all the important aspects of the relationship between trade and industrialisation. In fact, we do not. Important subjects for further inquiry include the following: the reasons for successes and failures in the transition from highly distorting to more rational foreign trade policies; the relevance of the country's size and natural resources endowment for the transition effort; the political economy of export promotion; the long-term economic implications of selectivity *versus* uniformity of export incentives; the sources of international competitiveness at the firm level; the role of domestic public enterprises, as well as that of foreign manufacturing firms and foreign buying groups, in this process and the pattern of structural change and adjustment within industry in the LDC context. Much more careful quantitative analysis is necessary to obtain a better understanding in these fields. The marginal return of the corresponding research efforts is still high.

NOTES AND REFERENCES

1.   The various investigations have focussed on five African countries (Egypt, the Ivory Coast, Ghana, Kenya and Tunisia); ten Asian countries (Hong Kong, India, Indonesia, Israel, Korea, Malaysia, Pakistan, the Philippines, Singapore and Taiwan); six Latin American countries (Argentina, Brazil, Chile, Colombia, Mexico and Uruguay); and three south European countries (Spain, Turkey and Yugoslavia). See Ian Little, Tibor Scitovsky and Maurice FG. Scott, *Industry and Trade in Some Developing Countries: a Comparative Study* (London, New York and Toronto: Oxford University Press, for the OECD Development Centre, 1970); Bela Balassa and Associates, *The Structure of Protection in Developing Countries* (Baltimore and London: Johns Hopkins Press, for the International Bank for Reconstruction and Development and the Inter-American Development Bank, 1971); Balassa and Associates, *Development Strategies in Semi-Industrial Countries* (Baltimore and London: Johns Hopkins Press, for the World Bank, 1982); Jagdish Bhagwati, *Foreign Trade Regimes and Economic Development: Anatomy and Consequences* (New York and Cambridge, Mass.: Ballinger, for the NBER, 1978); Anne O. Krueger, *Foreign Trade Regimes and Economic Development: Liberalization Attempts and Consequences* (New York and Cambridge, Mass.: Ballinger, for the NBER, 1978); Krueger *et al.* (eds), *Trade and Employment in Developing Countries: Individual Studies* (Chicago: University Press, for the NBER, 1981); Juergen B. Donges and Lotte Müller-Ohlsen, *Aussen wirtschaftsstrategien und Industrialisierung in Entwicklungsländern*, Kieler Studien, 157 (Tübingen: J. C. B. Mohr, for the Institut für Weltwirtschaft an der Universität Kiel, 1978). In addition to these comparative analyses, many country studies have been published separately. This essay has drawn mainly on the Kiel research, to which Professor Herbert Giersch has given considerable encouragement. The comments by Sanjeev Gupta, Klaus-Werner Schatz and Dean Spinanger on an earlier version are gratefully acknowledged.

2.   This objective was articulated in the so-called *Lima Declaration and Plan of Action on Industrial Development and Co-operation*, which was adopted by the Second General Conference of the United Nations Industrial Development Organisation (UNIDO) in March 1975. The Lima Plan postulates the achievement of at least 25 per cent of the growing world industrial output by LDCs by the year 2000; in 1981, the LDCs' share was almost 11 per cent.

3.   Very often, the import-substitution policies originated in balance-of-payments deficits, the correction of which was not attempted by means of exchange-rate devaluation and internal deflation. Thereafter it almost invariably turned out that the import restrictions became permanent even if they were announced as temporary measures.

4.   For references, see note 1. Although the evidence from the countries that have been researched is not without ambiguity, it, none the less, provides a firm basis for being sceptical about the alleged virtues of import-substitution policies.

5.   This last point is usually overlooked by the critics of the transfer-pricing practices actually or allegedly pursued by vertically integrated multinational corporations from industrial countries.

6. Similar experiences were met by the south European countries, which also fostered their industrialisation around highly protectionist import-substitution policies. Spain (until 1959), Yugoslavia (until 1965) and Turkey are cases in point. See Donges, *La Industrialización en Espana—Politicas, Logros, Perspectivas* (Barcelona: Oikos-Tau, 1976); Charles R. Chittle, *Industrialization and Manufactured Export Expansion in a Worker-Managed Economy: the Yugoslav Experience*, Kieler Studien, 145 (Tübingen: J. C. B. Mohr, for the Institut für Weltwirtschaft an der Universität Kiel, 1977); and Krueger, *Foreign Trade Regimes and Economic Development: Turkey* (New York and London: Colombia University Press, for the NBER, 1974).

7. The reference to South Korea and Taiwan as instances illustrating the potential advantages of efficient import substitution frequently evokes the criticism that both countries are dictatorships. The interaction between the political system of a country and its economic performance is difficult to formulate accurately with the given state of the art. It is not difficult, however, to look at the map of the Third World and find most LDCs ruled under authoritarian (communist or fascist) regimes (at present as well as in the past). As repression is the rule, why then was the South Korean or Taiwanese approach not imitated more widely? It should also be noted that private-enterprise-oriented South Korea and Taiwan have been quite successful in meeting 'basic' human needs—accomplishments which have usually been associated with the People's Republic of China alone. This country, in turn, reportedly now wants to give a greater role to market forces in steering the economic development process, after decades of experiencing the deficiencies of autarky and central planning.

8. For more detailed analysis of LDCs' manufactured export performance, see, apart from the references in note 1, Donges and James Riedel, 'The Expansion of Manufactured Exports in Developing Countries: An Empirical Assessment of Supply and Demand Issues', *Weltwirtschaftliches Archiv*, Kiel, Vol. 113, No. 1, 1977, pp. 58-85; Balassa, 'Export Incentives and Export Performance in Developing Countries: A Comparative Analysis', *Weltwirtschaftliches Archiv*, Vol. 114, No. 1, 1978, pp. 24-60; Hollis B. Chenery and Donald B. Keesing, *The Changing Composition of Developing Country Exports*, World Bank Staff Working Papers No. 314 (Washington: World Bank, 1979). Note here too that the considerable rates of manufactured export expansion extend also to those south European countries which have recently become more outward-looking—Spain in particular. This country exported industrial goods worth US$13,331 million in 1979 as compared with US$380 million in 1965 (sources as in Table 14.1).

9. Long-term rates of only 5-6 per cent for manufactured exports were considered feasible at that time, partly due to the fact that the shift from anti- to pro-trade policies made by various LDCs in the more recent past was not foreseen. See Balassa, *Trade Prospects for Developing Countries* (Homewood, Ill.: Richard D. Irwin, for The Economic Growth Center at Yale University, 1964).

10. For references, see, once again, note 1. Note that the evidence about the impact of foreign trade policies on domestic equity is mixed in some cases and rather ambiguous in others. Whenever the basic human

needs have not been fulfilled, the personal income inequalities accentuated, or the regional development paths extremely unbalanced, no clear causal relationship to any type of foreign trade policy appears. Obviously, these issues are multi-dimensional, and pro-trade as well as anti-trade policies are presumably too weak to have significant and lasting (positive or negative) consequences here. This being as it may, received trade theories do not explain unequivocally the distributional implications of smaller and larger involvement in international trade either.

11. For a more detailed discussion, see Donges, 'A Comparative Survey of Industrialization Policies in Fifteen Semi-Industrial Countries', *Weltwirtschaftliches Archiv*, Vol. 112, No. 4, 1976, pp. 626-57, and Krueger, 'Trade Policy as an Input to Development', *The American Economic Review*, Menasha, Wisconsin, May 1980, pp. 288-92.

12. See Benjamin I. Cohen, *Multinational Firms and Asian Exports* (New Haven, Conn. and London: Yale University Press, for The Economic Growth Center at Yale University, 1975); Deepak Nayyar, 'Trans-national Corporations and Manufactured Exports from Poor Countries', *The Economic Journal*, Cambridge, March 1978, pp. 59-84; Donges and Müller-Ohlsen, *op. cit.*, pp. 149-57.

13. See James Riedel, 'The Nature and Determinants of Export-Oriented Direct Foreign Investment in a Developing Country: A Case Study of Taiwan', *Weltwirtschaftliches Archiv*, Vol. 111, No. 3, 1975, pp. 505-26. Riedel has also shown that export-oriented DFI in the manufacturing sector need not lead to the creation of an enclave apart from the local economy, as critics often contend, and that it can make the country better off even if the investment entails additional requirements of imported intermediate inputs. See his *Factor Proportions, Linkages and the Open Developing Economy*, Kiel Working Papers, No. 20 (Kiel: Institut für Weltwirtschaft, 1974), subsequently published in abbreviated form in *The Review of Economics and Statistics*, Cambridge, Mass., November 1975, pp. 487-94. It remains true, however, that when competition among LDCs for DFI is very strong, much of the direct and indirect benefits of foreign investments may be given away in the form of 'too' generous concessions.

14. Valuable information is provided in Balassa, André Barsony and Anne Richards, *The Balance of Payments Effects of External Shocks and of Policy Responses to these Shocks in Non-OPEC Developing Countries* (Paris: OECD Development Centre, 1981). See also Balassa, 'The Newly-Industrializing Developing Countries After the Oil Crisis', *Weltwirtschaftliches Archiv*, Vol. 117, No. 1, 143-94. This study shows again that existing export opportunities are given up, once the response to the external shocks consists of slipping back into excessive import substitution (like Brazil) or of stimulating excessively domestic demand and providing undue incentives for capital-intensive investment projects (like South Korea). For a comparative analysis of these two countries, see also Peter Nunnenkamp, 'Negative Weltmarkteinflüsse und Anpassungsreaktionen in Brasilien und Südkorea', *Die Weltwirtschaft*, Tübingen, No. 1, 1979, pp. 111-34.

15. UNIDO's Lima-Plan for accelerated industrialisation calls for an annual rate of growth of manufactured exports from LDCs of 13 per cent in real terms until the year 2000. See *Industry 2000—New Perspectives*

(New York: United Nations, 1979), pp. 218-21. More cautiously, the World Bank expects these exports to increase annually at 20.5 per cent in real terms until 1990, which is still faster than the forecast for the LDCs' total exports and the manufactured exports from the industrialised countries. See *World Development Report 1980* (Washington: World Bank, 1980), pp. 6-8.

16.   And yet, inter-LDC trade in manufactures increased annually at 14.4 per cent in the period 1965-79 in real terms. In 1979, about one-third of LDCs' total manufactured exports went to other LDCs (sources as in Table 14.1).

17.   Small wonder that the LDCs' manufactured exports into the CPEs increased at an annual rate of only 7.4 per cent in real terms from 1965-79 and accounted for a meagre 1.8 per cent of the total in 1979 (sources as in Table 14.1).

18.   They refer to customs valuation, subsidies and countervailing duties, import licensing procedures, government procurement and technical standards. For details, see *Activities in 1979 and Conclusion of the Tokyo Round Multilateral Trade Negotiations (1973-1979)* (Geneva: GATT Secretariat, 1980).

19.   For a detailed evaluation of the Tokyo Round results, with particular reference to LDCs, see Bernd Stecher, *Zum Stand der internationalen Handelspolitik nach der Tokio-Runde*, Kiel Discussion Papers, No. 69 (Kiel: Institut für Weltwirtschaft, 1980); and Balassa, 'The Tokyo Round and the Developing Countries', *Journal of World Trade Law*, Twickenham, March-April 1980, pp. 93-118. Balassa takes a rather optimistic view, whereas Stecher is more ridden by fears. Both interpretations are sensible and precisely this fact may generate additional uncertainty among LDCs' manufacturers making investment decisions with a significant export-capacity content.

20.   This is not to say that the spread of protectionism has not hurt manufactured exports from LDCs, as is sometimes contended. As we do not know how these exports would have developed under less new import barriers, we ought to state that, *in the aggregate*, the export opportunities of LDCs were not brought to insignificance—and this is so because the supply side looms a great deal. In this respect, it was perhaps unwise that the Report of the Independent Commission on International Development Issues (Brandt Commission), in dealing with North-South trade, has put emphasis only on the actually or potentially damaging import restrictions imposed by the industrial countries; LDC governments should have been told that their own protectionism is in general more severe and therefore more inimical to their own industrialisation interests. See The Report of the Independent Commission on International Development Issues under the Chairmanship of Willy Brandt, *North-South: a Programme for Survival* (Cambridge, Mass.: MIT Press, 1980; and London and Sydney: Pan Books, 1980), ch. 11.

21.   Interesting examples of such grading-up-adjustments are provided by Taiwan, which is setting up a technology-intensive industrial estate, and by Singapore, which is promoting the development of software technology. This runs counter to the popular 'fallacy of composition' argument. For

cross-section analyses supporting the notion that changes in comparative advantage tend to follow a fairly constant pattern, see Ranadev Banerji and Donges, *Economic Development and the Patterns of Manufactured Exports*, Kiel Discussion Papers, No. 16 (Kiel: Institut für Weltwirtschaft, 1972), and Balassa, 'A "Stages Approach" to Comparative Advantage', in Irma Adelman (ed.), *Economic Growth and Resources—National and International Policies* (London: Macmillan, for the International Economics Association, 1979), pp. 121-56.

22. This criticism dates back to the early and extremely influential writings of Raúl Prebisch and Hans W. Singer and it has been stressed time and again in UNCTAD and UNIDO documents related to the role of LDCs in the world economy. The point has recently been re-emphasised by a group of distinguished development economists and practitioners from various countries. See Gerald K. Helleiner, *Economic Theory and North-South Negotiations on a New International Economic Order*, a Report on the Refsnes Conference (Oslo: Norwegian Institute of International Affairs, 1980). In the Federal Republic of Germany, the relevance of the comparative-costs principle for development purposes has most strongly been challenged by leftist economists and neo-Marxist political scientists concerned with the problems of LDCs, mainly from the Free University of Berlin, the University of Bremen and the Max-Planck-Institut zur Erforschung der Lebensbedingungen der wissenschaftlich-technischen Welt, Starnberg.

23. It is important to note that, while most of the professional main-stream takes the existence of externalities for granted, particularly in LDCs with regard to learning-by-doing effects, we know little about the precise nature of such externalities and whether they are generated by particular firms, by specific industrial branches or by the manufacturing sector as a whole. If, under these circumstances, governments give incentives on infant-industry grounds which are not uniform among industrial activities, but show a high inter-industry dispersion (the common case in practice), they run the risk of fostering industrial development in unintended or wrong directions.

15 Impact of the Energy Crisis on the Third World and the Prospects for Adjustment

Lutz Hoffmann

This essay reviews the energy situation as well as future prospects of the developing countries. It then discusses the determinants of the development of energy demand in order to assess the scope for demand adjustment to rising fuel prices and resulting balance-of-payments problems. Finally, the possibilities for adjustment on the supply side are investigated with the emphasis being placed on the financing requirements and potential financing sources for investments in the energy sectors of these countries.

ENERGY SITUATION AND PROSPECTS

About one-eighth of global primary commercial energy is used in the developing countries. Although this is only a small share, the importance of developing countries rests on the assumption that their energy requirements will increase at much faster rates than those of the rest of the world. There are several factors behind this expectation. First, the developing countries are likely to maintain higher economic growth rates than the rest of the world. Second, rapid economic growth tends to be accompanied by increasing industrial production and urbanisation, which are generally energy intensive. Third, as income levels increase, demand for various energy consuming amenities (automobiles, electric appliances, et cetera) could rise dramatically from present low levels. Fourth, substitution of commercial for non-commercial energy is likely to continue.

Besides commercial energy, non-commercial energy consisting of fuel wood, charcoal, dung and agricultural waste is of major importance in most developing countries. According to a recent country-by-country study,[1] non-commercial energy is estimated to account for 80 per cent of total energy consumption in West Africa, 77 per cent in Central and East Africa, 55 per cent in South Asia, 51 per cent in South-east Asia, 24 per cent in South America and 22 per cent in the centrally-planned developing economies.

There are hardly any data available on the long-run development of energy demand in developing countries. This is particularly the case for non-commercial energy. For commercial energy, data have been collected by the United Nations for the years since 1950. They show that growth rates of demand in these countries have been roughly 50 per cent higher than in the industrial countries. Demand for commercial energy increased at an annual rate of 7 per cent between 1960-65 and 7.4 per cent between 1965-70. Unlike the industrial countries, the developing countries maintained high growth rates of commercial energy demand during the 1970s. Between 1970 and 1975 the annual growth rate was 6.2 per cent and, between 1975 and 1978, 7.0 per cent. Future growth rates have been projected somewhat lower because of the oil-price increase, but they are still substantially higher than in the industrial countries.[2]

There have been few attempts up to now to project future growth of the demand for non-commercial energy. Although demand for non-commercial energy is likely to grow far less than that for commercial energy, substantial further growth can be envisaged. According to a study by Jean-Romain Frisch, of Electricité de France, non-commercial energy grew between 1960 and 1976 at an annual rate of 2.4 per cent in Africa, 3 per cent in Asia and 1 per cent in Latin America. Hence, in Africa the growth rate roughly corresponded to the growth of population, in Asia it was even higher and in Latin America lower. The relationship between the growth rate of the demand for non-commercial energy and that of population is affected by the relative availability of non-commercial and commercial energy sources, the purchasing power of the population and the process of substitution of commercial energy for non-commercial energy. Apparently these three factors are closely interrelated. For the future, Mr Frisch envisages a growth rate of 2.2 per cent for Africa, 2.0 per cent for Asia and 0.1 per cent for Latin America over the period 1976-2000.

The future production potential of non-commercial energy is rather limited in most developing countries. In some countries the problem is extremely serious. Dung which is badly needed as fertiliser is burnt instead. The cutting of fuel wood substantially exceeds the rate of reforestation in many countries, leading to the creation of wastelands, with very detrimental consequences for agricultural soil and food production. It has been estimated that 'nearly a third of the original tropical forest area has been destroyed within recorded history, and it has been predicted that by the year 2000 or shortly thereafter virtually all humid tropical forests will have been transformed into deserts and unproductive wasteland. Large parts of Indonesia now have less than an eighth of their original forest cover. In the Philippines less than a fifth of the land area is still forested. Aerial photographic surveys show a 30% reduction in area of the Ivory Coast's dense rainforest during the decade from 1956 to 1966. At present rates of deforestation, the last trees would disappear from Niger within about 150 years—even allowing for present reforestation programs'.[3]

For commercial energy the outlook is better in principle. The developing world as a whole is well endowed with energy resources. About two-thirds of the global proven crude oil reserves and at least 60 per cent of the estimated ultimate reserves are located in developing countries. They possess about 40 per cent of the natural gas reserves, half of the global hydro-electric potential, one-third of the uranium reserves and at least one-tenth of the total coal resources. Although not fully developed by the standards of the Organisation for Economic Cooperation and Development (OECD), these resources already account for one-third of world primary energy production and 60 per cent of crude oil production. Although the situation looks favourable for the developing countries as a whole, there are tremendous supply problems for individual countries and different country groups. In more recent discussions of this problem, a distinction has therefore been made between oil-exporting and oil-importing countries. As the former cannot be said to face an energy crisis, they will be omitted from further discussion in this essay. Among the oil-importing countries, one distinguishes between the industrialising countries and the very poor agricultural countries, mainly in Africa.

All oil-importing developing countries have in common the problem of how to balance their domestic energy supply deficit and how to finance their own energy production facilities. But the poor non-oil developing countries, which have been the object of most of the recent attention, face the additional problem of a likely rapid increase of the deficit if growth is not to be impaired. As these countries are just on the brink of industrialisation, they have the periods of rapid increases in commercial energy demand still before them. Even if they were able to invest large amounts in the development of commercial energy sources, the long gestation period for such investments would prevent significant additions to supply before 1990 or even later. Hence, these countries will have to import increasing amounts of commercial energy and up to now this has been oil. The switch to coal would be difficult in most countries and would require heavy investment because existing power stations and industrial producers usually lack dual-fired boilers. Consequently, energy imports will continue to have a strong negative effect on the balance of payments of these countries. The ratio of oil imports to exports of goods and services which now ranges from 25 per cent to 40 per cent in the low-income countries of Asia and Africa, south of the Sahara, can be expected to rise to over 50 per cent. This would contribute to a rapid increase in the debt service ratios (debt service to exports). These payments problems might have the effect that the import of investment goods needed for further development will have to be curtailed and that economic growth will therefore slow down. The foreign debts of these countries have increased in the last decade by a factor of ten, or by 22.4 per cent annually, on average.

In order to investigate whether the growing energy deficit of the oil-importing developing countries could be reduced, several studies have recently been undertaken to analyse the energy demand of these countries as well as the possibilities of speeding up the growth of supply. I will deal here with demand issues first and then try to focus on what seem to be the crucial supply problems.

DETERMINANTS OF ENERGY DEMAND AND ITS FLEXIBILITY

The size of a country's energy demand depends essentially on the energy intensities of its various economic activities, including private household operations, its economic structure and its economic size measured by gross domestic product (GDP). The changes of demand therefore can be analysed in terms of intensity changes, structural change and growth.

Energy Intensities

Total energy consumption per capita (including non-commercial energy), measured in tons of coal equivalent, varies from 0.6 for the Far East to 0.62 for Africa and 1.43 for Latin America. The average for the developing countries is 0.68. In comparison, the developed countries have an average energy consumption per capita of 6.03.[4] The total energy intensity, however, measured as energy consumption per million dollars real GDP (data from Irving B. Kravis, of the University of Pennsylvania),[5] shows, rather, little variation. The average for the developing countries is 1,305 and that of the developed countries 1,804. If we use income data converted into dollars on the basis of official exchange rates, the energy intensity of the developed countries (1,727) is even lower than that of the developing countries (2,204).

Energy is not only consumed directly but also by imported commodities. Preliminary estimates of this indirect energy consumption have been undertaken by Alan M. Strout, of the Massachusetts Institute of Technology.[6] According to his estimates, indirect energy consumption incorporated in imports less that of exports as a percentage of total estimated apparent consumption is quite large in a number of countries. The percentages range from 4 per cent for India to 32 per cent for Pakistan, 53 per cent for Morocco and 70 per cent for Nigeria. In the industrial countries this percentage hardly exceeds 10 per cent and usually is even lower.[7]

Aggregate energy consumption per capita or per unit of output is a useful starting point for comparisons between countries and groups of countries, but it obscures differences in sectoral energy intensities and in the structure of economic activity which certainly influences the level of energy consumption. The orders of magnitude of sectoral energy intensities can, however, be derived as described in the following paragraphs.

An attempt has been made by Joy Dunkerley, of the Center for Energy Policy Research, Resources for the Future,[8] to make a comparison for the years 1973-75 for the sectoral energy consumption shares by including non-commercial energy. If one takes energy consumption net of non-energy uses, one obtains a share of 36 per cent for industry, 27 per cent for transport and 38 per cent for others in the industrial countries; and 30 per cent for industry, 20 per cent for transport and 50 per cent for others in the developing countries.

Thanks to the work of Hollis B. Chenery, at the World Bank, Washington, Moises Syrquin, of Bar-Ilan University, Israel, Gerhard Fels, Klaus-Werner Schatz and Frank Wolter, all of the Institut für Weltwirtschaft, Kiel, and Simon Kuznets, of Harvard University,[9] there are sufficient data available on typical sectoral GDP shares at different levels of development. With increasing income, the share of industry increases from a low level while the share of agriculture, here included in 'Others', declines from a high level. No clear trend is visible for transport.

Assume the average GDP shares for industrial and developing countries to be as shown in Table 15.1:

TABLE 15.1

Average Shares in GDP: Industrial and Developing Countries

Sector	Shares in GDP (%)	
	Industrial countries	*Developing countries*
Industry	42	24
Transport	7	6
Others	51	70

If we take the primary energy consumption data per unit of Professor Kravis's GDP as quoted above, the assumed average GDP shares and the energy consumption shares including non-commercial energy, as estimated by Mrs Dunkerley, we can calculate the following sectoral energy intensities (Table 15.2):

TABLE 15.2

Sectoral Energy Intensities: Industrial and Developing Countries

Sector	Sectoral energy intensities	
	Industrial countries	*Developing countries*
Industry	1,550	1,580
Transport	5,430	4,500
Others	1,280	822
GDP	1,804	1,308

The surprising result is that the differences between industrial and developing countries are rather small. In industry there is no difference at all. Indeed, Mrs Dunkerley found almost the same energy intensity in industry for India as for the United States, which is higher than that of the United Kingdom and of West Germany. Mexico's energy intensity corresponds to that of the United Kingdom, and Brazil's to that of West Germany. An independent calculation by Ashok Desai,[10] of the National Council for Applied Economic Research, New Delhi, produced comparable results.

In the transport sector, the energy intensity is rather higher in the industrial countries, which is, however, entirely due to the high energy consumption of the United States transport sector (road transport). In the 'Others' sector, the industrial countries also have a higher energy intensity. This results partly from the higher energy intensity in agriculture (which, in West Germany for instance, is almost equal to that of industry) and partly from greater energy consumption in heating and air conditioning (primarily in the United States). If non-commercial energy were omitted, the difference between industrial and developing countries would be much larger in this sector.

Impact of Structural Change and Growth

Having identified some of the basic differences and similarities in energy consumption between industrial and developing countries, it may be useful to look at the mechanisms which change energy demand in the process of development. Only if these mechanisms are properly understood will it be possible to assess the flexibility of these countries' energy demands and their repercussions on the development process. Unfortunately, knowledge about these mechanisms is still in an embryonic stage and I can therefore only sketch some major trends as they are seen at present. Let us first assume a very low income level ($200 per capita or less) with little or no industry. Commercial energy consumption will then be very low, usually significantly less than 100,000 barrels per day (b/d), which is about one-sixth of the capacity of the refinery at Abadan, Iran. This is the situation in the majority of African countries. The energy share of industry may be relatively large, as we saw above, but this only reflects the fact that the other sectors, in particular agriculture and households, consume so little commercial energy. If, for instance, we found for East Africa an overall non-commercial energy share of 80 per cent, that means that the share approaches 100 per cent in agriculture and households.

An increase in the per capita income of such an economy can originate basically from three developments: either the agricultural sector becomes modernised and produces cash crops for export, or a mining sector develops, or a manufacturing industry emerges which in its early stages may process agricultural products or imported semi-finished products. Some of these changes may, of course, take place simultaneously. For instance, it seems unlikely that agriculture should become modernised without entailing at least some primary processing of its products. Mining industry can also be expected to generate some manufacturing activities.

Modernisation of agriculture as such, even when it involves large-scale irrigation programmes, does not usually affect a country's energy consumption markedly, although local unavailability of suitable energy may forestall such programmes. As long as chemical fertilisers are not produced domestically, the energy consumed in their production does not show up in a country's energy balance. The effect on the energy consumption of the transport sector, however, may be considerable. There is, first, the transport of the agricultural produce to the harbour or station at the national border from which it is exported. This involves transport activities which consume energy in the form of petroleum products or coal, depending on whether there is a road or a rail connection.

Secondly, there is the substitution of tractors for draught animals. This, however, takes place at a much later stage in agricultural modernisation and may be interpreted as substitution of commercial for non-commercial energy with a correspondingly low impact on total energy consumption. Statistically, though, this change would be recorded as additional energy consumption, since animal power has so far not appeared in any statistical energy balance.

The rural population's improved standard of living, resulting from agricultural modernisation, also affects energy demand; with rising income, private households will switch from non-commercial to more convenient commercial energy sources. The increased consumption of kerosene, LPG, coal or gas and rural electrification is a common manifestation of agricultural modernisation. Again, this does not represent so much an increase in total energy demand— at least not one disproportionate to the increase in income—as it does a substitution of commercial for non-commercial energy.

Major increases in energy consumption begin to appear when an agrarian economy takes up industrial production. Country studies suggest that, given low levels of income, commercial energy consumption per unit of output is more than ten times as high in manufacturing as it is in agriculture. The same can be expected to hold for most mining activities. Hence it is obvious that structural change in favour of industry, with a relative decline of agriculture, must accelerate the expansion of energy demand, whatever efforts to save energy may be made. By contrast with agriculture, the observed increase in commercial energy demand is almost equal to an increase in total energy demand. The industrialisation process raises the income level and thereby increases the energy demand of private households in a similar manner as does agricultural modernisation. There is, however, an important difference. Whereas agricultural development does not change the distribution of population significantly, industrialisation leads to migration to urban areas, where the necessary infrastructure, wage labour and commercial services for industry are available.

The urbanised population no longer has access to non-commercial energy sources and becomes dependent on commercial energy. In those cases where non-commercial energy is still available, it becomes increasingly commercialised, because the concentrated urban demand puts a heavy strain on local supply. The commercialisation process, for example that of firewood, has been observed in several countries. The high price demanded for firewood need not reflect the market situation of excess demand, but can also reflect high real costs. With rising urban demand, local forests either have to be replanted or firewood has to be transported from more distant areas by paid labour.

The increased mobility of the population leads to a rapidly rising demand for transport facilities. The failure to plan for public transport needs and the relatively low private (versus social) costs of individual motor cars result in transport largely taking the form of private passenger cars, although this is by far the least energy- (and socially-) efficient mode of passenger transport. Passenger transport adds to the transport needs of industry and commerce which also grow rapidly as the industrial sector expands.

Impact of the Strategy Choice
Although there is no doubt that industrialisation raises energy demand far more than agricultural development does, the pace of this process can vary substantially, depending on how industrialisation proceeds. It is well known that the principle of comparative advantage, derived from economic efficiency considerations, sug-

gests that the developing countries should produce labour-intensive commodities and, where a choice of technology exists, use labour-intensive technologies. The technology recommendation is particularly relevant for indispensable activities, such as infrastructural services, which tend to consume large amounts of capital.

The emphasis on labour-intensive production gains new topicality in light of the energy debate, because theoretical considerations as well as empirical observation[11] have led to the conclusion that energy use for productive purposes is closely related to the use of capital. It is machinery, and not human labour, which consumes fuel in its operation. Capital intensity therefore tends to go along with high energy intensity, whereas the reverse is true for labour-intensive production.

In the past, many developing countries were, for a variety of reasons, unable or unwilling to achieve a satisfactory industrial growth based on predominantly labour-intensive activities. The widely favoured import substitution strategy of the 1960s indiscriminately promoted all kinds of mostly capital-intensive industries by means of high import barriers, including such heavy energy consumers as basic metals (in particular iron, steel and aluminium), cement and industrial chemicals. In Brazil, for example, these three industries alone account for more than one-fourth of the country's entire commercial energy bill.[12]

A more labour-intensive strategy, however, was followed by some smaller countries which stimulated industrial growth by expanding the export of labour-intensive products. Import substitution in these countries was less capital-intensive and more limited, exports became a necessity for growth at an early stage of their industrialisation and policies tended to reinforce relatively low capital intensity. By contrast, large countries find it difficult to resist the temptation of import substitution. For some time it seems to them to be the easiest way to promote industrial growth and it appears to be particularly attractive (although this is often an illusion) if the balance of payments is tight. The structure of industrial production—the kind of products to be substituted—is in this case crucially dependent on the distribution of income. The more unequal the distribution, the more the substitution process concentrates on capital- and energy-intensive durable consumer goods. Capital-intensive production tends to aggravate distributional inequality. Hence unequal distribution of income and capital-intensive production reinforce each other and thereby accelerate energy consumption. If government can stop this process through appropriate policies, import substitution need not be so energy-intensive.

After a phase of import substitution with consumer goods and simple producer goods, industrialisation tends to spread backwards into intermediate and capital goods. This is when the crucial decision has to be made whether the country is to consume energy directly in the production of energy-intensive intermediate or capital goods, or indirectly, by importing these commodities. This decision, of course, is not influenced by energy considerations solely, although they could play an important role if the problem is realised. It is also possible that the country is prepared to directly consume only those types of energy of which it has abundant resources and to indirectly consume the others. Several South American countries, for instance, have abundant hydro resources and could, if the resources were developed, easily produce such energy-intensive products as aluminium, whereas the production of oil- or coal-intensive products in these countries does not seem advisable from an energy-cost point of view.

In the past, the export-oriented strategy was predominantly labour intensive. As such it hardly posed decision problems with respect to energy consumption. The aluminium example, however, shows that this need not be so. Proposals have already been made to shift at least some of the energy-intensive industries from the industrial to the developing countries which have command over reproducible or vast non-renewable energy resources. Proponents of this strategy, in so far as they come from the industrialised countries, believe that it would be more efficient for the industrialised countries and that the supply would be more secure, if they were to consume energy indirectly by importing energy-intensive products instead of directly by producing these goods at home. Hence an export-oriented strategy *per se* provides no more a guarantee for less direct energy consumption than does a carefully planned import-substitution policy. A sensible energy demand policy has to be based on the evaluation of the various strategic alternatives available under the circumstances prevailing in a particular country. No simple, generally valid strategy recommendation is possible.

In conclusion, one can say that there is certainly some flexibility in the course a developing country's energy demand will take, depending on the development strategy it will pursue. The actual range of this flexibility still has to be assessed. It is equally certain, though, that whichever strategy might comply with the developing countries' broad targets of socio-economic development, their energy demand, and in particular that for commercial energy, is bound to grow at considerable rates. Unlike the industrial countries, the developing countries have no possibility whatsoever to plan for a significant deceleration or even stagnation of their energy demand over the next one or two generations if the ultimate extinction of poverty and human misery is ever to be achieved in these parts of the world.

Price Response, Technological Change and
Conservation

Up to now, few estimates of the price elasticities of energy demand of developing countries have been available. The estimates made by myself and Matthias Mors[13] suggest that commercial energy demand is slightly more price-elastic in developing countries than in developed countries. This is contrary to the frequently voiced opinion that the price elasticity ought to be lower in developing countries because energy is widely used there as a subsistence good. This view, however, seems to overlook certain factors: on the one hand, that non-commercial energy can be resubstituted for commercial energy in developing countries if the price of the latter rises faster than that of the former, and on the other hand, that the higher income level in developed countries implies a lower sensitivity to price increases and the more sophisticated energy-consuming equipment in these countries makes a fast reaction to price changes difficult. With regard to the reaction of other productive factors to energy-price changes, I found, in a statewise cross-section analysis for Brazil,[14] a confirmation of the results which Ernst R. Berndt, of the University of British Columbia, and David O. Wood, of the Sloan School of Management, Massachusetts Institute of Technology,[15] as well as Edward A. Hudson and Dale W. Jorgenson, of Harvard University,[16] obtained for the United States—complementarity of energy and capital and substitutability of energy and labour.

Apart from the direct price response, an indirect reaction to rising energy prices reflected in the balance of payments and a retardation of economic growth is generally expected. Although such a reaction by now seems pretty obvious in the industrial countries, it has not been so clear in the developing countries.

Whereas real growth of GDP per capita in the industrial countries was curtailed by one-third between 1970 and 1978 as compared with the previous decade, the developing market economies, not belonging to the capital-surplus Organisation of Petroleum Exporting Countries (OPEC), were able to maintain real per capita growth at an annual rate of 3.1 per cent.[17] For individual countries the empirical evidence is even more controversial. Of the three countries (Brazil, Korea and Spain) which account for almost one-third of the developing countries' total oil imports, two (Brazil and Korea) managed to increase their real growth considerably during the 1970s.

The empirical evidence, therefore, seems to contradict the hypothesis that oil-price hikes lead to balance-of-payments problems with detrimental consequences for economic growth. In order to determine whether this impression is correct, one must take a look at the reasons that allowed the developing countries to maintain their growth rate. One possibility is that these countries found sufficient finance on the international capital market to balance their growing payments deficit. The financing requirements of the developing countries resulting from the higher oil prices, although enormous from these countries' point of view, indeed proved to be manageable by the private international capital market. It has become known that major private banks in Western Europe as well as in the United States increased their loans to developing countries much more than was thought possible a couple of years ago. If these banks become reluctant to do so in the future, the countries will either have to find other sources or apply import restrictions which would then certainly affect growth. The result would be that the past favourable performance of the developing countries would not be repeated.

Another explanation for the differing price response of the developing countries and the industrial countries is that the former are more accustomed to absorbing external shocks. The history of almost all developing countries, which are major primary commodity exporters, is characterised by regularly occurring heavy external shocks due to strong price fluctuations on the commodity markets. In principle, it does not matter whether a country's external liquidity is abruptly squeezed by a sharp decline in export prices or by a rapid price increase of essential imports. Hence, one could argue that if these countries' economies were able to grow in the past, in spite of external shocks on the export side, there is no reason to believe that the oil-price shock on the import side will lead them into the doldrums. This may be due to the fact that a young economy, with a rapidly changing output and employment structure, can much more easily adjust to sudden external shocks than an industrial economy, with its very rigid and mature economic structure. All this, of course, is rather speculative, in particular as the oil-price changes might turn out to be a long-run rather than a cyclical phenomenon.

There is practically nothing known about the impact of technical progress on the energy consumption in developing countries, because the required data are unavailable. It is certain, however, that energy demand growth, compared to income growth, will in the future be substantially lower in the developing countries than it was in the history of the industrial countries' development, because the former can make use of today's much more efficient energy conversion technologies.

The latter argument points to the fact that, in most developing countries, the problem of conservation, too, is not so much a question of improving efficiency in present energy use, as it is one of avoiding inefficiency in the transition to a more diversified and sophisticated economy. In addition, these countries need to avoid further deforestation which is caused by an extensive use of non-commercial energy.

FLEXIBILITY OF ENERGY SUPPLY

There certainly exists some short-run (upward) flexibility in the energy supply of the developing countries as a whole. This is particularly the case in the capital-surplus oil-exporting countries. From a development point of view, however, more interest is directed at long-run flexibility, which essentially depends on the availability of resources, the capability to plan adequately and implement energy projects, and the possibilities for obtaining the finance required for the necessary investments.

Availability of Resources

The world's proven oil reserves are estimated to be between 570,000 million[18] and 640,000 million barrels. Of this amount the capital-surplus OPEC members possess 46 per cent, the capital-deficit members 23 per cent and the non-OPEC developing countries 9 per cent. The ultimately recoverable reserves are estimated to be three to four times as large. Of the world's proven gas reserves

(2.5-10^{15} cubic feet), capital-surplus OPEC possesses 8.6 per cent, capital-deficit OPEC 29.8 per cent and the non-OPEC developing countries 7.2 per cent. Four capital-deficit OPEC countries own 0.6 per cent and the non-OPEC developing countries 10.6 per cent of the world coal reserves which total 800 to 900 gigatons. In addition, the developing countries as a whole own one-third of the world's uranium and have substantial untapped hydro resources. The problem of supply flexibility is thus not so much a matter of resources, but of how to create the necessary production and transport facilities.

Financing Requirements

Leaving aside the issue of adequate project planning and implementation, one is still confronted with the problem of meeting the financing requirements of the necessary investments. This need arises in addition to that for finance to cover higher oil-import costs. Tentative calculations indicate that these requirements will be enormous. For the non-OPEC developing countries they will have to come mainly from foreign sources and will thus augment the debts which are already high for some of these countries. We need not worry very much about the problem of financing in the OPEC countries and therefore I will again omit them from the discussion.

The financing requirements of the non-OPEC developing countries for their planned investments in energy-producing capacities (reserve capacity included) can be estimated roughly. The resulting capacity increases for oil, gas and coal have been projected by Efrain Friedmann, Ali Ezzati and Matthew J. Mitchell, of the World Bank.[19] Between 1980 and 1990 the capacity increase for oil will be 7.1 million b/d, for gas 1.7 million b/d of oil equivalent, for coal 2.7 million b/d of oil equivalent, and for electricity 274 gigawatts (GW). An alternative projection by the World Bank[20] places the increase for oil and coal at a somewhat lower and that for electricity at a higher level.

The OPEC countries' investment costs for one b/d of oil are estimated at $4,000 to $5,000 on average, expressed in 1980 prices.[21] Outside OPEC the costs amount to $8,400 for the net exporters of oil and $15,500 for the net importers. The higher figure for the latter is due to higher expenditures on exploration and development. If these figures are multiplied with the respective capacity increases one obtains a cumulative investment volume of $74,000 million for upstream production in the non-OPEC developing countries. For downstream processing (refining, transport and distribution) one has to add another $49,000 million. A corresponding calculation for gas results in $15,000 million for upstream production and $10,000 million for downstream processing.

The investment costs for coal vary between $15 and $70 per ton of annual capacity in strip mining and $30 and $90 in underground mining. If one takes as an average for the non-OPEC developing countries $52 per ton for investment in production capacity and $26 for the necessary infrastructure (transport), one obtains a cumulative amount of $15,000 million.

The investment costs for electricity vary substantially according to type of power plant. The costs are highest for nuclear (boiling or pressurised water) power plants, amounting to about $1,880/kilowatts (kw) in 1980, followed by $1,700/kw for large-scale hydro power plants and $1,130/kw for fossil-fired plants. Present plans envisage an additional capacity of 46 GW for nuclear plants, 131 GW for fossil-fired and 97 GW for hydro power plants, amounting to a cumulative investment volume of about $400,000 million.

In total, the financing requirements for investments in order to expand commercial energy capacity will, between 1980 and 1990, amount to $560,000 million expressed in 1980 prices or to $56,000 million annually on average. This is slightly less than the amount these countries—that is, the non-OPEC developing countries— paid for their oil imports in 1980. In the light of the World Bank's alternative projections referred to above, these estimates are conservative. The World Bank projects a total investment requirement of $425,500 million between 1980 and 1990 for the oil-importing non-OPEC developing countries alone and of $683,000 million for the developing countries as a whole.

Between 1966 and 1975, upstream investments in energy in the developing countries amounted to less than 5 per cent on average of total national gross investment. If downstream investment is added, one obtains 7 to 8 per cent. Total real gross investment of the developing countries has been projected at about $450,000 million annually on average for the years 1980 to 1990. This implies an increase in the share of energy investment to more than 12 per cent of total investment.

The Debt Problem

The energy investments will have to be financed partly from domestic and partly from foreign sources. In the past, roughly one-third of the finance came from domestic savings and two-thirds from capital import. The shares of individual fuels are shown in Table 15.1. It can be seen that some $37,000 million annually will have to come from foreign countries. This amount almost equals 10 per cent of the non-OPEC developing countries' foreign debts at the end of 1979. Hence, energy investments alone will double these countries' foreign debts (in 1980 prices) by 1990 and account for an annual growth of about 7 per cent. If the present rate of international inflation continues, the annual growth rate of debts in nominal terms will come close to 14 per cent and the foreign financing of energy investments will more than treble foreign debts.

TABLE 15.3

Projected Investment Requirements of the Energy Sector in Non-OPEC Developing Countries, 1980-90, 1980 US $ prices (thousand million)

	Average annual investment	Foreign-exchange requirement	
		Annual average	Share %
Upstream			
Oil and gas	8.86	7.08	80
Coal	0.97	0.63	65
Electric power	26.04	15.69	60
Hydro	10.72	5.37	50
Thermal	9.63	5.77	60
Nuclear	5.69	4.55	80
Total	35.87	23.41	65
Downstream			
Oil and gas	5.90	4.72	80
Coal	0.49	0.25	50
Electric power	14.03	8.48	60
Hydro	5.77	2.91	50
Thermal	5.18	3.11	65
Nuclear	3.07	2.45	80
Total	20.41	13.45	66
Total energy sector			
Oil and gas	14.76	11.81	80
Coal	1.46	0.88	60
Electric power	40.06	24.17	60
Hydro	16.49	8.28	50
Thermal	14.81	8.88	60
Nuclear	8.76	7.01	80
Total	56.28	36.85	65

SOURCE: Efrain Friedmann, Ali Ezzati and Matthew J. Mitchell, 'Energy Financing of Non-OPEC Developing Countries', World Bank, Washington, 1980, mimeograph.

This raises the question of whether such a high increase in foreign debt is feasible and whether the finance will be forthcoming. There are various aspects under which this question can be considered. If we consider the re-cycling of OPEC dollars and assume (conservatively) that the oil price will remain at $32 per barrel in 1980 prices over the coming decade, an oil equivalent of 3.2 million b/d, which is about 12 per cent of OPEC's present exports, would be required. Since several OPEC countries do not fully absorb their oil revenues, it does not appear to be unfeasible—although it is rather unlikely—that they might hold a share of, say, 50 to 70 per cent of the required amount in the form of assets of the developing countries. OPEC has recently increased its special fund for loans to developing countries from $1,600 million to $4,000 million, which is only 11 per cent of the amount needed.

Another aspect is whether the debts and the debt servicing might become too high for the developing countries. At the close of 1979, the debt ratio (debts minus reserves divided by current exchange revenue) of the non-OPEC developing countries was 0.6, which was lower than in 1970 (1.0) and 1975 (0.8) but higher than in 1973 (0.4). By contrast, the European Council for Mutual Economic Assistance (CMEA, or Comecon) countries had a debt ratio of 1.1, with some countries running as high as 1.7 (German Democratic Republic), 1.9 (Bulgaria) and 2.5 (Poland)—not counting the substantial loans (after the strike) to Poland.[22]

The debt service ratio (debt servicing to current exchange revenue) of the non-OPEC developing countries increased continuously in the past, and now stands at 18 per cent. Some countries, however, have reached such high percentages as 43 per cent (Chile in 1978) and 50 per cent (Brazil, also in 1978). For the Comecon countries the ratio is 33 per cent with some countries reaching 55 per cent (Bulgaria) and 65 per cent (Poland).

Hence, if one takes the non-OPEC developing countries as a whole, their debt problem does not yet seem to be critical. It has also been argued that the debt ratio was much higher in Australia and Canada in the nineteenth and early twentieth centuries than in the Chiles and Brazils of today. There may be problems for individual countries, however, because foreign private banks become unwilling to lend, or the government regulatory agencies will not give them the permission to lend, or because the countries themselves consider their debts too high. Finally, one should not forget that there are thousands of non-energy projects in the developing countries which lead to foreign debts and with which the new energy projects must compete in the struggle for foreign capital.

One might also ask whether the investment costs could not be reduced without lowering the capacity increase. There are considerable doubts about the feasibility of increasing the nuclear capacity by 46 GW over the period from 1980 to 1990. These doubts are based in part on the problems of acceptability and finance, but to a greater extent on the difficulties of handling such a highly sophisticated technology.[23] Even in the industrial countries the outage ratio of nuclear power plants at present is about 35 per cent of capacity on average.

If we thus assume that all planned additional nuclear power capacity will be replaced by fossil-fired plants instead, we then obtain a net reduction of $3,500 million annually in investment and of $2,300 million or 6 per cent in the annual foreign-exchange requirement—which, indeed, is not very much. A possibility of reducing investment costs might also exist in the construction, at a substantially lower cost, of a larger number of small and medium-sized instead of large-scale hydro power plants. Little can be said at present, however, as to whether this could be done without knowing whether capacity targets would be impaired and what the size of the cost reduction would be.

Sources of Foreign Finance

The question then remains of where the foreign finance can be expected to come from. This has to be discussed for each major fuel separately, because the investment pattern differs markedly for each fuel.

For the period 1975-80, foreign oil and gas investment in the non-OPEC developing countries has been estimated at $1,800 million annually in the form of direct investments and $1,600 million annually in the form of supplier credits, loans from financial institutions and official multilateral and bilateral loans. If one assumes a 10 per cent annual increase in foreign direct investment between 1980 and 1990, this source would contribute about $4,800 million annually or about 41 per cent of the amount needed, which is less than in the period since 1975 (53 per cent). Assuming that the World Bank loans $1,300 million on average (the Bank itself has projected $1,000 million in 1985), other regional banks loan $700 million and OPEC $1,000 million from special funds, we would have another $3,000 million or 25 per cent of the amount needed.

Official bilateral loans may be expected to amount to $1,300 million or 11 per cent. This would leave $2,700 million or roughly 23 per cent to be covered by private financial institutions and supplier credits, approximately two-thirds of it coming from the former and one-third from the latter. In the past (that is, over the last five years), official loans accounted for 14 per cent, financial institutions for 27 per cent and supplier credits for 6 per cent. Hence, it is expected that the burden of adjusting to a higher foreign financing requirement will have to be borne primarily by official loans.

The amount needed for investment in coal is small compared with the overall foreign financing requirement, namely, 2 per cent of the latter, but large in view of past investments which only averaged some $20 million annually in the second half of the 1970s. Considerable efforts will therefore have to be undertaken to reach the annual target of $900 million. About $550 million will probably come from official loans, roughly half of them being multilateral. Direct investment is not assumed to be very high ($45 million). Financial institutions and supplier credits will have to share in the remaining almost $300 million. Compared with those of the past, all these figures are very high. For the period 1975-80 the annual average of official loans was estimated at $11 million, that of direct investment at $1 million and that of financial institutions and supplier credits at $8 million.

Substantial increases will also have to be made in foreign electricity financing which in the recent past amounted to $3,000 million annually. In the past, official loans constituted the largest proportion (50 per cent) of this amount, which is due in part to the public ownership of utilities in developing countries (as well as in most developed countries). Direct investment was practically nil. Financial institutions accounted for 34 per cent, supplier credits for 12 per cent and bonds for 5 per cent. It is very difficult to say what kind of pattern will emerge in the future because the required increase is enormous, that is, six to eight times as large as the present level of the foreign financing requirements (the exact factor depending on whether or not nuclear power plans will be realised). If we apply the pattern of the past, official sources would have to contribute $11,600 million in loans (two-thirds being bilateral), whereas bonds and loans from financial institutions would have to amount to $9,600 million and supplier credits to $2,800 million.

Finally, one may ask whether the investments envisaged here would considerably improve the developing countries' energy and balance-of-payments situation. Unfortunately, the answer is no, they would not. The present plans for capacity expansion on which the calculations are based would only help to prevent a more serious deterioration of these countries' energy balance and balance-of-payments situation. If the plans are realised, the non-OPEC developing countries can be expected to still import some 11 million b/d of oil by 1990. Given an oil price of $32 b/d (in 1980 prices), the oil import bill for that year would amount to $125,000 million. This would roughly correspond to 30 per cent of these countries' revenue—if the present trend continues—as compared with about 20 per cent at present.

CONCLUSION

The energy situation of the oil-importing developing countries is serious, at least during the 1980s. Downward flexibility of demand is rather limited if major development targets are not to be seriously affected, although a proper choice of strategy could help to prevent an undue acceleration of demand. The problem of the poorer developing countries is that the development phases of rapid increase in energy demand, resulting from structural change, still lie ahead of them. These countries will have no choice but to increase their energy supply—thus, their investment requirements will be enormous. The private capital markets will have to channel financial resources to the developing countries to an unprecedented extent, but this alone will not suffice. Official grants and loans will also have to be stepped up considerably. How this is to be achieved in a period of slow growth and heavy financial constraints on the public budgets of the industrial countries is a question that still awaits an answer.

NOTES AND REFERENCES

1. Jean-Romain Frisch, 'Third World Energy Horizons 2000-2020: A Regional Approach to Consumption and Supply Sources', paper presented at the 11th World Energy Conference, Munich, 8-12 September, 1980.
2. Lutz Hoffmann and Matthias Mors, *Energy Demand in the Developing World: Estimation and Projection up to 1990 by Region and Country, World Bank Commodity Models*, Vol. 1, World Bank Staff Commodity Working Paper No. 6 (Washington: World Bank, 1981).
3. Philip F. Palmedo *et al.*, *Energy Needs, Uses and Resources in Developing Countries* (New York: Brookhaven National Laboratory, for the Agency for International Development, 1978), p. 53.
4. For the following data, see Joy Dunkerley, 'Comparative Analysis

of the Energy Sectors of Industrialized and Developing Countries', Washington, 1979, mimeograph.

5.   Irving B. Kravis, Alan W. Heston and Robert Summers, 'Real GDP Per Capita for More Than One Hundred Countries', *The Economic Journal*, Cambridge, No. 350, 1978.

6.   Alan M. Strout, 'The Hidden World Trade in Energy', Cambridge, Mass., undated, mimeograph.

7.   Joel Darmstadter, Joy Dunkerley and Jack Alterman, *How Industrial Societies Use Energy: A Comparative Analysis* (Baltimore and London: Johns Hopkins University Press, for Resources of the Future, 1977).

8.   Dunkerley, *op. cit.*

9.   Hollis B. Chenery and Moises Syrquin, with the assistance of Hazel Elkington, *Patterns of Development, 1950-1970* (London and New York: Oxford University Press, for the World Bank, 1975); Gerhard Fels, Klaus-Werner Schatz and Frank Wolter, 'Der Zusammenhang zwischen Produktionsstruktur und Entwicklungsniveau: Versuch einer Strukturprognose für die westdeutsche Wirtschaft', *Weltwirtschaftliches Archiv*, Kiel, No. 2, 1971; and Simon Kuznets, *Economic Growth of Nations: Total Output and Production Structure* (Cambridge, Mass.: Belknap Press of Harvard University Press, 1971).

10.   Ashok V. Desai, 'Development and Energy Consumption', *Oxford Bulletin of Economics and Statistics*, Oxford, No. 3, 1978.

11.   See, for example, Ernst R. Berndt and David O. Wood, 'Engineering and Econometric Interpretation of Energy-Capital Complementarity', *The American Economic Review*, Menasha, Wisconsin, No. 3, 1979, which is a considerably shortened version of *idem, Engineering and Econometric Approaches to Industrial Energy Conservation and Capital Formation: a Reconciliation*, Massachusetts Institute of Technology Energy Laboratory Working Paper, No. MIT-EL 77-040WP, Cambridge, Mass., November 1977.

12.   Hoffmann, 'Energy Demand and its Determinants in Brazil', in W. D. Cook and W. D. Kuhn (eds), *Planning Processes in Developing Countries: Techniques and Achievements* (Amsterdam: North-Holland, 1982).

13.   Hoffmann and Mors, *op. cit.*

14.   Hoffmann, *op. cit.*

15.   Berndt and Wood, *op. cit.*

16.   Edward A. Hudson and Dale W. Jorgenson, 'U.S. Energy Policy and Economic Growth, 1975-2000', *The Bell Journal of Economics and Management Science*, New York, No. 2, 1974.

17.   Boem Jong Choe, Helen Hughes and Adrian Lambertini, 'Energy Prospects for the Developing Countries', World Bank, Washington, 1980, mimeograph.

18.   *Survey of Energy Resources 1980*, prepared by the Federal Institute for Geosciences and Natural Resources of the Federal Republic of Germany for the 11th World Energy Conference in Munich, 8-12 September 1980 (London: World Energy Conference, 1980).

19.   Efrain Friedmann, Ali Ezzati and Matthew J. Mitchell, 'Energy Financing of Non-OPEC Developing Countries', Washington, World Bank, 1980, mimeograph.

20.   *Energy in the Developing Countries* (Washington: World Bank, 1980).

21.   Most of the following data are based on Friedmann *et al.*, *op. cit.* All data, however, have been updated and in some places adjusted by the present author.

22.   Source of the data: Deutsche Bank.

23.   Elis Roth, 'Criteria for Nuclear Electricity Generation in Developing Countries', Hoover Institution on War, Revolution and Peace, Stanford, California, 1980, mimeograph.

Part VI

Economic, Social and Political Thought

16 The Perception of Man and Justice and the Conception of Political Institutions

Karl Brunner

A protracted battle is taking shape in the political arena of all Western democracies. Moreover, a corresponding battle is proceeding on the intellectual plane. Its outcome will determine the future of our society and the patterns of life encouraged or suppressed by its prevailing institutional arrangements.

BATTLE FOR THE FUTURE OF WESTERN SOCIETY

This intellectual and socio-political conflict is concerned fundamentally with the role and form of 'government'. Those on one side of the battleline argue for social coordination based on market processes. They also express substantial reservations about political institutions and insist on constitutional restrictions to limit the range of their operation to the absolute minimum. Those on the other side reverse this pattern. They favour a social system which coordinates its affairs mainly within the context of political institutions operating in a political process with few, if any, constitutional constraints.[1]

Socio-political and Intellectual Scene

A socialist trend has been gathering momentum since it emerged in the mid-1960s and has found strong support among the intelligentsia and the mass media. Advocates of this trend oppose the social coordination of human affairs based on markets within a system of private property rights and a minimal set of political institutions controlled by a constitutional census. The socialist standpoint argues for a wide-ranging and open-ended replacement of spontaneous market arrangements by an array of political agencies. Thus, it assigns a powerful and central role to 'government', which we understand here as the gradual incorporation of all relevant social decisions within the political process.

This conflict in the public arena and the intellectual market place is usually interpreted, at least by the media which address a broader intelligentsia, as reflecting some basic 'ideological commitments'. This characterisation conveys the pervasive impression that the ongoing disputes occur essentially on the plane of religious visions or political commitments, beyond any rational assessment. Advocates of a revealed truth tend, of course, to describe alternative conceptions of the world as ideologies, which express the false consciousness unavoidably suffered by the unenlightened. Such explanations of the conflict, however, hardly survive probing examination. The social and intellectual battle involves aspects beyond the grasp of such metaphysical interpretations. Ideological commitments nevertheless play an important role in this context. They occur as attitudes and dispositions which reject determinedly any rational assessment of socio-political views of positions on the grounds of inter-personally valid analysis and evidence. But the prevalent rejection of a rational assessment does not determine its non-existence or its impossibility. We do possess the intellectual means to penetrate beyond 'ideologies' and 'ideological commitments' to the substantive core of the issues shaping the conflict. This essay should be regarded as an attempt to penetrate the ideological fogs of the intelligentsia market. It attempts, in particular, to relate opposing views on the 'role of government' to two fundamental and rationally assessable strands of thought.

*First Strand: the Perception of Man and
the Conception of 'Government'*

Two major alternatives pertaining to the perception of Man dominate our thinking. One alternative, the 'Scottish' model of Man, was introduced by the Scottish philosophers of the eighteenth century and developed into the choice-theoretic foundation of economic analysis. The other alternative derives from the French enlightenment of the same century and was ultimately shaped into a sociological view of Man. Both perceptions of Man permeate the social sciences, but with differing frequency of occurrence in the various fields and branches. The sociological version, however, clearly dominates the public arena with the intelligentsia. For our purposes, we may summarise the major differences between the two alternatives with the following passages from a previously published paper.[2]

'According to the Scottish intellectual tradition, man is

foremost a maximizer. He is not indifferent. He cares about the world around him. He differentiates, sorts, and orders states of the world, and in this ordering he reduces all entities encountered to a commensurable dimension. Things valued positively are preferred in larger magnitudes. Moreover, the evaluation depends on the context. Any given increment of a positively valued object suffers a lower evaluation as the total available to the individual rises. Man is willing to trade off in all dimensions. He is always willing to forfeit some quantity of any given valued item for a quantity of some alternative item which he values more highly. His evaluations tend to be transitive, expressing a consistency in his value system.

'Maximizing man recognizes, moreover, that all resources are limited, including his own time. Whatever his resources, man attempts to achieve the best position he can under the constraints facing him. This optimization occurs on the basis of less than perfect information, and it recognizes that decision making itself involves costs.

'Lastly, the resourceful aspect of man is analytically the most troublesome to handle. Resourcefulness emerges whenever man is confronted with new and unfamiliar opportunities, or when man searches for ways to modify the constraints and opportunities. Coping, groping, and learning all express man's resourcefulness and form an essential aspect of his systematic behavior.

'The REMM model [that is the model characterising a Resourceful, Evaluating and Maximising Man] does not describe man as a brainy, but heartless, calculating machine. Charitable behavior, love of family, compassions, can be consistently subsumed. Man appears as a search organism, responding systematically to incentives and stimuli. These are systematically associated with institutional arrangements surrounding man. Market and non-market institutions can be analyzed in terms of the incentive structures they generate. In contrast with the other models, the REMM model explains man's behavior as a consequence of interaction between the *individual's* value system [that is, preferences] and constraints or opportunities. This formulation is usually supplemented with the assumption that the variability of the constraining conditions dominates the variability of the preference system.

Changes in behavior are thus dominantly attributed to variations in opportunities and not to variations in values.

'The basic ideas of the REMM model were introduced more
than 200 years ago by Mandeville, Ferguson and Adam Smith.
The idea of REMM was an essential building block in the
analysis which led them to conclude that a social equilibrium
results as an unintended by-product of the interaction of "self-
seeking" men.'[3]

The French tradition offers a remarkable contrast to the Scottish
perception.

'Sociological man is conformist and conventional. His
behavior is a product of his cultural environment; the taboos,
customs, mores, traditions, etc., of the society in which he is
born and raised. . . . If behavior is determined by acculturation, then choice, or purpose, of conscious adaptation are
meaningless. . . . Sociological man is not an *evaluator*, any
more than ants, bees and termites are evaluators.

'Cultural conditions and historical forces certainly affect
human behavior, but the sociological and the REMM model
differ in their treatment of this effect. In the REMM model,
acculturation conditions the constraints and the preferences
of the individual in his coping, groping, and interested
behavior. In contrast, the sociological model asserts that
individual behavior is directly determined by social factors
and cultural conditions. Man is neither resourceful nor an
evaluator, he is a conformist enslaved by conventions.

'Structuralist interpretations of sociology reveal some basic
properties of the model. Members of a society are essentially
viewed as role players. Society determines an array of social
positions which determine roles assumed by members of society
with specific role obligations. Social anticipations concerning
the performance of specific role obligations are supplemented
with appropriate sanctions to assure adequate performance.
The interaction between social positions, role anticipations and
sanctions determines individual behavior. There is no room
for adaptive creativity, or for evaluating responses to incentives.
The sociological model attributes a crucial significance to the
exogenous existence of social values and social norms. These
values and norms establish the social order independently of
individuals.

'The sociological view of man is particularly prominent in

Marxian writings. Lukasz stresses the role of "social totality" as an entity above and beyond all individuals and their interaction. This view is repeated by Adorno who maintains that all social phenomena, including the individual, depend on the social totality. Others argue that a reduction of social phenomena to the behavior of men, i.e., the explanation of social phenomena in terms of individual behavior, is basically false and inadmissible. These scholars insist that individual behavior be traced to a social whole. Society determines individual behavior, not the other way around.'[4]

Perception of Man and the Analysis of
Political Structure

The alternative perceptions of Man should be regarded as empirical (or potentially empirical) theories about Man's position in society. The substantive differences that characterise the conflicting strands of thought are best revealed by their respective implications relating to important socio-political problems of our time. They result, for instance, in radically different propositions concerning crime, corruption, marriage, divorce and a host of further issues. Moreover, these differences reach substantially different conclusions concerning suitable social policies involving a wide array of political issues. Lastly and, for our immediate purposes, most importantly, the two perceptions also yield radically different evaluations relating to the working of markets and the operation of political institutions or political processes. The 'Scottish' model typically produces an entirely different view of the operation of non-market institutions from the sociological perception. The latter implies a vision attributing substantial virtues to non-market institutions which contrast with the many vices assigned to the market processes. An intellectual approach to the world conditioned by the sociological model of Man typically encourages, under the circumstances, an open-ended and essentially unlimited expansion of political institutions. An expanding government with a shrinking private sector and eroding private property rights necessarily emerges from social policies guided by the sociological perception of Man. Moreover, a detailed examination of the host of socialist viewpoints establishes that, without exception, they share the sociological vision of Man. This perception may not offer a sufficient condition for any particular version of socialist views, but it certainly forms a necessary condition. The denial of the sociological model as an empirically valid hypothesis about Man would thoroughly destroy the case for a socialist society.[5]

Second Strand: the Perception of Justice

The perception of Man, however, does not form the only intellectual strand underlying the conflict about the future of our society. It is supplemented by a closely related, but still very distinct, strand of thought. This second strand involves the perception of justice. A survey of many versions of socialist thinking exhibits a close connection between the sociological model of Man and some broad notion of justice. The role of the perception of justice in our battles relating to the future of democratic societies needs to be examined in more detail at this stage. The opposing perceptions of Man which control our views of political institutions are matched by two fundamentally distinct conceptions of justice. The Nobel laureate Friedrich A. von Hayek and Robert Nozick, of Harvard University, have contributed a penetrating clarification to the structure of these conceptions in their recent work.[6] The remainder of this essay deals with the relationship between the perception of justice and the conception of government.

AN EXPLORATION OF THE SECOND STRAND

Many discussions of social issues proceed with the implicit assumption that only one particular view of justice is possible. The form of the discussions would also suggest that the particular view more or less implicitly advanced offers its own justification. A survey of the discourse on the evaluation of social structures, however, reveals that two broad, but very distinct, notions summarise an array of specific views. One notion typically contains 'end-state' or 'outcome conceptions' of justice, whereas the other notion embraces 'process views' of justice. These alternative perceptions of justice involve radically different approaches to various forms of social organisations. They also imply very different evaluations of political institutions and the effect that moral arguments have on socio-political aspects.

Two Notions of Justice

The first notion, that is, the 'end-state' view, anchors justice in terms of specific outcome patterns of the social process. The criteria for justice involve pre-conceived specific outcome patterns relating directly to the actions of individual members of society. Social justice is defined as obtaining the nearest possible result to the established outcome pattern which defines justice. The alternative notion of justice completely disregards any outcome pattern. According to this notion, any outcome pattern is consistent with social justice, *provided* the process generating the outcome satisfies specific properties constituting the defining characteristics of justice.

The 'process' conception may be exemplified with the aid of a court trial. Justice has traditionally been defined by the very nature of the task confronting a court in terms of the properties of the trial procedure. It is hardly possible to define a 'just trial'—that is, a trial which satisfies some criterion of justice—in terms of its outcome. An end-state conception is quite impossible under the circumstances. It would require the information to be examined before any trial and judgment to be formed after it. Reliance on an end-state criterion implies that the trial itself is really irrelevant and unnecessary. All we would need under such circumstances is the pronouncement of the penalty and possibly an award to the damaged party. An end-state principle of justice cannot be reconciled in this respect with the independent operation of courts.

This argument, however, requires further elaboration. It has been argued that a case for a process conception cannot be developed independently of the outcomes typically produced by the process mechanism. The trial procedures of the court usefully exemplify the required elaboration. The choice between alternative process views, characterised by different criteria stressing various properties of the process, is rationally influenced by the expected consequences produced under alternative process structures. In the context of criminal trials, the possible range of process criteria associates vastly different combinations of the two fundamental risks—the risk of condemning innocents and the risk of absolving the guilty. The variety of risk combinations produces very different social consequences. Advocates of a process conception of justice should thus acknowledge that the choice between specific elements of the broad notion depends very much on a comparison and evaluation of the expected consequences. This does not mean, however, that the process conception essentially coincides with an outcome conception or that it, at best, forms a special case of the one and only acceptable position of justice. The difference is made clear in that the end-state approach usually requires specific details of the outcome pattern. By contrast, the process approach requires only a broad outline of the outcome for its evaluation of justice. We note, moreover, that the process view involves a commitment to the selected process criteria irrespective of specific possible outcomes. Such a commitment would not be accepted by the end-state theory of justice.

Another example may illustrate further the difference between the two perceptions of justice. Suppose that underlying changes in supply and demand conditions modify relative prices and produce windfall profits (or losses) in the context of an open competitive market mechanism. According to the widespread egalitarian belief characterising a dominant example of end-state views, windfall profits are inherently unjust. They push the outcome of the social process further away from the outcome patterns satisfying the criterion of justice. A process conception, by contrast, finds that windfall profits do not violate, *per se*, the canons of social justice. If such profits emerge in the context of a process satisfying the criteria of (processual) justice they pose no ethical or moral problem. This example clarifies the issue considered above. The end-state view demands a detailed outcome pattern relating to the actions of all individual members of society. Departures from the detailed pattern express the extent of prevailing social injustice. The process view, by contrast, emphasises the question whether windfalls occur in the context of contrived monopoly situations or in open competitive markets *irrespective* of the pattern and distribution among the members of society. Judgment depends simply on the broad properties of the process and *not* on specific and shifting allocative details produced under the acceptable properties of the process. A process view would, of course, be guided in the present case by the recognition that windfalls serve an allocative social function in competitive contexts. This judgment would hardly be affected by the recognition that chance may assure an overlap in the set of achievable outcome patterns consistent with open competition and with a state containing occasional monopolies.

Notions of Justice and the Role of Political Institutions

The two notions of justice determine very different attitudes towards the state and the role of political institutions. A process conception is compatible with a minimal state. It is, in particular, consistent with the basic definition of a constitutional government— that is, a government with a range of political institutions explicitly and deliberately limited to the broad functions of protection and the provision of the most obvious 'public goods'. A process conception hardly justifies detailed interventions or the extensive replacement of market mechanisms by political institutions based on budget or police powers. On the other hand, the required patterning of outcomes produced by the social process under an end-state conception requires extensive structuring with the aid of political agencies. In the absence of political institutions arranging or controlling the use of resources, the required patterning of outcomes will necessarily fail. Voluntary private transactions, in general, produce results which deviate substantially from any particular end-state principle. The enforcement of this principle can thus only proceed in the context of political institutions controlling the use of resources with the application of appropriate police powers. The range of political institutions associated with any end-state principle implies, moreover, that the range of voluntary transactions and private opportunities is coercively reduced to a very small range. Professor Nozick concludes on this point that 'end-state and most patterned principles of distributive justice institute (partial) ownership by others of people and their actions. These principles involve a shift from the classical liberals' notion of self-ownership to a notion of (partial) property rights in other people'.[7] The partial loss in self-ownership follows unavoidably from the operation of the political institutions according to the intentions of the end-state principle selected.

The analytic tradition of economic analysis based on the REMM model reveals the fundamental flaw built into the end-state conception of justice. It shows quite clearly that political institutions are not governed by their original intentions and justifications. Every institution characteristically develops specific incentives and disincentives embedded in the arrangement. The people manning the institution and exercising the police powers associated with the institution respond to these incentives and disincentives. Under the circumstances, unintended and unanticipated behaviour patterns emerge which threaten the realisation of the end-state principle. Further institutionalisation of police power will be necessary to correct these unintended outcomes in order to modify the results according to the requirements of the end-state principle.[8]

*Fundamental Ambivalence of Political Structure
and the End-state Principle*

The problem addressed in the preceding paragraph deserves some further discussion. An examination of the theory of justice by John Rawls, of Harvard University, may clarify some relevant aspects.

Professor Nozick convincingly argued that Professor Rawls' criterion of justice (the difference principle) operates in the nature of an end-state principle. The difference principle imposes a constraint on the admissible distribution of resources or entitlements. Social arrangements are ranked according to this principle by the comparative position of the least endowed or least 'entitled' social group. The discussion of Rawlsian theory proceeds in this context according to a long philosophical tradition which essentially disregards any institutional environment. But these contexts form the crucial material for the proper examination of the social consequences associated with any attempt at institutionalisation of end-state principles. Such principles do not operate automatically and by themselves in an institutional vacuum. They do not require an array of political institutions to attend to the application of the principle. But new opportunities for political manipulation are unavoidably created with any political agency designed to enforce the patterning required. These opportunities result from the fundamental ambivalence of all political structures. I have described this problem elsewhere in the following words:

'The starting point is the fundamental ambivalence of government. This ambivalence is expressed by the mixture of benefits and risks associated with a political structure. Hobbes and others have eloquently described the state of anarchy. We also note that anarchy or unstructured social processes appear at most as transition phases. Nozick and Buchanan offer a lucid and detailed analysis of the transition from anarchy to elementary forms of political structure. Both authors demonstrate that anarchy is not a viable state and spontaneously evolves forms of political structure. This spontaneous evolution requires no mysterious "social" forces beyond man's interest and resourceful endeavors. The social interaction between self-interested men produces the transition into patterns of political structure.

'The benefits to individual members of these associations are very substantial indeed. Their security is enhanced and the political structure encourages an economic organization raising the productivity of labor and thus improving the standards of living. This story is clear enough. But the emergence of political structure shifts opportunities and incentives in a peculiar way. Nozick addresses this aspect when he notes that already the constitution of a "minimal state" unavoidably involves some measure of coercive redistribution of wealth. In a state of anarchy each individual has essentially three options: to engage in productive activity or voluntary exchange, to allocate efforts to protect his product and possessions, or to engage in piracy and acquire wealth through violent extraction from others. It should be obvious that only the first option determines the brutal uncertainty of anarchy and the vanishing incentive to invest any resources of efforts for returns beyond the immediate horizon. The appearance of political structure replaces this vast uncertainty, confronting the individual with some "rules of the social game" represented by specific political institutions. The crucial fact requiring some emphasis in this context bears on the range of options available to individual members of the political association. These options include, of course, the application of resources controlled by individuals to produce wealth. The evolution of political structure enhances and safeguards this option. But the very nature of political institutions cannot prevent alternative options. Their existence offers opportunities to invest resources in political activity, guided by implicit (or explicit) rules of the institutions, in order to extract wealth from other members of the political association. The occurrence of this option implies the existence of a last option, i.e. investment in political activities designed to fend off extraction of wealth threatened by the political activities of other groups. Under both anarchy and a state of political structure individual agents can thus acquire wealth by productive effort and voluntary exchange or via extractions from others. The ambivalence of political structure is defined by the persistence of socially non-productive private wealth extraction. This kind of wealth acquisition does not distinguish anarchy from systems exhibiting political structure. The crucial difference appears in the range of uncertainty and the existence of rules confining the processes of wealth extraction in the context of political structure. Such rules lower the uncertainty confronting individual agents. This difference implies that opportunities for socially productive wealth acquisition via productive efforts and voluntary exchange are enhanced. Such enhancement assures the viability of the political structure. Viability is endangered whenever political institutions develop complex and pervasive incentives for potential wealth extraction. There emerge under the circumstances ever widening organizational efforts to exploit the political process for persistent acquisition of wealth at the expense of others. The change from anarchy to political structure may also be formulated as a shifting mixture of a positive-sum game (productive effort) and a negative-sum game (piracy). The negative-sum game looms so large under anarchy that most political structures offer a better mixture of positive and negative sum games. But the crucial fact is that every political structure necessarily contains characteristic incentives yielding its own peculiar range of negative-sum games.'[9]

The fundamental ambivalence of the political structure thus releases forces which make it quite unlikely that any institutionalisation of an end-state principle will offer a stable solution settling around the desired pattern. The existence of political institutions tears down the 'veil of ignorance' and encourages their extensive manipulation for the self-interested purposes of all those with better information and access to these agencies and their respective police powers. The consensus established behind the 'veil of ignorance' and expressed by a class of distribution will thus eventually dissolve when members of the social group actually confront the institutional reality of the end-state principle. This dissolution of the consensus implies, furthermore, that the end-state principle remains a ritualistic invocation with an essentially different reality. This reality will remain intractable relative to the demands of the end-state principle, even with systematic attempts to enlarge the police powers and rectify the 'aberrations'. The sociological model of Man fails to recognise these problems and thus offers an excellent support for any end-state conception. Moreover, it offers an explanation for the inherent failure of the end-state principle's realisations. According to the sociological view, this can always be (and usually is) attributed to the prior corruption of the people associated with the political institution by their exposure to commercial values and the 'customs of the market place'. According to this view, the failure of the end-state principle results from the failure of people to accept the educational influence of political institutions.

Process Conception of Justice

Consider now the contrasting view represented by the process conception. In this context, Professor Nozick elaborated the entitlement theory of justice with great care. His theory is anchored by three principles: the principle of justice concerning transfers of entitlements, the principle concerning the original acquisition of unowned objects and, lastly, the principle of rectification. Any distribution of resources existing at any moment, whatever its characteristics or outcome patterns, satisfies the canons of justice, provided it results from an original acquisition and a sequence of transfers which are just. The justice of the present entitlement structure thus depends in principle on its complete history. It follows that any violation of the principle of just acquisition and transfer in the past must be rectified among the current entitlement holders. This argument, although appealing in many aspects, raises some difficult problems. These problems relate essentially to the historical character of the argument. The principle of original acquisition poses a fundamentally unanswerable question. We can hardly ever expect to settle, in any meaningful way, disputes over the justice of original acquisition. Similarly, the principle of rectification covering a long historical sequence of transfers, raises irresoluble questions. Attempts to apply these principles would require political institutions which create strong incentives perennially to raise questions about the justice of any given entitlement's historical background. The phenomena discussed above, associated with the ambivalence of political structure, also extend to this case. The possibility of challenging any prior steps in the sequence leading to any particular current entitlement offers opportunities to exploit the institutions designed for adjudication of such claims. A permissive interpretation of the principle of rectification covering a long historical span encourages attempts to extract wealth independent of productive effort.

The problems inherent in Professor Nozick's entitlement theory suggest that the historical emphasis may be eliminated from a useful conception of justice. The social cooperation within a group requires some basic 'rules of the game' which are generally understood and can be adjudicated without posing unanswerable questions or creating pervasive and strong incentives to modify the governing framework incessantly. The rules of the game assure both coherence and social cooperation for the social group. Thus, they contribute to the great benefits accruing from social organisation. They also influence the distribution of the resulting benefits. A wide variety of distributional patterns, however, is consistent with the general rules stated below. They cannot be defined in terms of any outcome pattern under the circumstances. The rules of the game controlling the social process that satisfies a criterion of processual justice are constituted by two sets of rights assigned to the members of the social group. Moreover, these sets of rights are anchored by a constitutional consensus determining the range and operation of political institutions. The assignment of rights so crucially characteristic for our purpose are described in the following passage:

'One class of rights which can be granted to individuals is limitless—limitless in the sense that granting a right to one person in no way limits the opportunity to offer the same right to others. Examples include the right to say or write what one wants (freedom of speech), the right to adhere to whatever religious convictions one chooses (freedom of religion), and the right to transfer rights that have been assigned to a particular individual or individuals to others (freedom of exchange). Everyone can be granted the right to say what they want. Everyone can be granted the right to transfer rights which they have to others. Everyone can be granted the right to hold whatever religious (or other) beliefs he or she chooses. All these rights can be granted to everyone without affecting the freedom of speech, exchange, or religion of anyone.

'The second class of rights available for assignment to individuals is limited and therefore scarce. The limitation is imposed on us by physical facts. Some actions which individuals take have physical consequences which forestall other actions. Two individuals cannot eat the same slice of bread. The same piece of steel cannot be embodied in two different automobiles. Two individuals cannot simultaneously stand or sit on the same spot at the same time. While two individuals can be given the right to say what they want, if they speak simultaneously in the same room at the same time, the sound waves they create will "interfere" in the ear of a listener. Nature imposes a set of constraints on the action we can take. When a scarce right is exercised alternative actions which might have been taken are physically eliminated from the set of possible actions, i.e., from the opportunity set.

'Physical incompatibility among actions creates a social problem. Some means must be found for resolving the question of which among many incompatible actions will be taken. Early humans probably resolved this question on the basis of physical prowess, but the central feature of what we call "societies" is the evolution of social institutions for resolving the conflict which physical incompatibility induces. In the end, some social institution, the law in any modern society, assigns the right to choose actions with specific objects to specific individuals or groups. Society sanctions or at least accepts the use of the police powers to enable individuals to exercise the rights assigned to them. Doing so, of course, means limiting the actions which others can take. Some individuals are thereby coerced into recognising the rights of others.

'Given what nature bestows on us, constraints of individual's actions will exist. Different societies can evolve different social institutions for determining who can take what actions with what objects, but nature's limitation on actions is inescapable. Freedom defined without regard to this fact would be a useless concept. Any sensible definition of freedom must sanction the use of coercion to resolve the physical incompatibility question.

'Using the distinction between scarce and non-scarce rights, we can define freedom so that it is not simply a question of robbing Peter to pay Paul. The definition contains two provisions: 1. Every individual must be granted all non-scarce rights, i.e., any denial of a non-scarce right to any individual is a violation of freedom; 2. All scarce rights must be assigned to someone, i.e., to deny to everyone in society a scarce right is a violation of freedom.

'To the authors, at least, this definition of freedom does not do violence to what most of us have in mind when we use that term. Moreover, the definition is not empty. It does enable us to say whether a particular constraint imposed by society reduces freedom.

'The moral foundation of this concept of freedom can be summarised in one simple principle. Nature provides man with a set of opportunities; it is morally wrong for society not to pass all of these opportunities on to individuals. Since non-scarce rights can be given to everyone, it is wrong to deny any individual those rights. Thus, the assignment of non-scarce rights under this definition, is egalitarian. Scarce rights, on the other hand, cannot be given to everyone, but it is morally wrong to deny a scarce right to everyone.'[10]

The basic rationale of political structure centres on the protection and adjudication of these rights. The resulting political functions include the essential provision of 'public goods'. All activities beyond this basic social role of political structure involve mainly redistributive operations which require an end-state principle for suitable justification. The constitutional consensus is thus required to formalise as a general understanding the crucial limitations on the range and operation of political institutions. The constitutional framework also has to specify the assignment of new rights made feasible as a result of new technologies. We also note that the first set of rights characterised above includes, in particular, provisions ensuring the maintenance of *open competition* within the political process and the social coordination emerging from market mechanisms. *Open competition*, in this context, forms an essential characteristic of the social process satisfying an alternative view of justice.

Unfortunately, this general outline has to be burdened with an unavoidable qualification. My previous discussion concerning the ambivalence of political structure implies that no social arrangement is protected against the incentives embedded in all political institutions. This problem afflicts all social arrangements. Social organisations differ, however, in terms of pervasiveness and magnitude of the affliction. The concentration of the state on its basic protective role maximises the cost of political activism or minimises the expected return from political investment. The process of modification remains comparatively slow and gradual under the circumstances.

Further Comparison of the Two Notions

The independence of 'processual justice' from specific and detailed outcome patterns renders it essentially unacceptable to ambitious political or 'socially committed' intellectuals. It should be obvious that this notion of justice clashes violently with any view requiring specific distributional results in one form or another. It certainly clashes with most of the prevailing justifications for a welfare state, with all justifications for a socialist society and with the array of actions and programmes subsumed under the title of 'energy policy' by the Carter Administration. It appears that the two opposite notions of justice could be evaluated usefully by some detailed examination of their respective consequences. In this respect, any application of the sociological model offers an inherent advantage over the end-state conception. It assures us that the outcome pattern satisfying the criterion of justice can be realised by

suitable institutionalisation. Moreover, the required social arrangement can be expected to be reasonably stable and well operated
apart from temporary 'human mistakes' associated with an inadequate choice of personnel. The sociological model also promises
that participants in the social game will eventually *learn* to prefer
this outcome pattern. Lastly, this model can only recognise 'chaotic
deviations' from the desired outcome patterns resulting under a
process conception justifying a vast programme of activist interventions by the government.

The REMM model implies, by contrast, a very different assessment. It emphasises that the rules of the game, defining the process
of social cooperation, produce a vast rise in real income per capita
compared with the 'state of nature'. It is possible, but hardly likely,
that a member of the social group who is actively involved in social
interaction does not benefit from the social productivity of social
organisation. Moreover, the rules of the game defining a minimal
state offer the strongest incentives for the intelligent use of human
and non-human resources and thus promise the largest *maintained*
increase of society's real income per capita. They allow and en-
courage a broader scope for the spontaneous emergence of a wide
array of private organisations aimed at coping with a variety of
social issues and private transfers. Furthermore, the REMM model
reveals insights into the consequences resulting from any attempted
institutionalisation of end-state principles. It alerts us to unintended
but systematic results produced by political institutions and makes
us appreciate that these consequences usually dominate the intended
results or motivating expectations. We are most particularly
cautioned by the fact that the patterned outcome of the social
process consistent with an end-state principle can hardly be achieved
with a stable range of predictably functioning political institutions.
An expanding range of political agencies creates new dimensions
and aspects of distributional patterns which deviate substantially
from the general idea reflected, for operational purposes, in the
specific criteria of justice. The occurrence of a large array of political
institutions discriminates, for instance, in favour of those participants in the social game who enjoy a comparative advantage in the
political market place. Any attempt to impose an end-state conception on the social game will eventually lower the social productivity
of social organisation. It also involves the endless pursuit of an
illusion with a persistent shrinkage of the range of private actions
available to individuals.

SELECTED ISSUES

A number of special aspects or issues still require more explicit explanation. The discussion here should clarify, in a somewhat more concrete context, the general remarks made in the previous sections. I am most particularly concerned with arguments advanced in justification of 'governmental regulation' beyond the range of the 'minimal state' described above.

Problem with Moral Discussions

Social and political philosophy is permeated with normative statements. Most discussions of the 'Good Society' consist of elaborate exercises in moral evaluations and judgments based on more or less developed arguments justifying the normative standards used for these purposes. It is unfortunate that these evaluations and judgments are usually sealed in a philosophical vacuum safely separated from any historical reality. Moral principles are adduced in order to justify the application or extension of political institutions, subjecting a larger part of the social organisation to the state's police power. Observed violation of some normative or moral standard is found to offer, *per se,* sufficient reason or justifiable grounds for the use of this power. But this philosophical exercise, which usually proceeds with intelligence and sincerity, rarely examines the nature of the required political institutions. Thus, it seems particularly oblivious to the incentive structures created by the institutionalisation of the legislated moral standards. This implies, moreover, that the actual consequences of the legislated moral principles are poorly conceived and thoroughly misunderstood. Most of the moral discussions of socio-political phenomena should be clearly recognised to be *either irrelevant, as they stand, or false.* They are irrelevant to the extent that they proceed totally within an institutional vacuum, conveying the impression that the moral principles are *somehow* transformed into distributional realisations. Many discussions of socio-political norms and the associated moral arguments can be re-interpreted, however, as an implicit background argument based on the sociological model of Man. A conjunction of moral precepts of socio-political standards with the specific form of the sociological view expressed by the 'goodwill' or 'public-interest theory' of government, actually yields a positive statement about the world. This statement is blatantly falsified, however, by the historical facts concerning the operation of political institutions.

A discussion at a conference held in 1979 exemplifies the 'institutional vacuum' so characteristically built into arguments proceeding in the tradition of moral philosophy.[11] A moral dilemma was presented to the listeners in the following terms. Suppose there is a lady with a wig and a man with a pot of water (don't ask why) participating in a social event. The wig catches fire and you, as a participant, must decide between violating the man's property right to the water (voluntary transactions are excluded by explicit postulation) in order to save the lady or letting the lady burn to death while acknowledging the man's property right. The rationale of the 'moral dilemma' elaborated over a lengthy period was very clear. Property rights should not be 'absolute'. They should be adjustable in response to evolving requirements imposed by the environment and in accordance with an implicit end-state principle. The institutional requirements of this theory with the associated social consequences and the expected adjustments in the social process were systematically disregarded by the philosophers.

A social scientist trained to use the tools of economic analysis would object to the transformation of a problem involving a *private* moral choice into a *social* problem. The participants at the social event do confront a moral problem: to violate a property right or to fail in a moral obligation to help. The philosophical arguments were designed to remove the *private* moral dilemma by sacrificing the private property right. But this ploy will not work without a sociological model of Man and a commitment to an end-state *principle*. Once we reject these two pillars we are forced to acknowledge the *private* moral dilemma of each participant from which there is no escape. He must decide either to rob the water and *pay the consequences* or let the lady burn and wrestle with his conscience and his god for the rest of his life. The processual view of justice thus leads to an understanding of the serious moral dilemmas facing *individual* members of a social group which cannot be resolved by a social contrivance. The *individual* bears the moral and resource cost of his decision. But this is ultimately what any reflection on moral behaviour involves in all fringe cases constituting the range of dilemmas. In this context the philosophers attempted to deny the occurrence of genuine *private* moral problems, once 'suitable' social arrangements prevailed. An implicit use of the sociological perception of Man supplemented with an end-state principle removes any further need for a searching analysis of the required social institutions.

N

A specific example drawn from an advocate of moral arguments in support of detailed regulatory actions may usefully illustrate my point. We learn that 'economists profess an unequivocal anti-paternalism that one suspects is influenced as much by the neatness of the mathematically deducible conclusions regarding social welfare that neoclassical micro-economic theory can produce given non-paternalistic assumptions . . . '.[12] The crucial point is hardly connected in any relevant sense with the neatness of 'mathematical deducibility'. It is related to the substance of the central core anchoring economic theory. This central core is expressed by the REMM model—which poses serious and somewhat unpleasant questions to any paternalistic position. The latter favours the systematic use of coercive police powers operated by some political institutions. The REMM model tends to expose the true, unintended and unanticipated (by the advocates of police powers) consequences of the resulting exercises with police powers. A defensible paternalistic position unavoidably requires some variant of the sociological model of Man as an intellectual basis. Economists with sufficient understanding of their subject matter thus object to paternalistic endeavours, not because they are devoted to mathematical neatness but because they suspect the empirical fallacy of paternalistic views justified by an implicit advocacy of a sociological model of Man. We may add, in the present context, that a paternalistic approach to policy is substantially conditioned under most circumstances by an end-state view of justice.

Normative Transformation of the Concept of Rights

The scarcity rights which, together with the rights to acquire and unload property rights, constitute the rules of the game and characterise a process conception of justice, do not possess any normative connotation. They involve positive descriptions of entitlements to resources or to specifiable aspects or dimensions of resources. Many recent discussions, however, reveal the ambiguity in the use of the word 'rights' which has evolved in the public arena. On many occasions, particularly in discussions of moral aspects or of socio-political norms associated with some concept of justice, the use of the word 'right' shifts subtly from a positive, descriptive connotation to a normative judgment. This shift changes radically the intellectual positions involved—sometimes, it appears, without the speaker or the author being aware of the problems involved. Some cases from recent discussions may illustrate the nature of the issue.

The role of a minimal state is generally recognised as being centred on its protective function, including the protection of property rights and adjudication of rival claims. A case for enlarging the admissible range of political institutions beyond the minimal state proceeds on the basis of subtle modifications of the term 'rights' essentially assuming a normative meaning. Some examples of this pervasive trend may be considered at this stage. It is argued in particular that the provision of 'public goods' unavoidably remains below a social optimum under the circumstances. The participants in the social game suffer from the typical characteristics of a 'prisoner's dilemma'. Everybody would be better off with the full provision of public goods, but no private supplier experiences an incentive to produce the public goods with the expectation of a serious 'free-rider' problem. The argument usually continues with the declaration that the state is the only agency capable of resolving the prisoner's dilemma. The police power associated with a political institution removes the free-rider problems and all participants in the social game enjoy an opportunity to benefit from the optimal provision of public goods. The argument is strengthened further by the assertion that the members of the social group possess (really) a right to the public goods. The non-provision of these goods in the context of a minimal state violates a basic right of the people, under certain circumstances. Suitable protection of the public by the state against such violation—the very function of the state—requires, therefore, an extension of governmental activities beyond the minimal state. But the right to 'public goods', so unobtrusively slipped into the argument, is not the same kind as the positive descriptive rights clarifying potentially rival claims on scarce resources. The 'rights' to public goods express a normative judgment in the nature of an end-state principle. Once we accept such extensions of the terminology there is hardly any social issue which could not be formulated as a 'violation of rights' requiring redress by suitable application of the state's police powers. Beyond the questionable extension of 'rights' the argument involves an essentially analytic-empirical problem. The provision of public goods is presented as an essential and unavoidable function of political institutions. Recent research, however, raises some doubts about the standard interpretation of public goods, their relevance and the necessary involvement of the state. Furthermore, we note that, once again, the whole argument predicates the sociological model of Man with a version of the public-interest theory of government. Lastly, we observe as an empirical fact that the provision of public goods beyond the protection of rights and their adjudication forms a negligible proportion of the government's activities. The government dominantly provides *private* goods and services to selected groups of participants.

Another example regarding the shift in meaning associated with the term 'right' may be noted here. Some authors assert that future generations have rights which justifiably call for our attention. The protection of these rights again requires powers to enforce these rights on the current generation. The juxtaposition of 'human rights' with property rights and the interpretation of these rights as allocative claims on specific resources to be guaranteed by the state, offer another example of the shifting usage of words. It should be clearly recognised, however, that these extensions are not innocuous, appealing as they may appear. Such extensions involve an implicit rejection of a process conception of justice and a corresponding acceptance of an end-state principle expressed by the array of 'human rights' laid down. The normative and positive meanings of the terms are difficult to reconcile. The normative meaning must be associated with a sociological view of Man in order to justify its relevance, whereas the REMM model is more typically associated with the positive descriptive notion. And, most importantly, the normative meaning establishes claims which essentially erode the content of the positive, descriptive rights regarding aspects or dimensions of scarce resources. Thus, the formulation of 'human rights' forms one of the most effective contemporary strategies in the political market-place for the transformation of society in accordance with end-state principles of justice.

Comparative Advantages of Government

The argument justifying an extended range of political institutions well beyond the minimal state occasionally invokes systematic advantages of one kind or another in the governmental provision of specific services. We may read that a government possesses a major advantage in the collection, preparation, interpretation and provision of information about a variety of aspects pertaining to our environment. Others argue that high transaction costs preclude the emergence of socially useful private transactions. High transaction costs also prevent the consideration of the 'undefined property rights' of third parties. Quite generally, a variety of market failures 'obviously' justifies the application of police powers exercised by an extended array of political institutions. Lastly, individual members of society frequently reveal by their actions a willingness to shift some dimension of their decision making pertaining to specific aspects of their life to other people or to agencies. The argument then progresses from this fact to the proposition that governmental agencies offer substantial advantages for the execution of such decision making on behalf of other people.

The fact brought out in the last point is, indeed, well observed. But advocates of the subsequent argument usually fail to recognise the nature of the agency problem associated with the delegation of decision making. The agency problem, embedded in agent-principal relationships of any kind, has recently been attracting increased research attention: the principal faces the perennial problem that he cannot reasonably expect his preferences to be fully and passively reflected by the agent. The latter expresses his own preferences and experiences his own interests. This discrepancy of interests and preferences poses a monitoring problem for the principal. The larger this problem, expressed by the costs of monitoring, the greater will be the potential leeway for the agent to satisfy his own interests at the expense of the principal. Perfect and costless monitoring occurs only in never-never land. The competitive market has therefore developed a large array of arrangements designed to cope with the unavoidable monitoring costs. Competitive suppliers of decision-making services offer, in their own interest, guarantees, information channels and other devices in order to lower the demanders' uncertainty. Competition thus induces a sharing of the monitoring cost between the parties. In the context of such competition, both demanders and suppliers can tailor the nature, dimensions and duration of the delegation of decision-making authority in many different ways. The market in decision delegation, however, continues to experience monitoring costs and some amount of fraud. The simple fact that resources must be allocated to any monitoring activity determines that the social optimum of monitoring costs and fraud, given the positive expected return from the agency relation, also remains positive.

A sociological model of Man implies a fundamental difference between the agency relation on the commercial market and the agency relation in the context of political arrangements. According to this view, monitoring costs and potential fraud result typically from the preferences and interest cultivated by the market place. The dissociation of political institutions from private ownership and private profits assures us, so it seems, that agencies in the political market place will attend faithfully to the *best* interests of the private principals. This judgement is subtly reinforced by pervasive end-state conceptions of justice. Such conceptions usually find the very occurrence of fraud morally offensive. The end-state principles require, in this context, a political structuring which removes fraud. In the public arena, the emotional force of Ralph Nader, the American consumer advocate, hardly emanates from the sociological view expressing superior attention to public interests by political institutions. It seems to result, to a large extent, from the sense of outrage that a perceived, just human condition is violated by the occurrence—however infrequent—of fraudulent transactions.

But the sense of outrage supported by an end-state conception of justice provides no relevant justification for the superior agency quality of political institutions. At this point the argument must invoke the sociological model. But the comparative success that economic analysis has achieved, over many decades and on a broad front, confirms the analytic-empirical superiority of the REMM model and the resulting analysis produces a radically different evaluation of agency relations in the political market. The monitoring costs confronting the principals are typically much higher in the political market than in the commercial market. Moreover, the agent frequently enjoys a much higher degree of monopoly power in the political market. We should therefore expect that the preferences of principals will be less effectively represented by a *political* agency relation. Invocation of end-state principles of justice by political agents' justifying actions for the *best* interests of others not really appreciated by principals (that is, citizens), enlarges the opportunities to disregard the principals' preferences. An analysis of the agency problem thus produces substantial scepticism about a justifiable extension of political institutions on the grounds indicated.

The arguments based on a comparative information advantage and on market failures suffer from the same flaws elaborated upon in the previous paragraph. The force of both arguments depends on the sociological model supplemented with an empirical assertion that the social cost of governmental operations is substantially below the market solution. These two strands of the justifying argument are actually, to some extent, interrelated. The alternative model emphasises, on the other hand, the externalities imposed by political institutions. It also reveals the pervasive incentives built into the operation of political institutions to 'dis-inform' the public. These incentives are not balanced by any inherent economic or techno-logical advantage in information production. Systematic lying, cover-ups and persistent distortion of facts are in general less likely and less successful in the competitive commercial market-place over the longer run than in the political market-place. The control mechanisms built into a competitive market system are substantially weakened in the context of political institutions.

Public Interest and the α-β Syndrome

The trend in the lower courts in the legal system offers remark-able material demonstrating the victorious sweep of end-state conceptions in our legal thinking. The following quote is significant for our purposes:

'What has happened, under the attempted due process rationale, is that property rights, as we have traditionally known them, are subserved to what is presumed to be the public interest or general welfare. The public interest is defined by the legislature. This means that the strong interests in a community . . . are able to influence social events via the manipulation of police powers.'

The positive explanation of these developments was outlined on another occasion and the reader is referred to the appropriate material on the growth of 'government'.[13] This analysis demonstrates that, by contrast with the sociological interpretation of non-(commercial) market events, the outcome of political action can hardly be assigned the connotation of 'public interest' with its usual undertone of moral approval and ethical justification.

Our attention at this stage should be addressed, however, to the 'ideology' expressed by the justification of the trend in lower court decisions. The interpretation of legislative actions as an expression of the public interest over-riding property rights, demonstrates an effective use of end-state conceptions for purposes of wealth re-distribution. It is immaterial at this stage whether everybody participating in the process fully believes in the end-state principle of justice involved. The very formulation of the legal argument reflects, however, the occurrence of at least some believers in the political market place. Whatever the distribution of believers may be, we find, under the circumstances, that end-state conceptions of justice are systematically exploited by manipulators of political institutions in order to extend the range of political control over resources. The progress ineradicably involves a persistent erosion of both non-scarcity and scarcity rights. The whole trend reveals most clearly that a system of positive rights is an obstacle to any end-state conception of justice. This obstacle can only be overcome with an open-ended extension of political institutions. Moreover, this extension must be buttressed in the market-place of ideas with the support offered by the sociological model and a suitable perception of justice.

The combination of end-state and sociological perceptions prevalent among the intelligentsia manning the political institutions also explains the frequency occurrence of the α-β syndrome. This syndrome is well expressed in the motivation for pharmaceutical regulation: a regulation justified in terms of the human cost incurred by dangerous pharmaceutical products. The argument is frequently enlarged with overtones from the sociological model. We are told that private producers enmeshed in commercial transactions governed by profit-seeking activities cannot be expected to control the health hazards of their products. It is suggested that profit-seeking producers systematically supply dangerous drugs. The moral outrage of the undeniable human cost reinforces the sociological interpretation. Under the circumstances, an end-state conception can comfortably argue that political institutions must replace the market and control the relevant resources in order to remove the hazards. The force of the justifying argument remains intact in spite of the fallacies of the sociological model used in this context. It is enhanced by the systematic commission of the human costs produced under the regulation. This regulation is designed to lower the likelihood of costly hazards associated with new drugs without ever considering the potential human cost unleashed by the regulation. The latter cost results from the curtailed rate of innovations and the decrease in supply of important drugs.[14] The syndrome has increasingly governed the decisions in lower American courts.[15]

This issue can be clarified with the aid of some statistical concepts drawn from the theory of hypotheses-testing. Any test situation facing two alternative and conflicting hypotheses involves two potential errors. The first (or α) error arises when the observations lead us to reject a true hypothesis and the second (β) error occurs whenever we accept a false hypothesis. Now consider any pharmaceutical innovation. The following decision problem confronts the regulator. He can either accept or reject the innovation and in either case he faces a social risk expressed by the matrix arrangement below.

states actions	hazardous	good
reject	o.k.	risk
accept	risk	o.k.

FIGURE 16.1

If he rejects a hazardous drug, no problem arises. But he may reject a good drug on the basis of his incomplete information. This means that more people will die or suffer from diseases as a result of unavailable drugs and cures. On the other hand, whenever he approves a new drug he may run the risk of accepting a hazardous drug. The risk of rejecting a good drug corresponds in this context to the α-error and the risk of accepting a hazardous drug measures the β-error. The incentives of the political market-place induce the regulator to minimise the β-error without much attention to the α-error. This behaviour is better explained by the REMM model than by the sociological model. Realisations of the β-error appear in the form of generally observable events and usually with some dramatic force on the public scene. The β-error thus triggers a strong feedback mechanism on the regulating agency via the political market-place. There is, however, no feedback mechanism encouraging the regulator to pay attention to the α-error. The media do not connect potentially preventable deaths and chronic diseases with non-produced drugs. Observations from Hearings in the United States Congress reveal that politicians suffer from similar inabilities.

The resulting asymmetry thus associates a large α-error with a small β-error. The combination of errors tends actually to be sub-optimal and the net effect produces a *larger* human cost and more unnecessary suffering. This result is crucially conditioned by the incentive structure of the political institutions. An end-state view of justice, motivated by the visible suffering emerging from β-errors and buttressed by an essentially sociological interpretation of regulatory activities, thus effectively justifies the extension of police

P

powers. Important aspects of the problem expressed are omitted by a determined disregard for the α-error.

CONCLUSION

The essay submitted to the reader's attention can hardly do more than alert him to some fundamental issues controlling the future of Western democracies. Its theme is simple: two pairs of ideas exert a subtle but powerful influence on the prevailing views about the role of political structure in the coordination of our social affairs. The sociological perception of Man, supplemented with an end-state perception of justice, effectively justifies an increasing political structure of pronounced reliance on such a structure as a medium of social coordination. The two perceptions reinforce and depend on each other in this context. The victorious sweep of these ideas produces—unavoidably, under the circumstances—a clear trend towards a socialist society. The combination of the two perceptions cannot be reconciled by advocating a minimal government controlled by severe constitutional limitations. Support for the latter case stems from the 'Scottish Model' of Man and a process perception of justice. Advocates of social activism, however, will hardly recognise any sense of social justice in this position and, of course, judged in the context of their views, this is well justified. But they fail to examine or understand the real consequences of their position. They favour a view of Man operating in a society which has no historical relevance and posit a notion of justice which is sadly only an illusion.

The alternative perceptions unfortunately offer little emotional satisfaction, but then, they are not offered to placate Man's ineradicable metaphysical drive. They describe an intellectual position within a society which relates social justice to freedom. In a way, this position erodes the concept of justice as a social concept guiding *public* policy via social structures. Justice, like morality and moral decisions, is a *private* concept expressing a private conscience.

A society with a minimal and widely decentralised political structure offers the only opportunity for genuine moral decisions and concerns of justice. The imposition of such 'decisions' and concerns with the aid of coercive police powers destroys the meaning of moral behaviour. A 'moral society' places the responsibility for moral decisions with individuals and their conscience and not with the police powers of the state's apparatus. This emphasis refers to issues not adequately elaborated in this essay. Serious questions and important aspects of the problem under consideration remain. We need to explore these problems on another occasion.

NOTES AND REFERENCES

1. Many discussions with William Meckling, of the Graduate School of Management, University of Rochester, New York, Allan H. Meltzer and Maurice Falk, of Carnegie-Mellon University, Pittsburgh, influenced my thinking in the range of problems covered in this essay. All three will still recognise aspects of the argument requiring further exploration in the future. A first draft was exposed to the critique of my colleagues at the seventh Interlaken Seminar on Analysis and Ideology, 1980. William Ryker also contributed valuable comments.

2. Karl Brunner and William H. Meckling, 'The Perception of Man and the Conception of Government', *Journal of Money, Credit and Banking*, Columbus, Ohio, No. 1, 1977.

3. *Ibid.*, pp. 71-2.

4. *Ibid.*, pp. 72-3.

5. You are referred to the paper authored jointly with Meckling, where the different approaches to political structure built into the alternative perception of Man are discussed in some detail.

6. Friedrich A. von Hayek, *Law, Legislation and Liberty: a New Statement of the Liberal Principles of Justice and Political Economy*, Vols 1-3 (Chicago: University of Chicago Press, various years) and Robert Nozick, *Anarchy, State and Utopia* (New York: Basic Books, 1974).

7. *Ibid.*, p. 172.

8. This issue involves a generalisation of the 'Lukasz effect', which is well established in the theory of stabilisation policy.

9. Brunner, 'Reflections on the Political Economy of Government: the Persistent Growth of Government', *Schweizerische Zeitschrift für Volkswirtschaft und Statistik*, No. 3, 1978, pp. 659-61.

10. Clifford G. Holderness, Michael C. Jensen and Meckling, 'The Logic of the First Amendment', paper presented at the eighth Interlaken Seminar on Analysis and Ideology, 1981, mimeograph.

11. The conference referred to was sponsored by the Liberty Fund (Indianapolis) and held in Santa Barbara, California, in November 1979.

12. Steve Kelman, 'Regulation and Paternalism', paper presented at the Liberty Fund conference, Santa Barbara, 1979, mimeograph.

13. Jensen and Meckling, 'Theory of the Firm: Managerial Behavior, Agency Costs and Ownership Structure', *Journal of Financial Economics*, Amsterdam, No. 4, 1976.

14. Norman Karlin, 'Some Economic Consequences of Substantive Due Process', draft paper prepared for the Liberty Fund conference, Santa Barbara, 1979, mimeograph.

15. The reader many consult Sam Peltzman, 'An Evaluation of Consumer Protection Legislation: The 1962 Drug Amendments', *Journal of Political Economy*, Chicago, No. 5, 1973.

17 Schumpeter and Hayek: on Some Similarities in their Thought

Erich Streissler

Herbert Giersch, as one of the leading members of the Mont Pélerin Society, founded by Friedrich A. von Hayek, and as one of the leading liberal (or libertarian) economists in West Germany, has always been close in his thinking to the Mises-Hayek tradition of economic philosophy. Yet recently he has become renowned for his enthusiasm for Schumpeter and the concept of the Schumpeterian innovator—the creative entrepreneur.[1] Is there not an inherent contradiction in such a double affiliation?

To some this would appear to be so. While Professor Hayek is certainly considered univerally as an economist in the tradition of the Austrian school of economics, many would deny that Schumpeter belonged to this school.[2]

In fact, a certain curious, modern American sect[3] has tried to pre-empt the term 'Austrian school', applying it only to those economists who were pupils of Ludwig von Mises, which Schumpeter never was. Some would like to exclude him from the Austrian tradition solely on the grounds that he was a founding member of the Econometric Society or because he thought Leon Walras the greatest economic theorist who ever lived.[4] Others regarded Schumpeter as a socialist[5] and wanted to exclude him from the Austrian tradition for political reasons. They were misled by the particular interest shown by Schumpeter—and many of the other great Austrian economists—in Marxist economics. They confused analysis of abstract thought with adherence to, or at least a certain contamination by, an ideology. The interest of Austrian economists in Marxist economics has, in fact, also received the opposite misinterpretation; that is, that the 'Subjective Value School'—the Austrian brand of the Marginalist Revolution—was purposely designed as an intellectual counter-revolution to the Marxist challenge in economics.[6] This misinterpretation can only have come about through the influence of Marxist economists who, in

356

their self-aggrandisement, thought that mainstream economists took them as seriously as they took themselves. The Austrian economists, along with Knut Wicksell's Swedish school (an off-shoot of the Austrian tradition), were the only ones to take any interest in Marxist economics. All the other mainstream schools simply ignored it. (Marxist economics did not, in fact, come to be more generally recognised until World War II.) The Austrian school was thus assigned the role of a reactionary counter-revolutionary movement.

The Austrians themselves did not become interested in Marxist economics until some time after the tradition had started—in 1871—but this was well before Marxism became politically important. Friedrich von Wieser, in his first book and Eugen von Böhm-Bawerk, in his second—both published in 1884[7]—considered Karl Marx an important economist to be analysed as such alongside the other great economists. They were the first mainstream economists to take notice of him.

Yet it appears that they became interested in Marx for a purely endogenous reason of scientific development: Marx, as a theoretician, was interested in exactly the same questions which were always of particular interest to the Austrian school—capital theory and monetary theory. For that very reason, Böhm-Bawerk's famous series of discussions throughout 1905-6 was attended not only by Schumpeter and Mises but also by leading Marxist and socialist economists such as Otto Bauer, Rudolph Hilferding and Emil Lederer. Also for this reason, theoretical strands of analysis found in Marx became intertwined with some of Schumpeter's ideas, just as they did with the ideas of Mises and Professor Hayek, whom nobody would classify as socialists. As Gottfried Haberler stresses,[8] Schumpeter never was a socialist on the ideological level. He was an economist in the liberal tradition—admittedly more in the somewhat muted tradition of Wieser than that of the austere Böhm-Bawerk, which Mises and Professor Hayek followed, but still he was decidely liberal.

Professor Haberler, in his great biographical article on Schumpeter, emphasises that he did not belong to any particular school; he was completely original.[9] Original ideas are, of course, contained within the thoughts of every great scholar, particularly if he has the same strong desire for originality that Schumpeter had. But if he develops his ideas in a cohesive intellectual climate with marked peculiarities of thought, he cannot help being influenced in many ways. It is true that Schumpeter, the *enfant terrible*, diverged from tradition on many points particularly dear to the leaders of the Austrian school, which tends to support the contention that he was not a member of the school. On the other hand, he took up so many of the ideas then current only in the Austrian economic tradition that any hypothetical historian of economic thought, not knowing Schumpeter to be an Austrian, could immediately trace him to this school. To mention only one of the ideas which link him to other protagonists of the same intellectual tradition: the innovative 'Schumpeterian' entrepreneur, the glorified leading figure of the capitalist process, is actually one of Wieser's ideas,[10] which Schumpeter merely amplified and embellished. I shall, therefore, attempt in this short essay to show some of the similarities in the basic ideas of Schumpeter and Professor Hayek. In pointing out these similarities, I shall endeavour to show that there is thus no contradiction at all in the deep admiration which Professor Giersch shows for both Professor Hayek and Schumpeter.

THE REAL EFFECTS OF CREDIT

One of the Marxist ideas which became intertwined in the web of ideas emanating from the Austrian economists in the first decade of the twentieth century was the importance of the role of credit to the real structure of economic development. Few historians of economic thought, though, would recognise this idea as Marxist, for as such it has no value connotation. It is, however, an idea which is decidely at variance with orthodox classical economics and, too, with the generality of neoclassical thought; that is, that part which John Maynard Keynes also termed 'classical'. These classical traditions see money as a mere veil and therefore deny that money and credit have any influence on real magnitudes. Marx, on the other hand, mixed a full measure of pre-classical, mercantilist thought into his brand of classical economics—see, for example, his denial of Say's Law. The transformation of capital goods into money and back into capital goods was of great interest to him. As early as the first volume of *Das Kapital*,[11] and even more so in the third,[12] he saw banks as foci of great importance in the capitalist process. True, the importance of banks for industrial development had been stressed in popular concepts of economic policy, particularly in the Crédit Mobilier movement of the brothers Emile and Isaac Pereire which emanated from France around the middle of the nineteenth century and took particularly strong root in Austria.[13] But it had not been recognised in high economic theory before Marx.

The Austrians' interest in, and their minute knowledge of, Marx and the practical civil service lore of economic policy in which its leaders—and particularly Böhm-Bawerk—were steeped, thus combined to produce an out-crop of ideas on the real effect of credit closely paralleling contemporary Marxist development. The importance of credit for causing cyclical fluctuations in the economy, the so-called Austrian business-cycle theory, was first presented in germinal form in 1912 by Mises[14] and later given substance by Professor Hayek.[15] In the same year, but at an earlier date, Schumpeter, in his famous *Theory of Economic Development*,[16] presented his analysis of the effects, on both long-run and cyclical development, of credit extended by the banks to newly founded enterprises. (His analysis of credit is more central to his main theme and much more extensive than that of Mises.) Two years later, one of the two doyens of the Austrian school, Wieser, incorporated an extensive analysis of credit into his comprehensive theoretical treatise;[17] and the other doyen, Böhm-Bawerk himself, defined the external credit extended by foreigners to Austria as the major factor in turning the balance of trade into deficit (although here the real culprit, in good liberal tradition, is the government deficit, which is financed by external credit).[18] The Marxist participants of Böhm-Bawerk's series of discussions can, however, claim priority over Schumpeter; Hilferding published *Das Finanzkapital* in 1910.[19] Ideas similar to those of the mainstream Austrians on the role of credit and banks in fostering cyclical movements were later propounded by Lederer[20] and also probably developed during his Vienna days.

Strange bedfellows make for strange ideas. None of the Austrians had any qualms about attributing important distributional consequences on income to monetary influences—and that was for the first time since Richard Cantillon, one of Professor Hayek's favourite authors.[21] Distributional consequences of credit creation form the basis of the analyses of Mises[22] and, subsequently, Professor Hayek no less than they do for Schumpeter. All of them picture the economic process as usually being out of equilibrium. In a situation of disequilibrium, individual incomes and functional income shares are not determined by marginal productivities. They are determined by disequilibrium prices (relative to the long-run static equilibrium) caused by the creation of additional bank credit. The idea that prices are not at any moment in time in long-run equilibrium came naturally to members of the Austrian school, for its founder, Carl Menger,[23] had already adopted this kind of disequilibrium thinking. Even Böhm-Bawerk claimed that distributional prices were determined by economic laws only in the long run.[24]

This means, however, that for Mises and Professor Hayek no less than for Schumpeter, actual everyday market prices embody a large measure of *wrong information*. The market interest rate misleads entrepreneurs when choosing the optimum capital intensity. The idea of divergence between the real return on capital and the market rate of interest for credit is attributed to Wicksell,[25] who is closely linked with the Austrian tradition, but who is also another thorough expert on Marx. He particularly stresses the *time* it was likely to take for this divergence to disappear.[26] Credit markets thus have decisive negative external effects. Other distributional prices, according to the later general Austrian tradition, do not correspond to long-run supply and demand factors either. As to relative commodity prices, Mises and Professor Hayek (in particular) never tire of stressing how these are warped and stretched out by monetary influences into strange disequilibrium shapes. Mises evidently was very proud of having instigated the 'Austrian' business-cycle theory; otherwise his pupil and admirer, Murray Rothbard, would hardly have stressed that he originated it.[27] (Schumpeter's version of cyclical development is, in fact, somewhat different, as he stresses innovation and not mere routine investment as the driving force of the cycle.) The consequence of the Austrian theory is that prices in a credit-oriented market economy embody a great deal of wrong information most of the time. In the case of Mises, it is particularly amusing to see him attempt to have his cake and eat it too. In his famous book *Die Gemeinwirtschaft*,[28] he bases his claim that a socialist society will inevitably be inefficient on the fact that it lacks a price system, the essential instrument for correct economic planning. This lack is particularly grievous under dynamic conditions. As he admits, 'eine stationäre Wirtschaft könnte nur zur Not ohne Wirtschaftsrechnung auskommen'.[29] He forgets that, according to his own analysis, in everything other than stationary situations economic agents in a market economy are not *correctly* informed by the price system.

THE PRICE SYSTEM

The Austrians stress repeatedly and in many contexts that the general public may be persistently misinformed. These ideas, no less familiar to Schumpeter than to Mises and Professor Hayek, seem strange to present-day neo-classicists. They appear to be in basic conflict with the modern notion of rational expectations.[30] There may certainly be some white noise in the perception of economic messages by the general public.[31] But is this not being gradually filtered out as time goes on and the unchanging social system is perceived more clearly?[32]

This is, in fact, a serious argument against Professor Hayek's notion that easy credit conditions cause entrepreneurs to embark on over-investment sprees in spite of the fact that they cannot complete the roundabout processes, as eventually credit runs out or, at least, becomes too expensive. Here the basic 'system' remains the same. Why, then, do entrepreneurs not learn from their experience? At best one can assume that it is always the newly emerging entrepreneurs who get bitten. Even so, it is difficult to understand why they do not learn from their predecessors.

Here Schumpeter's concept is on surer ground. He explicitly assumes 'spontane und diskontinuierliche—"ruckweise"—Veränderungen' and 'eine plötzliche Veränderung der Daten ... Anlass ... für andere als schrittweise Anpassungen [des] Verhaltens'.[33] Sudden and large changes in the economic system occur and are perceived to occur, making any attempt at step-by-step approximation to the new situation appear nonsensical. Precisely because of such discrete changes in the environment, together with the inability of the economic agents to formulate expectational rules, it is impossible to postulate the necessity of convergence to rational expectation equilibria.[34] The concept behind Schumpeter's assumed situations of partially wrong beliefs is thus logically consistent, although possibly factually wrong. Schumpeter also implicitly offers a link between the idea that, in a market economy, prices frequently yield wrong information (as propounded in the Austrian theory of the business cycle) and the other, no less Austrian theory, first propounded by Wieser[35] and later by Professor Hayek,[36] that prices are inestimable instruments of decision taking, that they secure the use of knowledge accumulated in society and that competition is a discovery procedure. Schumpeter always saw two sides to everything and this, in particular, distinguishes his thought from that of the other economists. The entrepreneur is the agent of creative destruction: he creates progress and destroys the outmoded, static capitalists who function merely in an administrative capacity. Inflation certainly is 'harmful' because of its distributional consequences; but it can also be a positive source of economic growth. The same is true of monopoly and so on. Nothing is an unmitigated good: everything has its cost.

We can thus find a compromise between the two contradictory ideas propounded by Mises and Professor Hayek in different works: the price system is both highly confusing and highly informative. It is confusing, particularly in its short-run aspects and the closer we get to purely financial markets; it is informative, particularly in its long-run movements. Such a compromise view also has important consequences for economic policy—it implies that extremes should not be sought after. A price system may be more informative on average if it does not react too quickly to changes in supply and demand. An economy may be more stable if economic agents do not react too quickly to price signals which, after all, may be false. Seen in this way, transaction and information costs, as well as a certain amount of inertia in response, may be aberrations from the model of perfect competition; yet they may guarantee the smoother working of the free enterprise system.[37]

NOTES AND REFERENCES

1. Herbert Giersch, 'Aspects of Growth, Structural Change, and Employment—a Schumpeterian Perspective', *Weltwirtschaftliches Archiv*, Kiel, No. 4, 1979.

2. See Gottfried Haberler, 'Joseph Alois Schumpeter', *The Quarterly Journal of Economics*, Cambridge, Massachusetts, August 1950, pp. 342-43 and p. 344. Professor Haberler says 'his earliest writings . . . show little specifically "Austrian" influence' (p. 343); I beg to differ on this point.

3. See Edwin G. Dolan (ed.), *The Foundations of Modern Austrian Economics* (New York: New York University Press, 1976). One might well ask how far the ideas propounded in this volume are either 'modern' or representative of the full Austrian tradition.

4. See Haberler, *loc. cit.*, p. 342.

5. Edgar Salin, for example, in the preface to the German edition of *Capitalism, Socialism and Democracy* (New York: Harper & Row, 1942), said 'Schumpeter ist Sozialist'. See Joseph A. Schumpeter, *Kapitalismus, Sozialismus und Demokratie*, 4th ed. (Munich: Francke, 1975), p. 8.

6. See Harry G. Johnson, 'The Keynesian Revolution and the Monetarist Counter-Revolution', *The American Economic Review*, Evanston, Illinois, No. 2, 1981. On p. 2 Johnson says: 'By contrast with the abundance of revolutions, counter-revolutions are hard to find in the development of economic thought. About the closest one can come to a counter-revolution . . . is to interpret the development of the Austrian theory of value as a counter-revolution against the socialist, and especially the Marxist, tradition of economic theorizing'. Evidently Johnson knew the work of the Austrians only from hearsay.

7. Friedrich von Wieser, in the preface to his book *Uber den Ursprung und die Hauptgesetze des wirtschaftlichen Werthes* (Vienna: Alfred Hölder, 1884), names only five economists: Ricardo, Jevons, Menger, Marx and Engels. In the text there are some fleeting references to Marx (which, however, as always with Wieser in this book, are made without mentioning his name explicitly). Eugen von Böhm-Bawerk, in *Capital und Capitalzins, Vol. I: Geschichte und Kritik der Capitalzins-Theorien* (Innsbruck: Wagner'schen Universitäts-Buchhandlung, 1884), allocates a substantial passage to Marx, but only as the author of one of the many theories to be refuted.

8. See Haberler, *loc. cit.*, p. 345, pp. 346-47 and especially p. 369, footnote 3.

9. *Ibid.*, p. 344. With regard to Schumpeter, Professor Haberler cites the philosopher Friedrich Wilhelm Nietzsche on Arthur Schopenhauer: 'Seht ihn nur an—Niemandem war er untertan'.

10. See Wieser, 'Theorie der gesellschaftlichen Wirtschaft', in *Grundriss der Sozialökonomik, Erstes Buch: Grundlagen der Wirtschaft I* (Tübingen: J. C. B. Mohr [Paul Siebeck], 1914), p. 63 and pp. 69-70. Wieser uses the same terminology as Schumpeter, but at an earlier point in time.

11. Karl Marx, *Das Kapital—Kritik der politischen Okonomie, Band I: Der Produktionsprozess des Kapitals* (1867) and *Marx-Engels-Gesamtwerk, Vol. 23* (East Berlin: Dietz, 1969), ch. 23, p. 655 and ch. 24, p. 783.

12. *Idem, Das Kapital—Kritik der politischen Okonomie, Band III: Der Gesamtprocess der kapitalistischen Produktion* (Hamburg: Meissner, 1894), chs 25-27.)

13. See Eduard März, *Osterreichische Industrie- und Bankpolitik in der Zeit Franz Josephs I., Am Beispiel der k. k. priv. Osterreichischen Credit-Anstalt für Handel und Gewerbe* (Vienna, Frankfurt and Zurich: Europa, 1968). See also a most important article by the same author, to which I owe very much: 'Zur Genesis der Schumpeterschen Theorie der wirtschaftlichen Entwicklung', in *On Political Economy and Econometrics: Essays in Honour of Oskar Lange* (Oxford and New York: Pergamon; and Warsaw: Polish Scientific Publishers, 1965).

14. See Ludwig von Mises, *Theorie des Geldes und der Umlaufsmittel* (1912), 2nd revised edition (Munich and Leipzig: Duncker & Humblot, 1924), pt iii, ch. iv, p. 6, and ch. v, pp. 4-5.

15. See Friedrich A. von Hayek, *Geldtheorie und Konjunkturtheorie* (Vienna and Leipzig: Hölder-Pichler-Tempsky, 1929). *Idem, Price sand Production* (London: Routledge, 1931).

16. Schumpeter, *Theorie des wirtschaftlichen Entwicklung* (Leipzig: Duncker & Humblot, 1912), ch. iii, 'Kredit und Kapital'.

17. See Wieser, 'Theorie der gesellschaftlichen Wirtschaft', *op. cit.*, pp. 46-49.

18. See Böhm-Bawerk, 'Unsere passive Handelsbilanz', *Neue Freie Presse*, Vienna, 6, 8 and 9 January 1914.

19. Rudolf Hilferding, *Das Finanzkapital: Eine Studie über die jüngste Entwicklung des Kapitalismus* (Vienna: Brand, 1910).

20. See Emil Lederer, 'Konjunkturen und Krisen', in *Grundriss der Sozialökonomik, Zweites Buch: Spezifische Elemente der modernen kapitalistischen Wirtschaft* (Tübingen: J. C. B. Mohr [Paul Siebeck], 1925).

21. See Richard Cantillon, *Abhandlung über die Natur des Handels im allgemeinen*, translated into German from the French edition of 1755 by Hella Hayek (Jena: Fischer, 1931).

22. See Mises, *op. cit.*, pt iii, ch. v, p. 3.

23. See Erich Streissler, 'To What Extent Was the Austrian School Marginalist?', *History of Political Economy*, Durham, North Carolina, No. 2, 1972, pp. 438-39.

24. See Böhm-Bawerk, 'Macht oder ökonomisches Gesetz?', *Zeitschrift für Volkswirtschaft, Sozialpolitik und Verwaltung*, Vienna and Leipzig, Vol. 23, 1914.

25. This is the basic idea of Knut Wicksell in *Geldzins und Güterpreise: Eine Studie über die den Tauschwert des Geldes bestimmenden Ursachen* (Jena: Fischer, 1898).

26. *Ibid.*, in particular pp. 98, 108, 125 and 134.

27. See Murray N. Rothbard's contribution, 'Von Mises, Ludwig' in David L. Sills (ed.), *International Encyclopedia of the Social Sciences, Vol. 16* (New York: Macmillan and The Free Press, 1968), p. 380.

28. Mises, *Die Gemeinwirtschaft—Untersuchungen über den Sozialismus* (Jena: Fischer, 1922).

29. *Ibid.*, 2nd ed. (Jena: Fischer, 1932), p. 101.

30. For an excellent survey, see Robert J. Shiller, 'Rational Expectations and the Dynamic Structure of Macroeconomic Models—a Critical Review', *Journal of Monetary Economics*, Amsterdam, No. 1, 1978.

31. See, for example, Robert J. Barro, 'Rational Expectations and the Role of Monetary Policy', *Journal of Monetary Economics*, No. 1, 1976.

32. This question was raised in Vienna in 1980 by Professor Bruno Frey, of Zurich, in criticism of Schumpeter's notion of persistent political misinformation of the public. It was in this discussion with Professor Frey that I got the idea for this essay.

33. Schumpeter, *Theorie der wirtschaftlichen Entwicklung—Eine Untersuchung über Unternehmergewinn, Kapital, Kredit, Zins und den Konjunkturzyklus*, 3rd ed. (Munich and Leipzig: Duncker & Humblot, 1931), p. 99. (The first edition is not quite so explicit on this point.)

34. See Shiller, *loc. cit.*, pp. 37-41.

35. The need to calculate accurately for purposes of economising, and the existence of a demand-determined price as a means to achieve this end, are the sole message of Wieser in *Uber den Ursprung und die Hauptgesetze des wirtschaftlichen Werthes, op. cit.*

36. See, for example, Hayek, 'The Use of Knowledge in Society', *The American Economic Review*, No. 4, 1945, pp. 519 *et seq.*, and *idem*, *Der Wettbewerb als Entdeckungsverfahren*, Kieler Vorträge 56 (Kiel: Institut für Weltwirtschaft, 1968).

37. See Streissler, 'Kritik des neoklassischen Gleichgewichtsansatzes als Rechtfertigung marktwirtschaftlicher Ordnungen', in *idem*, Christian Watrin (ed.), *Zur Theorie marktwirtschaftlicher Ordnungen* (Tübingen: J. C. B. Mohr, 1980).

Index

365

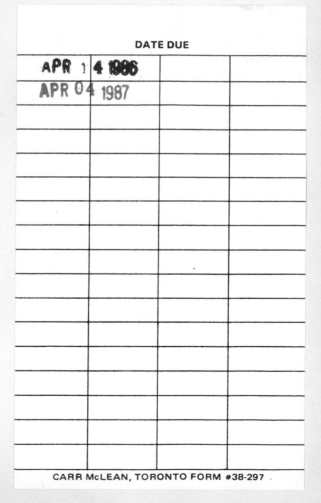